Waging War on War

Waging War on War

Peacefighting in American Literature

GIORGIO MARIANI

UNIVERSITY OF ILLINOIS PRESS
Urbana, Chicago, and Springfield

Earlier, shorter versions of chapter 2, chapter 5, and chapter 6 were published, respectively, in *American Literary History* 21 (2009), in *Ungraspable Phantom: Essays on "Moby-Dick,"* edited by John Bryant and Mary E. Bercaw (Kent, Ohio: Kent State University Press, 2006), and in *Letterature d'America* 26, no. 113–14 (2007). Parts of chapters 4 and chapter 7 appeared, in Italian, in *Ácoma: Rivista Internazionale di Studi Nord-Americani* 20 (2000) and in *Fictions: Studi sulla narratività* 2 (2004), while a rather different version of chapter 8 was included in *Vietnam e ritorno: La "guerra sporca" nel cinema, nella letteratura e nel teatro*, edited by Stefano Ghislotti and Stefano Rosso (Milan: Marcos y Marcos, 1996).

Library of Congress Cataloging-in-Publication Data
Mariani, Giorgio, 1954-
Waging war on war : peacefighting in American literature / Giorgio Mariani.
    pages   cm. — (Global studies of the United States)
Includes bibliographical references and index.
ISBN 978-0-252-03975-1 (hardback) —
ISBN 978-0-252-09785-0 (e-book)
1. American literature—History and criticism. 2. War and literature—United States. 3. Peace in literature. 4. Peace movements in literature.
I. Title.
PS169.W27M37   2015
810.9'358—dc23   2015020401

*In memory of my brother-in-law Zulfikar Alatas,
peacefighting doctor without borders in Afghanistan, Rwanda,
Israel/Palestine, the former Yugoslavia, and elsewhere*

The cause of peace is not the cause of cowardice. If peace is sought to be
defended or preserved for the safety of the luxurious and the timid, it is a sham,
and the peace will be base. War is better, and the peace will be broken. If peace is
to be maintained, it must be by brave men, who have come up to the same height
as the hero, namely, the will to carry their life in their hand, and stake it at any
instant for their principle, but who have gone one step beyond the hero, and will
not seek another man's life;—men who have, by their intellectual insight or else
by their moral elevation, attained such a perception of their own intrinsic worth,
that they do not think property or their own body a sufficient good to be saved by
such dereliction of principle as treating a man like a sheep.

—Ralph Waldo Emerson, "War" (1838)

Strike against all ordinances and laws and institutions that continue the
slaughter of peace and the butcheries of war. Strike against war, for without
you no battles can be fought. . . . Be not dumb, obedient slaves in an army of
destruction. Be heroes in an army of construction.

—Helen Keller, speech at Carnegie Hall, New York City, January 5, 1916,
under the auspices of the Women's Peace Party and the Labor Forum

Contents

Preface

This book, originally conceived as a study of U.S. war literature, began early on to morph into a somewhat different project. My intentions had never been encyclopedic—I never wished, that is, to write a full-blown survey of the manifold literary texts (poems, plays, and fictions, but also autobiographical accounts) dealing with war from the seventeenth-century clash between Puritans and Pequots to the so-called War on Terror. Moreover, I was aware that at a time when the twin notions of the literary canon and of literature itself were being called into question from a variety of cultural and theoretical perspectives, the category of "war literature" was also rapidly changing. Until recently, studies of American war literature focused on a number of fairly well-known novels, stories, or poems in which either the experience of combat and/or that of army life featured in a prominent way. Since the late 1970s, however, the canon of war literature began to open up: one need only think of the tremendous difference that Women's and Feminist Studies have made in not only the ways we see war but also how we *define war* in the first place. For example, even as invaluable a work as Paul Fussell's landmark *The Great War and Modern Memory*—as Lynne Hanley has argued—ignored women's writings altogether, on the grounds that there were no female soldiers in the belligerent armies. Yet it should be enough to read a few pages from the books by nurses like Mary Borden or Ellen La Motte (just to note two American examples) to realize not only the extent to which women directly participated in World War I but also the sophisticated understanding they had of war's murderous logic and of its numerous political and ideological implications. The "gendering" of "war talk" (Cooke and Woollacott) has greatly expanded the field of war literature, which has grown larger also with the rise of Cultural Studies. When we speak of war literature today, we refer not only to "great" autobiographies, fictions, or poems, but also to diaries, newspaper accounts, essays, as well as to formerly marginalized popular genres like the graphic novel, the cartoon, and song lyrics. In short, the field has become so diverse that any study of American (or any other) war literature aiming to discuss individual texts in some detail must necessarily be a highly selective one.

The question for me thus became what principle I would follow in limiting my field of inquiry. I soon discovered that, for the most part, the works I was interested in discussing were those that, in one way or another, belonged to what is sometimes referred to as the subgenre of "anti-war literature"—works, that is, ostensibly engaged both in writing about war and violence and in writing *against* war and violence, works waging war on war in often subtle and intellectually stimulating ways. Somewhat paradoxically, however, what drew me to such texts was the belief that the notion of anti-war literature is a deeply problematic one. As I argue in the first chapter, even though the qualifier "anti-war" is often applied to a large number of both literary and cinematic productions, so as to give the impression that we are referring to relatively solid genres such as, say, the Western film, the gothic novel, or the romantic lyric, I know of no systematic studies on the morphology or the philosophy of anti-war literature (or cinema, for that matter). My first impulse was to abandon altogether this poorly theorized and confusing label, but eventually I realized that, whether or not anti-war literature exists as a genre or subgenre, the question of the moral and political stance a text takes toward the war and the violence it describes remains crucial. Of course we may not be able to establish whether that stance is truly anti-war, mostly because we are likely to disagree on what constitutes evidence of an anti-war perspective. But that may be precisely the point. While the meaning of a text hangs considerably on what it says, its anti-war credentials rest to no small extent on the type of interpretive and discursive strategies we apply as critical readers.

My premise is the perhaps obvious one that today we consider the war we read about or see in films to be contrary to nearly everything we believe in, or we are supposed to believe in, as we go about our "normal" everyday existence as "civilized" human beings. As Robert Holmes has noted, we are all against war, we all think wars are wrong, we are all opposed to violence . . . but very often we "proceed to say that although we all hate war, nonetheless, some wars are necessary to avoid greater evils. And in any event, there have always been wars and always will be, and you cannot change that unless you change human nature" (15). Holmes believes that "this combination of views—that war is immoral but nonetheless necessary—effectively removes the need to question the morality of war. Its wrong-ness has already been conceded in a way that allows for the continuation of war and even for a belief in its inevitability" (15). War literature may be seen as one of the places where this "inevitability" is both sanctioned and questioned, where the immorality of war is taken up and debated rather than simply "removed." Yet war literature, including literature commonly considered to be "anti-war," always entertains an ambivalent, contradictory, troubled relation with the violence it is asked to represent. Its complexity may exceed the narrow confines of a binary pro-war *vs.* anti-war logic but—this at least is the argument of my book—*all* war texts are at risk of feeding on the very violence they purportedly wish to denounce. No war text can altogether repudiate war, though some not only try to resist it in more convincing ways than others but also acknowledge their inescapable moral and rhetorical shortcomings.

In selecting the literary texts discussed in the second part of the book, I singled out a number of narrative and poetic acts of war against war that punctuate the his-tory of U.S. literature from the early nineteenth century on. By characterizing these texts as imaginary efforts to wage war on war, I wish precisely to call attention to the aporia lurking in any anti-war perspective. The problem is at once linguistic, conceptual, and political. How can one inhabit the metaphors and the language of war in such a way that the struggle for peace does not become a continuation of war by other means? To what extent can peace be freed from being too often conceived as the lengthened shadow of war? What are the limits of non-violence, not only at the level of theory but also in terms of its practice? The texts I discuss in the pages that follow have been chosen because the stories they tell and the rhetorical operations they perform address in various ways these and other related questions. This is by no means to say these texts are unique and no other work in the U.S. literary tradition was worthy of inclusion in my study. Nor do I wish to argue that the texts I chose are more rigorously anti-war than others. While this book discusses forms and strategies of war resistance and peace building in the world of American letters, such efforts can never be free of contradictions. My intent is not to show that my select American war writers are all distinguished members of an imaginary literary war resisters' league. What I do wish to contend is that their work provides a fertile ground for investigating the question of what it means to oppose war and violence—for interrogating, that is, both war and the practice of writing critically about war. I realize that some may find my choice of texts eclectic, as I move across historical periods and through many genres (epic and lyric poetry, short story, and novel). This choice, however, provides me with an opportunity to comment on how the attempt to denounce and condemn war and violence is either enabled or complicated by a specific cultural context as well as by the use of a given literary form.

War is nearly always a "transnational" phenomenon. This means, among other things, that war literature is an object that can be profitably studied from a comparative, international perspective. The reason for limiting my focus on a small number of U.S. texts is in part circumstantial. My academic field is American literature, and even though I am familiar with some war literatures of other nations, I feel more comfortable discussing works belonging to a literary tradition I have been studying and teaching for some time. Thus, while I agree that literary studies should try to extend beyond the nation-based ontology on which they have been traditionally established, I feel also that as long as texts are not read as metaphors of some "typical" national trait or spirit, there is nothing wrong in seeing them as also connected to a country's specific history and culture. But there is a further reason why I have chosen to restrict my analysis to U.S. texts. The United States—at least to the eyes of someone who is to a considerable extent an outsider—stands out as a political and cultural power investing a great deal in the *symbolic* import of war and violence. I have italicized the word symbolic because I am not qualified to deal in depth with the more properly sociological side of the problem. It would stand to reason that specific features in U.S. history and society play a prominent role in the national imaginary of war and violence. As Richard Maxwell Brown writes in the opening essay of *Violence in America: An Encyclopedia*, "Scholars have concluded that during the nineteenth and twentieth centuries the United States was by far the most violent of its peer group of nations—the economically advanced democracies of the world. This is not because Americans are an innately violent people, but because a combination of factors from the colonial period on has created the juggernaut of American violence" (2). This position is not shared by all. Yet even someone who holds a different view on this matter—John Schwetman, for example, who maintains that "the U.S. has not historically been more violent than any other country" (310)—concludes that "violence does play a particular role in the nation's conception of itself. . . . America distinguishes itself from other countries not by being more violent but by situating violence so centrally in its self-conception" (315).

Though their views may differ, both Brown and Schwetman lay the ground on which a sort of American exceptionalism in reverse could be erected. Rather than being celebrated for being exceptionally virtuous, the United States could be vilified for being exceptionally bad. This position, however, is by no means one I am interested in defending. As the title of Geoffrey Perret's well-known book has it, the United States is no doubt "a country made by war." Yet to paraphrase the caustic remarks made by Melville's Ishmael regarding the Killer Whale, exception might be taken to the descriptive clause bestowed on America by Perret, on the grounds of its indistinctness. *All* nations, to a greater or lesser extent, have been made by war. War and nation building are inseparable. The history of any nation and of nationalism is in large measure violent, and, especially if we take a long-term view, little is exceptionally or uniquely bloody about the history of the United States. Since the War of Independence America has gone from being a country whose political elites and public opinion "evinced a pronounced ambivalence about the very existence of a standing army and the career soldiers who led that army" (Bacevich 221) to being not simply the only remaining world's superpower but one armed to its teeth, with military bases in nearly every corner of the planet and a "defense" budget almost equal to that of the rest of the entire world. The Founding Fathers believed that America's relation to the rest of the world should be established "on terms conducive to the well-being of the republic, steering clear of the ambitions, rivalries, interests, humors, and caprices of other nations" (Bacevich 214). Nowadays only the achievement of "Full Spectrum Dominance" would seem to satisfy its security needs.

If we confine ourselves to the history of the past 120 years—basically, from the Spanish-American War forward—the United States' imperial ambitions would be hard to deny, and such ambitions have often seen the American army or other branches of its security apparatus like the CIA involved in violent activities. Under these circumstances—as I argue in chapter 2—we may be tempted to see America almost exclusively as a "gunfighter nation" inhabiting a "fatal environment" in which "regeneration through violence" was the rule rather than the exception not only in recent history but since the early days of John Smith and William Bradford. I do not wish in any way to underestimate the invaluable work done on this count by Richard Slotkin, whose indispensable trilogy on the mythology of the frontier I have just invoked. Plenty of historical evidence buttresses Melville's claim that the United States of America has too often proved to be "civilized in externals, but a savage at heart" (*Israel Potter* 120). From Mark Twain's attack on "the United States of Lyncherdom" and his dismissal of patriotism as "a word which always commemorates robbery" (*Notebook* 295) to John Dos Passos's assault on war as being "the fullest and most ultimate expression" of that "vast edifice of sham" that is "civilization" (*Three Soldiers* 175), America's best writers have incisively, and frequently, condemned the country's participation in war. These unveilings of the legacy of violence in American history are important reminders of the existence of a national countertradition of peace seekers and justice seekers who oppose war and try to practice or imagine non-violent ways to transform the world. As I insist particularly in chapter 2, the international peace movement is in major ways intellectually indebted to U.S. thinkers and activists. In particular, we must give credit to Ralph Waldo Emerson—yes, the same Emerson who would later turn into a ruthless advocate of total war against the South—not only for imagining in one of his early essays a peaceful America where the heroes of old would be superseded—as mentioned in this book's epigraph—by greater figures, whose courage would consist in the readiness to *renounce* rather than engage in violence. Emerson was also the first, to the best of my knowledge, who defined peace not negatively, as the mere absence of war, but positively, as a moral force grounded in courage and the struggle for justice.

From Emerson to Martin Luther King, we can trace the emergence of an anti-war tradition that, by trying to imagine peace as the fight for truth and justice, works hard to turn war against itself. King may be said, like both Emerson and Gandhi, to rely on terms taken from the vocabulary of war (courage, heroism, struggle, force, strategy, and tactics). However, his politics of non-violence demonstrates at the level of practice what Kenneth Burke (as I argue in chapter 3) preached in terms of rhetorical theory: we may never be able to renounce the rhetoric of war, but we can still "purify" it so as to make it less harmful and dangerous. Indeed, we may turn this purified language into a resource for opposing war and violence, and for evoking a peace that would be no longer subservient to war. While even non-violence is not altogether free from contradictions—as can be seen especially in the fact that some of its pronouncements are still couched in the language of sacrifice—there can be no question that the early Emerson, Thoreau, Jane Addams, King, and many others all belong to a countertradition of peacefighters who offer an alternative to the legacy of the "gunfighter nation." Yet, while it would be a terrible political and cultural mistake to underestimate the significance of this alternative tradi-tion, in the present context we must ask ourselves what contributions, if any, can the idea of peace as a force equal and even stronger than war give to the study of war literature. Narratives of peacefighting can of course be found in many of the texts, autobiographical and otherwise, written by advocates of peace, and they may overlap with stories of mutiny like the one William Faulkner recounts in *A Fable*, which I discuss closely in chapter 7. Moreover, when war writers appear to follow Kenneth Burke's advice and show the "human side" of war, they sometimes get out a more hopeful anti-war message than if they had focused only on its bestial-ity. By creating "heroes" whose bravery has little to do with combat, war texts may be said to take, however tentatively, that extra step "beyond" that Emerson wrote about. It would be wrong to see all the works discussed in the second part of this book as coherent efforts to realize this peace-building program. However, to the extent that all the texts analyzed call attention—for the most part in rather explicit ways—not only to their anti-war efforts but also to the difficulties encountered in pursuing their critical intentions, they provide significant occasions for exploring the paradoxes and antinomies of war literature.

I begin with *The Columbiad* (1807), as Joel Barlow's struggle to accommodate the epic genre to a discourse of peace exemplifies a problem so many writers of war would confront over the course of the centuries to follow—how do you rec-oncile a form meant to celebrate the virtues of a bellicose spirit with the desire to project peace as the only worthwhile goal of a national and an international community? The difficulties Barlow faced in writing his epic, which is by now mostly (but unjustly) forgotten, were bequeathed to later critics of war and especially to the writer whose 1851 "mighty book" is nowadays considered as *the* great American epic novel. In chapter 5, I read *Moby-Dick* as a text that, though in many ways as critical as Barlow's *Columbiad* of humankind's history of violence, is infinitely more skeptical regarding efforts to curb human violence. Though not a traditional war novel, *Moby-Dick* may be considered a "symbolic poem of war and peace" (Adler 55), provided we understand that the "peace" this novel envisions cannot be disentangled from the sacrificial logic underwriting the narrative.

The question of sacrifice is also central to my interpretation, in chapter 7, of William Faulkner's *A Fable*—a work that notwithstanding the Pulitzer Prize and the National Book Award it earned in 1955 is constantly criticized and even vilified. In my reading I recover what I see as the implicit critical theology of the novel, which attacks the sacrificial logic of historical Christianity, and I argue that in Faulkner's view Christian civilization has been unable to resist war-making because it embraced a view of the Passion of Christ as a sacrifice when, in fact, the mission of Jesus was that of obviating sacrifice. As I have chosen to arrange the chapters of the second part of this book chronologically, my reading of *A Fable* is preceded by the discussion of an extraordinary and seldom-studied collection of short stories by Ellen La Motte, appearing in 1916, stories literally devoted to the wounds of the Great War. La Motte served as a nurse in a hospital near the Belgian front, and in *The Backwash of War* she paints a devastating picture of the psychological and moral degradation caused by World War I. Yet she also acknowledges how even her own critiques, no matter how intransigent, are always at risk of feeding back into the machinery of war on both ideological and practical grounds. As a nurse, La Motte was forced to wonder to what extent she was helping to heal the ravages of war and in what measure, on the contrary, her contribution was a way to oil the horrible meat grinder of trench warfare. And as a woman, she understood quite well how war discourse strategically exploits the opposition it sets up between the peaceful virtues of womanhood and the warlike instincts of masculinity by constructing the protection of the former as a license for the latter.

Even though, as I illustrate in chapter 8, by the time of the Vietnam War the cultural and social conditions in which military conflict came to be waged and narrated had changed a great deal, some old questions continued to surface in the work of writers who took part in the war. As Tim O'Brien writes in *If I Die in a Combat Zone*, though he sincerely wishes that his book "could take the shape of a plea for everlasting peace" and hopes that it might persuade "my younger brother and perhaps some others to say no to wrong wars," he doubts nevertheless that, as a foot soldier, he has anything to teach others "merely for having been there" (23).

All he can do is "tell war stories." In "How to Tell a True War Story," perhaps the best-known chapter in *The Things they Carried*, O'Brien pursues a search for "truth" that allows him to explore in a meandering though compelling way many of the moral and rhetorical dilemmas of the would-be anti-war writer, which I connect to the acknowledgment by "Tim" in another story of the book, that his decision to go to war was an act of cowardice, not of courage. The narrator, that is, realizes he was not brave enough to take that Emersonian step beyond military heroism.

The sense of frustration that Vietnam War writers often felt regarding the ability of their works to prevent the next war seems to be vindicated by the state of the contemporary United States, a country which—with brief intervals—has been at war in one form or another since the First Gulf War, when, in George Bush's words, it finally kicked "the Vietnam syndrome." Sold to the public opinion with perhaps more lies and media manipulation than the war in Southeast Asia, the Iraq War could not be prevented or stopped before hundreds of thousands would be killed or maimed, and not before the U.S. invasion devastated a whole country, with repercussions we are still feeling. However small the consolation may be, some contemporary writers are engaged, as much as their colleagues of a previous generation, in an effort to bring home the error and madness of the Iraq War, as well as the further tragedy endured by those returning soldiers whose fate is too often ignored, except for the occasional article about yet another veteran's suicide. In chapter 9, after a discussion of Maxine Hong Kingston's *The Fifth Book of Peace*, a meditation on the difficulty of matching anti-war writing with some much-needed imagining of what peace might look like when disengaged from a context of war, I read Brian Turner's poetry and Helen Benedict's novel *Sand Queen* (2011) as two "cosmopolitan" responses to the Iraq War. As I see it, both the soldier-poet who has been to war and the female writer who has researched the war with a special attention to the condition of women soldiers present the reader with an account of war that is not limited to showing the sufferings of "our side" but struggles to make us aware of how war feeds on ignorance and prejudice against the Other.

In a much-discussed book of some years ago, Richard Rorty observed that "those who hope to persuade a nation to exert itself need to remind their country of what it can take pride in as well as what it should be ashamed of. They must tell inspiring stories about episodes and figures in the nation's past—episodes and figures to which the country should remain true" (*Achieving Our Country* 3–4). As readers of this book will see, I share Rorty's position. It is politically self-defeating for any progressive movement worthy of its name to insist only on the shameful legacy of the United States, or of any other country, or of humankind as a whole, for that matter. Yet Rorty underestimates the degree to which writers and critics must insist on the hypocrisy of American mainstream culture and politics due to what governments continue to say and do. When, for example, a U.S. president, elected with the support of many of those same people Rorty sees as no longer interested in politics and resigned to a morose mood of unending hopelessness, receives the Nobel Peace Prize but apparently has no qualms about continuing a pointless and unwinnable war in Afghanistan, or about stepping up the so-called "drone war," and, to boot, launches a thirteen-year-long commemoration of the Vietnam War in which he describes not the war itself as a "national shame" but the way in which the country supposedly failed to pay homage to its "heroes," I wonder what else can peace seekers and justice seekers do but protest as loudly as they can?

Still, Rorty is right in calling attention to the need for safeguarding a cultural and political tradition one may take pride in. To be proud of a tradition, however, does not mean to be blind to its limitations or to the ways it can be improved on. I believe that the works I discuss in this book are all acts of the imagination animated by a sincere hope to promote peace but are also at the same time reflections on how such acts often fall short because of the limitations of one's language, culture, and history. At least in my reading of it, U.S. "anti-war" writing may satisfy both Rorty's request to spread a degree of hope nourished by an alternative national tradition and the need to temper that pride with the realization that even critiques of war and violence can quickly dissolve dreams of "peace" into calls for further war.

Just a few more words about the spirit in which I have approached the issues and materials discussed in this book. Though I have lived in the United States for more than ten years of my adult life (from 1980 to 1991), plus a period of one-and-a-half years as a third- and fourth-grader, I grew up and spent most of my life in Italy. Most important, I was in high school and university between 1968 and 1978—during, that is, the most turbulent yet exciting decade in post-war Italy. My interest in issues of "war and peace" dates back to those years, when I was busy protesting the Vietnam War and demonstrating for nuclear disarmament but was also affected in my daily life by the tangible consequences of Italy's disastrous involvement in World War II and especially by the legacy of the bitter civil war that marked its ending. I was a direct witness of police and state violence, not to mention the aggressions carried out by neofascist groups tolerated and at times directly sponsored by sectors of the state. The question of how to confront, respond to, or defuse such violence was a very concrete and urgent one, and equally pressing and dramatic was the question of what to do and say about the catastrophic choice made by a tiny (though unfortunately significant) minority of the Italian New Left that embraced armed struggle and terrorism. Discussions about violence, non-violence, and its limits, as well as about the different strategies called for by Lenin and Gandhi, Che Guevara, and Martin Luther King, were anything but academic debates. Compared to the political and pragmatic urgency of those heated, at times furious meetings on "tactics and strategy" the readings I perform in this book are certainly tamer confrontations with the questions of war, peace, and violence. I do hope, however, that some of the passion and concern still animating my older days has percolated into this book, which to the extent that it deals mostly with literary matters and questions of representation may appear somewhat removed from outright political issues. Personally, I like to think of this book as a way in which I have continued to ask myself many of the old questions. The object of my inquiry is U.S. literature, history, and culture, but the ethical, political, and historical problems I raise remain, or so I think, very much rooted in the experiences I lived through in my younger days.

Please note: (1) Whenever I use the terms *anti-war*, *non-violent*, and *non-violence*, I always employ the hyphenated spelling, consistent with my emphasis on the problematic, dialogical nature of the concepts they stand for. When quoting, of course, I follow the spelling of the original. (2) Unless otherwise indicated, all translations are mine.

Acknowledgments

Over the many years it has taken me to complete this book, I have benefited from the advice, knowledge, and encouragement of so many people that to list all of them here would be impossible. The support of some people, however, has turned out to be essential. Jane Desmond and Virginia Dominguez not only suggested I submit the book for publication to the series they co-edit, but they also granted me the privilege of being a visiting scholar with the International Forum for United States Studies at the University of Illinois at Urbana-Champaign, on three separate occasions. There I had the chance to present my ideas in public lectures and discussions, as well as the opportunity to conduct extensive and intensive library research. Jane and Virginia's generosity, friendship, and willingness to listen for hours to the various aspects of my project provided the foundation of the present book. I am also very much indebted to Donald Pease: his kind invitations to the Futures of American Studies Institute at Dartmouth afforded me the possibility to air some of the basic concepts underlying this study. Indeed, I am happy to acknowledge that the idea for this book began to take shape as I prepared my first Dartmouth lecture, back in 2006. I am also grateful to Djelal Kadir and his wife, Juana Celia, for many years of friendship and intellectual exchanges. By introducing me to the exciting scholarly community of the International American Studies Association, of which Djelal was the founding president, they contributed not only to the shape of the present project but also to that of my whole academic career.

It is a joy for me to express my deepest gratitude to Donatella Izzo and Stefano Rosso, lifetime friends on whose patience, intelligence, and affection I have been lucky enough to rely for so many years. They read early drafts of the book, they saw its flaws and its potential, and they made key suggestions. Most important, they were, in the best and most genuine sense of the word, fellow travelers who shared from the start the spirit, both intellectual and political, of my endeavor. For reading and commenting on parts of the book, I wish also to thank Sara Antonelli, John Bryant, Paola Cabibbo, Roberto Cagliero, Bruno Cartosio, Giordano De Biasio, Daniele Fiorentino, Cristina Giorcelli, Alba Graziano, Gordon Hutner, Richard Kidder, Daniele Niedda, Gordon Poole, Alessandro Portelli, Anna Scannavini, Igina Tattoni, and Marilyn Young. I learned a great deal from all of them, as well as from the thoughtful reading of the entire manuscript provided by the two generous anonymous reviewers chosen by the University of Illinois Press. I would also like to express my gratitude to all the people at the University of Illinois Press I had the pleasure of working with. They were always both helpful and cheerful. In particular, I wish to thank my editor Dawn Durante for her tact, patience, and enthusiastic support of the project, and my manuscript editor Julie Gay for being such an attentive and sympathetic reader of my work.

I have been a member of the editorial board of *Ácoma*, the Italian journal of American Studies, for twenty years. The experience has been rewarding on so many fronts, and to the wonderful people who are part of this adventure (many of whom I have already mentioned above) I wish to express my gratitude for making my scholarly work meaningful beyond the world of academia. To my students at the "Sapienza" University of Rome I am indebted in ways they may not suspect. They have helped me think harder about my ideas because, as my sons and my parents have repeatedly impressed upon me, you cannot claim to know something until you can explain it clearly and engagingly to someone else.

A significant part of my research was conducted at the Alexander Library of Rutgers University, my American alma mater, and at Cambridge University. In New Brunswick, I could count on the friendship and hospitality of Thomas Regan and his family. In England, I was privileged to rely on Paola and Nicola Cabibbo's wonderfully cozy retreat of "Scellirò," where numerous parts of this book were actually written. I am also happy to address a most sincere *merci beaucoup* to François Specq, who offered me a visiting professorship at the *École Normale Supérieure* of Lyon, where I could share some of my ideas with his colleagues and students and enjoy many days of intensive work that allowed me to complete the original draft of the manuscript.

Convention has it that family members are thanked last in the acknowledgments pages—I am not sure I understand why that should be the case, but without breaking this tradition I will say that it should be the other way around. The greatest debt is always to those who have to put up with you on a daily basis—understanding your anxieties; providing comfort when you are on the verge of breaking down; knowing how to say the right word at the right time. I have been blessed with parents who have always gone out of their way to support my scholarly efforts. Moreover, their decision to move to the United States from late 1962 to 1964 has obviously had lasting consequences on my choice of a career. My wife, Masturah Alatas, a writer and a rigorous critical thinker in her own right, has edited, proofread, and commented on so many different versions and parts of this book. Her patience and endurance have been much greater than I could ask for. Also, I owe so much to her sense of humor—as always, she was able to make me laugh at myself and my mistakes. My sons, Giordano and Dario, have provided me with a constant, healthy reminder that there are other important matters besides finishing a book. They were also curious, however, to understand where my interest in issues of war, violence, and non-violence came from, and that gave me a chance to revisit my growing up in Italy in the late 1960s and early 1970s. I am thankful to them for listening. I know it is a foolish hope, but I think it is one worth cultivating: may the world that they, and their children, grow up in have no use for heroes.

PART I

Theory

CHAPTER 1

Anti-War?

Notes on a Ghostly Concept

"Poo-tee-weet?"

> There is nothing intelligent to say about a massacre. Everybody is supposed to be dead, to never say or want anything ever again. Everything is supposed to be very quiet after a massacre, and it always is, except for the birds.
>
> And what do the birds say? All there is to say about a massacre, things like *"Poo-tee-weet?"* (Vonnegut 9)

The cryptic, both innocent and sardonic, chirping of *Slaughterhouse-Five*'s bird may be seen as Kurt Vonnegut's warning to whomever, in whatever capacity, wishes to narrate war. What intelligent things can be said on that endless string of massacres that is war? Wouldn't it be better to remain silent and let an unintelligible sound stand as the only adequate objective correlative of the senselessness of armed conflict? By granting to onomatopoeia the last "word" of his World War II novel, Vonnegut emphasizes both the impossibility of drawing a conclusion from his narration and the need never to lose sight of the absurdity and meaninglessness of war.

If, however, there is no war without its massacres, wars amount to more than "senseless" killing. Massacres are carried out, and often carefully planned, by human beings within historical conditions in part given and in part shaped directly by them. Indeed, from a historical/cultural viewpoint—which is different from the literary/existential perspective embraced by Vonnegut—it is indeed possible to say something "intelligent" about a massacre. I am thinking, for example, of Giovanni

De Luna's book on the handling of the bodies of killed enemies, an important historical and anthropological study of twentieth-century massacres, noteworthy on a documentary basis but also on an interpretive level. The insistence on the "meaninglessness" of war's violence is an understandable ethical posture meant to resist any justification of the horrors of war, but as a whole Vonnegut's novel wishes to resist rather than sustain this perspective.[1] *Slaughterhouse-Five* has a subtitle—"A Duty-Dance with Death"—rather explicit in reminding us about the *obligations* of those who choose to bear witness to war's atrocities. No matter how much he may poke fun at the regenerative or healing powers of Art, by ridiculing it through his bird's unintelligible chirping, Vonnegut does *not* give in to the quietness that follows a massacre. Instead, he speaks out, prompted by a sense of duty evidently stronger than any fear of the inadequacy of his language.[2]

Slaughterhouse-Five, however, features also a second (double) title—"The Children's Crusade"—that appears to have been fashioned, as we learn in the first chapter, precisely to meet the concerns of Mary, the wife of the author's war buddy Bernard V. O'Hare. Mary is worried that, after all, also in Vonnegut's novel, "war will look just wonderful, so we'll have a lot more of them. And they'll be fought by babies like the babies upstairs" (11). Like many writers of war stories, Vonnegut would want his book to be not only a document of the horrors he has witnessed, or an account of how he coped with a trauma both individual and collective, but also an instrument that may help prevent future wars. Yet he knows this is largely a naïve hope. When someone suggests that he write an "anti-glacier book" rather than an "anti-war book," the narrator hastens to add: "What he meant, of course, was that there would always be wars, that they were as easy to stop as glaciers. I believe that, too" (3). Vonnegut is aware of the antinomy at the heart of his novel, and if he hesitates in calling it an *anti-war novel*, this is probably because he himself does not know what exactly this literary object consists of.[3] Is it a tale that indignantly attacks the madness of war, even though wars need to be fought? A story that promotes a wholesale condemnation of War—*any* war, no matter how "just"? Or is it a narration that purports to help us understand the causes of war? Should an anti-war novel unambiguously rail against the monstrosity of human slaughter? Or, as many would argue, should a war narrative only present the real or imagined thoughts and actions of men and women at war, leaving explanations to politicians and historians?

Whoever has read any of the countless Western narratives dealing with war—the *Iliad*, Shakespeare's history plays, *War and Peace*, *A Farewell to Arms*, just to mention a few memorable examples—or watched even a small sampling of the hundreds of war movies shot since the birth of the movie industry knows there are no easy answers to these questions. Even though writers and critics constantly speak of the "pacifist novel," of "poetry against the war," of "anti-war literature" and "the anti-war movie," such labels are generally used in a casual way and, as a rule, they tell us precious little about the structure and the content of a text. Scholars sometimes refer to anti-war literature as a "subset" of war literature, but I have never come across any sustained attempt to identify its contours, either from a morphological or a philosophical point of view.[4] It is perhaps symptomatic that whereas we have dozens of book-length studies whose titles mention "war writing," "war poetry," the "war novel," the "war story," and so on, the qualifier "anti-war" is less frequently employed as an umbrella term. This seems to suggest that, while most critics would acknowledge the presence of anti-war feelings in literary works devoted to war, they harbor also an implicit mistrust of "anti-war" as an all-encompassing category. This attitude is understandable. To set apart certain texts as being "anti-war" would in a sense entail that those works not belonging in the "anti-war" group should be considered as "pro-war," a drastic conclusion few would probably endorse. This is why, I think, the term "anti-war" (or the different though related term "pacifist") is used for the most part locally, to identify specific works, since a more systemic use of the term would entail the tracing of a clear-cut line between a literature that is anti-war and one that is not. To speak more generally of war writing is safer, as it allows one to side step rigorous and hard-to-maintain distinctions between what is anti-war and what is "simply" war literature, assuming that an unambiguous pro-war stance may be confined—at least as far as modern literature is concerned—to works of propaganda.

Even though anti-war literature remains to this day largely untheorized, the label continues to be employed and to complicate most discussions, whether scholarly or not, of both war literature and war cinema. It seems that if on the one hand we cannot describe *all* war literature as anti-war, on the other we feel uncomfortable with any account of warfare that does not unequivocally condemn the killing and injuring of other human beings.[5] While many would probably agree that the term "anti-war" may easily turn into a straitjacket and fail to register the multilayered aesthetic and intellectual accomplishments of a text by privileging its didactic qualities, one could quote dozens of examples showing that the term continues to matter. Indeed, the archive of war-literature studies is full of pronouncements pushing texts from the "neutral" field of war literature into that of anti-war writing, and vice versa. We need only think of the ur-text of Western war literature. There is ample evidence to argue that the *Iliad* celebrates a civilization founded on war, the cult of the hero, and the glory of death in battle. All of this did not prevent, at the outset of World War II, a scholar of the classical world like Simone Weil from seeing in the Homeric poem a heart-rending representation of the horrors of war, or, to quote her own words, of the "force before which man's flesh shrinks away" (3). Seen from Weil's influential viewpoint, the *Iliad* is both the "ur" war *and* anti-war text of the Western tradition, since it unflinchingly illustrates the bloody mess of the battlefield as well as the devastating impact of war on civilian life. More recently, the psychiatrist Jonathan Shay has discovered in Homer's epic a strikingly realistic account of what happens to men in battle, extremely helpful in confronting the traumas of Vietnam War veterans. Shay knows that "Homer's poem does not mean whatever I want it to mean" (*Achilles* xx). Yet the parallels between the stories of the combat veterans he treats and those in the *Iliad* have reinforced his conviction that "there is no contradiction between hating war and honoring the soldier" (*Achilles* xxiii).[6]

Of course, the fact that the *Iliad* may be read as a poem that glorifies as well as condemns war is in many ways far from extraordinary. It could be seen as simply yet another demonstration of how a text may take on different, even starkly divergent meanings, depending on the perspective from which it is read, and on the historical and cultural contexts surrounding it. To students interested in connecting the epic to the worldview of classical Greece, the *Iliad* may well show the brutality of war—Homer's *polemos kakos* (evil struggle)—but it makes little sense to turn its celebration of a warrior society into anti-war poetry. For Weil, on the other hand, its display of an impersonal, terrifying "force" is a warning "not to begin a new Trojan War," to quote the title of another one of her essays.[7] And for Shay, the poem's mapping of combat trauma provides an illustration of "how war damages the mind and spirit," thereby encouraging us to "change those things in military institutions and culture that needlessly create or worsen these injuries" (*Achilles* xxiii). What makes all these readings—in this, as well as in many other cases—legitimate is to a large extent the rather vague status of the "anti-war" concept, which here stands revealed as being essentially an *evaluative* rather than a descriptive category. In the same years Weil, in France, was busy rescuing from the *Iliad* a pacifist message, in Italy the Fascist regime promoted the study of Greco-Roman classics as a way to celebrate the greatness of a former empire, foreshadowing the rejuvenation of the nation under the Duce's leadership. Whether a poem, a novel, or a film may be said to be anti-war or not ultimately depends on the ways they are decoded—and the ways they are decoded, to a considerable extent, hang in turn on the protocols of reading sponsored by a given culture, whether hegemonic or resistant. Within pacifist circles, the *Iliad* may be read as an anti-war text; within an imperialist culture, it is a poem extolling the manly virtues of the warrior.

To accept the idea that ultimately there are no anti-war texts but only anti-war *readings*, however, means obviously to kiss goodbye to the concept of anti-war literature as a definite subset of war literature. To many this would be an acceptable solution that avoids confining many different war stories into too narrow a category, and one could cite several critical discussions of war literature that avoid programmatically the war/anti-war debate by focusing on textual features that bypass such inflexible categorizations. Yet the question will not go away, no matter how much we want to ignore it. Whether one is analyzing issues of form (the war novel as *Bildungsroman*, for example), of trauma and guilt (a standard feature of many war veterans' memoirs and novels), or of gender (how masculinity is constructed and deployed in war literature, for instance), one keeps ultimately going back to modulations of the basic war/anti-war dilemma. What does it mean to "become a man" (or to fail to become one) while fighting a war? To what extent can one forgive oneself, or ask to be forgiven, for having been a participant, or a participant-observer, of the atrocities of war? How do characters relate to the aggressive masculinity sponsored by war propaganda? These are all, to be sure, essentially political questions that simply refuse to be confined within a sanitized "literary" precinct. Most educated contemporary readers may feel uncomfortable about pacifist tirades on the evils of war, but they would nevertheless object to a narrative endorsing a dehumanizing description of the enemy or one that ignores the bloody mess of the battlefield. As I will argue time and again in this book, this is not to say that a narrative that recognizes the humanity of one's enemy or openly depicts the horrors of warfare can be ipso facto considered an anti-war text. Such features may often be found in texts that would be awkward to define as anti-war. However, since war texts represent and debate a practice felt to be the quintessential negation of civilized life, readers and critics must in the end wrestle with the same basic question: what kind of image of war does the text offer? We may conclude that the answer to this fundamental narrative problem exceeds the binary logic of a somewhat Manichaean pro-war/anti-war juxtaposition, but these categories, however camouflaged, will continue to resurface in our debates. To use Vonnegut's terms, as long as war birds will keep on *Poo-tee-weeting*, war writers and critics will never be able to escape duty-dancing with death.

Ghostly Demarcations

In the title of this chapter, I refer to the *ghostly* nature of the anti-war concept in literary studies. Its incorporeal features may be registered on at least three levels: (1) whether invoked as the cornerstone of a subgenre or, more modestly, as a narrative point of view, the contours of the anti-war stance are vague: to take a firm hold of the concept seems as hopeless as Marcellus's attempt to strike with his "partisan" the elder Hamlet's ghost; (2) as a veritable specter, the text's anti-war perspective is both present and absent, seen by some, invisible to others; (3) the concept has something disruptive and disturbing about it, as it constantly threatens to turn the complexity of the literary text into straightforward propaganda. Especially in academic discussions, it is marginalized, and yet it keeps reappearing in one guise or another. Like Freud's uncanny, it has a paradoxical quality, as if it were something we both want the text to be and not to be.

In order to put some textual flesh around these incorporeal notions, I would like to show how they manifest themselves in two recent studies of war literature, Kate McLoughlin's *Authoring War: The Literary Representation of War from the* Iliad *to Iraq* and Cynthia Wachtell's *War No More: The Antiwar Impulse in American Literature, 1861–1914*. These are in many ways two excellent, original books, well written and packed—especially *Authoring War*—with insights that will greatly benefit future students of war writing. My intent in what follows is not so much to criticize them as to use them as test cases to reinforce the main argument of this chapter: the concept of anti-war literature remains poorly theorized, and it counts more as a symptom than as a cognitive tool. Some might think we would be better off dispensing with this category altogether. The fact is, we can't. As Peter Jones wrote several years ago, war literature "is almost always an ethical forum, expressing outrage or describing a search for meaning in the dilemma of war" (9). Hence, whenever we talk about war literature, we are always, however implicitly, also talking about the question of how war is either resisted, accepted, or both. Posed in one form or another, the anti-war question will always be there. As I will suggest in the final section of this chapter, perhaps a partial way out of this conundrum may lie with a more rigorous conceptualization of both war and *peace*. After all, if we take seriously the anti-war preoccupations of war literature, we should ask ourselves if, and how, the latter may manage to evoke what would be the anti-war perspective par excellence—the perspective of peace. Drawing on Nick Mansfield's *Theorizing War*, I will insist that a better understanding of the relation between "war and its other" may help us move beyond the war/anti-war dichotomy without sacrificing the moral implications of our interpretations.

McLoughlin's *Authoring War* provides a wide-ranging analysis of the rhetorical and narrative strategies through which war writing confronts the enormously complex task of representing the proverbially unspeakable reality of war. Cutting through literary genres, historical periods, and nationalities, McLoughlin—as she explains in her introduction—seeks "firstly, to identify what makes war impossible or very difficult to write about and, secondly, to explore the means by which it has, nevertheless, been written about with some success" (8). The result is one of the most stimulating and useful books on the subject of war literature I have ever read. McLoughlin carefully attends to a number of key formalist features found in a vast array of war texts. By focusing on "the representational challenge" facing any war writer—whether he or she be a soldier, a war reporter, a nurse, or a somewhat detached observer—the book offers "both close analysis of the rhetorical devices that have been deployed in response to the various challenges and structural comparison of them" (19). Whether discussing issues of time and space, "the phenomenon 'of not writing about war'" (18) as a response to the difficulty of finding the right words, or the function of laughter as a way to confront war's absurdity, McLoughlin's observations are both insightful and persuasive. Though her approach is formalist, she does not ignore that there are specific, extraliterary reasons writers take on a subject that "is the greatest test of a writer's skill of evocation" (9). McLoughlin refers to the "multitudinous" reasons that make war representation "imperative," but the numerous items on her list can perhaps be summarized under two main objectives. Writers choose to confront war because, first, they hope—in myriad ways—to inject meaning into an event usually perceived as the quintessence of meaninglessness; and, second, because they wish "to warn; and even, through the warning, to promote peace" (7).

The word "peace" may be said to bracket McLoughlin's entire project. After appearing in the introduction, the term returns, at the end of her list of reasons for writing war, in the book's conclusion, titled, "To Perpetual Peace." There, after rehearsing the "ends" of war writing, she returns to literature's overall anti-war intentions by asking the question, "Can war literature stop war?" (190). In order to answer this question, as she immediately recognizes, one would need to gauge "literature's extratextual impact," something notoriously very difficult to do. Nonetheless, McLoughlin suggests that "Make lit, not war" might be an effective pacifist strategy, as the reading of war literature might dissuade people from resorting to arms to solve their disputes and also show "the cost of armed conflict" (190). Even though adjectives like "pacifist," "anti-war," or "anti-militarist" are conspicuous by their absence in her analyses, and even though she is ultimately aware that the promotion-of-peace-through-literature project is to a large extent futile, McLoughlin advances a rather sweeping proposition: "If a war literature existed that had any hope of stopping war, it would be clear-eyed and purposeful. It would probably be messy. It would disconcert. It would do its best to convey the horror and misery of conflict. . . . It would find the task difficult and go off the point. . . . It would be very like the texts encountered in the course of this book" (191). Here the term "anti-war" is not employed, but the reader is led to believe that virtually all the writers discussed in the book have an implicit anti-war agenda, and, even more problematic, that any war writing sharing some of the formal features outlined in her study is *intrinsically* a declaration of war against war. In other words, considering the breadth and diversity of the texts mentioned throughout *Authoring War*, the passage comes dangerously close to saying that *all* war writing is at bottom anti-war writing. As I suggested above, even though critics may push the anti-war question to the margins of their argument—as is literally the case in McLoughlin's study—the dilemma resists being erased. It would seem that it is important for the author to indicate that the writers' skills all serve a superior ethical purpose. Whether one succeeds in stopping war by making lit is not important as long as one has tried. War writing, in her account, always tries to do the ethically correct thing.

What I described as the ghostly substance of the anti-war concept haunts McLoughlin's summation of her considerable achievements. She does not explain how the formal strategies highlighted in her book may advance the hope of stopping war. She simply states that those strategies would be part of any book aiming to stop war, heedless of the fact that certain rhetorical features appear in war writing pursuing different objectives. Homer's *Iliad* and Ernst Jünger's *Storms of Steel* may both depict "the cost of armed conflict" as effectively as Tim O'Brien's Vietnam War writings, but it would be hard to argue that Homer's and Jünger's overarching intentions are the same as O'Brien's. At the same time, one may note that O'Brien understands war's dark appeals as much as his two predecessors. How such recognition may be squared with the "make lit, not war" slogan is never discussed. Perhaps also because *plot* is not one of the textual features analyzed in *Authoring War*, we never learn how, either rhetorically or structurally, a text may advance its utopian wish to put an end to war. To be sure, McLoughlin can hardly be unaware that some critics have called into question the supposed anti-war content of several of the texts she discusses, as well as underlined the contradictory nature of apparently anti-militarist texts like Joseph Heller's *Catch-22*.

This impasse in no way diminishes the remarkable insights of her book. If I call attention to the impalpable pacifist contours she claims for an incredibly long and diverse tradition of war writing, it is simply to reiterate the point that even though McLoughlin offers no precise definition of what makes a war text anti-war, she still feels a need to argue that the promotion of peace features as an important, though perhaps hidden, scope of all good war writing. She does acknowledge that "war representation can also occasion delight in violence," and she also refers to Nick Mansfield's argument that rather than dwelling on peace and war as two discrete concepts, we would do better to scrutinize "what configuration of the peace-war complex embroils us" (191) at any given time. However, these observations are largely afterthoughts, with no explicit connection to the formal analyses of the preceding 190 pages. Most important, McLoughlin almost casually hints at a spectral feature of anti-war writing that I omitted from my list, and which may in fact turn out to be the most important one. After noting the ultimate hopelessness of literature's effort to stop war, she suggests that "some more *positive* claims can be made for war writing" (191). I have italicized the key word of this sentence as it implicitly points to what is probably the main reason the anti-war concept is intrinsically nebulous. It is largely a reactive, negative concept, whose lack of substance is implicit in its parasitical nature. It is meant to express discomfort and resistance, but unlike the term it confronts, it does not point to something equally objective and ontologically consistent. This is not to say that war is not a contested term—far from it. However, in most war literature, war *is*, whereas anti-war is at best an effect which, through certain narrative and rhetorical strategies, the text aims to produce *in the reader*. The positive, non-ghostly substance that McLoughlin justly invokes is of course *peace*: peace neither as something utterly removed from the war at hand nor as a concept (like anti-war) nearly enslaved to its dialogical counterpart.

How Old is Anti-War Literature?

In her introduction to *Authoring War*, McLoughlin acknowledges that all wars are different and that arguments could be made about each war having "its own poesis." However, she believes also that even though each war confronts writers with its own specific challenges (writing about Homeric hand-to-hand combat is of course different from trying to describe trench warfare or aerial bombardments), representational strategies display a remarkable degree of similarity across different cultures and historical periods. Moreover, not only "perceptions (as well as representations) of warfare are shaped by previous representations" (13), but even war theorists usually approach war "as a monolithic concept" (15). In short, the truism that all wars are different should not deter the pursuit of "a structural tropological methodology extending from the *Iliad* to poetry about the wars in Iraq" (16).

McLoughlin's point about the rhetorical similarities in war writings across time and space is substantiated by her findings and readings. Rhetorically speaking, war writing is marked by a number of significant continuities. On the other hand, such analogies may convey rather different meanings as cultural and historical contexts change. "War" and "peace" have meant different things to different cultures, and while it may be legitimate to "refunction" the *Iliad* into a sort of "anti-war" text from *our* perspective, it would make very little sense to maintain that the critique of armed combat *we* find there was shared by readers of the classical and premodern ages.[8]

This is one of the main points made in an essay originally written by Leslie Fiedler as an introduction to Jaroslav Hašek's *The Good Soldier Schweik*. The anti-war novel is a literary byproduct of World War I and should be considered as its "chief lasting accomplishment" (vi). Fiedler notes that though "it had been prophesied in the first two thirds of Stephen Crane's *The Red Badge of Courage*," "before the 1920's that genre did not exist" (vi). The uniqueness of authors like Ernest Hemingway, Henry Barbusse, Erich Maria Remarque, and others lies also in their having lived "in the interval between two conventional ways of understanding war" (vii):

> For a thousand years or so, roughly from the time of Charlemagne to 1914, the wars
> of Christendom, whether fought against external enemies or strictly within the
> family, had been felt and celebrated in terms of a single continuous tradition. And
> those who lived within that tradition assumed without question that some battles

at least were not only justifiable but holy, just as they assumed that to die in such battles was not merely a tolerable fate but the most glorious of events. Doubts they may have had, but these could scarcely be confessed to themselves, much less publicly flaunted. (ix)

Fiedler admits there may have been contradictions within this "single continuous tradition" ("what, after all, had any military code to do with the teachings of Christ?"), but in his view it was only "the literature of disenchantment that followed World War" that put an end to the celebration of the Christian hero and the concept of Honor. Though "the antiwar novel did not end war" (ix), it sprang to life at the moment when "men, still nominally Christian, come to believe *that the worst thing of all is to die*," or perhaps, more exactly "that no cause is worth dying for" (ix). To be sure, the Christian heroic tradition had been slowly dying all along, but it was only "under the impact of total war" that those who fought were "shocked into admitting that perhaps they no longer believed what they fought for" (vii).

Fiedler's historicizing may be accused of downplaying any literary denunciation of war before 1914, but he is right to insist that it was only after the devastating experience of total war that criticism began to speak of the anti-war novel as a genre (or subgenre) of modern literature. Again, one may object to the loose use of the term "genre." Fiedler does not offer any morphology of the anti-war novel, and he may have been wiser to use a term like "mode" or "attitude." Still, Fiedler is correct to point out that the experience of prolonged trench warfare brought about an unprecedented revolt against war that cast in a completely different light many old *topoi* of the Western literary tradition.[9] For example, no one would deny that in Western literature there have been characters "who have believed that death was the worst event and honor a figment" (ix) long before the Great War. The Falstaffs and the Sancho Panzas of the past, however, were creatures of "low comedy" who trembled in front of Prince Hal and Don Quixote, and who represented "not a satirical challenge but precisely a 'comic relief'" (x). One must assume, therefore, that as much as Fielder would have enjoyed McLoughlin's treatment of the *gelotopoios* (laughter-maker) as a recurring figure in war writing from Homer's Thersites and Shakespeare's Falstaff to Joseph Heller's Yossarian and Tim O'Brien's Cacciato, he would have objected that, on both a functional and a cultural level, it is only after World War I that the comic character can rise to "heroic" stature. As Philip Metres has also noted, Thersites may be the prototype of all war resisters, but we should not forget that his protest "is dispensed with quickly" and, to boot, ridiculed by the surrounding narrative context (1).

Even though Cynthia Wachtell's *War No More* refers to Fiedler's periodization only in a footnote, it could be said that her whole book is meant to call into question its validity. As the dates (1861–1914) of her book's subtitle imply, for Wachtell anti-war literature—at least in the United States—has a longer history and originates with the American Civil War. However, whereas Fiedler evokes the notion of genre and focuses on the novel, Wachtell speaks more generally of a "common impulse to rewrite and redefine war" shared by "the antiwar authors" studied in her book—an impulse that cut through different literary genres. She notes that a close look at the historical record shows that "the meaning of war is in the eye of the beholder" (4), and, for example, while in 1637 Captain Underhill saw in the destruction of a Pequot fort "the hand of God helping the New England colonists," during the following century Benjamin Franklin "was appalled" by the massacre of a group of Conestoga Indians at the hands of white Pennsylvanians and called the latter "Christian white savages" (5). *War No More* thus provides a useful corrective to interpretations of American history and culture emphasizing exclusively the gun-fighting impulse. No one before Wachtell had so carefully illustrated how many writers—well-known ones as well as many now seldom read—devoted their energies to denouncing the folly and the hypocrisy of war in general, and of American wars in particular.

While *War No More* shows that anti-war feelings and rhetoric predate by decades World War I, one may wonder whether the "impulse" Wachtell wishes to recover was able to crystallize into something like a literary tradition, and whether the difference between pre– and post–World War I anti-war literature is only one of degree—as Wachtell seems to believe—or else also one of a kind, as Fiedler argues. To answer these questions we need first to understand how *War No More* identifies anti-war literature. What are the common features shared by "dissenting interpretation[s] of war's violence" (6) produced since the Civil War? The ways U.S. anti-war writers waged war on war are essentially two: they "questioned the fundamental morality of warfare" (2), and "they did their best to strip military training, combat, and death of all romantic rhetoric" (6). One may object that this is a touch too vague. At least since Augustine, just war theorists have never denied that war is, in essence, immoral. War entails the taking of people's lives and therefore to call moral war *as such* would not do. This is not to say that just-war theorists are by any stretch of the imagination "anti-war." "The just war theory says that if certain conditions are met, it is permissible to go to war; and it says further that if certain other conditions are met, one's manner of conducting the war is moral" (Holmes 174). This does in no way moralize killing, but it does subordinate the immorality of killing to the morality, the "just cause" (*jus ad bellum*) of a specific war. As long as the cause is just and "just rules" (*jus in bello*) are respected in the way a war is waged, the latter is morally acceptable. The question, therefore, is not so much whether a text finds war "fundamentally" immoral, but whether it subordinates the immorality of war to the conditions that theoretically justify war. As for the second feature Wachtell sees central in anti-war writing—the attack on romantic rhetoric—it suggests that with the advent of realism and its debunking of chivalric images of warfare, literature became ipso facto anti-war, a proposition that is hard to substantiate and one that in fact Wachtell herself does not really care to defend.

As the term "impulse" suggests, most if not all the "antiwar writers" discussed in *War No More* rejected war in a sort of unpremeditated, instinctive way. Thus, after identifying many of her writers as "antiwar," Wachtell is quick to add that their anti-war feelings were far from being consistent and continued over time. For example, while Herman Melville, John William De Forest, and Walt Whitman gave through their writings a non-idealized picture of the Civil War, all three of them "felt conflicted about the morality of the war" (7) and did not dare to openly criticize a conflict they felt was inevitable. Moreover, while they distrusted romantic attitudes, there was much they found admirable in the conduct of individual soldiers. Rather than opposing the Civil War, they opposed "the way in which it was represented in print" (78). No wonder that what is announced at the outset as a study charting "the rise of antiwar literature in America from the Civil War to the eve of World War I" (2) is, a few pages later, reassessed as an examination of "American writers' complex, contested, and frequently self-conflicted understanding of war" (8). With very few exceptions (Mark Twain, Ernest Crosby, George Kirkpatrick) all the authors discussed turn out to have been only relatively and contradictorily "antiwar." In sum, while *War No More* convincingly shows that the works "prophesying" the anti-war novels of the 1920s and 1930s extend far beyond "the two thirds of Stephen Crane's *The Red Badge of Courage*," it treads too lightly on the "antithetical" views of war entertained by authors whose work is considered both "antiwar" and, upon closer scrutiny, not always and unreservedly so. Writers like Melville, Whitman, Bierce, and De Forest were appalled by the reality of warfare, and yet not only could they "neither fully reject nor fully embrace the popular literary norms of the war era" (41) but, crucially, they were never really opposed to the Civil War to begin with. Even though their contradictory stances are not explored in depth, Wacthell's discussion shows that Melville and Whitman would be better described as just-war, rather than anti-war, writers. They frankly depicted the horror of the battlefield but never questioned the necessity of fighting. To call them anti-war writers is to render the concept of anti-war essentially meaningless.[10]

Writing "impulsively" and intermittently against war, many authors discussed in *War No More* painted war as an ugly affair—but so did William Tecumseh Sherman and Robert E. Lee, and many other military commanders before and after them. Opposition to romantic views of war as a glorious affair can hardly count as a sign of pacifism. Here it may be useful to remember that Stephen Crane's Henry Fleming joins the Union army eager to partake in "Homeric struggles" only to discover the brutality and ultimate confusion of modern mechanized warfare. However, regardless of how Crane felt about his character, Henry never turns into an anti-war rebel. Readers may wonder whether by the end Fleming is deluded in feeling he has achieved "a quiet manhood," but regardless of how *we* feel, *he* seems to have accepted a war that is not Homeric but remains nonetheless fascinating (Mariani, *Spectacular Narratives* 139–71). Wachtell correctly notes that "whether Crane's book constitutes an antiwar novel has been much debated" (104), but we never hear her opinion. The problem is not that here we have yet another writer whose anti-war credentials are at the same time evoked and undermined but that we are faced with yet another instance of how problematic the concept of anti-war writing is to begin with.

Like other studies of war literature, *War No More* suggests that gruesome accounts of war count as anti-war statements. Yet the authors of such anti-war pronouncements could not outright reject war in their writings. This was especially the case with the Civil War authors. Wachtell claims that writers like Whitman and Melville "boldly questioned the consensus view of the war as morally righteous" (109), though she earlier stated that "Melville did not condemn the Civil War. Indeed, he did not publicly oppose the Civil War at all," which he considered a "just war" (49). How could Melville condemn the righteousness of a war he thought was just? Similarly, Wachtell maintains that "if the Civil War record was whitewashed by contemporary writers, Whitman was complicit. He added his own artful strokes to the collaborative paint job" (89). This is nicely put, but what happens to the "bold" questioning of the consensus view of the war he deserves praise for? I quote these inconsistencies not to make light of a scholarly work whose merits are considerable but to call attention to the fact that also in *War No More* the concept of anti-war is deployed in such a contradictory way as to carry virtually no cognitive value whatsoever.

True, when the term is applied, in the book's second half, to Mark Twain and the largely forgotten pacifist writer and activist Ernest Crosby, it seems fully justified. How else would one describe a text like Twain's "The War-Prayer" or Crosby's *Captain Jinks, Hero*, if not as anti-war satires mocking America's imperial ambitions in Cuba and the Philippines and reinterpreting "war as plain bloodlust" (146)? Of course it was easier for Twain and Crosby to write devastating critiques having the Spanish-American war in mind—a conflict that could hardly be painted as "just," no matter how vehemently the jingoists argued about its necessity. Though their pronouncements did not found a "genre" or tradition of anti-war writing the way post–World War I soldier-writers did in Fiedler's account, Twain and Crosby display something more radical and thorough than a mere "antiwar impulse." Texts like Twain's "The War-Prayer" or Crosby's *Captain Jinks*, or Crosby's poetry collection *War Echoes*, are so relentless in their attack on the viciousness and monstrosity of war that they certainly deserve to be called anti-war manifestos. Their rhetoric is so unambiguous it could be described as propaganda, if it weren't for the fact that the term has acquired—interestingly enough, only after World War I—a pejorative meaning.

War Literature and Symbolic Action

The anti-war stance of a Twain, a Crosby, or a Kirkpatrick is so unequivocal that it casts a critical light on the first half of Wachtell's book as well as on Fiedler's own claims for the "anti-war" novel of the 1920s and 1930s. As compared with the clarity with which not only the war in Cuba and the Philippines but also war in general is condemned by Twain and Crosby, the tortured attempts by Civil War writers to reconcile war and justice, violence and morality, can be seen as belonging to an altogether different narrative world. The same may be said of the post–World War I novelists Fiedler refers to. Their efforts always entailed a degree of complicity with war that prevents their texts from acquiring the straightforward rhetorical clarity of Twain's or Crosby's satirical onslaughts. This is not to suggest that outright critiques of war are morally superior to "self-conflicted" poems or novels like those of Melville, Crane, or Hemingway, nor have the former proved to be more effective than the latter in stopping war. My argument is that they should be described as two different types of what Kenneth Burke calls "symbolic action." In advancing his idea of "literature as an equipment for living," Burke proposed we see literary works as "proverbs writ large"—as linguistic constructs designed to confront a social, cultural, or existential problem. Just as proverbs "are designed for consolation or vengeance, for admonition or exhortation" (Burke, "Literature" 304), also works of literature may be considered "as strategies for dealing with situations" (296). Following Burke, I suggest we see war writings as ways to "handle" the intractable reality of war, and that we distinguish them, like proverbs, on the basis of their prevalent rhetorical strategies. Some war novels have a therapeutic, cathartic function, similar to those of proverbs whose aim is to console. Others may instead have a more explicit admonitory tone and "size up" the war situation in a different way. As Burke explains, these categories are not by definition mutually exclusive. A proverb, or a work of literature, may be initially perceived as having a consolatory function and then later be "taken over" for vindictive or admonitory purposes. Overlaps are possible but for the most part only when a proverb or a text is considered at an abstract level. Once it situates itself in a specific communicative context, one meaning usually takes precedence over latent ones.

As mentioned earlier, McLoughlin touches on a nearly identical concept when discussing the ends of war literature. The "multitudinous" reasons "that make war's representation imperative" (7) may be filed under two main "strategies." On the one hand war writing purports "to impose order on the chaos of conflict and so to render it more comprehensible," "to give some meaning to mass death," "to provide cathartic relief," "to memorialize," and so forth. All these ends share one encompassing strategic aim: to assign meaning to an apparently meaningless event—war. The second aim listed by McLoughlin—"to warn; and even, through the warning, to promote peace" (7)—falls squarely under a different rubric. Warnings are verbal constructs meant to dissuade people from doing something and may be classed as "rhetoric" in its purest Aristotelian sense. Of course one may wish to argue—as McLaughlin does—that by showing people, for example, what an atrocious thing war is, you are encouraging them to choose more peaceful means to settle their disputes. However, such indirect warnings are hardly ever unambiguous in most war literature, and especially in novels, with their multiplicity of voices, points of view, and levels of discourse. As I noticed apropos the *Iliad*, often the same war text may be read either as a warning or as an incitement to further violence. Plenty of war stories may be read as cautionary tales, but only occasionally their admonitions acquire the force and bluntness of a direct "warning." To put all this in a simple but hopefully clarifying formula, the warning issued by most war literature could be summed up by the sign, "Danger—War Zone. Enter at Your Own Risk," whereas the sign introducing an explicit anti-war text like Twain's "War-Prayer" would be more like a prohibition: "War Zone—Do Not Enter."

In *The Difference Satire Makes*, Fredric Bogel notes that traditionally "criticism of satire has insisted on its clarity, its stability, and its ultimate if not apparent lack of ambiguity" (4). While irony is constructed as inherently ambiguous, satire is usually seen as a strategy of direct attack on the satirist's object of scorn, and therefore free from the "interpretative uncertainty" (67) accompanying irony. Challenging this concept of satire as a form of "relative ethical simplicity" (4), Bogel insists that irony's "intrinsic structure of doubleness" (67) has "its satiric counterpart in the connectedness that is . . . the very precondition for the sort of aggressive effort of separation that is identified with satiric attack and the satiric making of difference" (68). Simply put, far from being a sort of "stable irony," satire's meanings are also fraught with ambiguity. We must therefore entertain the possibility that even a text like Twain's "The War Prayer" may be marked by some degree of ambivalence. One could note, for example, that Twain's attack on war mongering and the "Christian" churches' role in promoting it is based on a contradictory image of the Almighty, who, according to the "stranger," is simultaneously willing to grant the congregation the victory it so eagerly desires and yet also sends a messenger to spell out "the unspoken part of the prayer" in the unlikely hope that, being confronted with the harsh truth, the faithful would change their minds. The Almighty's envoy makes clear that to ask for victory is to ask "for many unmentioned results which follow victory" ("War Prayer" 262). It is to ask the Lord to help "us . . . to tear their soldiers to bloody shreds with our shells; help us to cover their smiling fields with the pale forms of their patriot dead; help us to drown the thunder of the guns with the shrieks of their wounded, writhing in pain; help us to lay waste their humble homes with a hurricane of fire; help us to wring the hearts of their unoffending widows with unavailing grief" (262–63). The satirist aims to unmask the violence hidden in the congregation's "prayer" but if He is willing to grant such a monstrous request, how can "the Most High" expect his children to exercise the moral discernment he appears to advocate? In sum, by using war to show the hypocritical, violent underside of American institutional Christianity, Twain shows a "connectedness" to the very object of his own indignation, thus displaying a degree of that doubleness Bogel sees also in satire.

Even though, as I will argue in the final pages of this chapter, a case could be made that Twain's text is anti-war but maybe not pro-peace, "The War Prayer" belongs to a class of satirical attacks on war that are a rare breed within the world of war literature. The "war literature" that is mostly taught and written about comprises novels, memoirs, and poems whose "symbolic action" is more complicated and ambivalent than Twain's direct rhetorical onslaught. Fiedler is surely right in seeing an anti-war ethos emerging from the "disenchantment" of the post–World War I era, but he is wrong to assume the novel form could unambiguously express it. He insists, for example, in seeing Hemingway's *A Farewell to Arms* as epitomizing the new genre when, as I maintain below, its representation of war is ambivalent, to say the least.

War and Form

As Antonio Scurati has observed, even passages like the famous one where Frederic Henry expresses his embarrassment upon hearing the words "sacred, glorious, sacrifice, and the expression in vain" (143), or the other one in which he announces he has made "a separate peace" (188), may be read not as voicing the protagonist's rebellion against war but rather as signs of his nostalgia for a lost epoch in which those words *were* meaningful and it was inconceivable to be detached from one's community. Upon signing his separate peace, Frederic does not experience any exhilarating sensation. He simply feels "damned lonely" (188). His famous farewell to arms expresses "neither indignant rejection nor joyous relief, neither condemnation nor freedom. It is only a melancholic farewell" (Scurati 309). Whether Scurati is correct in seeing an analogy between Hemingway's mourning for the "loss of war as a cultural form" and Carl Schmitt's nostalgia for the post-Westphalian, juridically regulated *guerre en forme*, he demonstrates that one cannot unproblematically identify *A Farewell to Arms* as an anti-war polemic.

The implications of Scurati's argument, however, go beyond his reading of Hemingway's work. Scurati agrees with Fiedler in seeing World War I as a watershed in Western representations of war, but, unlike Fiedler, he argues that what total war broke away from was not a millennial Christian tradition but the Schmittian "ritualized," regulated war of the *Jus Publicum Europaeum*. The "loss" of this "classical" form of warfare, which began with the Napoleonic wars and was sanctioned by

World War I, generated a parallel loss of the cultural forms that traditionally narrated and "contained" war. In Scurati's view the tragedy of the "lost generation" was not only that it was decimated by war but that it also lost the possibility of thinking war "a cohesive form imposed on the formlessness of violence" (Scurati 312). The concept of a "separate peace" is from this point of view absolutely tragic, as it sanctions the impossibility of ever again confining war "within its traditional formal limits" (Scurati 309).

Scurati's reading of the post–World War I novel may be accused of too closely following Schmitt in conceiving of "classic" war as the only way an apparently ineradicable will-to-violence may be channeled into a "civilized" or "limited" form of sorts.[11] However, Scurati's construction of both war and war literature as ways to "give shape" and "set limits" to violence—as attempts not to "outlaw" armed conflict but to confine it within a set of legal and rhetorical conventions—is a useful one. As seen from this perspective, the task of representation is not that of outright rejecting any form of violence but, on the contrary, that of containing a potentially endless and purely destructive violence into the "disciplined" form of war. Of course, given that total warfare is irreducible to the older (both narrative and juridical) paradigms of "classic" war, the modern war novelist may give the impression of rejecting war altogether, as testified by Hemingway's thrashing of the notions of honor, glory, and courage. Yet to the extent that also modern war literature must *narrate* war, to think of it as being nearly automatically anti-war is a contradiction in terms. As Scurati argues, the war novel cannot oppose war but must exist *side by side with war*. The war novel may well criticize—as Hemingway undoubtedly does in *A Farewell to Arms*—the emptiness of an older martial rhetoric, but it can do so only by resorting to a new rhetoric that will inevitably be in a relation of *both opposition and proximity* to war.

The insistence on the war novel's connectedness to the object it supposedly wishes to paint in a condemning light appears homologous to satire's ambivalent relation to the target of its rhetorical barbs. In both cases, the attacker and the attacked share a common ground—a point emphasized by Kenneth Burke's concept of rhetoric in general and of the dialectic in particular. To employ Burke's own terms, we might say that war is "consubstantial" with the war novel, the latter being necessarily "a part of" the real or imagined experience the war writer also wishes to break "apart" from (*Grammar of Motives* 406). As Burke reminds us by quoting Coleridge, *inter res heterogeneas non datur oppositio* (414). The critique of war can never come from a standpoint wholly external to it. War writing is always entangled with war and to the extent that it may indeed be argued that the former's bona fide intent is to promote peace, one should qualify this statement by observing that—as we shall see in a moment—peace itself is always inevitably entangled with war. And just as all war writing must offer a representation—no matter how partial or unsatisfactory—of war, it always by the same token needs to project a vision of war's dialectical counterpart. War novels should therefore always be read also as *war-and-peace* novels. Unlike the "pacifist novel"—which I take to be that extremely rare object expressing a loathing for war in any form—the "peace novel" would be a war novel one reads with the intention of assessing not only its representation of war but also what image of "war's other" (as Nick Mansfield aptly describes peace) the text either implicitly or explicitly constructs.[12]

Peace and War / Peace *Is* War?

> O peace! how many wars were waged in thy name.
> —Alexander Pope

Let me begin with the following proposition: if a narration can often slide from the field of war literature to that of the anti-war story, that may well be due to the fundamentally ambivalent and contradictory use of the term "peace." Nowadays, probably to an extent much greater than at any other time in history, most of us emphatically declare to be peace lovers, and it is next to impossible to find someone willing to admit that he or she is in way of principle a war enthusiast. While theorists and pundits have repeatedly insisted that war continues to be necessary, political leaders of all stripes are always careful to present themselves as reluctant warriors. However, much as we may be tempted to liquidate the promotion of peace through war as a paradigmatic case of Orwellian double-speak ("war is peace"), hypocrisy is only part of the problem. A cursory consideration of world history should be enough to realize that any peace that the peoples of our planet have been lucky enough to enjoy has been generated by historical processes shaped by strife and war. In the words of Italian philosopher Augusto Ponzio,

> The world in its current shape is the outcome of war. There is no national territory, state, community, or union of states that is not the result of war. Any current configuration is sanctioned by war. Any peace is a war's peace, a peace gained by war. So far there are no boundary lines that are not the outcome of war. War requires and sets boundaries, so that it may reproduce itself. To keep the peace is to keep a status quo reached through war. (7)[13]

It may be objected that, occasionally, settlements are reached through peaceful negotiations, though one could retort not only that agreements are usually reached after wars have broken out but also that they are heavily influenced by the outcome of the armed conflicts preceding them. In short, Augustine's notion that "one wages war in order to have peace" cannot be liquidated as sheer bad faith or propaganda.[14] Even though we intuitively think of war as the opposite of peace, the historical record suggests that while war and peace are not the same thing, they must be grasped as part of the same historical and theoretical continuum.

In *Theorizing War*, Nick Mansfield eloquently illustrates to what extent "the deployment of the term 'war' is inevitably a deployment of something else as well, the 'other' of war, something called variously peace, or civil society, or sovereign authority, or love or friendship" (2). This "other" of war is *not* "a simple opposite of war, something that we aim to protect from war or retrieve from it somehow" (2). This other—which we will refer to with the umbrella-term, "peace"—is what war needs to constantly refer to "in order to make sense at all" (3). Through an enlightening discussion of theories of war and peace from Hobbes and Kant to Clausewitz and all the major poststructuralist theorists, Mansfield shows the "ineluctable interpenetration" of the twin concepts of peace and war. His point is not to suggest that the difference between the two concepts has been completely eroded, an idea he rejects along with "the associated view that only by restoring this difference can we make peace really available" (6). Mansfield's position is that the distinction between peace and war is not the one "on which our hope of perpetual peace rests, but the difference that makes war potentially meaningful and that is constantly referred to by politicians in their rationalizations of aggressive policy" (6). We must therefore reject both the idea that peace can be defined without reference to war and the seemingly opposite yet attendant notion that war has somehow cannibalized peace. As each other's Other, peace and war remain different yet connected, inseparable yet in a permanent state of tension.

Analogously, in *The Transformation of Peace*, after lamenting that peace "is rarely conceptualised, even by those who often allude to it" (2), Oliver Richmond goes on to argue that, especially today, it has become apparent

> that war is a tool of a shifting conceptualisation of peace, inextricably linked to its creation and expansion, and used to achieve a version of peace acceptable to the hegemonic few, or to the many. . . . Types of war may provide the impetus for types of peace: versions of peace may provide the impetus for violence. . . . There seems to have been a shift from efforts to establish and preserve clear distinctions between peace and war . . . to an acceptance that the two can also essentially be ambiguous hybrids. (13)

Richmond's "ambiguous hybridity," like Mansfield's "ineluctable interpenetration" of peace and war, does not mean—as I stated above—that we must resign ourselves to the Orwellian nightmare of acts of war sold to public opinion as missions of peace. As Mansfield puts it, "Our rejection of war, like our purported commitment to democracy and human rights, is not merely hypocritical. It must be understood as part of a complex in which war and its other emerge together in a double relationship *in which they both encourage and refuse one another*" (163, emphasis added). In Kenneth Burke's wordplay, peace is both historically and conceptually "a part of" war and "apart from" war. We are always caught in what Mansfield describes as an "aporetic entanglement" (98): if we cannot, on the one hand, "take refuge in the sentimental idea of an achievable perpetual peace," on the other "we cannot simply resign ourselves to the idea that war is either inevitable, productive or meaningful" (99).

As we shall see in chapter 2, many peace activists have been struggling with this paradox for a long time. Their efforts to fashion a non-violent way to fight violence have come up against similar tensions and contradictions. Here, however, I would like to draw some tentative conclusions apropos the literary and cultural implications of the situation I have been describing. Given that not even peace can provide us with an Archimedean point from which we may view war at a safe distance, what might be the advantages of reading war writing at one and the same time as *peace* writing? In order to answer this question it may be helpful to consider the contribution that the relatively new field of peace studies brings to the study of literature. As Laurence Lerner has argued, what distinguishes the field of peace studies from the related fields of war studies or military history is "the fact that it is being undertaken from a committed position, the view that war is an evil which we are trying to learn how to eradicate" (643). The purpose of peace studies is that of producing "pacifist" readings of texts, whether literary or otherwise.

The first task that peace studies as applied to literature should set for itself is that of investigating how war has been represented in literature. Interestingly enough, whereas many critics feel that war literature is usually written *against* war, Lerner's starting point is, to the contrary, that "traditional representations of war are not pacifist" (643). Perhaps because most of his examples come from the pre-Enlightenment world of Shakespeare and Milton, Lerner believes that a great deal of literature does indeed glorify "military prowess" the way, for example, Shakespeare does in his history plays. The pacifist critic must therefore be a resisting reader. Confronted with works animated by a fascination with the martial spirit, he or she needs to respond in two ways. First, "by measuring . . . [the text] against criteria which, as readers, we bring to bear on it" (647), and, second, by "exposing the fissures and contradictions within a text" (648) that may subvert what appears to be its surface meaning. The pacifist reader must register and indeed "emphasize" the literary text's endorsement of war, but she may at least in part console herself with the knowledge that, very often, even texts like Shakespeare's histories or Homer's *Iliad* can be read against the grain. In sum, the pacifist critic has to take note of both the pro- and anti-war arguments that a text makes, "by measuring it against criteria which, as readers committed to a contrary ideology, we bring to bear on it" (647).

The peace studies agenda Lerner illustrates would not seem to be markedly different from that of studies of war literature produced from a less openly committed perspective. We might indeed say that, thus constructed, the business of pacifist literary studies is no other than war. Lerner acknowledges this problem by noting that "to restrict ourselves to the representation of war would be to limit the possibilities of peace studies for literary criticism" (648). Besides devoting their labors to the critical study of war literature, pacifist literary studies should investigate "how far militarism informs our conceptualizing of other experience" (648). Here Lerner's proposal opens new, interesting possibilities. As Lerner shows in his reading of *Paradise Lost*, a Peace Studies approach will ask questions such as, in Milton's version of universal history, "How far is God a general?" (648). Or, on a larger plane, to what extent is the spiritual battle described in the poem—a true mother of all battles if ever there was one—"seen in terms of actual fighting" (651)? By asking the reader to consider the virtual omnipresence of war metaphors and violence in texts we would not usually class as "war writing," peace studies may indeed break new ground. Questions similar to the ones we put to war literature—as I hope to show in the chapters devoted to Joel Barlow's *Columbiad* and Melville's *Moby-Dick*—can be usefully employed to interrogate literary texts that are ostensibly not primarily concerned with armed conflict.[15]

Lerner's essay focuses, for the most part, on how pacifists may respond to the representation or the language of war. R. S. White's *Pacifism and English Literature: Minstrels of Peace*, instead, though making "no claim that there is a coherent and sustained tradition or 'school' of pacifist literature in English," concentrates on literature from the Middle Ages to the present whose subject is the celebration of peace "as a natural condition for human existence" (1). This book is noteworthy because to White literary peace studies should not be concerned only with the question of how war and violence are represented in literature but also raise the question of what it means to represent *peace*. Even though I am not convinced by White's argument that a pacifist literary criticism should not trouble itself with distinctions among different conceptions of pacifism—which he sees as "artificial categorisations" (9)—his effort to retrieve representations of peace is both admirable and original.[16]

In his introduction White writes of how often, in researching pacifism, he would encounter in book indexes the phrase, "Peace: see War." He is of course right in lamenting the fact that while those who wish to study peace can hardly escape devoting much time to the study of war, the reverse is not usually the case with students of war. Yet he too must acknowledge, example after example, that peace is discussed by poets and novelists first and foremost in relation to war. In order to grasp what peace looks like, also peace writers—writers whose primary objective is not to think war but peace—are inescapably forced to confront war. One fine example of this is provided by White's discussion of Denise Levertov's "Making Peace," certainly one of the most compelling poetic explorations of this theme in the English language.

As White notes, one must pay attention to the poem's "implicit" as well as "explicit" messages. Implicitly, Levertov suggests that so far poetry has been unable to think peace without having recourse to a language indebted to a rhetoric of violence. Anti-war poetry—including much of the poetry written by Levertov herself—is oppositional and angry, and "the imagination of peace" remains locked in a struggle against "the imagination of disaster." On a more explicit level, however, her argument is, according to White, "that the radically different message of peace poetry requires not only a new perspective but also a new vocabulary and a range of poetic means" (20). The poem of peace cannot get "there" before peace does, and yet poetry may provide an important stimulus to restructure "the sentences our lives are making."

Levertov's effort to think peace as a "presence" (and not as "the absence of war"), echoing Johan Galtung's classic distinction between "positive" and "negative" peace (*Peace* 109–34), is not free from a contrastive reference to war.[17] Even in the final lines—with their Dantesque evocation of vibrating light—the Utopian "energy field" of peace is grasped as something "more intense than war." The "forming crystal" of peace begins to take shape by showing itself to be *stronger* than war, or better, in light of the etymology of the word "intense," by having a capacity to *stretch* and *resist* superior to that of war. As White perceptively observes, the poem's tone is "tentative, hypothetical, groping for something without quite maintaining confidence that it can ever be found. The search is for a poetry which is obliquely *against* war while being fundamentally a poetry *for* peace" (20). White here calls attention to a crucial distinction between works written against war and a genuine literature of peace which, though it may still need to refer to war, would do so *obliquely*, indirectly, as its main scope would not be so much to condemn war as to praise the virtues of peace as a *positive* social and existential state. Of course even "pro-peace" writing can be defined as such only when seen as a response to a war-ridden world—there would be no need to sing the beauty of peace if that were the normal state of affairs in human life. Still, there are examples of a poetics of peace—some poems by Adrienne Rich and Maya Angelou, for example—that show the pacifist artist refusing to confront war on its own ground in order to concentrate "upon details of everyday life" or on peace as a "practical implementation of natural law" (White 256).

In his conclusion White has to admit that most of the writing discussed in his book falls under the rubric of "anti-war" literature—literature written in opposition "to a particular war in its historical and political specificity" (258). However, he insists that there exists a body of literature "that discards war altogether as an aberrant, unnatural and irrational activity, not only unworthy of human beings but, more fundamentally, a threat to the continued existence of the species" (258). What interests me here is that this pro-peace poetics is described by White as anti-war, and not obliquely so. The most significant difference between the pro-peace and the anti-war positions is no longer that one manages to do without any explicit reference to war while the other borrows the language of conflict in order to fight against war. The difference is now located at the level of ideology, with anti-war literature opposing a specific war (but perhaps condoning another, "just" or "inevitable" war) and pro-peace literature opposing *any* war as a denial of human beings' truest nature. In the end, therefore—and this is by no means a criticism of White's rich study—we must accept that, however admirable his or her search for "the imagination of peace," the pro-peace writer can never really leave far behind "the imagination of disaster."

White's insistence that war resistance should be grounded in a set of *positive* pacifist values offers an important corrective to those who believe that to promote peace is enough to declare war evil. As I will insist throughout this book, if we wish to grasp the critical (anti-war/pro-peace) aspects of war literature, we cannot restrict our analysis to the ways in which war is represented. We must also investigate how peace is implicitly (as is often the case) or explicitly constructed. However, while we should heed White's invitation to think of peace as presence, the only way to avoid encountering "the imagination of disaster" would be to study texts extolling the virtues of Arcadian contentment. As long as our critical business is with war texts, the images of peace found there must be assessed against Mansfield's peace-war complex. When reading war literature, that is, we need to understand the extent to which the peace projected by the text is continuous with the text's imaging of armed conflict. Because even though the war-peace nexus can never be completely broken, some war texts do allow peace to speak in a voice that does not merely echo that of war.

An Ambiguous Peace: Two Examples

I noted above that if there is a text in American literature that is unquestionably anti-war, that is Mark Twain's "War Prayer." Yet I added also that Twain's text showcases a rather troubling image of God. The text mounts an implacable attack on the hypocrisy of the so-called Christian churches, always ready to enlist God on America's side. By providing the prayer uttered by the congregation with its unspoken subtext, Twain's stranger performs a textbook example of ideology critique. He shows that to ask God for victory means to ask him to visit unlimited suffering upon the enemy. By underlining that this is done "in the spirit of Love"

("War Prayer" 263), the stranger calls attention to the disfiguration of Christ's original message. Yet if that is what these Christians really want, we are told, God will grant them their request. This detail implicates "God" in the wars of humankind. According to Edward J. Blum, "The silent prayers approached God as a murderer and a nationalist. And this God, Twain implied, could not be the God of the Bible" (35). Unfortunately, as everyone who has read the Bible knows, there are several occasions in the Bible were God is invoked precisely as a murderer of enemies and as a hypernationalist interested exclusively in his own followers' well-being. Twain was well aware of this, and it is no accident that the "Prayer" itself mentions both that "a war-chapter from the Old Testament was read" and that the congregation addresses this Biblical God as "all-terrible" ("War Prayer" 261).[18] While this Warrior God is by no means the *only* God of the Bible, it is certainly *one* God who is also found there.

The story does not sponsor completely the idea of God as commander-in-chief. Unless we consider the stranger a lunatic—but then we would be adopting the perspective of the people who are the target of the story's satire—we must accept the man as the Almighty's messenger and, moreover, that he was sent on Earth because God is sincerely trying to convert His followers. Some readers even consider the possibility that this stranger may be a Messiah of sorts (see Eutsey). Whether this is the case or not, the stranger stands out as the spokesman of a "just and fair" God—a God who is *also* in the Bible and who is not easily reconcilable with his incarnation as God the Warrior. But also Twain's God appears to be contradictory. His benevolence prompts Him to send a messenger to enlighten His people, but His willingness to consent to the congregation's request, no matter how monstrous, is puzzling and implicitly calls into question His merciful side. It could be argued that here Twain is advancing a materialist argument by suggesting that God the Warrior is nothing but a projection of human beings' perverted, bloody desires. Yet one must also note that by constructing an ambivalent image of God, Twain is depriving his text of the only possible location for true Love and Peace. No human being, excepting the stranger, can see the war-prayer's hidden truth. Only God can. But the God who sees the truth will not renounce violence.

Twain's "War Prayer" is of course a powerful, biting, and unfortunately long-ignored attack on the ideology of war akin to the ones unleashed by Swift in *Gulliver's Travels* or, two centuries later, by Dalton Trumbo in *Johnny Got His Gun*. The text is unquestionably anti-war, but, in R. S. White's terms, it would be hard to describe it as pro-peace. Not a single member of the Church's audience is able to get the stranger's message, and on His part God is willing to issue warnings but powerless to side with peace. While the story reveals how the only "love" the community knows is a narcissistic love of itself, and therefore the only peace they can aspire to is a victor's peace, it seems to confirm that human beings are so depraved that they will in the end get all the war and violence they deserve. If that is what they want, God will see to that. The only "peace" of the story seems to reside with a holy, but very distant, immaterial, and rather contradictory God. Overall, the scenario Twain paints is indeed as "ghastly" as the stranger.

Let me now move on to another "ghastly show," to use Catherine Barkley's description of the Battle of the Somme in *A Farewell to Arms*. One of Fiedler's prototypical "antiwar novels," Hemingway's text presents us with a more explicit engagement with the concept of peace. As mentioned earlier, after the defeat of the Italian army at Caporetto, Lt. Frederic Henry decides he has had enough of war and announces he has made "a separate peace" (188). Fiedler believes this makes of Frederic a new kind of "hero"—the "antiheroic hero" of a world "in which men begin wars knowing their avowed ends will never be accomplished" (x). Frederic's desertion, however, is only *a* "farewell to arms," the act of an isolated individual who, moreover, is far from imparting any specific anti-war significance to his desertion. "I had taken off the stars, but that was for convenience. It was no point of honour. I was not against them. I was through. I wished them all the luck. There were the good ones, and the brave ones, and the calm ones and the sensible ones, and they deserved it. But it was not my show any more and I wished this bloody train would get to Mestre and I would eat and stop thinking" (181). Frederic's "separate peace" is not an act of rebellion, just a somber withdrawal from a "show" he does not want to be a part of any longer: "I had the paper but I did not read it because I did not want to read about the war. I was going to forget the war" (188). My point is not so much that Fiedler's paramount example of the new disposition of the "antiwar novel" has no pacifist vision but that, just as "war never emerges outside of a relationship to some conceptual other" (Mansfield 162), also peace is always defined in relation to a specific understanding of war. The question we need ask, therefore, is what is the war context that allows Frederic's "separate peace" to emerge?

Scurati's provocative reading of Frederic as a man deprived, like other men of his generation, of the opportunity to fight a "classic" *guerre en forme* provides us with a possible answer. Even though I find his wholesale acceptance of Schmitt's theoretical framework problematic, I think Scurati is right in suggesting that the verso of Frederic's "separate peace" is the notion of a "separate war." He may be overstretching the point when he argues that the post-Caporetto scenario of Hemingway's novel reflects the Schmittian disintegration of a regulated form of interstate warfare, to be replaced by a new type of war in which various de-regulated "armies" (partisans, "special forces," terrorists, and the like) will conduct their own "private wars." While it is true that Frederic signs his separate peace only after he narrowly escapes being shot by the Carabinieri as either a spy or a traitor, it is debatable whether the execution without trial of all officers "of the rank of major and above who were separated from their troops" (175) really provides an illustration of what happens when a Schmittian, "regulated" war gives way to "civil," indiscriminate warfare. After all, both the perpetrators and the victims of the violence Hemingway describes—as well as the protagonists of the other violent episode I discuss below—wear uniforms, and the Carabinieri are neither terrorists nor partisans, but military police acting under orders. The scene may suggest not so much the coming apart of the political, juridical, and cultural form of Classic War, but a higher stage of that state of exception that is war, whether "Classic" or not.[19] Yet there is no question that Frederic's "separate peace" is affirmed not only after he has risked being executed, but also after he has actively engaged in an act of "separate war" that precedes the battle police's shooting of the officers. This is an episode that Scurati fails to mention, and yet it is one that could be more legitimately read as an anticipation of the "civil war" scenario Schmitt sees as superseding the age of Classic warfare.

During the chaotic retreat following the Austrian breakthrough at Caporetto, Frederic shoots the two sergeants for refusing to help in getting a jeep out of the mud, and for breaking away from the group. "You can't order us. You're not our officer" (158), they tell Frederic, but, with Bonello's help, he murders one man and tries to kill the other one as well. As Margot Norris has argued in a splendid essay ("The Novel as War: Lies and Truth in Hemingway's *A Farewell to Arms*"), this episode parallels the one where the Carabinieri try to dispense the same treatment to Frederic (58–77). He is not merely a victim of a civil war scenario: he actively initiates it by waging his "separate war" on the two sergeants. His separate peace emerges out of this re-defined context, one in which the "hero" behaves in a truly "antiheroic" way by shooting an innocent man in cold blood. Following Mansfield's thesis on the "inseparability of war and its other" (164), we might see the emergence of Frederic's separate war as contiguous with the deployment of his separate peace. They literally "facilitate the emergence of one another, even in their defiance of one another" (Mansfield vi). We must therefore resist both the inclination to see Frederic's separate peace as indistinguishable from his separate war, and the associated temptation to recover an absolute difference between the two. Instead, both must be grasped as shaped by a specific historical and political context in which the enemy is no longer a *justus hostis*—a legitimate adversary who could be killed but who was also entitled to specific rights and a certain respect— but a criminal or "unlawful combatant."

So much, then, for the alleged anti-war disposition of Hemingway's antiheroic hero. It should be noted, however, that though Frederic is the narrator-protagonist of his own story, he dialogically shares the narrative stage with his lover. In fact, a standard reading of the novel is the one emphasizing how Frederic's farewell to arms is balanced by his taking refuge in the arms of Catherine. While there is no textual evidence to construct Frederic's desertion as an instance of pacifist rebellion, it is tempting to see the values of peace embodied in the woman with whom he flees to the neutral haven of Switzerland. As Sandra Whipple Spanier has persuasively argued, Catherine has the courage, the intelligence, and the maturity that distinguished Hemingway's ideal soldier. However, she is *not* a soldier, nor does she cultivate any illusions about the war that has killed her former fiancé. When Frederic mentions to her the dictum, "The coward dies a thousand deaths, the brave but one," she immediately undercuts this platitude by replying, "The brave dies perhaps two thousand deaths if he's intelligent. He simply doesn't mention them" (111). She may be the novel's true antiheroic hero, the one genuine "brave" of the narrative ("dear brave sweet" are the very last words Frederic addresses to her). Unlike Frederic, in the "war" she has to fight while trying to deliver her and Frederic's baby, she cannot afford the luxury of making a separate peace. As Gayle Whittier points out, "Catherine cannot escape from pregnancy because the 'enemy' is inside her, because she *is* the ritual battlefield. Her labor therefore reactivates imagery of war" (259). Unlike the soldiers in chapter 1, who "marched as though they were six months gone with child" because the ammunitions "bulged forward under the capes" (8), Catherine is literally "gone with" the child/weapon that will kill her.

Whether or not, as Whittier believes, the final suppression of Catherine allegorizes the male artist's appropriation of women's procreativity, there is overwhelming evidence that the narrator's metaphorics of war undermines the reader's desire to construct Catherine as a figure of "peace." One might say that, by reconceiving the experience of childbirth as a kind of war, Frederic makes a desperate effort to "handle" the otherwise meaningless, unacceptable death of his loved one. To see Catherine as a soldier who accepts bravely her fatal Caesarian wound is in a sense to have at least a language—though it is a language Frederic had earlier by and large rejected—through which the absurdity of her death can be narrated and somewhat "contained." At the same time, however, Catherine's "war" may be seen as something as private and "separate" as Frederic's own war and peace. No wonder that Frederic, standing in front of her dead body, remarks, "It was like saying good-bye to a statue" (256). The war monument she has become is only an empty form, removed from any communal context that would impart meaning to it. The peace she ultimately signifies is akin to the "perpetual" one satirically inscribed "on a Dutch innkeeper's sign upon which a burial ground was painted," referred to by Immanuel Kant in the opening line of his 1795 essay on "perpetual peace."

These sketchy observations on two texts that, though quite different, are commonly perceived as examples of anti-war writing, are not meant to exhaust the ways in which the deployment of "peace" can complicate our reading of them. My point is simply to suggest how, while peace can never be imagined independent of its other, it is all the same a concept we cannot do without when reading war literature, especially if we see it as either overtly or covertly anti-war. Yet war-literature criticism has traditionally devoted little attention to how specific images of peace may either contribute to or resist the production of attendant images of war. The problem is not only that, from a peace studies perspective, it could be lamented that criticism has been more interested in the anti-war rather than the pro-peace elements of war literature; what criticism has too often forgotten is that inasmuch as war needs at all times to define itself through the production of its other, also war literature needs to balance its obscene content with the moral consolation of some "pacifist" message encoded in the text. Yet, as we have seen, the "peace" produced by the war text may turn out to be disappointingly indebted to the imagination of war—and not "obliquely" so. This is why in this book I prefer to think of war resistance (literary or otherwise) as an antinomic "war against war." *All* "anti-war" texts may be shown to harbor ideological blind spots and contradictions, including the ones discussed at some length in the second part of this book. They were chosen not because they amount to unequivocal anti-war statements but because they self-consciously try to come to terms with the moral and intellectual paradox of waging war on war. And by so doing they may remind us of that more combative, militant peace that has significant roots, as we shall see shortly, in the history of the United States.

CHAPTER 2

Ad Bellum Purificandum

Giving Peace a Fighting Chance

A Very Short History of an Academic Scandal

Published by Alfred Knopf in September 2000, Michael Bellesiles's *Arming America: The Origins of a National Gun Culture* was immediately enthusiastically endorsed by the likes of Stewart Udall, Michael Kammen, Robert Dykstra, and other well-known scholars.[1] As Garry Wills put it in his review in the *New York Times*, Bellesiles's book dispelled "the darkness that covered the gun's early history in America" by providing overwhelming evidence that the American gun culture was created during the Civil War era, and that in the eighteenth century guns were much less significant. "Guns are [so] central to the identity of Americans, to their self-perception as a rugged and violent people, as well as to their representation of others," Bellesiles wrote in his introduction, "that the nation's history has been meticulously reconstructed to promote the necessity of a heavily armed American public. . . . [W]hat if we discovered that early American men did not have that special bond with their guns?" (9). Judging by the tempest that followed, and to some extent even preceded, the book's publication, if it could indeed be proved that—as Bellesiles intended to show—"America's gun culture is an invented tradition" (13), that would make no small difference to how many Americans perceive themselves. Bellesiles seems to have had a point when he closes his introduction by noting that "there exists a fear of confronting the specifics of these cultural origins, for what has been made can be unmade" (15). In other words, Bellesiles realized that since today the gun is "the axial symbol of American culture, absolutely integral to the nation's self image and looming even larger in plans for its future development," by showing that "it was not always that way" his research might stimulate an unmaking and remaking of American culture along less gun-owning lines (15)—an intellectual and political project that would obviously not go unchallenged.

I have been using the conditional mood because, as is well known, *Arming America* stands today in the eyes of most readers as an utterly disgraced book. Prestigious historians like Garry Wills and Edmund Morgan, after initially lavishing it with praise, have more or less explicitly retracted their earlier endorsements. In December 2002, Columbia University voted to rescind the Bancroft Prize awarded to *Arming America* a year before. Finally, also at the end of 2002 and following the report of the review board appointed to investigate the soundness and honesty of his research, Michael Bellesiles resigned from Emory University.[2] A number of scholars discovered serious discrepancies between Bellesiles's sources and their use or reproduction in the book. In particular, two lengthy reviews appearing in the *William and Mary Law Review* (by James Lindgren and Justin Heather) and the *Yale Law Journal* (by Lindgren alone) raised objections regarding the alleged scarcity of guns in the probate records Bellesiles claimed to have examined and which, at least in some cases, appeared to be nonexistent. Bellesiles admitted he may have made mistakes in handling some of his data, yet one academic review after another called into question every single claim on which Bellesiles's thesis rested—his readings of gun censuses, militia muster records, and homicide rates. Without going into the details of what has become known as "the Bellesiles scandal," it will suffice to recall the conclusions reached by the review board appointed by Emory to investigate the case. Asked whether Bellesiles had engaged in "intentional fabrication or falsification of research data," the board—while "seriously troubled by [his] scholarly conduct," and believing that Bellesiles's research in probate records was "unprofessional and misleading" as well as "superficial and thesis-driven," and furthermore that his explanations of errors "raise doubts about his veracity"— found it impossible to state conclusively that Bellesiles had fabricated or falsified his evidence. In other words, while firm in condemning his "sloppy" scholarship, the review board had to suspend its judgment regarding the question of Bellesiles's good faith.[3]

Some believe that, no matter what his mistakes may have been, Bellesiles was subjected to an unusual amount of criticism because his book was a de facto attack against the pro-gun lobby.[4] Being by nature skeptical about conspiracy theories, I cannot believe the NRA may have enlisted a significant number of professional historians to find at all costs some flaws in *Arming America*. On the other hand, considering the overall tone of many non-academic critiques of Bellesiles's book, it is not hard to believe he may have indeed received insulting emails and threats of one sort or another. What I find most interesting in the Bellesiles story is less the academic scandal per se than the heated debate surrounding it. In particular, I want to call attention to the angry reactions drawn by his thesis on the historical rather than mythical status of what is evidently perceived as a key component of the U.S. national character.

Even before experts called into question Bellesiles's findings, *Arming America* was criticized in newspapers, magazines, and on the Web as a "foolish" attack on what Charlton Heston—at the time president of the NRA—described as a "useful myth" of America's past. Bellesiles was accused in several reviews of pursuing a "liberal-leftist" political agenda: of wanting, that is, to challenge from a historical perspective the notion that gun owning was understood as an individual right in the Second Amendment. Most of this early criticism did come, as Alexander Cockburn has noted, from "NRA types . . . [and therefore] their often cogent demolitions were initially discounted as sore-loser barrages from the rednecks." Once the academics came on the scene, they by and large decided to stick to the more or less objective flaws in Bellesiles's scholarship, declining to take issue with the alleged politics of the book. Yet the relish with which many conservative commentators welcomed the scholarly demolition of Bellesiles's thesis is worth a few considerations. It is easy to understand why columnists for *Guns and Ammo* or the *National Review* should rejoice at seeing the fall from grace of a man who had dared criticize the NRA's interpretation of the Second Amendment. One can also understand why the right wing would celebrate that a book written by a "liberal" academic was being exposed as fraudulent. Indeed, it was perhaps inevitable that Bellesiles would end up being characterized by some as a prototypical "postmodernist" historian with no respect for facts and trying to garner academic laurels by spinning a politically correct yarn.[5]

Yet there is still something somewhat puzzling about the Bellesiles affair. Not a single conservative commentator seemed to have even remotely wished that Bellesiles's thesis were at least partly true. No one, in other words, praised *Arming America* for correcting what is after all a rather negative image of the United States as one of the most violent and heavily armed countries in the world, by suggesting that originally Americans were not that much in love with firearms and had only later turned into a gun-loving people. This may have had much to do with the fact that, as Corey Robin has documented, "Throughout the 1990s, the lead item of intellectual complaint, across the political spectrum, was that the United States was insufficiently civic-minded or martial, its leaders and citizens too distracted by prosperity and affluence to take care of its inherited institutions, common concerns, and worldwide defense" (282).[6] At a time when the old Cold War scenario was disintegrating, Bill Clinton's dream of free-market globalization was attacked by conservatives for its refusal "to embrace the murky world of power and violent conflict, of tragedy and rupture," and "pagan courage and an almost barbaric *virtù*" were promoted "over the more prosaic goods of peace and prosperity" (Robin 283), it is perhaps only natural that Bellesiles's contention that early America was relatively violence-free would meet with more than a sneer. A typical review appearing on the *BrothersJudd* website, for example, chides Bellesiles because in his book, "rather than rapacious conquerors and brutes, the early Americans seem downright pastoral." Perhaps my views on this matter are influenced by my position as a scholar who looks at American culture from the outside, but at first I was so naive to think that the picture of a kinder, gentler early America should have appealed not only to liberals in favor of tighter gun control but also to at least some conservative and patriotic U.S. citizens who may resent being portrayed as the descendants of "rapacious conquerors and brutes." In fact, in the same review, the author—while all along attacking Bellesiles as an example of how "the modern academy has been thoroughly corrupted by Leftist ideology"—cannot fail to notice that, were Bellesiles's thesis on a relatively violence-free early America true, it would deny "most of the crimes that the Left has laid at our collective doorstep over the years."[7]

Here the reviewer raises an important, albeit contradictory, point. Aren't many contemporary scholars and critics charged with being "anti-American" when they focus on the unpleasant traits of U.S. history or society, of indeed "hating" their object of study so much that the field should be renamed "Anti-American Studies"?[8] This is the case inside as well as outside the United States. In Italy, for example, especially since 9/11, critics of U.S. foreign policy are systematically accused of being obsessed with the aggressive, warlike legacy of American history. The self-appointed guardians of what, along with my colleague Alessandro Portelli, I have elsewhere described as "Mythic Philoamericanism" are always ready to denounce anyone who calls too much attention to the United States as a violent or gun-loving country as being "anti-American." Yet, rather than appreciating at least Bellesiles's intentions, conservative reviewers usually seemed outright offended by the simple suggestion that early Americans may not have been armed to their teeth. Their attacks on *Arming America* were of a piece with a wider conservative polemic against those U.S. citizens "too consumed with their own comfort and pleasure to lend a hand—or shoulder a gun—to make the world a safer place" (Robin 282).

However, I believe that the point duly noted by the *BrothersJudd* reviewer still holds. Had it been widely accepted, Bellesiles's thesis might have caused some problems not only for the gun-loving front but for several left-leaning historians and cultural critics as well. It is worth remembering, for example, that in his introductory pages Bellesiles does not take issue only with the views of the NRA, but he refers also to Richard Slotkin's *Regeneration through Violence* (1973) as an example of what he considers a common misrepresentation of early American history and culture. In fact, Bellesiles clearly implies that studies like Slotkin's encourage the notion that "we have always been killers." According to Bellesiles, by insisting that from a "Hobbesian heritage of each against all emerged the modern acceptance of widespread violence," Slotkin's approach ends up supporting the views of those who think that "little if anything, can be done to alter America's gun culture" (5). Perhaps Bellesiles's criticism of Slotkin is not altogether fair. However, whatever the pitfalls of *Arming America*, the resentful response with which the book met seems to suggest that the image of a gun-loving, and ultimately rugged, violent America is as important to the Right as it is to the Left, depending on the ideological perspective from which one looks at it. This is why, perhaps, a quintessential American genre like the Western has been studied with equal passion by conservatives and liberals. To the former it is the precious record of the heroic and epic struggle of the American people to turn the wilderness into a New World garden; to the latter the Western offers a wonderful display of the workings of American ideology. In both cases, however, the mythology of the frontier, with its legacy of mythicized violence, is seen as standing at the center of U.S. culture.

As I hope should be clear, my point is not that if early America was as much in love with guns and as violent a world as the post–Civil War United States, we should simply choose to believe in Bellesiles's fiction because at least it offers us the glimpse of an inspirational, peaceful golden age to which one day we may be able to return. We cannot, that is, make up a non-violent America just because it may be politically convenient to do so. What we can and should do, however, is give more visibility to the non-violent and nonconformist side of American history and culture than many literary and cultural critics have done of late. Let me dwell just one more time on the Bellesiles story. In his damning review of the book, Clayton Cramer pokes fun at Bellesiles because "he would have us believe that by the 1830s, a pacifist movement, fiercely hostile not only to gun ownership, but also to a military and hunting of any form, was becoming a major influence on American society." To be fair to Bellesiles, he nowhere argues that in antebellum America pacifism was a dominant ideology, though he insists that there were both individuals and groups intent on criticizing the institution of war and calling for a politics of non-violence. This is a point few scholars would dispute. We usually think of non-violence as a philosophy first conceived by Gandhi and Tolstoy, and later imported into the United States by Martin Luther King Jr. However, according to Staughton Lynd and Alice Lynd, editors of *Nonviolence in America: A Documentary History* (1996), there is "a distinctive [American] tradition of nonviolence [that] runs back to the British colonies in the seventeenth century. Thoreau's influence on Gandhi is well-known. Tolstoy, too, was indebted to North American predecessors. In 'A Message to the American People,' written in 1901, Tolstoy stated that 'Garrison, Parker, Emerson, Ballou, and Thoreau . . . specially influenced me'" (xi).[9]

Obviously, to argue that there is in the United States an important anti-war intellectual and political tradition grounded in Christian pacifism, and that this tradition reached a marked visibility in the 1830s and 1840s, is by no means to deny the reality of a "gunfighter nation," with its legacy of slavery, racism, and imperialism. Yet, just as no one would dream of writing the history of the Vietnam years and leave the anti-war movement out of the picture, one should also not forget that the ideal of non-violence and a deep dislike for war have been significant, albeit not hegemonic, features of U.S. culture since at least the late eighteenth century. Some may think that when arguing that "the United States has more often been teacher than student in the history of the nonviolent idea" (xii), Lynd and Lynd may be overstating their case. Yet, in light of what I have learned from the Bellesiles affair, I would submit that, especially in the post-9/11 climate, the reclaiming of a non-violent U.S. tradition would be a more culturally and politically effective weapon than yet another "black book" on the crimes of American domestic and foreign policies from the Pequot War onward. Despite all the complaints against the practitioners of "anti-American studies" for focusing on U.S. imperialism, slavery, genocidal policies against the Indians, and so forth, it is quite clear that many of those who support the so-called global war on terrorism prefer to think of their forefathers as "rapacious conquerors and brutes" rather than people who, among other things, wondered whether a key feature of a genuine New World should be the abolition of war. After all, at the end of the eighteenth century, when the United States were born, "princes, armies, and perpetual war defined Europe. The absence of these things was to provide a point of departure for defining America" (Bacevich 32–33).[10]

I am not arguing we should forget what Michel Foucault, neo-Marxism, and the New Historicists have taught us concerning the ways power operates to preempt oppositional stances, or that we should ignore the ways, as Sacvan Bercovitch (29–67) has insisted, "the myth of America" operates even in what strive to be counterhegemonic practices. Yet a necessary skepticism regarding the limitations and contradictions of any intellectual or political movement wishing to challenge the status quo, especially on a fundamental issue like the use of state violence, should never obscure the rich, and by no means naive, tradition of anti-war thinking visible in many strains of U.S. culture. So, while we should continue reading Richard Slotkin's trilogy on the myth of the frontier, I would welcome a greater familiarity with such works as Peter Brock's *Pacifism in the United States: From the Colonial Era to the First World War* (1968), a volume that, despite leaving out almost one hundred years of U.S. history, runs to nearly one thousand pages. One may object that, important as they might be, studies like Brock's are not half as exciting a read as *Regeneration through Violence* or *Gunfighter Nation*. Many of us are more likely to find discussions of the role of violence in *The Last of the Mohicans* (1826) or interpretations of *The Wild Bunch* (1969) as an allegory of U.S. Third World interventionism more captivating than the perusal of Quaker journals or of the writings of Elihu Burritt, one of the few abolitionists who opposed the Civil War on pacifist grounds. However, as we saw in the previous chapter's discussion of Cynthia Wachtell's *War No More*, the influence of this pacifist culture was not limited to a few radical circles, and it left its marks on the work of several major authors. Regardless of my reservations concerning her use of the "antiwar" label, Wachtell in *War No More* demonstrates that, as Werner Sollors was already arguing some years ago, although "there may be no American *Lysistrata*, and American literature may not be concerned with peace as was the book of Psalms . . . there is a tradition of American imaginings of 'peace' that could be profitably studied and taught" (34).

As the scare quotes around the word *peace* imply, Sollors is aware of the controversial and largely derivative status of "war's Other." Notwithstanding efforts to construct positive rather than merely negative images of peace, the latter can never fully disentangle itself from its dialectical counterpart. However, the reverse is also true. "Imaginings of peace" can be found as a rule also where war dominates. Take, for example, Cooper's *Last of the Mohicans*. In the bloodiest of his frontier novels, during their wanderings through the forest Leatherstocking and company meet one David Gamut, a bizarre "psalmodist" who expresses Christian pacifist views that are resolutely opposed to Natty Bumppo's wilderness philosophy. A few chapters before killing Magua, Natty tells Gamut that if he were to be scalped by the hostile Indians, his death would be avenged. Gamut, however, objects: "I am an unworthy and humble follower of one who taught not the damnable principle of revenge" (Cooper 274).[11] Challenged by such a clear moral position, Hawkeye is incapable of articulating an answer. He heaves "a heavy sigh" and declares that somehow he too wished he could live by conforming to such noble principles, so different from "the law of the woods," concluding that in his heart he would really like to treat an Indian as "a fellow Christian" but that "it is not always easy" (274). Though he remains sympathetic toward Hawkeye, and though he continues to see Indians—both the "good" and the "bad" ones—as tainted with a natural predilection for barbarous practices, Cooper cannot hide the fact that, by imposing their own civilization, Americans must resort to bloody and savage means, thus trampling upon those Christian principles which—as testified by Natty's dialogue with Gamut—are only superficially adhered to.

An awareness of the significance of peace-loving culture in early-nineteenth-century America is obviously not enough to turn Cooper into an advocate of nonviolence. Nevertheless, it is an illustration of how Natty's "American soul," which D. H. Lawrence (65) waxed lyrically about, could triumph over the Indians only by defeating alternative values that were also part of his own culture. Such explicit antipacifist connotation of the tale of Western adventure would continue to be one of its distinguishing features as this genre developed in the course of the nineteenth and twentieth centuries. As Jane Tompkins has shown, the Western can be fruitfully interpreted as a male and patriarchal "answer" to the domestic novel—as "the antithesis of the cult of domesticity that dominated American Victorian culture" (39). From the Molly of Owen Wister's *The Virginian* (1902) to the Jane of Zane Grey's *Riders of the Purple Sage* (1912), or, to move from literature to cinema, from *High Noon*'s Amy (dir. Frank Zinneman, 1952) to *Shane*'s Marian (dir. George Stevens, 1953), the Western is crowded with heroines who go from pacifism to the arms of a man who has just committed a homicide, as if the most important goal of the story were not so much the slaying of the bad guys as the woman's renouncing of her Evangelical values. In Tompkins's words, "It cannot be fortuitous that the shoot-out is staged time and again in Westerns as a direct violation of what the woman in the story wants" (143). In order to sponsor the idea that only violence can solve social conflicts and submit the will of the woman to the masculine imperative, the Western has nevertheless to admit the existence of an alternative ideology.

These examples are meant to suggest that, whatever the degree of bellicosity of American culture and society, the recourse to violence has never gone unchallenged. That even Western narratives had to stage time and again the subjugation of the would-be-pacifist to the gunslinging male hero is an indication that the recourse to violence has to be justified even in those texts where it is most at home. Still, one would hope that American literature could provide us with more affirmative images of both peace and its advocates. The problem is that, notwithstanding the central place usually assigned to the idea of peace in both the individual and the collective consciousness, as already mentioned in the previous chapter, its aesthetic appeal has always been a very limited one. In one of the rare essays on this subject, the Italian literary scholar Vanda Perretta has eloquently argued that, compared with the soldier or the fighter, the man or the woman of peace usually appears to be dull and living in a sort of fantasy world. Like Cooper's Gamut or Wister's Molly, these figures and the "feminine" values they stand for are no match for the strong masculine hero. Peace—and that, according to Perretta, is true of literature as much as of the figurative arts—has never reached the status of an autonomous "aesthetic object." A famous "peace" monument like the Roman *Ara Pacis*, for example, is nothing but a form of "regime art" designed to celebrate the *military* victories of Augustus. The *Pax Augusta* was simply a synonym for the supremacy of the Roman Empire. Indeed, the greatest Western "peace painting" of the modern era may be Picasso's *Guernica*, which is of course not a portrayal of peace at all, but in many ways exactly its opposite: a critical, powerful representation of the "imagination of disaster."

In his recent *The Glorious Arts of Peace*, John Gittings tries to state a different case. Arguing that "the study of peace can be as exciting as the study of war" (7),

Gittings acknowledges that peace is often celebrated in the arts as that which is not war, but this does not mean peace has no independent aesthetic and moral status. He refers, for example, to a fresco by Ambrogio Lorenzetti in Siena's Palazzo Pubblico, overlooking its famous main square, which has come to be known as an allegorical representation of "good and bad government" but in medieval times was simply known as "Peace and War." On one side of the fresco, "we see a city with empty streets and rough soldiers, houses in disrepair, women being raped, and, outside the city gates, abandoned fields, buildings set alight, and looters at work" (84). On the other side, Lorenzetti painted an altogether different city: "The population throngs in the streets but there are no soldiers in sight, the houses are well kept, with flowerpots in their windows" (84), people go about their daily activities, some even play chess, and the fields beyond the walls are well tended. Similarly, in Rubens's *Minerva Protects Pax from Mars* (1629–30), Peace is depicted as "a Venus-like figure . . . feeding at her breast the young child Ploutos, god of wealth. A helmeted Minerva, goddess of wisdom, protects Peace/Venus from Mars" (99). Here, as in Rubens's later *Consequences of War* (or *Horrors of War*, 1637–38), in which Peace/Venus tries to restrain War/Mars, who has broken out of the Temple of Janus, Peace is the aesthetic, beautiful object, whose very existence is threatened by the fury and madness of War. True, peace is rarely depicted as victorious: as in the literary examples Gittings discusses, Peace is honored, but, whatever its superior ethical and aesthetic qualities, it is not able to prevent War from having its way. While, unlike Perretta, Gittings insists that peace has been often celebrated as a positive notion—as something richer than the mere absence of war—he too must admit that authors like Homer and Shakespeare voiced their criticisms of war in response to destructive forces that could not be halted. However, by emphasizing the significance and indeed omnipresence, along the familiar discourses of war, of many "countervailing narratives" of peace, Gittings's study encourages us to rethink the representation of the war-peace opposition.

Even though peace has been painted often as a noble but impractical ideal, destined to suffer defeat at the hands of a more realistic gunfighting spirit, once—as Gittings and other Peace Studies scholars ask us to do—we stop associating peace with passivity and see it as a source of energy and creativity, we may more easily reject the customary association of violence and American culture. There is a "peace" that may appear "downright pastoral," a condition of "no-war" subordinate to the ideology of war. Indeed, from the *si vis pacem para bellum* of my own rapacious Roman forefathers to Michel Foucault's clever inversion of Von Clausewitz's view on the relation of politics to war, "peace" has been often understood as the continuation of war by other means.[12] Against this image of peace as either a temporary suspension of war or, even worse, a camouflaged form of violence, we must rediscover a different kind of peace—a peace that, far from shying away from conflicts, *promotes* confrontations, though its means are obviously different from those of war. This "fighting peace" is by no means a uniquely American invention, but it has deep roots in the U.S. imagination. As we shall see, from Ralph Waldo Emerson to William James, Jane Addams, Richard Gregg, Kenneth Burke, and beyond, many American writers, thinkers, and organizers have struggled to deconstruct the peace-war opposition, knowing full well that all too often the ideal of non-violence can and indeed must be spelled out in a metaphorics of war.[13] By repeating the rhetorical and political gesture of Jean Paul's 1809 *Declaration of War on War* and anticipating Ernst Friedrich's 1924 cry, *Krieg dem Kriege!*, these thinkers have waged an intellectual war against war, thereby paving the way for a non-violent yet militant and uncompromising opposition to the cant of militarism and nationalism that has been an important feature of twentieth-century American political movements.[14]

Disarming America, "Arming" Peace

As many readers would have recognized, the title of this chapter replicates the epigraph Kenneth Burke chose for his *A Grammar of Motives* (1945). The book's motto registers its author's desire to celebrate sociopolitical conflict by "purifying" it of its potentially destructive nature and "channelling" it along less warlike lines. From this point of view *A Grammar* is the logical continuation of an idea Burke had already expressed in *Attitudes Toward History* (1937), where the entry "Control" in his "Dictionary of Pivotal Terms" reads as follows:

> To control a bad situation, you seek either to eradicate the evil or to channelize the evil. Elimination vs. the "lightning rod principle," whereby one protects against lightning not by outlawing lightning but by drawing it into a channel where it does no damage. . . . When liberals began to think, not of eliminating war, but of finding "the moral equivalent for war," liberalism was nearing the state of maturity. (236)

In developing this idea in his work of the 1940s and 1950s, Burke explored at some length the "war is peace" paradox. He believed that while we should always call attention to the rhetorical strategies deployed by war in order to masquerade itself as a form of peace, the deconstruction—or, as Burke called it, the "debunking"—of militaristic thought was not enough. What we should do, instead, is "treat 'war' as a 'special case of peace'—not as a primary motive in itself, not as essentially real, but purely as a derivative condition, a perversion" (*Rhetoric of Motives* 20). War, in Burke's eyes, should be understood as the "ultimate disease of cooperation," as "a disease or perversion of communion." Thus, while we need never deny what he calls "the tyrannous ubiquity in human relations" (20) of strife and enmity, we must also resist the temptation to make of war our "representative anecdote."

"For," as Burke argues, "if we took war as an anecdote, then in obeying the genius of this anecdote and shaping an idiom accordingly, we should be proclaiming war as the essence of human relations" (*Grammar of Motives* 329).

As we have just seen, Burke acknowledges his debt to William James's essay on "the moral equivalent of war," and in the next chapter I will discuss both James's and Burke's contributions to the rethinking of the peace-war opposition. Here I would like to suggest that the intellectual and moral fountainhead not only of both Burke's and James's thinking but, more generally, of a U.S. tradition of militant anti-war thinking is in fact Ralph Waldo Emerson. This claim will probably strike some as surprising. With a few exceptions, Emerson has been lately portrayed either as Richard Poirier's "philosopher of language," for whom "the revolution worth pursuing is the continuous act of turning and overturning the page" (*Renewal of Literature* 170) or as an unwitting spokesman for westward expansionism, laissez-faire capitalism, corporate individualism, and so forth.[15] Standing somewhat astride both the apolitical Emerson of the former tradition and the ideologically suspect Emerson of the latter one, one finds the Nietzschean, and perhaps even Foucauldian, Emerson of George Stack, Michael Lopez, and others.[16] All these different versions of Emerson have some merit, yet the Emerson of most interest to me here is the "philosopher of power" discussed at length in Lopez's *Emerson and Power: Creative Antagonism in the Nineteenth Century*. In particular, I would like to call attention to Lopez's brilliant discussion, in chapter 5 of his book, of Emerson's rhetoric of war.[17] Though Lopez argues that "real war was for Emerson, in principle at least, a violation of the common soul of all men" (192), the bulk of his investigation suggests that Emerson fully, if perhaps unwittingly, participated in the Romantic "poeticizing of war" (193) that eventually led to the unspeakable disasters of two world wars.

Much as I admire Lopez's clever exploration of Emerson's rhetoric, it seems to me that—in Burke's language—he treats war as Emerson's "representative anecdote," thereby giving no credit to what I believe is Emerson's attempt to deploy war metaphors against the institution and the practice of war. Lopez, for example, does not mention that one of Emerson's most important early statements on the subject—the 1838 essay "War"—was delivered as an address sponsored by the American Peace Society. Indeed, some insights of Emerson's essay are as valuable today as they were nearly two hundred years ago. Howard Zinn has included an excerpt of Emerson's address in *The Power of Nonviolence* (8–14), and the contemporary pacifist thinker Michael Nagler continues to draw on it in his "search for a nonviolent future." What makes this essay important is, first, Emerson's warning that "along the passive side of the friend of peace" there is "his activity" ("War" 168). Peace is not synonymous with inaction. On the contrary, peace can be achieved only through a nonmilitary militancy. As Emerson put it in a passage with which

William James was likely to have been familiar, "the peace principle . . . can never be defended, it can never be executed, by cowards. Everything great must be done in the spirit of greatness. The manhood that has been in war must be transferred to the cause of peace, before war can lose its charm, and peace be venerable to men" (171). By "manhood" here, as often elsewhere, Emerson means "self-dependence," which he believes is what we really admire in the Greek and Roman heroes. Yet, if "self-subsistency is the charm of war," its highest form is the one that can do without all military trappings—"without any flourish of trumpets, titles of lordships or train of guards" (173).

The hortatory conclusion of Emerson's address deserves to be remembered as the forerunner of a modern tradition of militant pacifism culminating in Gandhi and King, and still alive in contemporary global anti-war movements:

> The cause of peace is not the cause of cowardice. If peace is sought to be defended or preserved for the safety of the luxurious and the timid, it is a sham, and the peace will be base. War is better, and the peace will be broken. If peace is to be maintained, it must be by brave men, who have come up to the same height as the hero, namely, they will carry their life in their hand, and stake it at any instant for their principle, but who have gone one step beyond the hero, and will not seek another man's life; men who have, by their intellectual insight or else by their moral elevation, attained such a perception of their own intrinsic worth that they do not think property or their own body a sufficient good to be saved by such dereliction of principle as treating a man like a sheep. (174)[18]

Here Emerson sketches a redefinition of heroism that will continue to preoccupy him in many of his writings. For example, in his essay "Heroism," "the charm of war" is operative in almost every sentence, beginning with the epigraph from Mohammed: "Paradise is under the shadow of swords." Read out of context, the quotation would seem to strengthen the notion that the bliss of paradise and the hell of battle are but two sides of the same coin. Yet if Emerson appears fascinated by the concept of holy war, the essay as a whole shows that Emerson's *jihad* is nothing but the "warlike attitude" of the soul opposing "external evil" ("Heroism" 374). In Jamesian fashion, Emerson calls attention to "the attractiveness of war" mainly to suggest how a vulgar, infantile militarism must be superseded by a "military attitude of the soul." "Self-trust is the essence of heroism," Emerson proceeds. "It is the state of the soul at war" ("Heroism" 374, 375). For Emerson peace is inextricably intertwined with war, yet the war he speaks of is essentially a metaphor for the ongoing spiritual and political struggle engaged by the nonconformist self against society, as we can also gather from "Self-Reliance," where he urges his readers to "enter into the state of war" if they hold dear their intellectual independence. An appeal to this kind of intellectual and moral warfare is also at the core of Thoreau's "Resistance to Civil Government" (1849), an essay some consider the greatest theoretical contribution the United States has made to the cause of world peace (Gruesser).

The resemblances between the position advocated by Emerson in these early essays and the Gandhian concept of non-violent civil resistance are striking. Emerson distinguishes between a "base" form of pacifism bordering on cowardice and a truly "heroic" non-violence that can be practiced only by those courageous enough "to carry their life in their hand." Similarly, Gandhi draws a clear distinction between the "non-violence of the weak"—the non-violence of those who are afraid to be violent—and "the active non-violent resistance of the strong"—the behavior of those who have come to understand that "non-violence is the mightiest force in the world" (*Non-Violence* 1:167). This explains why, like Emerson, Gandhi was attracted to the symbolic dimension of military bravery (as displayed, for example, in the *Bhagavad Gita*) and why, also like Emerson, he believed that "cowardice is impotence worse than violence" (*Non-Violence* 2:148).[19] As H. J. N. Horsburgh has noted, for Gandhi "the violence which springs from courage is morally superior to the non-violence that is an expression of cowardice" (64). Or, in Gandhi's own words, "My nonviolence does not admit of running away from danger and leaving dear ones unprotected. Between violence and cowardly flight, I can only prefer violence to cowardice. I can no more preach nonviolence to a coward than I can tempt a blind man to enjoy healthy scenes. Nonviolence is the summit of bravery" (quoted in Borman 252–53). For both Emerson and Gandhi the worst temptation is, finally, not violence but cowardice. Hence the ambivalent attraction both felt for war not only as a "poetic" fact but also as a display of actual bravery.

Gandhi may have been more outspoken than Emerson in defining war as a form of "unmitigable" evil, yet it is striking how Emersonian he was in praising the "good," admirable qualities of war: "War is unmitigated evil. But it certainly does one good thing, it drives away fear and brings bravery to the surface" (quoted in Borman 189). When Emerson published his address to the Peace Society he chose to change its original title ("The Peace Principle"), to its current one ("War"), an indication of how in his mind the struggle for peace had to come to terms with the psychological—aesthetic appeal of the martial spirit. Similarly, Gandhi noted that "if war had no redeeming feature, no courage and heroism behind it, it would be a despicable thing, and would not need speeches to destroy it" (quoted in Borman 189). Gandhi, in other words, fully shares Emerson's desire to transfer to the cause of peace "the manhood that has been in war." Like William James, Gandhi too is searching for a "moral equivalent of war," though Gandhi's substitute for war is probably closer to Emerson's formulation than it is to James's. If, as Horsburgh and others have suggested, *satyāgraha*—that is, a method of resistance practically and ethically distinct from war—is Gandhi's own "moral equivalent of war," he is not so much thinking of what may take the place of national armies and tame the martial spirit—arguably James's major preoccupation—as he is striving to enroll Emerson's "military attitude of the soul" on the side of social change and the fight for justice. Gandhi's emphasis on a "warlike" self-reliance closely resembles Emerson's, and it is no accident that the Mahatma not only insisted that satyāgraha should be seen as an expression of soul-force, but he also identified *Ahimsā* (literally, non-harming, non-killing) as a *weapon*, often employing in his writings the phrase "the weapon of non-violence."[20] Finally, for both Gandhi and Emerson the value of "peace"—militantly defined not as the mere absence of war but as a "higher," purer, non-violent form of "war"—cannot be divorced from the notion of truth as moral authenticity. For Gandhi "moral authenticity means the effort to bring inner states and outer conduct into congruence by speaking and acting one's convictions" (Borman 74).[21] This most Emersonian premise can help explain why Gandhi found cowardice far more despicable than violence and why at times some of his statements may be puzzling to those who think of him as an apostle of unconditional non-violence. When Gandhi notes, for example, that "where there is only a choice between cowardice and violence, I would advise violence" (quoted in Bondurant 28), one is tempted to conclude that Gandhi's paramount value is truth rather than non-violence, even though, of course, Gandhi's simultaneous equation of the two suggests that the courage of those who cannot use non-violent means to their just ends is at most a second-best form of bravery, just as Emerson in his "War" essay maintains that any act of violence (treating a man like a sheep) will always be "a dereliction of principle."

I am aware that the *ad bellum purificandum* perspective of the early Emerson is only one aspect of his rhetoric of war. During the Civil War and the crisis that led up to it, Emerson often poeticized *real* war. At times his praise of the martial spirit borders on jingoism, though we should always keep in mind that, even when Emerson speaks of war in general, what was on his mind was largely a specific armed conflict targeting the daily violence of slavery.[22] While for several years Emerson's preoccupation was no longer the purification of war but rather war as an instrument of purification, I would basically agree with the conclusion reached more than sixty years ago by the earliest student of Emerson's "philosophy of war and peace," William Huggard: "Emerson desired to stand neither for war nor peace, but always for truth, which is a thing greater than any particular war or any peace, and which may afford sanctions or condemnation for either" (72).[23] Yet, while this strikes me as a balanced summary of Emerson's lifetime reflections on the question of war and peace, I would insist that Emerson's most lasting and innovative contribution in this area lies in his attempt to imagine peace as an active force in the service of individual and social transformation. Emerson's invitation to inject a warrior spirit into the pacifists' ranks lays the foundation for the crucial shift from an essentially "passive" resistance to war grounded in religious belief to the "active," more explicitly political anti-war ideology of modern peace movements. His redefinition of peace as the cause of those "brave men" capable of going "one step beyond the hero" stands behind not only James's search for a moral equivalent of war but is also the foundational statement of an American intellectual and political tradition grounded in the distinction between the non-violence of the weak and the non-violence of the strong (see Chernus).

For example, in the very first lines of *Newer Ideals of Peace* (1907) Jane Addams writes: "The following pages present the claims of the newer, more aggressive ideals of peace, as over against the older dovelike ideal. These newer ideals are active and dynamic" (3). In Emersonian fashion, Addams wishes to convince her audience that the struggle for peace is by no means a "dovelike" affair. Having little patience with "the old dogmatic peace," she insists that

> The word "non-resistance" is misleading, because it is much too feeble and inadequate. It suggests . . . the goody-goody attitude of ineffectiveness. The words "overcoming," "substituting," "re-creating," "readjusting moral values," "forming new centres of spiritual energy" carry much more of the meaning implied. For it is not merely the desire for a conscience at rest, for a sense of justice no longer outraged, that would pull us into new paths were there would be no more war nor preparations for war. *There are still more strenuous forces at work reaching down to impulses and experiences as primitive and profound as are those of struggle itself.* (7–8, emphasis added)

Addams's wish to enlist the martial spirit in the service of peace replicates the intellectual and political move advocated by both Emerson's "War" and William James's "Moral Equivalent of War" (to which she refers in her introductory chapter). Rhetorically speaking, it is an excellent example of Burke's "lightning rod principle." By "channelizing" the evil of war in the fight for peace, Addams rejected "the heroism connected with warfare and destruction," suggesting that "the same heroic self-sacrifice, the same fine courage and readiness to meet death may be displayed without the accompaniment of killing our fellowmen."[24]

Giving Peace a Chance

The legacy left by Emerson's, James's, and Addams's reflections on war and peace has had a lasting influence on the American, and indeed the international, movements for peace and social justice. One need only think of the work done by figures like Clarence Marsh Case, the University of Iowa sociologist who, in 1923, published a book, *Non-Violent Coercion: A Study in Methods of Social Pressure*, in which he tried to show how peace and practical force need not be thought of as opposites, and especially of the work by Richard Bartlett Gregg, author of *The Power of Non-Violence* (1935), a book that deeply influenced Martin Luther King Jr., who himself would never tire of distinguishing, in Gandhian fashion, between "negative" and "positive" peace, and who insisted that non-violent resistance could never be embraced by cowards.[25] Gregg's definition of non-violent direct action as a "moral jiu-jitsu" that could turn out to be an "effective substitute for war" was directly indebted to Gandhi's example (43, 93), yet it can also be seen as standing squarely in the tradition of Emerson and James, especially when Gregg insists that the virtues required of the peace fighter are similar to those one admires in great military heroes. This lesson would not be lost on many great U.S. "peace heroes" of the past few decades—Dorothy Day, Helen Keller, Daniel and Philip Berrigan, A. J. Muste, Elizabeth McAlister, Cesar Chavez, George Lakey, Cindy Sheehan, and many, many others who have "strenuously" fought non-violently against war and injustice. In this light it is all the more surprising that, to quote Sollors again, peace has never managed to become a buzzword in American studies. Perhaps, he surmised, this is because "American Studies may be first and foremost a child of war" (23). The two World Wars, and then in decisive ways the long Cold War, were key factors in the development of American studies both at home and abroad. It was only during the interlude of the 1960s that, in response to the Vietnam War, "peace actually moved to the foreground of American Studies" (Sollors 28). However, one could argue that a good deal of the literature stimulated by the Vietnam disaster was more concerned with locating the war within America's imperialist legacy than focusing on ways to build peace. This kind of rhetoric is wonderfully epitomized by a famous passage in Michael Herr's *Dispatches* (1978), where he writes, "You couldn't use standard methods to date the doom, might as well say that Vietnam was where the Trail of Tears was headed all along . . . might just as well lay it on the proto-Gringos who found the New England woods too raw and empty for their peace and filled them up with their own imported devils" (51). This intellectual perspective informs Slotkin's work, from *Regeneration through Violence* to *Gunfighter Nation*, as well as many other texts written since Vietnam—texts that rightly denounce the wrongdoings of the U.S. war machinery but that, perhaps unwittingly, reinforce an essentialist image of America as a sort of "natural born killer." One must be careful, in other words, to avoid the "paradox" in which, according to Burke, run those doctrines too "zestful in building an admonitory image of our warlike past," thus contributing their part "to usher in precisely the gloom they thought they were ushering out. For the only substance represented with any fullness in their statements [is] that of the warlike past—and so, what we [are] admonished against [is] just about the only tangible thing there for us to be" (*Grammar or Motives* 331–32). It is hard to oppose war if one constantly projects an image of the United States as a nation in which peace has virtually no place and whose "deeds of gift," as Robert Frost famously wrote in his "The Gift Outright," always amount to "many deeds of war." "The continued and relentless militarization and colonization of everyday life can be resisted, but this takes more than simple demystification" (Deer 7).

This is not to say that everything is fine and good with the "aggressive" pacifist tradition I have summarily sketched. For example, even though Emerson's coupling of courage and non-violence opened up the possibility of defining heroism in nonmasculine ways, his pacifist rhetoric remains confined within the pale of an idealized American manhood. One may wish to note that there were—especially in nineteenth-century America—compelling tactical reasons for highlighting the "strenuous" and specifically "masculine" character of peace. As Aaron McLean Winter has shown, while "doves" opposed war on essentially moral grounds, the "laughing doves" expressed their opposition through an aggressively masculine writing strategy. Besides offering evidence that—no matter how many guns American males owned—anti-war sentiments in the nineteenth-century United States were more widespread than most people suspect, Winter shows that "in an era that strongly associated aggression with political masculinity," satire provided "a form of compensatory violence—a boot in the ass of flag-waving war propagandists" ("Doves of 1812" 1563). The laughing doves, that is, prevented hawks "from monopolizing a claim to political masculinity" ("Laughing Dove" 2). For instance, during the War of 1812, for authors like William Cullen Bryant, "the central project of U.S. anti-war satire was to invent a muscular pacifism that could revenge itself on the Republican usurpers by somehow revaluing their war against Britain as an act of cowardice" ("Laughing Dove" 60). This combination of manhood and pacifism would carry over in the satires written to denounce both the 1848 War with Mexico and the end-of-the century U.S.-Philippine War, and it is still operative nowadays. "As war retains its association with normative masculinity in a postliberal or neoliberal United States, anti-war satire remains, to a great extent, a compensatory assertion of masculinity" ("Laughing Dove" 72). The insistence of an Emerson, but perhaps of a Gandhi as well, on the "manhood" of the "heroic" peace-fighter, must therefore be understood not only as a sign of individual male chauvinism but also as part of a more general fear that the feminization of anti-war dissent might expose peace activists to accusations of being wimps and cowards. An excellent example of this is provided in a passage by Ernest Crosby quoted by Winter, where this labor organizer, pacifist, and writer, in order to emphasize that "the principle of non-resistance is not cowardly or effeminate," forcefully argued, "Peace is a god, not a goddess, a man not a woman—a brawny, bearded man of might" (Crosby, *Swords and Plowshares* 21). To our postfeminism eyes this narrative strategy appears paradoxical, as it reinforces the very gender stereotypes that sustain war propaganda and that anti-war discourse should subvert. Yet it could be argued that as long as force continues to be associated with masculinity, a "feminine" peace remains open to the charge of being ineffectual. Of course feminist theorists and activists have worked hard to show that peace need not wear a beard in order to oppose war. Yet the manipulation of masculinity and femininity in order to promote wars, and the promotion of war-making in order to reinforce gender roles, are well-engrained, millennial social practices whose disarticulation will take a long time.[26]

In light of war's longstanding association with manhood, the militant pacifist will always confront contradictions of the kind outlined above. There is no way around it, just as one cannot magically bypass the peace/war continuum analyzed in the previous chapter, and that always threatens to cannibalize peace as—to quote another satirist studied by Winter—nothing but "a period of cheating between two periods of fighting."[27] I will return to the aporetic features of both the theory and practice of peacefighting at the end of this chapter. First, one more word on the problem of peace's supposed lack of aesthetic appeal. When critics observe that peace as such is seldom celebrated, they obviously do not imply that art and literature never offer us peaceful sceneries. Pastoral literature and art, for example, celebrate the virtues of a simple life removed from strife and enmity. It is only when the tranquility of the self-enclosed rural retreat is either implicitly or explicitly juxtaposed to war's "anti-pastoral" (Fussell 231) or "inverted pastoral" (McLoughlin, *Authoring War* 84) landscape that the pastoral context takes on a strong connotation of "peace." Peace is celebrated *as such* only, that is, when its anti-war connotations are perceived.[28] That is what does *not* happen with traditional "peace" monuments, which usually celebrate military victories. Conversely, Picasso's "Guernica" is perceived as a "peace" statement because in its devastated landscape peace is conspicuous by its absence. This is also the case with literature, and in particular with narrative. To the extent that all storytelling hinges on conflict, perpetual peace (like happiness, harmony, or requited love) may be virtually impossible to narrate. However, if peace is reimagined as the *struggle for peace and justice*, it becomes both as narratable and "spectacular" as war. It is no accident that what we find appealing in the lives of figures like Addams, Gandhi, and King is first and foremost their readiness to be women or men of action. Whether speaking of "soul *force*," "the *power* of love," "the soul *at war*," or "spiritual *energy*," all the pacifist theorists we have mentioned, as well as many we have not, always struggled to detach peace from its semantic associations with passivity. In sum, rather than despairing because one cannot be defined without reference to the other, we should emphasize how the vexed connection between peace and war can be confronted in two alternative ways. One is to try to restore an irreducible difference between the two terms, so that peace may be emancipated from its dialectical counterpart. The other way—the way embraced by all the thinkers and militants mentioned above—is to turn the rhetoric of war against itself by making peace a more strenuous combatant than war.

As we go about reassessing the legacy of U.S. pacifist/anti-war discourses and their rhetorical and conceptual features, we must avoid both "the essentialist idealization of America as devotional object" and "the equally essentialist reification of a dark side of America as compensation for our chagrin at demystification and disenchantment" (Kadir, "Defending" 151). Pitting a "good," peace-loving America against a "bad" United States-as-global-sheriff always ready to draw its gun would not only mean falling into the essentializing trap but would also fly in the face of the historical record. As witness for example the crisis of the American Peace society on the verge of the Civil War, a devotion to the cause of peace may at times come into conflict with a nearly irresistible state of war. It may be shocking for us to see not only Emerson but so many former "non-resisters" like William Lloyd Garrison turn the same evangelical language they had earlier used to condemn the abomination of war into a call to annihilate the devilish forces of the rebel, slave-owning states. Yet there were also pacifists who, like Angelina Grimké, were capable of giving a more sober assessment of the war:

> Although the shedding of human blood is utterly abhorrent to my mind . . . yet the tame surrender of a helpless victim up to the fate of the slave is far more abhorrent. . . . In this case, it seems as though we are compelled to choose between two evils, and all that we can do is take the least, and baptize liberty in blood, if it must be so. . . . A temporary war is an incomparably less evil than permanent slavery.[29]

Grimké believed she had no choice but negotiate the nonnegotiable prohibition to resort to violence. A century later, the anti-war movement of the 1960s also had to question some of its non-violent practices. Some pacifists, for example, considered that burning draft cards—as the Berrigan brothers and the other "Catonsville Nine" did in May 1968—or destroying property was not inconsistent with a commitment to non-violence. Others, more problematically, maintained that street rioting was justified both as a way to call attention to the anti-war cause and as a form of violence incomparably smaller to that of the war in Indochina.

Pacifists have often denounced the hypocritical language deployed to justify war in the name of peace. For example, when in March 2003 George W. Bush announced that the airstrikes against Iraq had begun, he claimed that America was "a peace-loving nation." It was easy for Arundhati Roy to slash such rhetoric with a reference to George Orwell's "war is peace," and she was of course right. But there is also a sense in which Bush's words were *not* hypocritical. The United States he represents does love "peace"—as long as it is a Pax Americana. Thus, just as pacifists point to the contradiction between the war machinery of the state and its supposed peaceful ends, the state often responds in kind by attacking the hypocrisy of a pacifist movement engaged in forms of resistance that are not always non-violent, or not rigorously so. Even a paramount figure of American non-violence like Martin Luther King Jr. was accused in his own day of "disturbing the peace" by promoting marches, rallies, and boycotts. More generally, all over the world, from at least the Vietnam War onward, there have been peace marches and demonstrations that should have been "peaceful" but often, for manifold reasons, turned violent. Pictures of students battling the police in anti-war demonstrations have often appeared in conservative and even liberal newspapers to ridicule the peace movement or, at best, to pressingly invite its leaders to "police" their own constituencies more thoroughly. A humorous reference to this can be found in one of Sherman Alexie's early stories, where the narrator's father, "dressed in bell-bottoms and flowered shirt, his hair in braids," is photographed during an anti-war demonstration in which participants "go to war for peace." "In his hand my father holds a rifle above his head, captured in that moment just before he proceeded to beat the shit out of the National Guard private lying prone on the ground. A fellow demonstrator holds a sign that is just barely visible over my father's left shoulder. It read MAKE LOVE NOT WAR" (Alexie 24–25).

The Limits of Non-Violence: From Theory to Practice

Much as I appreciate Alexie's ironic portrait, as he himself knows all too well (see his controversial novel *Indian Killer* [1996]), the relation between violence and non-violence is *always* aporetic as the one between war and peace examined in the previous chapter.[30] There, following Nick Mansfield's *Theorizing War*, I privileged the conceptual dimension of the problem. Here I would like to argue that not only the theory but also the *practice* of non-violence, as it has historically unfolded, should be seen as part of a violence/non-violence continuum, or "economy," akin to the peace/war continuum analyzed by Mansfield. While it is important to distinguish between the two, just as it is important to resist the cynical move of equating war and peace, it is often hard to trace a clear-cut line between what is violence and what is not. As Judith Butler has shrewdly noted, "It is precisely because one is mired in violence that the struggle exists and that the possibility of non-violence emerges. . . . Non-violence . . . denotes the mired and conflicted position of a subject who is injured, rageful, disposed to violent retribution and nevertheless struggles against that action (often crafting the rage against itself). The struggle against violence accepts that violence is one's own possibility" ("Claim of Non-Violence" 171).[31] This conceptual, practical, and political problem is compounded by the fact that the Western media and its culture industry have promoted, over the years, a veritable "myth of non-violence." Figures like Gandhi, King, and even Nelson Mandela have been constructed as examples of a noble, peaceful way the oppressed should always confront injustice and seek redress of their grievances. In the case of Gandhi, for example, his promotion to "good" Third World leader over the likes of Ho Chi Minh, Castro, Arafat, and others who condoned and encouraged the use of revolutionary violence had already begun in the 1960s. In a similar fashion, in the United States and elsewhere, King has irresistibly emerged as the alternative to Malcolm X and the Black Panther Party. More recently, Mandela also has been hailed as the wise leader who chose non-violence, with no mention of the fact that he endorsed armed struggle as long as the white government refused to enter into serious negotiations with the ANC.[32] The Western media seem to forget that, when King and Gandhi were alive and protesting—let alone Mandela—they were painted by their opponents as anything but peaceful. "Provocateur," "fanatic," "subversive," and "totalitarian" were terms applied by Winston Churchill to Gandhi, and similar adjectives were used to attack both King and Mandela. Indeed, as late as April 2008 Mandela would have not been able to obtain a visa to visit the United States, as he was on a terrorist watch list.[33] If we wish to assess seriously the philosophy and practice of non-violence, we must move beyond the opportunistic exploitation of figures like Gandhi and King and look in a more objective and scholarly fashion at the textual and historical record. In this regard, a recent book by the Italian philosopher and historian Domenico Losurdo can be of help. Losurdo carefully documents how not only Gandhi and King but also other advocates of peace and non-violence conceded that non-violence was not always an option.[34] Most important, both Gandhi and King realized that non-violent means could not always guarantee non-violent ends, and that even the practice of the most rigorous non-violent tactics entailed at times not only a willingness to be the target of someone else's violence but were in fact predicated on the expectation that one's opponent would engage in violent behavior. Both Gandhi and King were fully aware that they were engaged in a *political* conflict, which required at times the negotiating of one's values and principles. My scope is not to prove that integral non-violence is impossible (that largely depends on how one defines violence) but simply to call attention to factual and textual evidence showing that the relation between violence and non-violence is as complex, contradictory, and intricate as that between war and its other.

Even though Emerson's thought continues to inspire some pacifists, his support of the Union during the Civil War is often seen as a repudiation of his earlier pacifism. What is less often mentioned is that Gandhi's attitude toward war was not only imaginatively but often also practically at odds with his espousal of non-violence. According to H. J. N. Horsburgh, the Mahatma's "belief that courage is a major index of moral stature . . . led him to accept the role of recruiting sergeant during several imperial wars—a role for which he has been widely criticized" (64n). After siding with the British Empire in both the Boer War and the crushing of the Zulu revolt in South Africa, during World War I Gandhi called on his fellow citizens to join the British Army. He hoped that, by taking part in this "necessary evil," India would be rewarded with independence. But he also argued that, by fighting the war, Indians would regain part of their lost manhood. Later in his life, Gandhi's commitment to non-violence seems to have been absolute, but there were also eminently political reasons at the root of his strategy. As Losurdo notes (92–94), Gandhi was the first to understand that by allowing his people to become the target of the occupants' brutality, he would prompt the moral indignation of the British and of the world's public opinion. He strategically created the conditions for violence to take place, as only the spectacle of violence passively and heroically endured by Indian protesters could provoke a worldwide moral condemnation of the colonizers—a lesson that, as we shall see, was not lost on his greatest American disciple. His embrace of non-violence went to such an extreme that in 1940, in an (in?)famous letter addressed "to every Briton," he wrote that the United Kingdom should

> fight Nazism without arms, or, if I am to maintain military terminology, with non-violent arms. I would like you to lay down the arms you have as being useless for saving you or humanity. You will invite Herr Hitler and Signor Mussolini to take what they want of the countries you call your possessions. Let them take possession of your beautiful island, with your many beautiful buildings. You will give all these but neither your souls, nor your minds. If these gentlemen choose to occupy your homes, you will vacate them. If they do not give you free passage out, you will allow yourself, man, woman, and child, to be slaughtered, but you will refuse to owe allegiance to them.[35]

However, in a letter to the viceroy dated July 27, 1944, Gandhi stated that "full cooperation in the war effort should be given by Congress," provided that India be granted immediate independence.[36] Again, he would have sacrificed the souls, the minds, *and the bodies* of his fellow Indians to reach the goal of independence.

Far from proving that Gandhi was either dishonest or a hypocrite, these all-too-brief observations illustrate a point he himself made in his *Autobiography*: "The saying that life lives on life has a deep meaning in it. Man cannot for a moment live without consciously or unconsciously committing outward *himsa*. The very fact of his living—eating, drinking, moving about—necessarily involves some *himsa*, destruction of life, be it ever so minute" (291). Gandhi knew that the practice of non-violence required, literally, the negotiation of the nonnegotiable principle of the sanctity of all life. This in no way diminishes his historical and intellectual accomplishments, though it is an important reminder of the fact that while the choice of non-violent means is praiseworthy, that choice will nearly always entail some degree of compromise with violence to be politically operative. While Gandhi's thought, and that of his several followers, deserves unconditional praise for providing an alternative to an often naïve, at best, belief in the virtues of revolutionary violence, it must not be enveloped in a mythical aura. Instead, Gandhi's and his disciples' example should be seen as part of an effort to promote a form of "disciplined" conflict that would be as non-violent *as possible*.

King's writings and speeches do not show, overall, the same fascination with the rhetoric of war that we find in Gandhi's work. However, he repeatedly condemned cowardice and spoke of resistance to evil as a "very strong force" (King, *Autobiography* 266). He also declared, "Those of us who love peace must organize as effectively as the war hawks."[37] And, like Gandhi, he was forced to admit that though war (World War II in his case) "could never be a positive or absolute good, ... [i]t could serve as a negative good in the sense of preventing the growth or spread of an evil force" (23). Also, King celebrated the Civil War for putting an end to slavery and identified with the bellicose biblical rhetoric of "The Battle Hymn of the Republic," "the fateful lightning of his terrible swift sword" (286) included. King recalled that, after reading Niebuhr, he "tried to arrive at a *realistic* pacifism" (27, emphasis added), which may explain why his commitment to non-violence approved the use of army or police force when it was employed for the protection, rather than the harassment, of the African American community: "I believe firmly in nonviolence, but, at the same time, I am not an anarchist, I believe in the intelligent use of police force" (109). Police force, however, was also intelligently exploited by King in Gandhian fashion. When the police beat protesters, King knew this would trigger the public's moral indignation.

> The newspapers of May 4 carried pictures of prostrate women. And policemen bending over them with raised clubs: of children marching up to the bared fangs of police dogs; of the terrible force of pressure hoses sweeping bodies into the streets.
>
> This was the time of our greatest stress, and the courage and conviction of those students and adults made it our finest hour. We did not fight back, but we did not turn back. We did not give way to bitterness.... In the face of this resolution and bravery, the moral conscience of the nation was deeply stirred and, all over the country, our fight became the fight of decent Americans of all races and creeds. (208–9)

As in Gandhi's case, King's tactic is morally problematic because children, who could not decide for themselves, were used to heighten the brutality of the police. Though civil rights protesters, unlike some of Gandhi's followers, did not go so far as exposing *infants* to the brutality of the police, children regularly took part in demonstrations and, of course, they were in the forefront of the battle for school desegregation. Even a liberal like Hannah Arendt ("Reflections") seemed troubled by the price that black children (and white ones as well, in her view) were being asked to pay for "forced integration."

More generally, one could argue that there is something paradoxical in the non-violent tactics of both Gandhi and King. For non-violence to emerge as both a moral force and a political weapon, the adversary *must* violently attack you. Non-violent resisters, that is, were asked not only to endure violence: they had in some sense to elicit it in the first place, so that they could submit to it later. In Christian terms I suppose one could even say that the pacifists were supposed to *tempt* their adversaries to engage in sinful behavior in order for the pacifists' righteousness to be manifest. In the more down-to-earth language of the society of the spectacle, the violence of the opponent had to be spectacular enough for the innocence of the victims to be on full display. In other words, non-violence could emerge as a useful political tool only by creating the conditions, paradoxically, for violence to occur. Another way of putting this would be to say that, at least in some cases, non-violence ends up generating a sacrificial scene. To the extent that opposition to violence requires a sacrifice of self, it paradoxically reinforces the logic it wishes to escape. As Kelly Denton-Borhaug has noted in a discussion of how we may find alternatives to the sacrificial system of war, proclaiming one's willingness to die for the cause of peace may be a way to reinforce rather than undermine the logic of sacrifice. This is obviously also the case with Emerson's new "hero," whose renunciation of violence takes on heroic proportions by virtue of his readiness to become a pacifist martyr.

While I do not wish in any way to call into question the sincerity of King's beliefs and actions, there is no doubt that his rejection of violence was—as he himself declared—*also* based on political calculus. As we noted, King was a pacifist as well as a realist. In recounting a meeting he had with Black Power activists influenced by Franz Fanon's belief in the liberating power of violence, after admitting that *The Wretched of the Earth* was a book "with many penetrating insights," King went on to observe:

> Now the plain, inexorable fact is that any attempt of the American Negro to overthrow his oppressor with violence will not work. We do not need President Johnson to tell us this by reminding Negro rioters that they are outnumbered ten to one. The courageous efforts of our own insurrectionist brothers, such as Denmark Vesey and Nat Turner, should be eternal reminders to us that violent rebellion is doomed from the start. In violent warfare one must be prepared to face the fact that there will be casualties by the thousands. Anyone leading a violent rebellion must be willing to make an honest assessment regarding the possible casualties to a minority population confronting a well-armed, wealthy majority with a fanatical right wing that would delight in exterminating thousands of black men, women and children. (329)

One might surmise that, given the context, King chose to focus on the political, rather than the ethical, side of the question. Yet the homage he paid to the violent rebellions led by Vesey and Turner seems sincere. In fact, King had words of praise as well for the Boston Tea Party, which he described as "a massive act of civil disobedience" (194), though it led to a revolution that was anything but peaceful. He also thought highly of the 1956 Hungarian revolution, though perhaps those revolutionaries were unable to make an "honest assessment" of the situation they faced. King always insisted that the civil rights movement could only succeed by embracing non-violence, but he admitted there were circumstances in which other options might be considered.

The goal of non-violence was, of course, to win—to obtain emancipation, voting rights, desegregation, and access to better jobs. This was the strategy. Tactically, however, the aim of non-violence was also to turn the state, with its own machinery of legally sanctioned violence, to the African Americans' advantage. Arendt was right on at least one count. The National Guard *enforced* desegregation, just as—though not always in a consistent way—the FBI conducted a "war" against the KKK. One of the objectives of non-violence was to mobilize the (legal) force of the state and have it do what, on their own, civil right activists could not do. This was definitely "an intelligent use of the police force." But one may want to take this reasoning further. The civil rights movement must be understood against the historical and political background of the Cold War, a confrontation in which America took on the role of leader of the "free world." Within this larger international context, the United States' handling of its "racial problem" was a delicate matter and often the source of embarrassment not only with decolonizing nations but with its Western allies as well. Historians have debated the degree to which the Cold War favored, hindered, or was relatively unimportant to the struggle for civil rights in America. Clearly, to exaggerate the impact of foreign criticism of the United States' handling of its racial problems would be to diminish the significance of the civil rights movement, whose strength did not hang on "foreign aid." However, the United States could not afford to leave the race card in Soviet hands for too long. To a level that is difficult to gauge, the U.S. government was also pressured to take action by the specter of its archenemy. As Mary Dudziak has put it, "U.S. government effort to contain and manage the story of race in America was a component of the government's broader Cold War policy of containing communism. Yet within this framework, the Cold War was simultaneously an agent of repression and an agent of change. . . . To the extent that reform was motivated by a desire to placate foreign critics, reform efforts that safeguarded the nation's image would best respond to that concern" (250–51).[38] In other words, the substantial non-violence of the movement was framed by a context of "war" that to a degree made possible (and in other ways made impossible) certain kinds of social and political changes.

Once again, the scope of these remarks is neither to diminish the moral and political achievements of non-violence per se nor to argue that non-violence is less non-violent than we realize. My point is simply that non-violence was part and parcel of a political struggle in which some degree of coercion and force had to be operative in order for the desired social change to occur. In conclusion, there are excellent reasons for figures as diverse as Ralph Waldo Emerson, William James, Jane Addams, Kenneth Burke, and Martin Luther King Jr., when engaged in an actual or theoretical pursuit of peace, couched their efforts in the language of war, heroism, strife, conflict, and power. Non-violence may be seen as the attempt to transfer the "purification of war" project from rhetoric to practice or as an attempt to realize Emerson's idea of peace heroes who would stand taller than war heroes. Non-violence may be considered as a "moral equivalent of war" different—as we shall see in the next chapter—from James's own, but animated by a similar spirit. Finally, and perhaps most important for the future of American studies, the "hybrid" conceptual and historical nature of non-violence is proof that the rediscovery of a non-violent, anti-war America has nothing to do with the rescue of an imaginary, "downright pastoral" world. Peace cannot be studied or understood without simultaneously studying and thinking war, and the same is true of violence and non-violence. The legacy of the gunfighter nation need not be denied but must be set alongside the historical, political, and intellectual legacy of an important *peace-fighting* tradition. To "purify" a Ciceronian phrase Kenneth Burke most probably knew: *Si pace frui volumus, bellum purificandum est.* If you wish to enjoy the fruits of peace, you must achieve the purification of war. Or, in the more recent formulation by peace activist and theorist Scott Ritter, in order to put an end to war, one must wage peace "as one would wage war" (15).[39]

CHAPTER 3

The Rhetorical Equivalent of War

William James, Kenneth Burke, Stephen Crane

> Batteries were speaking with thunderous oratorical effort.
>
> —Stephen Crane, *The Red Badge of Courage*

Words and Swords

"Words to Swords"; "Belles Lettres and Belligerency"; "Troops versus Tropes"; "Fiction and Friction." Over the past decades, wordplay of this kind has become increasingly common in studies of the relationship between literature and war, and, more generally, between language and violence. What all these formulations share is an emphasis on the continuity between the battlefield and the province of rhetoric that overturns, more or less radically, an older approach that saw language and literature always falling short of the intractable, ineffable, chaotic violence of war. In terms of the war/peace, violence/non-violence continuum discussed in the first two chapters of this book, recent literary criticism has been actively participating in the erosion of the border between war and its Other by suggesting that, far from being powerless or simply neutral vis-à-vis the armed conflicts it seeks to represent, language is complicit with violence. Indeed, in some radical versions of this argument, language itself *is* violence. Words always fall under the shadow of swords, so to speak, because "an a priori violence . . . inheres in language *as such* . . . and . . . insofar as it determines the (negative) conditions of possibility governing all individual speech acts, threatens to de-rail the speaker's implicit claims to authority, intentionality, sovereignty, and autonomous subjecthood" (Hanssen 165).

This understanding of the relationship between language and violence has been usefully filed by James Dawes under the rubric of "the disciplinary model"—a model that conceives language and violence "as mutually constitutive" (1). To this way of seeing the relation between rhetoric and force, Dawes juxtaposes the disciplinary model to "the emancipatory model, which presents force and discourse as mutually exclusive" (1). His overarching thesis is that we should learn from both models without accepting either in its entirety. Dawes acknowledges that the disciplinary model has much to commend itself, as "wars are born and sustained in rivers of language about what it means to serve the cause, to kill the enemy, and to die with dignity; and they are reintegrated into a collective historical self-understanding through a ritualistic overplus of the language of commemoration" (15). At the same time he is also drawn to the emancipatory model, not only for obvious ethical reasons—who would be against a democratic language emancipating us from a realm of pure force?—but because this model "recurs throughout the literature of war," which can be seen *also* as an attempt to undo, through language, the work of violence. Dawes's conclusion is that we have no choice but to try, on the one hand, to inhibit language's "more coercive potentials" while, on the other, "to maximize its emancipatory ones" (23).

Though I share Dawes's interest in linking "specialized modes of verbalization to the deceleration of violence" (23), my focus will be restricted to investigating what would appear as a specifically American wish to fashion a "substitute" or "equivalent" of war, which I read as an *ante litteram* effort to circumvent the emancipatory-versus-disciplinary-models dilemma. No matter how reluctant we may be to endorse the Heraclitean notion of war as "the master of all things," and hence of language as well, our resistance should not aim at reestablishing an absolute difference between language and violence, rhetoric and war. We should, instead, cut across the war/peace, violence/non-violence opposition by exploring how the rhetoric of war may be turned *against* war. In the previous chapter, I focused on the ideological concepts of non-violence and war resistance as these have been constructed and mobilized by a number of U.S. thinkers and activists in order to sustain the struggle for peace and justice. Here I return to rhetoric and literature. After reviewing the "violence of representation" position, I show how, following in the tracks of Emerson's "War," first William James and, in a more sustained, complex way, Kenneth Burke, imagine ways the hard facts of war and violence may be both acknowledged and worked through. Burke's *ad bellum purificandum* project acknowledges that power, language, and force are often entwined, but it also envisions ways in which such interconnections may be disarticulated and reconfigured. By refusing an originary status to either peace or war, Burke provides us with a template for understanding the tension as well as the cooperation between these two seemingly irreconcilable terms. Finally, in the concluding section, I test the usefulness of some of Burke's recommendations for literary studies through a reading of Stephen Crane's "A Mystery of Heroism." Set on a battleground of the

Civil War but devoted largely to exploring an instance of nonmilitary "heroism," the text provides an apt illustration of how in war writing the rhetoric of weapons may find in the weapons of rhetoric not only an ally but also an opponent. To use the terms of the Crane epigraph chosen for this chapter, in war the guns' "thunderous oratorical effort" may silence or replace the human voice, but as is implicit in the metaphor, language can also reverse the tables and turn its force against that of the guns. If, as Michel Foucault insists—and as in several ways Burke had already argued some decades before—"we have to interpret the war that is going on beneath peace" (*"Society Must Be Defended"* 49), we should not forget that also beneath war there is a peace waiting to be uncovered and critically understood.

To readers of war literature, the notion that language is coterminous with violence may at first appear odd. From Homer onward, war writers' common complaint has been that the magnitude, confusion, and monstrosity of warfare cannot be adequately represented in literature. As Kate McLoughlin points out, this disclaimer is what rhetorical handbooks call adynaton, "the impossibility of addressing oneself adequately to the topic" (*Authoring War* 152). This sense of frustration, of course, has not prevented writers from continuing to address the subject of war. Homer, for instance, as a rule shifted attention away from battles as a whole to the duel between two carefully individualized figures, a narrative and representational strategy he bequeathed to later epic writers, from Virgil all the way down to Tasso, Ariosto, and Milton. A focus on the individual combatant has remained a staple of war literature even in the age of total and cyber warfare, but war writers have hardly stopped complaining about the impossibility of containing war within the universe of letters. Walt Whitman famously remarked apropos the Civil War that "the real war will never get into the books," though he seemed somewhat relieved that "future years will never know the seething hell and the black infernal background of countless minor scenes and interiors . . . it is best they should not" (778). Some decades later, Walter Benjamin could not find anything redemptive in the unrepresentability of war, and observed that "[w]ith the [First] World War a process began to become apparent that has not halted since then. Was it not noticeable at the end of the war that men returned from the battleground grown silent, not richer, but poorer in communicable experience?" Benjamin did not ignore "the flood of war books" published in war's aftermath, but these, to him, contained "anything but experience that goes from mouth to mouth" ("Storyteller" 84). The war was for Benjamin an event that epitomized the break with "the epic side of truth." War marked the rupture with a world where sense and meaning could be "experienced" and communicated. Years later, addressing the same problem of a war beyond the reach of language, in *The Great War and Modern Memory* Paul Fussell also observed, "One of the curses of the war, of course, is the collision between events and the language available—or thought appropriate—to describe them" (169). He went on to add, "Logically, one supposes, there is no reason why a language devised by man should be inadequate to describe any of man's works," and yet "the presumed inadequacy of language itself to convey the facts about trench warfare is one of the motifs of all who wrote about the war" (170). From Fussell's viewpoint, "the flood of war books" was paradoxically able to communicate at least one thing: the incommunicability of the war experience.

The pervasiveness of the adynaton trope in war literature, no matter how "illogical" it may appear, is consistent with the notion that where violence and brute force prevail, language—the instrument of intersubjective communication par excellence—falls silent. Acts of violence can be described, of course, but they are felt to be that which language cannot contain. As Hannah Arendt put it in *On Revolution*, "violence itself is incapable of speech, and not merely that speech is helpless when confronted with violence" (quoted in Hanssen 163). Yet, as Mary Louise Pratt has noted, if "common sense locates, and often theorizes, violence as that which lies beyond words, that which erupts when words fail," it is also the case that "where there is violence, language is nearly always present, supplying meanings and alibis and inflicting injuries of its own" (1516). In obvious disagreement with the notion that language may be "the city gate that separates us from violence" (Dawes 19), Pratt suggests that if "the horror of war lies beyond words," this "may not be because language cannot capture the horror but because language is embedded in it. [. . .] The embedding of violence in language and language in violence is what makes it social" (1516). Pratt's inquiry privileges military sources, and perhaps it is not meant to invest that specialized form of language known as literature. Her overall theoretical framework, deriving from poststructuralist thought, however, suggests otherwise. Seen from a Foucauldian perspective, literature may in fact be the place where, as Nancy Armstrong and Leonard Tennenhouse have noted, the line "between forms of violence that are represented in writing and the violence committed through representation" is often blurred. Apprehended as "but one more symbolic practice among the others that make up cultural history," "writing is not so much about violence as a form of violence in its own right" (2).

Such thoroughgoing formulation of the disciplinary model immediately brings to mind the terms employed by Foucault to highlight the difference between his analytic method and that of both structuralism and Derridean deconstruction. In his view, the focus on language as an autonomous or semi-autonomous realm inevitably ends up obfuscating the role of power and force in the shaping of the symbolic field. "One's point of reference should not be to the great model of language (*langue*) and signs, but to that of war and battle. The history which bears and determines us has the form of a war rather than that of a language: relations of power, not relations of meaning" (*Power/Knowledge* 114). Against the liberal tradition best exemplified by Arendt, "for whom violence is to be located outside the arena of democratic politics and the precinct of language" (Hanssen 162), Foucault insists that power relations must be seen "in terms of conflict, confrontation, and war . . . Power is war, the continuation of war by other means" (*"Society Must Be Defended"* 15). In Foucault's theoretical imagination—at least as it unfolds in *"Society Must Be Defended"*—there is no outside to war, and "peace" is an optical illusion. "While it is true that political power puts an end to war and establishes or attempts to establish the reign of peace in civil society, it certainly does not do so in order to suspend the effects of power or to neutralize the disequilibrium revealed in the last battle of the war" (*"Society Must Be Defended"* 23). According to Beatrice Hanssen, despite Foucault's "repeated insistence that every desire to transcendentalize 'war' into a suprahistorical category would be thwarted, it appears that he did not fully succeed in keeping the specter at bay. 'War,' it seemed, started to operate as more than simply modernity's privileged grid of intelligibility or a codification of power—as he called it in *The History of Sexuality*—functioning at times as a grounding, foundationalist principle of sorts" (Hanssen 136).

Whether Foucault's analysis of power relations embraces a metaphysics of war, or, less drastically, it may be said to treat force as historically situated, his writings have helped promote what Hanssen describes as "the critical/mythical grid war/force" (137). Furthermore, regardless of how Foucault envisioned his project as distant from Derrida's language-centered critique of logocentrism, as Teresa de Lauretis has argued, one can trace a specular relation between their respective views on the matter.

> From the Foucauldian notion of a rhetoric of violence, an order of language which speaks violence—names certain behaviors and events as violent but not others, and constructs objects and subjects of violence, and hence violence as a social fact—it is easy to slide into the reverse notion of a language which, in itself, produces violence. But if violence is in language, before if not regardless of its concrete occurrences in the world, then there is also a violence of rhetoric, or what Derrida has called "the violence of the letter." (240)[1]

For the Derrida of *Of Grammatology*, violence is everywhere "writing" is and therefore practically everywhere language is, since, unlike Levi-Strauss, Derrida does not consider the absence of a written alphabet a sign of innocence. "Writing" as a means of classification and imposition of proper names, Derrida insists, is to be found also among primitive societies, and therefore it existed long before the intrusion of Western cultural anthropology—it is what in a sense founds and institutes culture as such: "To name, to give names that it will on occasion be forbidden to pronounce, such is the originary violence of language which consists in inscribing within a difference, in classifying, in suspending the vocative absolute. To think the unique *within* the system, to inscribe it there, such is the gesture of the arche-writing: arche-violence, loss of the proper, of absolute proximity, of self-presence" (*Of Grammatology* 112). The violence of language is thus found not only where easily detectable, as in insults, hate speech, and threats, but in language *as such*. Violence would be inherent in the mechanism through which language suppresses and disposes of difference.[2]

In a timely critical engagement with the "naming is violence" argument, Dawes notes that while for poststructuralist theory "the act of naming is a matter of forcibly imposing a sign upon a person or object with which it has only the most arbitrary of relationships" (192), article 16 of the International Covenant on Civil and Political Rights (ICCPR) unambiguously establishes that what guarantees one's personhood before the law is precisely an individual identity. Moreover, section 2 of article 24 states, "Every child shall be registered immediately after birth and shall have a name" (quoted in Dawes 193). While to poststructuralist critics "to be named is to suffer violence," in terms of international law and universal rights, "to be named is the foundation of human dignity" (Dawes 193). This comparison delivers a sharp critique of theory's readiness to conflate power with force, but Dawes does not rule out the possibility that, in given contexts, naming might indeed be a form of violence in its own right. Whether naming may be interpreted as an act of force or as the bedrock of human dignity would have to be adjudicated case by case, depending on the social, historical, and legal frameworks the named subject is a part of.

Even more interesting is Dawes's discussion of how certain uses of language can be seen as *resisting* rather than enabling violence. He focuses in particular on the international laws of war, which he sees as deriving "from the notion that language, deployed in a particular fashion, can be made equivalent to force—or, rather, can so effectively inhibit the reflex toward violence that disputes can be resolved, as Jürgen Habermas has put it, through the 'unforced force of the better argument'" (207). In Dawes's opinion, for instance, the Geneva Conventions should be viewed "as producing a counterlanguage to war" (210). This emancipatory force of rational argumentation is sustained by the use of a referential language that painstakingly tries to avoid confusion and the blurring of borders (both physical and conceptual), which is one of war's specific features. For example, Dawes observes that numerous articles are meant to render as rigid as possible the distinction between military objectives and civilians, and he observes that while earlier versions of these laws "centered on the concept of *aiming*, thus prohibiting the subjective intent directly to harm particular categories of noncombatants . . . [t]he revision of Article 51 ingeniously overcame distinction's vexed problem of subjectivity by pointing to the 'method and means of combat' rather than the intent of the combatant as the relevant evidence in determining the threshold of discrimination" (212).

Without cynically discounting the importance of the Geneva Conventions, one must note the perverse, inverted relation between the ever-increasing "ingeniousness" of the lawmakers, on the one side, and the growing number of civilians killed in war, on the other. It appears that, no matter how unambiguous the international laws of war may be, they have little effect on the civilian casualty rate, which has gone since the end of World War II from 2:3 (two civilian deaths for three soldier deaths) to a staggering 8:1.[3] Even though this is, somewhat surprisingly, something Dawes fails to mention, he *is* on the other hand quick to note,

> The laws of war from their inception functioned as much to justify violence as to prohibit it. Centuries later, things are much the same. The United States, for instance, managed to quell much of the criticism and dissent against its war with Iraq [the first Iraq War] by asserting through selective video evidence that its use of "smart" weapons complied fully with Geneva restrictions—indeed, complied to such an extent that the war could be imagined as "clean" and almost casualty-less. The conventions can be turned into a weapon for any military's propaganda arsenal. (214)

The evidence accumulated over the past few years, from Afghanistan to the Second Iraq War, not to mention Operation Cast Lead, would suggest that as long as you claim you are employing a "smart" weapon, you can "ingeniously" overcome the ingeniousness of the law. A smart weapon is by definition one whose intention is not to cause civilian deaths, which on this count are always unintentional.

It is not surprising that, as Dawes writes, some critics believe that the "essential nature" of the Geneva Conventions is to facilitate rather than mitigate violence, while others, more guardedly, argue that the problem lies simply with "the strategic *misuse* of the laws of war" (214). Yet this discussion, though important, is vitiated by the fact that, *pace* Habermas's "unforced force of the better argument," there is no truly independent court of law capable of adjudicating whether a law of war has been respected or not.[4] It is virtually impossible for an argument, no matter how "good," to be universally accepted, and all the more so in a war context. A "better argument" *can count as such* only to the extent that *it is enforced*. We may strongly believe that the way the United States has been conducting military operations in both Iraq and Afghanistan has been responsible for many civilian casualties, but our argument can become a counterforce capable of inhibiting violence only to the extent that it is registered and accepted by those who have the power to make changes in military policies. Until that happens, it would be hard to detect any "unforced force" in what (to me, though not to others) would be the better argument.

Language may shield us from violence just as it can, vice versa, be a tool for its implementation. Judging from the very terms Dawes employs in order to evoke the emancipatory versus the disciplinary potential of language, it would appear that, rather than being two alternative models, they actually exist along a continuum, just like peace and war (as we saw in chapter 1) and violence and non-violence (as we saw in chapter 2). Notice that in the same sentence in which Dawes evokes the power of the language of law "to inhibit" violence, language is imagined as "made equivalent to *force*" (emphasis added). The term needed to stress the emancipatory potential of language is one of the disciplinary model's keywords. Similarly, the Habermas quotation is exemplary in its simultaneous appeal to and erasure of force. Also in Arendt one can find similar passages where, for all her commitment to tracing an unambiguous line between politics and war, she acknowledges that while violence and coercion must be distinguished from "the political" (*das Politische*), they are "the means employed to protect, establish, and widen the political space" (see Esposito 44). Or one may think of the most famous instance of emancipatory language in U.S. history, Lincoln's 1863 Emancipation Proclamation, as an illustration of how its liberating potential and its power to inhibit the violence of slavery were backed by the force of a president who was also "Commander-in-Chief." No wonder the Emancipation Proclamation is described by Lincoln as a "war measure" (Guelzo 294).

Similar tensions may be traced in actual instances of disciplinary language as well as in theorizations of the disciplinary model. Laws are, to be sure, a primary example of language used with the aim of disciplining people's behavior. Yet all laws are by their very nature duplicitous because their intent is both to protect and to condemn, to defend people from being abused and to punish abusers. The language of the law is therefore intrinsically both disciplinary and emancipatory. Analogously, even hardcore exponents of the "language is violence"/"power is war" school do not see their theoretical work as politically disabling. While poststructuralist theory appears to its critics as endorsing a disciplinary model that cancels out any hope for amelioration, from the point of view of theory the disciplinary model is necessary to assess realistically the world we live in. More important, whatever the merits and shortcomings of theory, notice that just as Habermas and Arendt raise the specter of force in the same turns of phrase that should lay it to rest, likewise Foucault and Derrida admit to the existence of something beyond violence and war. When, for example, Foucault invites us to unearth "in the filigree of peace the signs of a war that has never ceased," is he not acknowledging that war must camouflage itself as peace in order to prolong its effects into our everyday lives? Is he not, at least implicitly, suggesting that if force must hide itself behind a peace mask, then war is not acceptable to people? Isn't he resurrecting the dream of a true peace in the same sentence in which he seems to bury it? And doesn't Derrida do something similar when, after noting that "discourse is originally violent," and that "the distinction between discourse and violence always will be an inaccessible horizon," concludes that "nonviolence would be the telos, and not the essence of discourse" (*Writing and Difference* 116)? Is he not invoking nonviolence as a worthy objective to pursue while all along maintaining that we must declare peace in the language of war?

My point is not that the differences between disciplinary-model and emancipatory-model adherents are not as great as they seem at first but rather to suggest that both models may be seen as ultimately sharing the same goal—to emancipate us from the reign of force—and as both betraying the same fear—that emancipation from force may in the end require the application of some kind of force. We may think the goal of emancipation is more consistently pursued by exponents of the emancipatory model, but as Dawes demonstrates in his use of theory to reveal the actual or potential shortcomings of international war laws, the disciplinary model can cooperate with, rather than hinder, the objective of inhibiting violence by revealing how international laws can be twisted to suit specific military needs. Conversely, we may feel that only the disciplinary model can register the pervasive influence of force, but also in Arendt we may find plenty of evidence that the emancipatory potential of language needs protection from the very force it is meant to liberate us from. As Roberto Esposito has put it, though *polis* and *polemos*, the citified space of politics and the chaotic sphere of war, are as a rule juxtaposed in Arendt's writings, there is hardly any question that the former *derives* from the latter (Esposito 43–50).

Though it may be difficult to reconcile the two models, we can neither ignore the lessons of poststructuralist theory nor, as Dawes rightly insists, do without the belief in the power of democratic debate to emancipate us from the subjection to sheer force. We cannot, that is, afford to remain trapped between the rhetoric of violence and the violence of rhetoric, and we cannot expect rhetoric to be intrinsically immune from the influence of force. In what follows I intend to show how, long before poststructuralism made its appearance on the world's intellectual stage, thinkers like William James and Kenneth Burke confronted the dilemma of how might a world in which war was the norm give birth to a genuine peace. Like latter-day poststructuralists, James and Burke cultivated no illusions concerning the possibility of a rigorous demarcation between peace and war. Well before Foucault, they discerned the marks of war in the filigree of peace. They also knew that—as Derrida would also later insist—rather than conceiving of peace and war as opposites, it was more productive to understand how, practically and conceptually, the two bled into each other. Finally, they were also aware that even though a conflict-free universe was impossible and perhaps even hardly desirable, conflict need not necessarily turn violent. Rhetoric could both promote and restrain the use of force.

William James: Troping War

William James's "The Moral Equivalent of War" (1910) is one of the high points of the philosopher's pacifist militancy, which led him in 1902 to join the Anti-Imperialist League, whose vice-president he would later become. It is also a text emerging from a historical period during which, on both sides of the Atlantic, war was incessantly poeticized and glorified. According to historian T. J. Jackson Lears

(123), James's essay demonstrates the difficulties encountered also by opponents of the triumphant "martial spirit" of the late nineteenth and early twentieth century. James shares many of his contemporaries' anxieties regarding the softness and meaninglessness of a modern life lacking the "spur" once provided by fear of God or fear of enemy. War may be immoral but—as Emerson had written decades before—it has long served a civilizing function, and James indeed calls it "the gory nurse that trained society to cohesiveness" (1283). Rather than wondering how to abolish war—a project that at the time James considered chimerical and counterproductive—one had better fashion an "equivalent of war" capable of taking on war's moral, sociocultural, and aesthetic functions with none of the bloodshed of actual warfare attached.

The best way to grasp the significance of James's essay is suggested by Richard Poirier: faced with a reality that seemed to respond to fundamental human needs, James "decides to treat it like a literary metaphor that needs to be troped" (*Poetry and Pragmatism* 116). As a good Emersonian, James acknowledges that if "history is a bath of blood" (1282), contemporary civilization can hardly claim to have nothing to do with war. Belligerency is not a useless archeological relic. On the contrary, "We inherit the warlike type; and for most of the capacities of heroism that the human race is full of we have to thank this cruel history" (1283). The "trope" destined to replace war—its moral as well as rhetorical equivalent—must therefore keep alive its role as "great preserver of our ideals of hardihood" (1285) and at the same time it need be able "to enter more deeply into the esthetical and ethical point of view" (1288) of those who extol the virtues of militarism. Only by understanding from the inside the cultural framework of their opponents and not by rejecting it outright, pacifists can make a real impact on the world.

One of the most significant points raised by James concerns the limits of traditional pacifist strategies. By insisting on showing "war's irrationality and horror" (1281), pacifists ignore that it is precisely its gory side that makes war a fascinating business. After introducing this concept in the first lines of his essay, James returns to it a few pages later in order to repeat that when confronted with the glorification of war, it is no use to emphasize obsessively war's immense economic and human costs. "The horror makes the thrill" (1287): it is the very horror to which pacifists draw attention that makes war a source of excitement and deep feelings. To try shocking citizens with the horror that is war's main source of psychological and aesthetic fascination strikes James as deeply illogical. "The military party denies neither the bestiality nor the horror, nor the expense; it only says that these things tell but half the story" (1287–88). The other half tells us that war is "worth" these sacrifices, and given that war taxes "are the only ones men never hesitate to pay, as the budgets of all nations show us" (1281), James despairs of convincing public opinion that war is nothing but a waste of human and financial resources.

In conclusion, if pacifists wish to stop wars, they must at least temporarily reason like militarists and show to all skeptics that the cultural and esthetic functions of war can be safeguarded by alternative, less bloody, practices.

James's critique of those who wish to educate the masses by treating them to healthy doses of the naked horrors of the battlefield is as valid today as it was a hundred years ago. The increased visibility of war's violence made possible by war journalism and photography, first, and then by cinema and television, and now the Internet, has only sporadically succeeded in educating public opinion. True, sometimes a picture may be worth a thousand words, but there is no conclusive evidence that images of atrocity succeed in turning war enthusiasts into pacifists. The limitations of James's diagnosis lie elsewhere, in the reification of what he describes as the "two unwillingnesses of the imagination, one aesthetic and the other moral" (1287). In his view the human mind is simply incapable of conceiving a future "in which the destinies of peoples shall nevermore be decided quickly, thrillingly, and tragically by force, but only gradually and insipidly by 'evolution'" (1287). What James imputes in the essay to a disembodied "imagination" is a failure of *his* imagination. Thus, while on the one hand he criticizes those who consider war a "biological or sociological necessity," "a permanent human obligation" (1285), on the other hand he himself sees war as fulfilling *innate* human needs, even sharing his adversaries' preoccupations regarding the risks that lack of military discipline may result in a spiritual degeneration of society.

James runs into a number of curious, adamant contradictions. He emphatically declares his belief "in the reign of peace and in the gradual advent of some sort of socialistic equilibrium. The fatalistic view of the war function is to me nonsense" (1289). Yet also on the same page he writes, "I do not believe that peace either ought to be or will be permanent on this globe, unless the states, pacifically organized, preserve some of the old elements of army-discipline" (1289). James fully shares many of his contemporaries' worries regarding the excessive "softness" of the modern world, and he seems genuinely worried by the idea that a "peace-economy" might amount to a "pleasure economy." Confronted with the hedonism of a nascent consumer society, James looks for an equivalent of war because he shares the anxieties of the militarists of his time vis-à-vis a world deprived of what is, after all, "the romance of history"—that unique combination of art, spirituality, perseverance, and willingness to sacrifice oneself that is war. In short, James asks us to adopt the militarist point of view because he shares some of its basic tenets.

Though, as Poirier argues, James approaches war as a metaphor in need of further troping, with a maneuver that in its essentialism may be seen as un-Emersonian, he finds the deep roots of the war metaphor in an absolute psychological and social reality. To James, "war results from militaristic sentiment, inbred pugnacity . . . war, as he puts it, 'is the strong life.' By that logic, ordinary folk not only fight the wars, they plan and start them" (*Poetry and Pragmatism* 117).[5] By rejecting the Clausewitzian notion of war as a political act, James finds the causes of human bellicosity in "nature" and, even more generally, in "life," thereby obliterating the concrete historical causes that lead to war. Moreover, Poirier finds especially troubling James's idea of replacing the military draft with a peaceful army "enlisted against *Nature*" (1291). What James has in mind is something similar to Baden Powell's Boy Scouts or the Peace Corps of John F. Kennedy's day—an organization in which the old martial virtues ("intrepidity, contempt of softness, surrender of private interest, obedience to command" [1290]) would continue to function as a social glue. This proposal, however, comes after James has declared, "There is nothing to make one indignant in the mere fact that life is hard, that men should toil and suffer pain. The planetary conditions once for all are such, and we can stand it" (1290–91). However, the hard life is endured almost exclusively by the poor and the laboring classes, while the well-to-do usually have no truck with it. As Poirier notes, "It simply never occurs to [James] that in America there can be any permanent, rooted enemy beyond whatever he means by Nature" (118). James equates in one stroke the toils of work and daily life to those of war, quietly discounting the possibility that such harsh conditions may be the consequence of some defect in the political arrangement of society. He therefore suggests that all should have a fairer share of the hard life, though not within the realm of work and production but in a clash with nature destined to resurrect a frontier that Frederick Jackson Turner had declared closed only a few years before. Poirier concludes that, for James, "the enemy is never within America's economic-social system, it is only whatever is opposed to America, even potentially. The mentality of the 'moral equivalent of war' sounds dispiritingly like a preparation for the mentality of the Cold War" (*Poetry and Pragmatism* 119).

One might add that James does not simply consider the hard life as an innate human necessity. He also sees it as part and parcel of a need for discipline and coercion that is characteristic of the human condition as well. The moral equivalent of war is explicitly described as a "substitute for war's disciplinary functions" (1288). "So far, war has been the only force that can discipline a whole community, and until an equivalent discipline is organized, I believe that war must have its way" (1292). Here James risks appearing, rather than an antimilitarist eager to find a peaceful alternative to war, a conservative frightened by the prospect that, with no tight control from above, societies would disintegrate into chaos. One may excuse James by noting that the disciplinary bulwark he believed was necessary to keep societies together should not be seen as the repressive apparatus of a police state but more as a cooperative effort meant to contain what he considered man's innate bellicosity. However, since James conceives "the martial character" as a conquest of civilization to be preserved, albeit cleansed of its bloodiest traits, his imagination cannot go beyond the dream of a pacifist-military utopia similar to Fourier's phalanx or the social organization depicted by Edward Bellamy in *Looking Backward*.

Notwithstanding its contradictions, James's essay marks a turning point in the history of U.S. pacifist thinking. Until then, with the important exceptions of the early Emerson, Thoreau, Jane Addams, and a few other, lesser-known figures, American pacifism had insisted on the horrors and immorality of war without heeding the motivations behind society's reluctance to renounce war. The most scandalous truth emphasized by James's essay is the one implicit in its title: in order to be able to imagine a *moral* equivalent of war, war's immorality must be seen as tempered by virtues that cannot, at least in principle, be immoral. A vision of war as nothing but horror and evil would risk obscuring the reasons why many people consider war not only a grim necessity but also a thrilling opportunity. For James war is, yes, the foremost expression of human cruelty, but it is also the context within which some of the highest moral qualities of humankind take shape. Devotion to the common good, altruism, the acceptance of suffering, the sense of belonging to something greater than oneself and one's private interests—these are, to James, human feelings and dispositions rather rare in peacetime but standard fare during times of war. One must not, in sum, see only the repugnant traits of bellicosity, thereby forgetting the utopian longings they manage to accommodate. Even though the "noble" traits of war do not magically turn the battlefield into a moral environment, they cannot be brushed aside too quickly, as they are needed by any healthy human community.

What is difficult to accept in James's reasoning is, of course, the idea that, without war, humanity would have never developed any spirit of solidarity. In this regard, one must call attention to the most glaring flaw of James's essay. He seems absolutely unaware that his point of view erases altogether women from history. Civilization in his essay stands out as the result of a martial and patriarchal dialectic leaving no room for women or for those activities traditionally associated with the feminine sphere. It is bizarre, to say the least, that James conceives the ability to endure pain, sacrifice for others, and give up one's selfish motives as deriving from "the *strong* life" and "life in *extremis*" without ever feeling the need to mention how women, without taking up arms, have contributed to generating and shaping values that are perhaps *also* found in war and in many other social and cultural contexts as well. James endorses a view of the martial conflict as being not only an important but *the* decisive motor of human progress. From a Jamesian perspective, peace is largely a continuation of war by other means—"the intensely sharp *preparation* for war . . . is the *real war*" (1283)—and the idea that it may be possible to overturn war dialectically, as Kenneth Burke would propose some years later, never strikes him as a possibility. Often, in short, James does sound very much like the hardcore

Foucault of *"Society Must be Defended."* The pragmatist, antifoundationalist James is willing, paradoxically, to make of war a foundationalist principle.

Even though the belief that the best heroic virtues of humankind have been largely forged on the battlefield can only strike us today as the price James paid to a hegemonic militarist culture, one may agree with him that *conflict*, though not war, is an indispensable ingredient of both social and intellectual life. Whoever thinks that peace should be thought of only "as the telos and not the essence of discourse"—whoever realizes, in other words, that the pacifist wager must be placed within an economy of violence, is likely to find James's essay inspirational even today. By troping war into a "monstrous work"—a human activity like others, though by and large horrific—James seems to resist with one hand the reification of war that his tracing the roots of war in the human spirit accomplishes with the other. James's imagination did not go far enough because it remained grounded in the belief that bellicosity was both a natural instinct and an innate psychological trait. And yet, however flawed, the essay represents an important link between Emerson's call to transfer "the manhood that has been in war . . . to the cause of peace" (171) and the more elaborate reflections on the war/peace continuum formulated by Burke, to whose work I now turn.

Kenneth Burke: Purifying War

Burke's more explicit and extended reflections on war and rhetoric may be found in the work he published in the 1940s but, as mentioned in the previous chapter, in a passage of his *Attitudes toward History* (1937), Burke was already pointing out that "when liberals began to think, not of eliminating war, but of finding 'the moral equivalent for war,' liberalism was nearing the state of maturity" (236). By connecting his own project to that of James, Burke suggests that any effort to trope war must be seen as part of a wider symbolic procedure bent on attenuating rather than uprooting evil. What Burke recommends adopting is—to employ a term from the second essay in *Attitudes*—a "homeopathic" approach, which, unlike an allopathic strategy, is based "on the feeling that danger cannot be handled by head-on attack, but must be *accommodated*" (45n).

Again in the 1930s, in a piece occasioned by a polemical exchange between Archibald MacLeish and Malcolm Cowley regarding the merits of a literary anthology on the Great War (*The First World War*, edited by Laurence Stallings), Burke moves from a similar Jamesian intuition in order to ask the question of what might be the best strategy to discourage the reading public's militarist, chauvinistic temptations. According to Burke, it is rather questionable that the cause of peace would best be served by focusing only on the most hateful and horrifying side of war. In words that explicitly echo James's essay, Burke argues that "the greater the horror, the greater the thrill and honor of enlisting." The feelings of "horror, repugnance, hatred" evoked by the war literature most committed to tracing a spectacle of death and destruction may perhaps convince someone that wars must be avoided at all costs, but, in Burke's view, it is more likely that such feelings "might well provide the firmest basis on which the 'heroism' of a new war may be erected" ("War, Response, and Contradiction" 239). The literature of war may be more likely to act as a deterrent of future wars not by presenting us with a nearly altogether inhuman reality but rather by offering us an image of war "*as a cultural way of life, as one channel of effort in which people can be profoundly human*" (240–41, original italics). Burke does not propose a *practical* alternative to war's destructive "heroism," but the continuity of his approach with the Jamesian perspective is obvious. Like James, Burke sees the extreme situations in which people find themselves during wartime as conducive not only to the worst but also to the best features of the human spirit. A literature that would exclusively or primarily emphasize the repellent aspect of the martial experience would risk, paradoxically, "partially clos[ing] the mind to the repellent. It may call forth, as its response, a psychological callus, a protective crust of insensitiveness" (241). If, vice versa, literature were to endeavor to depict a "human" war with feelings like "gentleness, companionship, humor, respect for courage (of the enemy as well as among one's own ranks), dignity in suffering, refusal to admire the jockeyings and elbowings for position which characterize so much of our efforts under conditions of capitalist peace" (240), it would perhaps encourage us to imagine another, non-violent environment, where feelings and attitudes analogous to the "martial" ones could prosper. Characteristically, Burke concludes "War, Response, and Contradiction" by calling attention to the split etymology of the word "virtue," a term that the Romans originally used to designate their warriors' courage. In time the term came to take on a moral and civic significance quite removed from the brutality of war. One might say that, through a "purification" of sorts, the English-speaking community has managed to overturn its original meaning.

This call not to forget that there is more than terror and bloodshed to war would form the basis of Burke's subsequent, more articulate ruminations on this problem. The mind immediately goes to the epigraph Burke chose for one of his most important works, *A Grammar of Motives* (1945)—*Ad Bellum Purificandum*, used as the title of the previous chapter. Given the book's date of publication, the motto may be read as suggesting that the rhetorical theories debated in the book are no mere academic exercise but rather attempts at responding to the devastation of worldwide warfare. As M. Elizabeth Weiser has carefully documented, the theory of dramatism expounded in Burke's *A Grammar of Motives* emerges from a war-torn context with the intent of providing "a specific response to the real threat of totalitarianism, both militarily from Nazi Germany and politically from the U.S.

response to that militarism." While total war demands "monolithic certainty in the role of the strong man," Burke's dramatism "encourages a poetic dialectic—the celebration of differing perspectives—and transcendence—the search for points of merger—in an effective parliamentary debate" (Weiser 287). While Weiser focuses mainly on dramatism's "parliamentary babel of diverse perspectives" (300) as Burke's alternative to war's suppression of differences and ambiguity, I will limit my remarks to key traits of Burke's "purification of war" concept by linking them to ideas he had already sketched out before the start of World War II. As mentioned above, Burke was aware that human society was unthinkable outside cultural and material conflicts. These conflicts could not be abolished, but they could be "channelized" in ways that would not forestall human communication and interaction. The main goal of his *A Grammar of Motives* was to disarm conflicts without trying to eliminate them—a political and rhetorical project centered on dialogue and the dialectical overcoming of violence.[6]

In what follows I do not discuss Burke's rhetorical project as a whole; rather, I concentrate on a few passages from both *A Grammar of Motives* and *A Rhetoric of Motives* (1950), where Burke explicitly confronts the issue of war's virtual omnipresence in human history as well as the problem of how such an unpleasant though undeniable fact may be best handled rhetorically. Moving from some considerations on "the imagery of killing" in Milton, Burke argues that the violence and brutality of certain images should not be taken literally but rather read as the symptom of a more general rhetorical war undertaken by the poet in order to solve on a figurative/symbolic plane his own personal and political crisis. We would be mistaken, Burke observes, to focus on images of violence, homicides, and revenge in order to reach conclusions—usually of a psychoanalytic tenor—regarding the primary and founding character of aggressive feelings in human personality. If we were to follow such an interpretive path, ethical or collaborative motivations would be discounted as simple cover-ups for deeper, more "essential" and ineradicable destructive impulses. While on a superficial level Burke seems to echo James in acknowledging the omnipresence of war, on closer scrutiny one realizes that he takes a firm stance against those who consider the martial spirit as providing *the* typical imprint for any human thought or activity. True, "rhetoric is *par excellence* the region of the Scramble, of insult and injury, bickering, squabbling, malice and the lie, cloaked malice and the subsidized lie," but it is equally true that rhetoric "also includes resources of appeal ranging from sacrificial, evangelical love, through the kinds of persuasion figuring in sexual love, to sheer 'neutral' *communication*" (*Rhetoric of Motives* 19).

Burke wishes therefore to translate/trope a rhetoric centered on images of death and violence into a language that does not magically erase conflict and contradiction but invokes aspirations that cannot be reduced to a purely destructive or homicidal intent. "We need never deny the presence of strife, enmity, faction as a characteristic motive of rhetorical expression. We need not close our eyes to their almost tyrannous ubiquity in human relations . . . yet we can at the same time always look beyond this order, to the principle of identification in general, a terministic choice justified by the fact that the identifications in the order of love are also characteristic of rhetorical expression" (*Rhetoric of Motives* 20). Unlike James, who remains prisoner of his metaphor and assigns an absolute and primary position to "the hard life," of which war is but an ancillary articulation, Burke insists on the simultaneous presence within rhetorical expression of two distinct symbolical and identifying strategies. The first is marked by a divisive and violent nature; the second is instead conciliatory and communicative. While James believes that peace should be considered as a kind of disguised state of war, Burke thinks of ways to move beyond this, albeit important, dialectical overturning. Peace may be at times a kind of war, no doubt, but at the same time "we can treat 'war' as a '*special case of peace*'—not as a primary motive in itself, not as *essentially* real, but purely as a *derivative* condition, a *perversion*" (20). War and violence are to be understood as perversions of the human aspiration to a peaceful coexistence, and they are therefore in principle amenable to "purification." War should not be, as we would put it today, essentialized, and it should instead be thought of as an "ultimate disease of cooperation" (22). At the same time, it would be hard to deny that human beings often fashion their identity by juxtaposing themselves to other human beings, conceived as fundamentally different. This othering process, Burke says, can and does often lead to "that most tragically ironic of all divisions, or conflicts, wherein millions of cooperative acts go into the preparation for one single destructive act" (22). Cooperation and communion should therefore be safeguarded against war and division, their perverse transfigurations.

Burke's dialectical approach to the problem of how to think and transcend war is further developed in ten or so dense pages of the "On Dialectic" section in *A Grammar of Motives*. Like any dialectician, Burke needs also to confront the problem of totality, an intellectual category he finds both necessary and problematic, especially within modernity. While in primitive communities ceremonies and tribal festivals were synecdochically representative, and in the Middle Ages the religious sphere functioned as a representative public space, with the advent of industrialism and consumerism it becomes difficult to find a communal event providing a basis for thinking the social totality. "Unfortunately, in the modern state, with its great diversity of interests and opinions, due to the dispersion of technological and commercial enterprise, the act that comes closest to the totality of tribal festivals and the agape is the act of war" (328). However, even modern war, taken as a general category, appears so complex and stratified that it amounts to "more of a *confusion* than a *form*" (329). This epistemological difficulty is augmented by an ethical one.

If we were to turn war, as Burke writes, into our "representative anecdote" (328)—the meta-language, that is, through which we may unify the multiple languages of modernity—we would seriously risk, in obedience to the logic of our rhetorical choice, "proclaiming war as the essence of human relations. And that choice is too drastic to be taken unless absolutely necessary" (329).

Here Burke anticipates the postmodern uneasiness regarding the notion of totality, which he sees not only as potentially "essentialist" but also as problematic from an ethical point of view. However, no matter how many reservations he may harbor about seeing war as a synecdoche of modern society, Burke believes that probably nothing else but war "draws things to a head as thoroughly as a suppurating abscess" (329). Being the outcome of myriad and distinct processes, war provides a privileged point of view for studying the functioning of the entire social and cultural body. Moreover, war is a significant presence "in all forms of theoretical or practical enterprises. In fact, when Heraclitus offered 'Strife' and 'War' as synonyms for his Universal Fire . . . was he not but saying, in a forceful way, that history is 'dialectical,' developing by the give and take of combat? And his very words for War and Strife survive as words for the dialectic in its most agonistic aspects: 'polemic' and 'eristic.'" (329). In our efforts to proceed toward the purification of war, therefore, we should keep in mind "the militaristic core" that remains operative "even during times of peace" (330). Peace, in other words, may indeed often appear as a thinly disguised form of war rather than a space of non-violence and tolerance.

For Burke the juxtaposition between war and peace must be refunctioned at a symbolic level by considering the effects one wishes to achieve through such rhetorical maneuvering. Returning to the theme of his earlier essay "War, Response, and Contradiction," Burke imagines that the intellectual and social energies, which are as a norm mobilized—often in the name of peace—in preparation for the next war, may instead form a basis for the edification of a genuine peace. If in this peace campaign we would still be relying on war to provide us with our basic "idiom"—we would, that is, be engaged in a war against war—war "would not be used primarily as a *constitutive* anecdote but rather as an *admonitory* anecdote. That is, an anecdote shaped about war would be designed not so much for stating what mankind *substantially is* as for emphatically pointing out what mankind is *in danger of becoming*" (*Grammar of Motives* 330). Burke detects an indelible remainder of violence in even the humblest appeal for peace. The temptation to turn war into the overarching metaphor to which all human experience can be traced back is therefore understandable, and yet Burke believes that it must by all means be resisted. While Burke anticipates both the Derridian denunciation of the ineradicable "violence of the letter" and the Foucauldian notion of politics as a state of potentially endless war, he resists embracing an unqualified skeptical perspective whereby only an ironic register may sustain an irenic attitude. The polar star of Burke's thought, on the contrary, must be found in what he calls "homeopathy" or "a certain medicinal kind of humanitarianism" energizing those constructive and "admonitory" linguistic strategies engaged in the translation of the rhetoric of violence into a less bellicose and, at least ideally, "purified" idiom (331). At the same time, Burke does not relent on what he calls "debunking," or what we would today describe as ideology critique. An important part of our critical task remains the laying bare of any violent and warlike impulse inherent in the languages of "peace" and the status quo.

All this does not make war as admonitory anecdote a problem-free choice. Burke acknowledges two limitations in his own proposal. In the first place, whatever its utility in terms of political and moral propaganda, evoking "*what one may become* is hardly the most direct way of discussing *what one is*" (331). By turning hortatory, language risks losing its grip on the actual world. Second, Burke adds, "it may be doubted whether a purely admonitory idiom can serve even the deterrent role for which it is designed; for it creates nothing but the image of the enemy, and if men are to make themselves over in the image of the imagery, what other call but that of the enemy is there for them to answer?" (331). In other words, if we insist on admonishing men not to become violent and bellicose by showing them plenty of images of their past as bloody warriors, "what we [are] admonished *against* [would be] just about the only tangible thing there for us to *be*" (332). It is not surprising that Burke would find considerably infected with militaristic imagery the language that should be the most distant from war: the pacifist idiom. As an ideal for which one should fight, or as an instrument of opposition to the danger of war, peace provides of course an indispensable reference point. This, however, should not blind us to the fact that all forms of more or less sincere "pacifism" that have so far existed have had to compromise morally and symbolically with the language of war. The only pacifism that Burke considers as undefiled by war is the one that has its roots in a rigorously Christian perspective—the only one, in Burke's view, that by ontologically identifying Peace with Being and arguing that "only insofar as people were peaceful did they actually partake of Being" (336) does not conceive the call for peace as a mere humanitarian invocation of a better future but as a categorical imperative to be acted upon in any instant of one's life.[7]

Though he admires the Christian position, Burke strongly doubts it can be translated into practice. As an example of the endemic state of human corruption in these matters, Burke refers to our inability to imagine the relation between war and peace in terms other than a struggle between the two terms, and not as "Peace and War at peace" (337). In agreement with Derrida, who argues that since discourse "is originally violent, can only *do itself violence*, can only negate itself in order to affirm itself, make war upon the war which institutes it" (*Writing and Difference* 146),

Burke maintains that a rhetoric of pure peace—assuming it could exist—would be incapable of describing "the world as we know it, the world in history" and therefore our "representative anecdote must contain militaristic ingredients" (*Grammar of Motives* 337). But if, by insisting that, in spite of appearances, "we are actually in a world at war" (337), Burke anticipated the poststructuralist suspicion that war is often hidden beneath a world of "peace," he also never stopped pursuing a strategy, at once political and rhetorical, that would not give us absolute peace but may at least be able to deliver a purification of war.[8]

A Constitutive or an Admonitory Anecdote?
Stephen Crane and the Mystery of Heroism

Surprisingly, the pacifist/pragmatist tradition that goes from Emerson to William James to Kenneth Burke has had little or no influence on the study of U.S. war literature. John Limon's *Writing after War* would seem to be an exception to this rule. Even though it makes no mention of Burke and devotes only a few cursory comments to James's essay, Limon's important study follows a critical path similar to what I describe. In his view, American writers are reluctant to produce martial epics. By rejecting the "metaphoric connection of war and writing, American fiction, eschewing epic prestige, likes to metonymize *from* war *to* writing" (11, original italics). Put otherwise, according to Limon, American war narratives substitute the direct description of military confrontations with the representation of other, bloodless types of conflicts. This substitution accounts for Limon's choice of texts, which are often not included in the canon of war literature and yet in his view are significant illustrations of those rhetorical strategies or "itineraries from war to peace" (7), through which writers replace—or, as Burke would have put it, sublimate—the brutal clashes of the battlefield with non-violent conflicts. As Limon writes, "War has a border with hunting, which has a border with sport, which has a border with play, which has a border with fabulation" (11). The ultimate goal of literature would therefore be that of troping the contest of swords into a contest of words.

Limon juxtaposes what he takes to be the metaphorical vision of the art-war relation in the writings of Carl von Clausewitz to Elaine Scarry's proposal that we see war, metonymically, as belonging to a wider class of conflicts and competitions where artistic competition also belongs.[9] Taking a stand against slogans like "literature is war" or "representation is violence," underwritten by Armstrong and Tennenhouse, Limon argues that, in a post-Homeric age, war has proved untranslatable in the symmetrical and captivating form of the duel. Even though von Clausewitz argued that at bottom war is "nothing but a duel on a larger scale" (quoted in Limon 15), in the end he was forced to admit that this much was true only of "pure," "absolute," theoretical war. Actual wars were an altogether different affair: confused, disordered events, which, unlike a duel, did not end with the utter destruction or complete subjugation of the enemy. For this reason Limon prefers following the path carved out by Scarry, and he points out how American literature has turned its back on a metaphorical aesthetics that would reduce war to a sort of duel of gargantuan proportions, by replacing war with forms of non-violent competition.

Far-reaching in its implications and historical breadth, and always intellectually stimulating in the interpretations it proposes, Limon's work is somewhat puzzling in terms of the literary texts it chooses to discuss. Limon privileges novels written "after war" not only chronologically but also from the point of view of their content; they are novels in which war recedes into the background or is present as memory rather than fictions that describe war in more direct and immediate ways. Thus he devotes more space to analyzing works like *The Bostonians, A Connecticut Yankee in King Arthur's Court*, and *The Great Gatsby* than classic war fiction like *The Red Badge of Courage, A Farewell to Arms*, or *The Naked and the Dead*. This choice is legitimate if one wishes to unearth the extent to which so much of literature may be reimagined as a sort of war literature, a notion that Burke might have found congenial. However, such a choice also risks erasing the category of war literature per se. Moreover, it is difficult to maintain that American literary texts are interested only in "metonymical" rather than "metaphorical" approaches to war. From a quantitative point of view, the opposite is probably closer to the truth: there are hundreds, probably thousands of war novels whose tone is resolutely "epic" and patriotic, or that at any rate wish to offer a very direct, face-to-face description of the real or imagined horrors of the battlefield. Limon is of course free to feel that, for instance, the most interesting "Vietnam War novels" are "sport novels" in which baseball or basketball function as mediating terms between war and peace. It would be hard, however, for anyone interested in the literary representation of the Vietnam War to ignore the dozens of books—factual, fictional, or semi-fictional—that portray the conflict in Southeast Asia in more iconic ways, from Michael Herr's *Dispatches* to the work of Tim O'Brien, Larry Heinemann, John Del Vecchio, Gustav Hasford, Philip Caputo, and many others. Limon evidently considers what is sometimes referred to as *combat novel* a narrative form too compromised with a bellicose language and a warlike imagination. Or, perhaps, he feels that because it inevitably fails at mirroring the violence of combat, such fiction is less interesting than a narrative that programmatically accepts its own representative impotence in relation to war. But if one may agree with him concerning the irreducible difference between the violence of war and that of literature, Limon seems to discount the fact that, as Burke would have recognized, "militaristic ingredients" persist in even the most peaceful of strategic retreats, whether the latter be real or literary. In Burke's own words, "*peace* is something we need to *fight* for," and though certain means may indeed be less bloody than others so as to give the impression of being peacefulness itself, "[i]t is wrong . . . to consider them as *essentially* peaceful" (*Grammar of Motives* 370). In sum, while it may make little sense to think of literature as war, this should not be taken to mean that literature can only "miss" war. As Tobin Siebers puts it in a perceptive review of Limon's study, it would appear that, paradoxically, "the only way to write about war is not to write about it," given that "the more literature embraces beautiful belligerence, the more it seems to express its own ineptitude before war" (507–8).

Even though Limon does not list Stephen Crane as a master of metonymical-strategic retreats from war to peace, and devotes only three pages to a discussion of *The Red Badge of Courage*, in the last section of this chapter I would like to show how one of Crane's best-known Civil War stories—"A Mystery of Heroism: A Detail of an American Battle"—may be read to an extent in Limon's terms, that is, as an attempt to carve a path, however winding and contradictory, from war to peace. This journey is done, however, by remaining close to the actual reality of the military encounter the story describes, so that if on the one hand the story is *also* about how literature can never fully grasp the violence and tragedy of war, on the other hand Crane insists that something *can* indeed be learned about war by narrating it. Though completely enmeshed in a war context, Crane's short story is an example of how, as the Russian formalists would have put it, war can be "made strange" in ways that would point toward a containment of its destructiveness. In my reading I will therefore resort to some of the Burkean concepts expounded above, as I remain convinced that only a dialectical approach can help us avoid the complementary traps of both the war-literature equation and that of their too-reassuring, gratifying distance.

"A Mystery of Heroism" begins, interestingly enough, with the narrator's attempt to imagine the battle as a sort of duel. The story's first sentence reduces the clash between the two armies to a gigantic one-on-one match: "The dark uniforms of the men were so coated with dust from the incessant wrestling of the two armies that the regiment almost seemed a part of the clay bank which shielded them from the shells" (623). Four paragraphs later, this imagery is picked up again in the simile of "some stupendous scuffle, as if two animals of the size of islands were fighting" (623–24). The Clausevitzian image of "a duel on a larger scale" is more explicitly invoked when the narrator describes the "frightful duel" in which "the battery on the hill" is engaged (624). The narrator, however, soon abandons any attempt to contain the chaos of battle within an ordered symmetry and proceeds to retreat strategically in search of what the subtitle of the story identifies as a "detail" of the battle. This choice may be described, from Limon's viewpoint, as an effort to leave behind the "stupendous" but untranslatable violence of the battlefield, in search of a rhetorical bridge from war to peace.[10]

The occasion for this switch in narrative perspective is provided by private Collins's decision to risk his life in order to reach a water well kept under constant fire by enemy artillery. The first "mystery" of the story concerns the reasons behind Collins's decision. His thirst seems to be only partly responsible, and the narrator is also by no means sure that Collins's reckless act may be imputed to the jeering of his comrades who, tired of his lamentations, defy him to go fetch some water.[11] Whatever the case, the substitution of the violent clash of war—a clash whose ultimate goal is always that of out-injuring your enemy (Scarry 63)—with a sort of "play" is unquestionably dangerous, but its objective, at least from Collins's point of view, has nothing *actively* criminal about it, since what is at stake is only his personal survival.[12]

The peaceful nature of Collins's desire is underscored by the image of the water well, a symbol of life and vitality with strong feminine and maternal connotations. Moreover, the well is surrounded by a "gentle little meadow," which the narrator compares to "the face of a maiden" (625), another symbol of innocence. The mad rush toward the well may thus be seen as the allegorical embodiment of Collins's desire to leave the world of war behind in order to return to the rural environment that is his original home. Indeed, when describing the soldier's race to the well, the narrator notes that "Collins ran in the manner of a farmer chased out of a dairy by a bull" (630). But the most important "detail" emphasizing the story's transition from war to peace is of course Collins's encounter, as he tries to make it back to his regiment, with a dying officer who asks him for a drink of water. Here we face a situation ideally suited to show, as Burke would have noted, the human and properly "cultural" side of war that escapes its destructive fury. This digression—or "metonymical digression," in Limon's terms—takes us away from the violence-drenched context of the battlefield, moving us toward a humanitarian and compassionate world of peace. For several critics this would be precisely the point where Crane unveils the story's "mystery of heroism." Collins becomes a hero not thanks to some decisive contribution he makes to the "duel" of war with which the story opens but by virtue of the courage and humanity he displays in attending to the wounded officer. According to this interpretation, Crane substitutes a competition in which striking the enemy is the measure of one's success for one in which heroism is gauged on one's willingness to take care of a wounded companion.[13]

Crane, however, takes war too seriously to believe that its belligerency may be so easily evaded. The story is hard to read as pacifist parable—or, in Burke's terms, as a straightforward "admonitory anecdote"—in support of a "translated," "purified," version of heroism because, on a practical level, Collins's humanitarian gesture is at best an interrupted one. Collins *is unsuccessful* in satisfying the dying officer's plea—a detail the text is careful to highlight: "Collins tried to hold the bucket steadily, but his shaking hands caused the water to splash all over the face of the dying man. Then he jerked it away and ran on" (631). Collins *is afraid*: he wishes to act as a "hero" but is simultaneously seized by a terror preventing him from completing his act. Is he then a hero, or not? According to Richard Halliburton, Collins's "inability to control the bucket undercuts his technical competence as hero, but in no way does it diminish the essence of his act. That is why his spilling of water, while regrettable, is not finally wasteful" (150). There can be no doubt that, however flawed, Collins's gesture is "an act beyond self" (150) which, after Emmanuel Lévinas, we may want to describe as Collins's encounter with the face of the Other.[14] Collins, who has so far been concerned only with his individual desire and his personal reputation, upon meeting the officer's "face contorted and blanched from pain" (630) recognizes a "*self . . .* which is not a *myself.*"[15] The face of the Other steers Collins toward the ethical. Asked for water by the dying man, he first screams, "I can't," but then he turns: "He came dashing back. His face had now turned gray . . ." as if his own face had come to mirror that of the wounded, destitute Other. With this episode in mind, we may conclude that Crane is describing war, in Burke's terms, "*as one channel of effort in which people can be profoundly human*" ("War, Response, and Contradiction" 240, original italics). Yet to be "profoundly," genuinely human means not only responding to the needs of the Other; it means also to be afraid. To the extent that Crane may be redefining the notion of heroism, he is doing something more complex than simply transferring the supposed fearlessness of the warrior from the battlefield to a humanitarian context. He also shows how ethics and emotions are at odds with one another, so that a word like heroism might be both necessary and yet not altogether adequate to describe the nature of Collins's act.

The term "hero," singular or plural, is used only seven times in the story, in a few short paragraphs describing Collins's state of mind as he sets out on his risky journey. This passage is the only instance in the story where the subject announced in the title is the object of an explicit reflection, and it is worth quoting in its entirety.

> It seemed to him supernaturally strange that he had allowed his mind to manœuvre his body into such a situation. He understood that it might be called dramatically great.
>
> However, he had no full appreciation of anything, excepting that he was actually conscious of being dazed. He could feel his dulled mind groping after the form and colour of this incident. He wondered why he did not feel some keen agony of fear cutting his sense like a knife. He wondered at this, because human expression had

said loudly for centuries that men should feel afraid of certain things, and that all men who did not feel this fear were phenomenal heroes.

He was, then, a hero. He suffered that disappointment which we would all have if we discovered that we were ourselves capable of those deeds which we most admire in history and legend. This, then, was a hero. After all, heroes were not much.

No, it could not be true. He was not a hero. Heroes had no shames in their lives, and, as for him, he remembered borrowing fifteen dollars from a friend and promising to pay it back the next day, and then avoiding that friend for ten months. When at home his mother had aroused him for the early labour of his life on the farm, it had often been his fashion to be irritable, childish, diabolical; and his mother had died since he had come to the war.

He saw that, in this matter of the well, the canteens, the shells, he was an intruder in the land of fine deeds. (628–29)

Collins initially reasons that since to be fearless, according to centennial wisdom, is to be a "phenomenal" man, and he feels no fear, then he too must be a hero. This account of what makes a hero would suggest that, whatever he may or may not have done during his encounter with the wounded officer, Collins did not behave heroically. He stops to give the man a drink, but he splashes the water because he "was all terror." He is not fearless; hence, he cannot be a hero. One also needs to add, however, that Collins himself implicitly questions the soundness of his definition immediately after formulating it. If what makes a hero is simply the absence of fear, then "heroes were not much." He realizes with "disappointment" that he too is capable of doing what he imagined was only the stuff of legend. If it is so easy to be a hero, something is wrong with the notion of the hero itself.

By making fearlessness its key feature, Collins constructs heroism as something that is largely, though not exclusively, performative. To be fearless is mostly to *act* in a certain way. In Collins's case, it is to "walk up squarely to the face of death" (628) and be aware of it, too. But being aware of danger and *feeling it* are two different things, as Collins discovers after reaching the well. Suddenly, he is "smitten with terror" and "all the power faded from his muscles" (629). Once he feels afraid, his body is affected, and he can no longer be heroic.

The second definition of the hero that Collins offers, on the other hand, is centered more on character and inner feelings than on performance. Disturbed by his discovery that heroes may not amount to much, he now thinks heroes should have spotless personal records, and since he feels ashamed for some of the things he has done in his life, he concludes that "he was not a hero." The narrator is obviously ironic, as Collins's "shameful" acts (not returning promptly the fifteen dollars he borrowed from a friend; being childish and irritable when his mother called him to work) are trivial and, moreover, they have nothing to do with his conduct in the war. Nevertheless, in this version, heroism comes down to a question of personal integrity over the course of one's lifetime, and past sins, though insignificant, cannot be redeemed by later conduct, no matter how impeccable.

What is "mysterious" in Crane's story is not only the nature of Collins's act—is it heroic or not?—but heroism as such. We may find Collins's ruminations amusing, but as a whole, Crane's story shows that the "heroic" act cannot be severed from the arbitrariness of the actual circumstances and the rhetorical strategies that are responsible for creating it in the first place. Collins's mad run, his humanitarian gesture, the risk he has taken are all real, material facts; the "mystery" lies in their not-necessary, non-essential connection with the term "heroism"—an act of symbolic designation imparting significance and cultural value to an event that remains insignificant and unexplainable in its contingency and arbitrariness. Both Collins's action and the term through which we choose to describe it are marked by ambivalence, something that from a Burkean perspective could be read as the story's "anti-war" message. As Weiser points out, "because conditions of war suppress ambiguity on all fronts, Burke's response highlighted it in the celebration of partial acts and multiple perspectives" (295). Crane's story, too, may be said to celebrate—literally—a "partial act" that invites multiple readings. One may feel that if the story's purpose were to reimagine the hero as a man of peace rather than a man of war, it would have been better if Collins had completed his act. But from a Burkean perspective, Crane should be praised for highlighting the incompleteness of Collins's act, since "we are capable of but partial acts, acts that but partially represent us and that produce but partial transformations" (*Grammar of Motives* 19). This partiality is exactly what happens with Collins: he is courageous and merciful enough to respond to the call of the Other, but the partial act he performs represents his courage only in part and produces only a partial transformation. He does not succeed in making the man drink, but he manages to elicit from him "the faintest shadow of a smile . . . as he looked at Collins" (631), a minuscule but significant sign that his generosity is acknowledged.

To close our discussion of heroism, we must consider the story's ending. Collins manages, after all, to bring some water back to his regiment, and the captain immediately orders him to give it to the men. The first to grab the bucket are "two genial, skylarking lieutenants" who, "play[ing] over it in their fashion," end up spilling on the ground the precious water Collins risked his life to obtain. "The bucket lay on the ground empty" (631)—the story's last sentence, and in particular its very last word, may suggest the overall futility of Collins's act. At this point, another Crane's story, "The Five White Mice," helps to gloss "A Mystery of Heroism": "Nothing had happened" (771). Or, to use a similar phrase from *The Open Boat*, we could argue that Collins's mad rush "is *apropos* of nothing" (891). It is not surprising that the image of the empty bucket has been read as a symbolic exemplification of the vacuity of heroism.[16] In this interpretation, the mystery mentioned in the story's title is essentially ironic—heroism hides *no* mystery since no heroic action is performed in the tale. Yet, while the image of emptiness adds a further note of ambiguity to the tale, what happens to the water once Collins is back with his regiment has no bearing whatsoever on the way we judge his attempt to meet the dying officer's plea. The loss of the water may well be a way to suggest the preciousness of the thing lost. "In the absence of the treasure the treasure is suddenly present: The value of [it] springs up and through its loss" (Halliburton 151).

The lieutenants' "skylarking" emphasizes once again, though now in a decidedly ironic key, the language of "play" first evoked to refer to Collins's risky race. I noted earlier that play may be read, after Limon, as a metonymic retreat from war. Here, however, play is what returns us to a context of war. The silly struggle between the two officers provides a kind of ironic, inverted mirror to the image of the duel from which we started. While the risky race may be seen as a rhetorical/moral equivalent of war—as an alternative way for Collins to test his manhood, especially once he feels the eyes of his comrades upon him—the lieutenants' boisterous and risk-free playing could be read as a caricature of war's destructive logic. In the former case, the story provides a metonymic displacement of war. In the latter, instead, the confrontation between the two officers is metaphorically reminiscent of the war that denies soldiers access to life's and nature's quintessential element. If we add to this that, in the Bible, the spilling of water is associated with death (something that the son of a Methodist minister like Crane could not fail to know), we may conclude that the story ends by projecting a rather negative image of "play."[17] More generally, Crane leaves the question open as to whether the language of "play" is a way of "resisting" or "acquiescing to" the language of war, just as the story is unclear as to what extent the term "heroic" may be applied to Collins's act, not to mention the doubts the text raises concerning the notion of heroism as such.[18] Interpreted on the basis of Burke's distinction between constitutive and admonitory anecdotes, "A Mystery of Heroism" may be said to oscillate between these two rhetorical strategies without finally privileging either. Collins's humanitarian gesture lies on the cusp between "what [he] is" and "what [he] may become" (*Grammar of Motives* 331). His act is certainly legible as the expression of a peaceful and perhaps "homeopathic" heroism through which the energies ill spent in war may be redirected toward nobler ends, but the story is unequivocal in reminding us that such an act is nevertheless circumscribed by a martial context. Indeed, seen from the perspective of our age of "humanitarian warfare," Crane's story may be read as a reminder that all humanitarian acts, as long as they are bounded by war, can never be rid of the war's contradictory nature.

If Crane's narrative strategy underwrites neither a simply constitutive nor an exclusively admonitory view of war, then, as far as the relationship between language and war is concerned, the story remains ambivalent. In its opening paragraph, the text imagines the human voice as thoroughly subjugated by the sound of violence. In an image strikingly similar to the one from *The Red Badge of Courage* used as an epigraph for this chapter, Crane projects a chiasmic relation between war and rhetoric: "On top of the hill a battery was arguing in tremendous roars with some other guns"—arguments are equivalent to blows, and blows are arguments in their own right. The violence of rhetoric is squarely mirrored by the rhetoric of violence. The human voice is reduced to the soldier's "wild and frenzied cheers" that parallel "the crashing of infantry volleys." As used by Collins's comrades, language continues to stand out as an instrument of coercion, pressuring him to risk his life for no real reason. For nearly the entire text, language is mostly used by characters to shout orders and oaths, and by the narrator to reinforce the idea that men are constrained by forces and emotions they have no control over. Throughout the story, Collins himself is under some kind of spell. First, when he decides to risk his life, he appears "as a man dreaming," "dazed," "dulled." Later, he is "smitten with terror." The representation of violence is matched by the violence of representation, as when the dying officer's "futile cries, wrenched from him by his agony, were heard only by shells, bullets" (630). Yet, somewhat implausibly perhaps, notwithstanding the "demon fingers . . . pressed into his ears" (629) and "the unspeakable noises of the swirling missiles" (631), a truly human voice does speak, apart from, and indeed above, the guns' roars, and this voice is almost magically heard by another human being: "Say, young man, give me a drink of water, will you?" (630). This may be the only instance in this brief story where language expresses a simple, spontaneous human desire free from any relation to the madness of war. The words exchanged between the dying officer and Collins might be seen as a momentary, fragile stay against the confusion of generalized violence—an illustration of how, if only for a few, precious seconds, language can decelerate the onrush of war. For once, the dying man's cry of agony is not "heard only by shells, bullets." For once, language strikes back at war.

PART II

Readings

CHAPTER 4

An American Counter-Epic?

War and Peace in Joel Barlow's *Columbiad*

Violent Beginnings

"The relevance of the problem of beginning to the phenomenon of revolution is obvious. That such beginning must be intimately connected with violence seems to be vouched for by the legendary beginnings of our history as both biblical and classical antiquity report it: Cain slew Abel and Romulus slew Remus; violence was the beginning and, by the same token, no beginning could be made without using violence, without violating" (Arendt, *Revolution* 20). In this well-known passage, Hannah Arendt underlines the paradox whereby politics originates from a constitutively violent beginning. The contradictory relation between war and politics, violence and power has been, according to Arendt, operative since time immemorial. Such tension, however, takes on special significance when, for the first time in human history, not only does war begin to appear as something different from a recurrent, inevitable human tragedy, but the effort to conceptualize peace takes place within a set of social and historical conditions that allow for a rational analysis of the international political situation. As W. B. Gallie has written in his *Philosophers of Peace and War*, before the late eighteenth century "international politics—centered on the use of the threat of war and the expansion of commercial and cultural contacts—hardly admitted of systematic study" (1). The turning point was Kant's famous essay, *Perpetual Peace*, published in Königsberg in 1795, in which the philosopher insisted that the goal of universal peace was not only a moral one but also one that could be concretely pursued.

The problem is of course that if, in the classical age, from the cinders of the Greek *polis* it was always possible to fan the destructive fire of *polemos*, also behind the origins of the liberal and republican right that sees, at least in principle, war as a form of evil, there is an act of violence. Kant himself had to confront a paradox similar to the one that Arendt would spell out a century and a half later: modern right is born with the French Revolution and, therefore, thanks to a bloody conflict and through eminently unrightful means. As André Tosel puts it in a study devoted to this Kantian "ambiguity," "right does not come into existence through the instruments of right. Its original and sustaining ground provides no juridical foundations. Revolution, this counter-violence which remains violent, reactivates the situation that the philosophy of history and the theory of right present as originary" (12). Moving from this premise, Kant arrives at "the realistic acknowledgment of the dramatic antinomy of history itself" (12).[1] The same thinker who, more than any of his contemporaries would struggle to define the contours of a credible, lasting peace, is altogether aware of the impossibility of thinking right without simultaneously evoking the specter of its opposite. It is not surprising that in *Perpetual Peace* Kant argued that peace was based upon the institution as well as the *enforcement* of moral law. As Nick Mansfield points out, for Kant "peace is instituted by violence to ward off a state of lawlessness that is constantly open to war, even equivalent to it, whether it is violent or not" (25). The Kantian paradox, then, is that only war delivers the possibility of peace.[2]

What Kant argues about the French Revolution as well as the peace-war nexus may be repeated about the American War of Independence. In fact, if one keeps in mind its messianic aspirations, shaped by that uniquely American mix of the Enlightenment of the Founding Fathers with the biblical rhetoric of the Pilgrim Fathers, the recourse to war—an act typical of Old World tyrannies—should appear even more contradictory.[3] American culture, however, is marked by a fundamental ambivalence regarding the paradox of its originating violence. A well-established cultural and historiographic tradition prefers—like Washington Irving's Rip Van Winkle—simply to sidestep the violence of the revolutionary violation.[4] As Robert Ferguson noted, the discourse on the origins of the new nation has been often subsumed under evolutionary metaphors, presupposing a natural progression from colony to province to state and, eventually, to a union of confederated states, thus avoiding those traumatic moments that would call into question the notion of an organic, quasi-spontaneous growth. Against this tendency to place war and revolution in parentheses, Ferguson invites us never to lose track of the "violence of the founding." Young, republican America had its birth "in the blood and agony and confusion of the Revolution" (Ferguson 249).[5] This does not necessarily mean that the United States had from its very beginning a special attraction to war and violence. It simply means that the American revolutionaries were well aware that their hopes were tied to the outcome of a military conflict. If American culture has traditionally sought to contain the symbolic and political implications of that original conflict, the fact that war would nevertheless turn out to be one of the key sources of a specific American identity should be a good enough reason never to lose sight of that inescapably violent beginning.

Literary scholars with an interest in the American Revolutionary War, however, must first come to terms with the relative low quality of works of literature dealing with that momentous event. There is no lack of poems and novels—both contemporary and late—on the War of Independence, but one has the impression that *the* great work of art on the Revolutionary War has never been written. As Sacvan Bercovitch has noted,

> The American Revolution plays a curious role in American classic literature. Like Beckett's Godot it is at once omnipresent and conspicuously absent. All contemporaneous accounts suggest that the Spirit of Seventy-Six was the muse of the American Renaissance. . . . Melville . . . returned obsessively to the theme of revolution . . ., as did Hawthorne, Cooper, and Poe. Yet no more than a handful of their writings—a few stories and minor novels—can be said to deal with the American Revolution, and even these do so obliquely, if not evasively.
>
> The forgotten popular writers of the time responded avidly (in romances, poems, plays, and epics) to the clamor for literature about the evolution. Those writers through whom the American imagination has been defined remained silent on the subject, or at most ambivalent. (169)

In keeping with his understanding that the specific traits of U.S. literary culture derive from its ability to turn radical threats into "rituals of consensus," Bercovitch explains that American writers repeatedly praise the revolution "yet they shrink from accepting revolution as a defining American characteristic; or more typically, they accept it by contrasting the American Revolution with other modern revolutions" (170). Against the idea of the revolution as rebellion, as "the clash between mutually exclusive" class interests and ideologies, American independence is imagined not as "the spoils of violence, but the harvest of Puritanism"—as the God-driven "progress" of "'the people' at large" (173). As Salvatore Proietti has incisively noted, "In order to make of 1776 an *American* revolution, the American *revolution* must be kept hidden" (29). What is worth noting is that Arendt also has done her best to deny the revolutionary character of the American War of Independence. In her view, the American Revolution is unique in that "the founding fathers . . . founded a completely new body politic without violence and with the help of a constitution." In her opinion,

> the act of foundation, namely the colonization of the American continent, had preceded the Declaration of Independence, so that the framing of the Constitution,

falling back on existing charters and agreements, confirmed and legalized an already existing body politic rather than made it anew. Thus the actors in the American Revolution were spared the effort of "initiating a new order of things" altogether. (*Between Past and Future* 140)[6]

Arendt believes that thanks to the homogenous social character of colonial America, issues of freedom had not come into conflict with problems of equality, thereby preventing the degeneration of the American uprising into the Terror of the French Revolution. The exceptional character of the American Revolution lies with the fact that what the Founding Fathers sought "was a restoration, the retrieving of their ancient liberties," so that "the movement which led to the revolution was not revolutionary except by inadvertence" (*On Revolution* 44). By first pushing the foundation back in time and then turning the revolution into a restoration, Arendt bypassed not only issues of class conflict but also the macroscopic question of slavery, not to mention the tragedy of the dispossession of the American Indians. Oddly enough, a secular and liberal theorist like Arendt lent credence to what Bercovitch has shown to be the *myth* of "a gradual, preordained movement toward redemption" (175) rooted in biblical typology. While American patriots may have seen the young republic as "Rome reborn on Western shores" (Shalev), it would appear that, for Arendt, Romulus (and Cain) had no New World counterparts. In the beginning, there was no fratricidal struggle, only a break so "inadvertent" that it was more a return to the past than an uncertain step into a shapeless future.

Joel Barlow's *Columbiad*: The Epic between War and Peace

Arendt's reading of the War of Independence shares some significant features with what U.S. writers had to say about it. In Michael Kammen's words, "By and large our authors have been rather conservative in their social outlook; and the net result has been to de-revolutionize the American Revolution" (211). Rather than as a traumatic and violent break, the revolution was mostly conceived as "a season of youth," celebrated in literary works that Kammen considers for the most part of poor quality. Many of the nineteenth-century novels or "romances" on the revolution he finds "rather banal" and even "stultifyingly mediocre" (145). As for poetry, he notes that while many of America's major poets devoted some lines to the revolution, "few wrote very much about it" (111). It is somewhat surprising that Kammen makes no mention of *The Columbiad* (1807), Joel Barlow's epic poem in ten books, four of which (5–8) are devoted to the Revolutionary War. Even though recently *The Columbiad* has been described by one critic as "one of the most complex and extraordinary long narrative poems in nineteenth-century American literature" (Blakemore 1), if I call attention to it, it is not because I consider it a forgotten masterpiece wherein the American Revolution features prominently. With the exception of a few fortunate lines, Barlow did not write great poetry. However, he attended closely to the historical and cultural implications of the revolution. *The Columbiad* registers with peculiar frankness some of the antinomies involved in *writing about* the American Revolution—in celebrating, that is, an act of war that the author saw as necessary to the creation of a unified world of peace. Barlow embraces a progressive vision of history that overlaps at least in part with the ideology of the jeremiad critiqued by Bercovitch, but he cannot be accused of "de-revolutionizing the Revolution" or of making it "non-replicable" by limiting its significance to an exceptional American context. In other words, one of the reasons Barlow's epic has never become canonical is that it does not fit into the dominant traditions that historians and literary critics have acknowledged as "typically" American. However, not in spite of but precisely *because* of its ideological and aesthetic tensions, *The Columbiad* is a text that deserves to be more widely taught and studied.

The ambivalence of Barlow's project is made evident right from his choice of the epic form. Epics were written to celebrate great wars, and if there is one thing Barlow detested, that was war. Yet he could not ignore that an armed revolution had taken place and had, like it or not, to be celebrated. Barlow's solution was to imagine his epic as an *anti-epic* of sorts, or, as I would like to suggest, as a *peace epic*. Both definitions are mine, not Barlow's, but I think they capture the author's ambition to inject a whole new spirit into a literary form he considered largely compromised by the Old World. It is precisely this awareness of the friction between form and ideology, between the strictures of tradition and the desire to break new ground, that makes the work in question worth reading even today. More to the point, given the overall concerns of this book, what is interesting in this otherwise often tiresome and wooden poem is the way it lucidly outlines some of the dilemmas American war writers would have to confront in the decades and centuries to come. Joel Barlow's epic is the first book-length example of the American effort to come to terms with the need to imagine and celebrate the virtues of peace by employing a literary form traditionally devoted—as the author knew all too well—to the promotion of a martial spirit antithetical to the author's self-proclaimed ideology. Barlow was by no means the only writer or thinker of the time who felt trapped between the need to sustain the new vistas of the American enlightenment and an Old World classical culture that could not be rejected outright. But he was the writer who most openly displayed the tensions between peace and war, between the hope to promote the former and the need to describe and even, to an extent, celebrate the latter. As seen from the point of view of the peace/war, violence/ non-violence continuum discussed in the previous three chapters, *The Columbiad* stands out as an archetypal text. It is the first work of the American imagination that aspired to be an anti-war manifesto and a hymn to peace. While in the end

Barlow's poem did not and—given its premises—*could* not emancipate itself from the weight of tradition, it is a text that unequivocally shows how at least one early American writer did not wish to make war the source of a specific national identity.

Born in Fairfield County, Connecticut, in 1754, Joel Barlow attended Dartmouth College and completed his studies at Yale University, later serving as a chaplain in a Massachusetts brigade during the revolution. He was initially associated with the "Connecticut Wits," a group of writers and intellectuals active around Yale in the late eighteenth century, best known for their attempt to bring to America the tradition of the British *Opposition poets* of the Augustan age.[7] In time, however, Barlow came to distance himself from the "classical republicanism," which William Dowling sees at the core of the Wits' ideological and literary practice, and embraced a form of Jeffersonian radicalism distant from his former associates' "retrospective radicalism" (Dowling 7).[8] As witness his early "rising glory poem," *The Prospect of Peace* (1778), Barlow always cultivated a desire to celebrate the "opening prospects of a golden age" following the "grand conflict" between America and England. The millenarian perspective informing this poem would also be the basis of his subsequent *The Vision of Columbus*, first published in 1787, which would in turn provide the template for his most ambitious work, *The Columbiad*, appearing in 1807.[9] As Steven Blakemore has noted, critics usually prefer *The Vision of Columbus* to *The Columbiad*, "maintaining that the former is the more interesting poem." However, "the revisions plus the additional political and ideological issues in *The Columbiad*, inter alia, the French Revolution and slavery, as well as the intertextual dialogues and the extended treatment of the American Revolution in book 6, make the latter superior both aesthetically and thematically" (16). I agree, and I would only add that the larger political and ideological scope of the poem results in its increased ambivalence, which I see as a virtue rather than a flaw of this odd but intellectually stimulating poem.

Before analyzing how *The Columbiad* addresses the historical question of the violence of the beginning, as well as the more specifically aesthetic question of the relation between literature and war, a few words on early America's quest for an epic are in order. The intellectual elites of the early republic—avid readers of the classics and convinced that, in George Berkeley's immortal verse, "Westward the course of empire takes its way"—believed that a great American epic was needed to put the new nation on par with the great civilizations of the past. As John McWilliams has written, "An American epic would be incontestable proof of cultural maturity; it would justify the sons' rebellion against the fathers, clarify the superiority of the New World to the Old, and show the autonomy of a formerly colonial literature" (*American Epic* 16). Invocations of an American Homer, Virgil, or Milton abound in postrevolutionary literature, and soon enough a number of writers would try their hand at long poems in heroic couplets (the meter used by Alexander Pope in his translation of the *Iliad*). Between the second half of the eighteenth century and the first half of the nineteenth, no fewer than nineteen epics were completed and published, while others appeared incomplete or were abandoned.[10] McWilliams argues that attempts at writing "heroic narratives" in traditional epic forms were doomed from the start and resulted in "elephantine poems crammed with the husks of epic convention but lacking the pressure of a significant credible heroic action" (*American Epic* 2). The epic, however, would die as a form but survive in very important ways as a literary mode, as witness the great novel-romances such as Cooper's *The Last of the Mohicans* and Melville's *Moby-Dick*, Whitman's poetry, and George Prescott's literary historiography. A truly "epic" literature would be written in America only after the dream of an exact equivalent of Homer's *Iliad* or Virgil's *Aeneid* had been set aside forever.

This is not the place to enter into a discussion of the extent to which the epic may be a literary genre that disappeared in the West with Milton's *Paradise Lost*, or else—as McWilliams and many others have argued—has managed to flourish as a *mode* rather than a fixed literary genre. What is interesting for our purposes is the short-circuit between form and ideology mentioned above. What McWilliams finds striking in early attempts at an American epic "is the consistency and vehemence with which Homer's world and Homer's morality were damned by those who simultaneously asserted that Homer was the first and greatest of poets" (*American Epic* 22). For a generation of American studies scholars who have grown up believing that the "American character" mostly took shape on the wild frontier, where the masculine hero cleared the wilderness and confronted the red savages, the cultural scene McWilliams reconstructs may sound surprising. In his view,

> The most acute problem of fitting the old form to the new muse was not formalistic but cultural: Americans' vision of their civilization did not suit the traditional substance of heroic narrative. For Americans, courage in battle was at best a barbarous means to the heroic end of creating an empire based upon rural virtues, profitable commerce, and libertarian politics. The nation's epic must portray the fields of valor on which the British father had been killed while somehow subsuming such scenes within an antimartial heroic code. (*American Epic* 34)

The America of this description is quite different from the one portrayed not only in critical works like Slotkin's *Regeneration through Violence* but also in the violence-ridden novels of Charles Brockden Brown or James Fenimore Cooper. It is an America that may not have been as pastoral as some of its early republican leaders and literati would have liked it to be, but it was the country where James Madison, in 1795, wrote, "Of all the enemies of public liberty, war is perhaps the most to be dreaded, because it comprises and develops the germ of every other. War is the parent of armies. From these proceed debts and taxes. And armies, debts and taxes are the known instruments for bringing the many under the domination of the few. . . . No nation could preserve its freedom in the midst of continual warfare" (quoted in Bacevich 7). What makes Barlow's *Columbiad* an exemplary text is the way it registers the need for new models of epic heroism and gives voice to the dream of a world forever free from the scourge of war, while at the same time realizing that these wishes must be expressed in forms that are hopelessly inadequate. However, Barlow's formal choices turned out to be ideological too. His adoption of worn-out epic conventions is not simply quaint but spells out a politics that runs against the grain of his peace-loving assumptions.

Barlow's initial plan was to devote his epic poem to Christopher Columbus and his voyages and explorations of the New World. Yet, for reasons unknown, he abandoned his original project and wrote a long prophetic poem in which the angel Hesper shows to a sad, imprisoned Columbus the astounding consequences of his discoveries. The poem was aptly titled *The Vision of Columbus*, and he himself described it as a poem "rather of the philosophic than epic kind." By the time he chose to expand and revise this work, Barlow had fully embraced the radical republicanism of the French Revolution. He was at the time convinced that his epic should celebrate a New World of progress, guided by human reason, science, and republican beliefs that would ultimately go beyond America itself. In his "Preface" he wrote that "*The Columbiad* is a patriotic poem; the subject is national and historical" (375). Yet the early books, devoted to the history of the rise and fall of the Inca empire, show from the start that his concerns were continental and not limited to the United States. Moreover, he closed his epic by evoking the image of a peaceful world, where people speak a common language and confederate in a "common league" that cannot but strike the contemporary reader as an improved version of the United Nations, and all countries prosper thanks to the fruits of what today we would describe as a globalized economy.[11] This is what neatly differentiates Barlow's epic not only from the most notable of all previous American attempts—Timothy Dwight's *The Conquest of Canaan* (1785)—but also from the tradition of the Puritan jeremiad studied by Bercovitch. Barlow's millennialism is secular and thoroughly rooted in an unshakable belief in reason and progress. One may argue that it preserves a religiously inspired notion of America as the land of futurity, but its Deistic outlook as well as its critique of the limits of nationalism make *The Columbiad* a unique text.

The poem begins by paying homage to epic conventions, with its opening lines explicitly echoing Virgil ("I sing the Mariner who first unfurl'd / An eastern banner o'er the western world," 1.1–4), and with a conventional invocation to the Muse, in this case appropriately identified with the Spirit of Freedom ("Almighty Freedom! give my venturous song / The force, the charm that to thy voice belong," 1.23–24). Then, after describing the sad predicament of the imprisoned Columbus, the poet introduces Hesper, the guardian spirit of the Western Hemisphere, who magically lifts the old explorer to the mount of vision, where he will be consoled by scenes displaying the drama and the remarkable prospects of the New World. Columbus, then, is not an epic hero like Aeneas or Achilles. He is the spectator rather than the protagonist of the epic tale. The epic celebrates the fortunate consequences of an action initiated by Columbus, but Barlow actually begins his narrative in pre-Columbian times, and only later does he describe the birth of the republic and, finally, a transfigured New World of global proportions. The first books (2–4) are devoted to the history of the Inca and Aztec empires, their ruthless destruction at the hands of Cortés, and the establishment of the first English settlement in Virginia. The central books (5–8) are devoted to the revolutionary war, while the last two illustrate the progress of science, commerce, and the arts, revealing that in due time the principles of republican democracy and the American constitution will be extended to the entire world.

The formal and ideological problems Barlow is confronting in writing an epic, and yet writing *against* the epic grain, are openly acknowledged in an important "Preface." Barlow notes that, even though he does not wish to enter into a wholesale discussion of the nature of the epic form, he has trouble deciding to what extent his poem may be indeed defined as an epic. To begin with, the events he describes—with the exception of the first books devoted to the discovery of America and the Spanish conquest of Peru and Mexico—are so recent "as to render them inflexible to the hand of fiction" (375). His materials lack what Mikhail Bakhtin (3–40) identifies as the "absolute temporal distance" of classical epic discourse. Most of the poem, in fact, is oriented toward the future rather than the past: the epic vistas of the poem are prophetic from Columbus's point of view, while the closing vision of a prosperous, peaceful world may be said to be located in an "absolute," Utopian future foreign to traditional epic narratives. What makes the epic status of the poem even more doubtful, however, is the complex interaction between its poetic and moral ends. In the *Iliad*, as Barlow explains, "the poetical object is to kindle, nourish, sustain and allay the anger of Achilles," and since Homer faces this task "with wonderful judgment," he manages to excite in the mind of the reader "not only a veneration for the creative powers of the poet" but also, unfortunately, "an ardent emulation of his heroes, a desire to imitate and rival some of the great actors in the splendid scene; perhaps to endeavor to carry into real life the fictions with which we are so much enchanted" (378). This is where the moral and political failure of Homer's work lies. Barlow has no doubts that, from a moral viewpoint, an epic like the *Iliad* can be in no way "beneficial to society." Quite the opposite. "Its obvious tendency was to inflame the minds of young readers with an enthusiastic ardor for military fame; to inculcate the pernicious doctrine of the divine right of kings; to teach both prince and people that military plunder was the most honorable mode of acquiring property; and that conquest, violence and war were the best employment of nations, the most glorious prerogative of bodily strength and of cultivated mind" (378–79).

In Barlow's eyes, while it may be difficult to ascertain with any precision "how much of the fatal policy of states, and of the miseries and degradations of social man, have been occasioned by the false notions of honor inspired by the works of Homer," it is fair to assume that such "monuments of human intellect . . . have unhappily done more harm than good." As if to underscore the cross-eyed theoretical perspective embodied not only in his prefatory remarks but, as we shall see below, in his poetic practice as well, Barlow states in his preface that though he is one of Homer's "most idolatrous readers," "his existence has really proved one of the signal misfortunes of mankind" (379). Barlow was so determined to emphasize the low opinion he had of Homer's cultural politics that he returned to this subject in one of the lengthy notes he appended to his poem. There he acknowledged that the works of Homer, "have called forth great exertions of genius in poets, artists, philosophers and heroes, thro a long succession of ages."

> But it remains to be considered what a fruitful source they have likewise been of those false notions of honor and erroneous systems of policy which have governed the actions of men from his day to ours. If, instead of the *Iliad*, he had given us a work of equal splendor founded on an opposite principle; whose object should have been to celebrate the useful arts of agriculture and navigation; to build the immortal fame of his heroes, and occupy his whole hierarchy of gods, on actions that contribute to the real advancement of society, instead of striking away every foundation on which society ought to be established or can be greatly advanced; mankind, enriched with such a work at that early period, would have given a useful turn to their ambition thro all succeeding ages. (848)

Here Barlow is confronting the narrative problem we have been discussing in the preceding chapters. Why should heroism be identified nearly exclusively with its military variety? Why did not Homer give us great farmer heroes rather than warrior heroes? Why cannot "a work of equal splendor" be written to celebrate a different code of honor and bravery?

Barlow formulates similar complaints regarding the other great epic poet of the classical world. Virgil, alas, "wrote and felt like a subject, not like a citizen" and the *Aeneid*—the artistic merits of which are also in this case not to be denied—ends up displaying a "moral tendency . . . nearly as pernicious as that of the works of Homer. . . . The real design of his poem was to increase the veneration of the people for a master, whoever he might be, and to encourage like Homer the great system of military depredation" (379–80). Even though the Latin poet was regarded by many "as the epic poet of judgment, decorum, and empire" (McWilliams, *American Epic*

22), Barlow was by no means alone in feeling that Virgil, too, had failed to overcome the pernicious lure of the martial spirit. John Quincy Adams, for example, expressed regret in his *Lectures on Rhetoric and Oratory* "to see the hero of Virgil, the pious Aeneas, steeling his bosom against mercy, and plunging his pitiless sword into the bosom of a fallen and imploring enemy, to avenge the slaughter of his friend" (quoted in McWilliams 23n41).

Barlow wished to offer his readers a poem that would polemically distance itself from the immoral, martial epic models he stigmatizes in his preface. If "the fictitious object of the poem" was "to sooth and satisfy the desponding mind of Columbus; to show him that his labors, tho ill rewarded by his contemporaries, had not been performed in vain," from a moral viewpoint what Barlow calls "the real object of the poem" has a much larger scope: "it is to inculcate the love of rational liberty, and to discountenance the deleterious passion for violence and war; to show that on the basis of the republican principle all good morals, as well as good government and hopes of permanent peace, must be founded" (382). While the epic "sanctions the strength and cohesion of a people starting from an act of war and the deeds of a hero who best symbolizes the value of his people" (Casadei, *Guerra* 10), the self-confessed scope of Barlow's counter-epic is to project before the eyes of the reader—just as Hesper does with Columbus—a bright future of freedom and peace in which, to quote from the poem's last book, "Swords, sceptres, mitres, crowns and globes and stars, / Codes of false fame and stimulants to wars / Sink in the settling mass" (10.607–9) and "all regions in the leagues of peace; / . . . confederate" (10. 622).

Now, it is all too obvious that Barlow's conviction that man will not fail to reach "the full reign of peace predestined at his birth" (10. 308), when reconsidered two centuries later, will at best be met with amusement. What could be more naïve than a blind faith in the inevitable progress of humankind? But of course Barlow's naiveté is something we may be more willing to forgive than his unshakable belief in a Reason that calls to mind the sinister dialectic of the Enlightenment outlined by Adorno and Horkeimer, whereby liberation from antiquity results in the imprisonment within the iron cage of modern capitalism. Moreover, that "One centred system, one all-ruling soul" destined to "live thro the parts and regulate the whole" in Barlow's utopia, and even his dream of a "total race" that "shall speak one language and all truths embrace" (10.400), would be all-too-easy targets for the conceptual artillery of contemporary postmodern theories of multiculturalism. In sum, ironically enough, Barlow's peace runs the risk of appearing in our eyes as a sort of reincarnation of the very *Pax Augusta* sung by Virgil and criticized by Barlow in his preface: as a totalizing and homogenizing status quo heedless of the customs and traditions of "un-enlightened" peoples. If we add to this that Barlow is absolutely confident that trade will be the force that will ultimately "[triumph] o'er the rage of war" (10.96, 160) and allow "a white flag of peace" to fly all over the world since "the spirit of commerce is happily calculated to open an amicable intercourse between all countries" (845), he will unmistakably appear to our eyes as a forerunner of contemporary enthusiasts of globalization or, worse still, of what political philosopher Alfredo Valladão described a few years ago as "World America."

There are indications in the poem that, though secularized, the sense of America's universal vocation survives in Barlow's epic. The "model" that "each land shall imitate, each nation join" is that of the "confederate states" (7.699, 696). However, the word "America" (or "American"), while appearing several times in the notes, the preface, and the introduction, is never used in the poem itself. Barlow's dream of unending progress lacks the cultural and religious inspiration of the jeremiad. Human advancement does not follow a biblical plan but rather, as William Dowling points out, the laws of the Newtonian universe, "impersonal and self-regulating and yet displaying traces of a divine benevolence" (105). Barlow's faith in Newton's nature is also continuous with his unassailable belief in the self-regulating virtues of the market, and it is mainly this vision of the world economy, rather than any residue of millennial Puritanism, that accounts for much of the poem's ideological closure. "The global market system" is grasped by Barlow as "a divine order immanent in history" (Dowling 124), and, oddly enough, the poet seems to ignore that trade may at times promote conflicts rather than cooperation. Thus, "*The Columbiad* comes to a close with the version of the progressive mythos that would then function as the governing ideology of American geographical and economic expansion for a century and more to follow" (Dowling 124).

Arms, Poetry, Indians

As a whole, however, the fundamental contradiction of Barlow's poem lies not so much with the ideological perspectives he explicitly embraces as with the tension between its cultural politics and its aesthetic form. In his preface Barlow must register how his own poem, notwithstanding its wish "to increase our natural horror for the havoc and miseries of war in general" (384), devotes some considerable space to scenes of war. His attempts to distinguish between moral and aesthetic principles are rather clumsy. The poet admits that while drafting an early version of his text, he felt uncomfortable because "the modern modes of fighting, as likewise the instruments and terms now used in war, are not yet rendered familiar in poetical language" (384–85). Moreover, "in respect to the dignity of the names of the weapons used in war, if not in their number and variety," he had the feeling that the ancients were at a much greater advantage than his contemporaries. Over time, however, Barlow has discovered that "the modern military dictionary is more copious than the ancient, and the words at least as poetical" (386). Finally, as far as contemporary fighting techniques are concerned, even though "poetically speaking" something has been lost because modern war allows for only few episodes of "individual prowess," one must notice that "in a general engagement, the shock of modern armies is, beyond comparison, more magnificent, more sonorous and more discoloring to the face of nature, than the ancient could have been; and is consequently susceptible of more pomp and variety of description. Our heaven and earth are not only shaken and tormented with greater noise, but filled and suffocated with fire and smoke" (386–87). As if aware that rather than lamenting the relation between war and epic he is now showing that even contemporary, supposedly progressive epics can safely continue to make a beautiful war central to their narrative efforts, Barlow argues that his discussion of arms and poetry, or, better, of the poetry of arms, is made necessary by those readers who, "being accustomed to seeing a long poem chiefly occupied with this sort of bustle conceive that the life and interest of such compositions depend upon it" (388). Yet there can be no doubt that, as a whole, *The Columbiad*, while registering the tension between the dream of peace and liberty America represents and the violence of a Revolutionary War without which that dream would have never come to pass, does not offer any sustained reflection on how means and ends may be reconciled. All Barlow can do is acknowledge the paradox whereby "war is the evil of kings but necessary to overthrow kings" (Camfield 143).

When Columbus is doubtful regarding the future of peace and prosperity traced by Hesper, Hesper reassures him by appealing to the "Sage science" that will guide with firm hand the destinies of humankind. In Barlow's eyes, war is nearly exclusively the product of ignorance and tyranny and is therefore destined to vanish as democracy and commerce expand their reach. At times, however, Barlow is drawn to a more dialectical approach to the problem of war. In Book 9, while tracing for Columbus the history of mankind's progression, Hesper refers to the time of the Crusades, when "Blind War himself, that erst opposed all good,/ And whelm'd meek Science in her votaries' blood, / Now smooths, by means unseen, her modest way, / Extends her limits and secures her sway" (9.547–50). On this occasion, against the conquering ambitions of the "mad Crusaders," war paves the way to the expansion of commerce between Europe and the Middle East. As Blakemore notes, "In Barlow's progressive formulation, even the violent ruptures in human history forward the harmonious future" (277–78). Yet this vision is not easily reconcilable with the simpler view of war as a consequence of superstition and authoritarianism. Indeed, in the lines I just quoted, War "smooths" rather than opposes the ways of Science. Moreover, if war is "blind," so in a sense is the reader (as well as the author), unable to grasp how the "unseen" hand of progress may turn the evil that "opposed all good" into the promoter of political advancement.

Barlow tries to handle the problem of war in two ways. One is to consider war incompatible with democracy and Enlightenment, and therefore destined to soon disappear. The other is to recognize that, in mysterious, providential ways, war can pave the way for progress, which is what happens with the American Revolution, of course, though—in keeping with his epic/anti-epic agenda—Barlow is careful to highlight that the American revolutionaries resorted to violence only to defend themselves from being conquered by an imperial enemy. In Barlow's logic, "war" is what is waged by England and her "savage" Indian allies. What the patriots fight, instead, is in some sense a war *against* war. This is clearly implied in the section describing the "demon War stalking over the ocean and leading on the English invasion" (as Barlow puts it in the Argument of Book 5). Here, as Blakemore argues, Barlow not only "deftly associates the British with the mythology of the past," but he also, "by refiguring Death, War, Famine, and Pestilence, into his allegory, alludes to the Four Horsemen of the Apocalypse in the sixth chapter of Revelation, suggesting that the War of Independence is an apocalyptic battle between good and evil" (118). If this is so, then Barlow's strategy stands out as an anticipation of equally ambivalent American denials of war and praise for peace, of which Barack Obama's Nobel Prize speech may be the most eloquent contemporary example. War *comes* to America: it is an invading force attacking the country *from the outside*. By repealing the imperial army, the American patriots are therefore not only fighting an assailant but the "demon War" itself. Americans stand for Peace, the British for War.

Analogously, "glory" can be a positive term when its beams play around "the crest" of Arnold in the Battle of Saratoga but be denounced as "false" when its dreams seduce the minds of British soldiers. The poem thus attacks the ideological frenzy that proves fateful to a young Scottish officer named Frazer, who, seduced by "false glory's fascinating call," throws away his life "like an errant knight" in "Wars not his own" (6.396, 401–2). The lure of glory makes Frazer an "errant" knight in at least three ways. First, he errs by virtue of his being a mercenary soldier, fighting somebody else's war. Second, as an "errant knight," he can only be a relic of the medieval past. Finally, he is inspired by a "false glare of glory," which in its martial contours stands opposed to the "solid glory, pure and bright" of peaceful and virtuous endeavors. But Frazer is of course an enemy, and while the object of merciful authorial sympathy, he remains the anti-type of the American soldier, who fights a war that is intimately his own and appears impermeable to ideological manipulations.

The poem, however, can scarcely hide its double standard. For all his dislike of Greek battle heroics, for example, Barlow does not hesitate to compare Arnold to Achilles, or, in the same book—as Blakemore has carefully shown—the American patriots to democratic "Greeks" fighting off an invading army of "Persian" Britons. By comparing the American soldiers to "Athenian youths" (6.331) who "fat their fields with lakes of Asian blood" (6.334), Barlow's language pays homage to the very Homeric tradition he declared to be writing against. Nor does he hesitate to paint in horrific details war's violence by staging an invented gory naval battle between an allied French vessel and a British ship, rich with "spatter'd brains" and "fresh brooks of blood" (7.532, 533). Thus Barlow makes true on his promise, in the preface, to show that modern battles can be "more magnificent, more sonorous, and more discoloring in the face of nature" than those of Virgil or Homer. His epic can count, so to speak, on the special effects granted by gunpowder, mighty cannons, and large ships, to go along with the more familiar ghastly show of severed body parts and spattered brains. Barlow tries to have his pacifist cake—by imputing the horror to an impersonal "War"—and to eat it too, by respecting the conventions of epic narrative.

What is rather disturbing in the way Barlow exorcises the violence of the founding as a form, in today's language, of postcolonial resistance, is that not only does he ignore the neo-colonial status of the United States, but he makes the American Indians the prototype of the war spirit his epic wishes to condemn both morally and historically.[12] For Barlow war is essentially a primitive practice, the consequence of prejudice and ignorance, and therefore typical of feudal society, or of what to Barlow appears as its American equivalent—barbarous Indian savagery. In a rhetorical and ideological move analogous to that whereby War is constructed as a foreign import to American shores, Barlow associates War with savagery. By this token, as the vanguard of an unfolding New World guided by the principles of reason, the United States does not fight a "war" but something like a war-that-is-not-a-war. "Ontario's yelling tribes," the "Insidious Mohawks," the "Scalpers and ax-men . . . from Erie's shore"—these are the "savage hordes" irresponsibly employed by characters like the "murderous" John Johnson, an American royalist fighting on the British side and, moreover, a mixed-blood by way of his "savage" Mohawk mother. If the fact that the majority of Indian tribes involved in the war chose to side with the Crown may help explain why Barlow depicted them in such unfavorable terms, one can scarcely fail to notice his silence regarding the anti-Indian violence of all European powers. Not only does the poet, as one would expect, praise Columbus's "paternal" attitude toward the natives, but while he dwells in considerable detail on Pizarro's bloody conquest of Peru, he has little or nothing to say about the relationships between whites and Indians in North America.[13] His treatment of the issue silently perpetuates a century-old discursive tradition that had seen the British colonists define themselves as a merciful and virtuous community vis-à-vis the savagery of both New World Indians and Spaniards. Such a "triangular" conception of identity—to use historian Jill Lepore's terminology—would form the basis of an emergent American nationalism in both the eighteenth and the early nineteenth centuries, when the British would replace the Spaniards as the third side of the triangle.[14] Notwithstanding its self-declared intention to criticize the ideology of war, *The Columbiad* is scandalously silent regarding the violence against Indians unleashed by Americans on the frontier as well as during the revolution.[15]

A Commonwealth of Peace

Although Barlow's portrayal of American Indians *is* quite troubling and may be easily interpreted as a resounding confirmation of the imperialist vocation of Western Reason, it would be unfair to conclude that his attempt to simultaneously praise the American Revolution and write against the ideology of war (which the Indians of the poem are made to embody more than the British army itself) is simply an expression of *mauvaise foi*. Unlike Madison's "gentle revolution to end all revolutions" (quoted in Kammen 212), Barlow's revolution is anything but a "gentle" or smooth affair—it unfolds "o'er the field of blood" and, most important, is definitely not meant to end but rather to *jumpstart* other revolutions all around the globe. Despite the bloodshed necessary to break away from the *ancienne regimes*, Barlow saw the republican revolutions of the late eighteenth century as ushering in a new era of world democracy that would consign war to the dustbin of history. Like Kant in *Perpetual Peace*, Barlow sees the establishment of republican governments as a *conditio sine qua non* for the rise of world peace, and though he is far more optimistic than Kant was, like his German contemporary he too sees the establishment of a world "league" as a prerequisite for finding peaceful alternatives to war. Furthermore, also like Kant, Barlow believed that the way to peace was through war, and though this kind of reasoning resonates in our contemporary ears as a thinly veiled form of American Newspeak, that was certainly not the way either Barlow or Kant intended it. Since only republican governments could be persuaded not to make war on each other, the revolution was the bloody, strait gate through which a new era of everlasting peace could enter into human history. And yet, for both Kant and Barlow, this new era of peace is in some sense also a return to a different kind of origin—an origin that is not human but divine. This is perfectly illustrated by the hymn to Peace with which Book 8 of the *Columbiad* opens.

> Hail, holy Peace, from thy sublime abode
> Mid circling saints that grace the throne of God!
> Ere morning stars his glowing chambers hung,
> Or songs of gladness woke an angel's tongue,
> Veil'd in the splendors of his beamful mind,
> In blest repose thy placid form reclined,
> Lived in his life, his inward sapience caught,
> And traced and toned his universe of thought.
>
> . . .

From scenes of blood, these verdant shores that stain,
From numerous friends in recent battle slain,
From blazing towns that scorch the purple sky,
From houseless hordes their smoking walls that fly,
From the black prison ships, those groaning graves,
From warring fleets that vex the gory waves,
From a storm'd world, long taught thy flight to mourn,
I rise, delightful Peace, and greet thy glad return. (8.1–28)

This hymn does much more than simply set aside the vengeful, militarist God of the Puritan imagination. In this passage, Barlow identifies the primordial state of Being with Peace itself. In terms that are virtually identical to those in which a contemporary liberal theologian like Matthew Fox has argued that "in the beginning there was joy," Barlow identifies the Logos (God's "creating voice") with joy, gladness, and harmony.[16] This is Barlow's poetic analogue to Fox's "original blessing": an argument in favor of the unnaturalness and irrationality of war and a call for humans to resume the place intended for them in the plan of Creation. God's primordial thought is Peace. The God of this hymn is incompatible with any act of violence, including Barlow's own occasional embrace of an apocalyptic imagery in support of the revolution. God's Peace radiates from "his inward sapience" toward the entire universe and stands in sharp contrast to the scenes of war recalled in the quoted second stanza. From a peace studies perspective (see chapter 1), we may say that here Peace is anti-war only "obliquely": in fact, it is not so much Peace that is anti-war, as war that is anti-peace, since Peace is in Barlow's imagination primordial. In its last three books, Barlow's peace epic may be said to finally come into its own, as the poet leaves behind Homeric scenes of war to chant the beauty of a human progress aided by advancements in agriculture, industry, and science. In the world that Hesper shows to Columbus as an eventual byproduct of his discovery of America—a world that now lies in the future not only for Columbus but for the reader as well—future poets will be rid once and for all of the pernicious epic heritage Barlow was forced to acknowledge and struggle with. The "epic song" of the future will be a Peace and no longer a War, or a War-and-Peace, song. This future world, with its interpenetration of God and nature ("the total God" 10.272), is one where the arts will be finally liberated from their subjugation to tyrants and their "rage of conquest." It is a world in which the epic of old—Barlow's name for war literature—will cease to exist and poets will be no longer forced to celebrate acts of violence.

Barlow's optimism is upheld by the belief that the "one great moral soul" that will eventually pervade all mankind emanates from the same divine energy that formed "every sphere." As in Kant, the moral law inside is at one with the starry

heavens above. For both Barlow and Kant peace is something that human beings will attain to the extent that they will commit themselves to universal moral
reason. By associating the progress of science and republicanism to the advent of
world peace, Barlow seems indeed to follow the Kantian maxim "Seek ye first the
kingdom of pure practical reason and its righteousness, and your end (the blessing of perpetual peace) will necessarily follow" (quoted in Mansfield 22). Though
Barlow is far more optimistic than Kant about the possibility of making the dream
of perpetual peace come true, their philosophical assumptions are essentially the
same: by realizing peace, humankind fulfills the divine decree. Barlow's God, also
like Kant's, is the bedrock of moral reason, not the God of a covenant with a chosen,
exceptional people. True, the future cosmopolitan world of Barlow's imagination
appears rooted in American-style republicanism, but this peaceful world, in which
"War's hosted hounds shall havoc earth no more" and "mutual love commands all
strife to cease, / And earth join joyous in the songs of peace" (10. 378, 493–94), is
by no means conceived as the lengthened shadow of an American identity but as
a *universal* transformation in which nationalisms are forever discarded, as we see
in the meeting of the world's assembly:

> Each envoy here unloads his wearied hand
> Of some old idol from his native land;
> One flings a pagod on the mingled heap,
> One lays a crescent, one a cross to sleep;
> Swords, sceptres, mitres, crowns and globes and stars,
> Codes of false fame and stimulants to wars
> Sink in the settling mass; since guile began,
> These are the agents of the woes of man. (10. 599–610)

Barlow knew that his inordinate optimism stood in sharp contrast to many of
the critical voices of his time, some of which belonged to those same "Connecticut
Wits" with whom he had long collaborated. He refused, however, to tone down his
polemics. "The notion that the social state of men cannot ameliorate . . . is pregnant
with infinite mischief. I know no doctrine in the whole labyrinth of imposture that
has a more immoral tendency. It discourages the efforts of all political virtue; it
is a constant and practical apology for oppression, tyranny, despotism, in every
shape. . . . It inculcates the belief that ignorance is better than knowledge; that war
and violence are more natural than industry and peace; that deserts and tombs are
more glorious than joyful cities and cultivated fields" (852n). While Kant is a more
cautious realist than Barlow, Barlow's indignation against the stubborn prophets
of doom is similar to Kant's impatience with those "political moralists" who, by
appealing to the pretext that human nature is incapable of the good that reason
prescribes, "do all they can do to make moral improvement impossible and to per-

petuate violations of law."[17] And just as Kant condemns such easy moralists who, on the basis of what man has been so far, forget "what he may become," so Barlow insists that "One of the most operative means of bringing forward our improvements and of making mankind wiser and better than they are, is to convince them that they are capable of becoming so" (852n).[18] The future of peace imagined by *The Columbiad* has not come to pass. Not only is the United States the most heavily armed nation in the world, but its relation with the United Nations and other international bodies (like the International Criminal Court) has often been a vexed one. Yet the value of Barlow's text lies not in the accuracy of its predictions. *The Columbiad* is an important literary and historical document because, first, it shows that there were writers who indeed considered Peace, not War, as a quintessential American value and aspiration; and, second, because it provides us with a virtual textbook illustration of the ambivalent, contradictory, multifaceted relation of the would-be anti-war writer to the object of his narration. His counter-epic ends with peace triumphant, but to get to it both poet and reader have first to wade through streams of blood. It was left to another kind of American epic to dwell in more painstaking detail on the war/peace, violence/non-violence conundrum. That epic is the subject of the next chapter.

"Cain's Ring"

Moby-Dick and the Narrative of Sacrifice

> There! The ringed horizon. In that ring Cain struck Abel. Sweet work, right
> work! No? Why, then, God, mad'st thou the ring?
> —*Moby-Dick*

In one of the final passages of Barlow's *The Columbiad*, we witness the unfurling of a white flag to celebrate the achievement of universal peace in a world envisioned as quickly moving beyond the nationalism of the American Revolution. One might say that Barlow's revision of the epic mode not only aims at refunctioning war as a momentary lapse on the way to a Kantian perpetual peace but also aspires to a global, transnational reach, which is also shared by the work most people would nowadays identify as *the* great American epic, even though it is an epic written in prose rather than verse. Herman Melville's *Moby-Dick* bears many signs of its Americanness, but it is also an "encyclopedic narrative" whose ambition is to take on the entire world.[1] The novel's global interests can be observed right from its very first sentences, where the reader is introduced to the odd compiler of the "Etymology": "The pale Usher—threadbare in coat, heart, body, and brain; I see him now. He was ever dusting his old lexicons and grammars, with a queer handkerchief, mockingly embellished with all the gay flags of all the known nations of the world. He loved to dust his old grammars; it somehow mildly reminded him of his mortality" (7). If we compare the pale Usher's hankie to Barlow's triumphant white banner of peace, we can begin to get a sense of the extent to which, despite their shared epic ambitions, the two texts are driven by different cultural persuasions. The "gay" colors of these national flags are neither transcended by nor easily reconciled with the implied whiteness of the background. If anything, the latter seems to anticipate that "dumb blankness, full of meaning" (165) to which Ishmael dedicates one of the greatest chapters of the novel. There, Ishmael observes that his "white-lead chapter about whiteness is but a white flag hung out from a craven soul" (164). Furthermore, Ishmael submits that "the concrete of all colors" is at one with the "visible absence of color" (165), thus retrospectively explaining why there is something fake ("mocking") about the flags' gay colors. When, in this crucial chapter, he refers to the "theory of the natural philosophers" that "every stately or lovely emblazoning colors" are only "allurements cover[ing] nothing but the charnel-house within" (165), Ishmael is speaking of "deified Nature absolutely paint[ing] like the harlot," but he could well be referring to the flags "emblazoning" the Usher's handkerchief, which now stand revealed as so many futile attempts at covering up the void on which the image of the nation erects itself.

Read from this angle, the flags' national colors violate the whiteness of the background, but to the extent that whiteness signifies "the heartless voids and immensities of the universe" (165), there is hardly anything peaceful about the flags' white background. Whiteness is constructed by Ishmael as the sign of a primordial violence done to man ("Though in many of its aspects this visible world seems formed in love, the invisible spheres were formed in fright" [164]), that ends up justifying "the fiery hunt" for Moby Dick. We know that, later in the novel, Ishmael will try to distance himself from this metaphysics of violence as an understandable response to a hostile, frightening universe, and he will appear to revoke his allegiance to Ahab. Yet the extent to which he is able to disengage his philosophical views from those of his captain's has been much debated. Ahab's world is unequivocally one of war, where appeasement is not an option. Ishmael, on his part, may crave peace, but his imagination, too, is obsessed with violence. As revealed by his vision of "one insular Tahiti, full of peace and joy, but encompassed by all the horrors of the half known life," Ishmael's island of tranquility is surrounded by "the universal cannibalism of the sea; all whose creatures prey upon each other, carrying on eternal war since the world began" (225). Ishmael's "mighty book" opens with a deceivingly conciliatory white flag but ends with the unfurling of a banner signifying revenge and disaster. Ahab's red flag, nailed to the masthead by Tashtego as the *Pequod* inexorably sinks, may be seen as Melville's dystopian counterpart to Barlow's utopian white flag saluting world peace. Though Melville probably valued peace as much as Barlow did, his own epic casts serious doubts regarding the possibility of curbing a violence that keeps frustrating mankind's best hopes from time immemorial.

Melville has been often identified as a forerunner of later anti-war writers—as an artist engaged from early on in his literary career in denouncing the destruction unleashed on the world by "the most ferocious animal on the face of the earth": "white, civilized man" (*Typee* 125). Joyce Sparer Adler's *War in Melville's Imagination*, perhaps the best study of the "war-or-peace" theme in Melville's imagination, forcefully argues that "abhorrence of war; belief that as long as brute Force remains dominant in the world, enslavement of human by human will continue; questionings about whether man's voice will ever be raised effectively against war—all these flow from beginning to end" (2) in Melville's oeuvre. While it would be hard to deny that "Melville's passion against war was a great dynamic in his imagination and a main shaping force in his art" (Adler 3), Adler's discussion of Melville's attacks on violence and war at times seems to ignore the ambiguity of Melville's critical voices. Just to quote two notable examples to which we shall return later in this chapter, both Tommo in *Typee* and Ishmael in *Moby-Dick* are often quick to discern the signs of violence in other people's behavior but less willing to contemplate the extent to which their views and actions are not altogether violence-free. This is in no way to argue that Melville's critiques of war, imperialism, racial violence, and so forth were not sincere. If anything, it is to suggest that his critique may cut even deeper, by investing the limitations of the would-be critic of violence. Melville's anatomy of violence is enhanced by his sophisticated understanding of the sacrificial dynamics human beings mobilize in order to rationalize their recourse to violence. This, I will maintain, is what makes Melville's approach to the question of violence especially valuable: his realization that—to resort to the terms employed by Kenneth Burke in *The Rhetoric of Religion*—in their effort to construct a peaceful Order, human beings "redeem" themselves by creating a "Cult of the Kill" that needs to feed itself on a victim. Melville is distressed by man's readiness to engage in wars and kills, but he is perhaps even more perplexed by the vicious circularity of "Cain's ring," where peace always hangs on victimization, and violence resurfaces precisely when one had hoped to be rid of it.

This tension runs through a great number of Melville's works, all of which culminate, or revolve around, acts of sacrifice. In addition to *Moby-Dick* and *Typee*, a preliminary list of Melvillean narratives brought to a close only through violence and the expulsion of sacrificial figures would include "Benito Cereno," with its execution of the rebel Babo, matched by the death of his victim and former victimizer Cereno; "Bartleby," with the gradual but nonetheless inexorable casting out of the eccentric scrivener; *Pierre*, with its tragic trajectory of the writer-as-outcast; the "Indian hating" section of *The Confidence-Man*, with the scapegoating of the Indian Mocmohoc; and *Billy Budd*, with its execution of the "handsome sailor." As well, Melville's most direct treatment of war, his *Battle Pieces and Aspects of the War* (1866), may be said to hang on a sacrificial dimension. As even Adler concurs, though Melville in the end calls for a reconciliation between North and South, he subscribes to the notion that "the spirit that urges the North is 'divine' while the 'evil end' of the South is the continued rule of Lucifer" (Adler 135). Just as in *Moby-Dick* the *Pequod* must sink to hell like Satan before Ishmael is saved, so in *Battle Pieces* peace can come only after the Satan of the South has been cast out.

In this chapter, except for a brief section on *Typee*, where I locate the blueprint of Melville's sacrificial narratives, I focus exclusively on *Moby-Dick*, of Melville's works the one where the logic of sacrifice is most extensively explored. Even though, ideologically speaking, Melville's novel may appear to be worlds apart from the Enlightenment optimism of Barlow's epic poem, both may be considered, to quote Adler's definition of *Moby-Dick*, "symbolic poems of war and peace" (55). Melville, like Barlow, is perplexed by humankind's bloody record of wars and violence, often describing whaling itself as a form of warfare, as when in one of the last chapters Ahab laments the fact that he has "forsaken the peaceful land, for forty years to make war on the horrors of the deep!" (405). However, unlike Barlow, he does not see war simply as a byproduct of superstition or as something alien to the New World. As the name of Ahab's craft indicates, Melville is aware that America has been founded on the genocidal attack against its original inhabitants. The novel has no lack of peaceful interludes—from Ishmael's and Queequeg's spell of "cozy" friendship to the great vision, before the final catastrophe, of the "enchanted pond," where Ishmael becomes privy to "young Leviathan amours in the deep" (303)—but these are mostly conceived as temporary retreats from an immutable and brutally aggressive world. What is even more troubling, as we shall see, is that resistance to violence seems to entail further violence, in an endless, tragic cycle of aggressions and counteraggressions. In Melville's world, no one can be entirely innocent—not even the author who, as he famously remarked, knew he had written a wicked book and yet felt spotless as the lamb. In what follows I try to unveil the cultural and narrative logic behind this paradoxical statement.

Father Mapple's Sermon

In the final chapter of *Violence and the Sacred*, René Girard discusses the biblical Book of Jonah to recapitulate the central argument of his study. The tempest sent by the Lord against the ship boarded by Jonah in his attempt to run away from his prophetic duties is read by Girard (312–14) as a textbook sacrificial crisis. The crisis brings about a breakdown of the religious order—"then the mariners were afraid, and cried every man unto his god" (Jonah 1:5)—and it can be solved only through the ritual expulsion of a scapegoat.[2] The crew wonders "for whose cause this evil is upon us" (Jonah 1:7) and goes on to cast lots to identify the culprit. The lot falls on the wayward prophet; yet the sailors are reluctant to sacrifice him, and they make an attempt to reach the shore by their own efforts. When they fail, they finally cast Jonah into the sea and the tempest subsides. Only Jonah's sacrificial expulsion saves the community. Jonah is, in Girard's terms, the surrogate victim whose sacrifice prevents the community from disintegrating and plunging into the utter chaos of reciprocal violence.

As we all know, the Book of Jonah is the text of Father Mapple's sermon in chapter 9 of *Moby-Dick*—one of the stories-within-Ishmael's-story on which much has been written but whose sacrificial logic, at least to my knowledge, has never been properly discussed. The connection between violence and the sacred is a major concern of both the sermon's narrative strategy—especially when the latter is considered in light of the major discrepancies between Mapple's reading of Jonah and the original biblical text—and of its relation to the novel as a whole. By focusing on this Girardian theme my aim is threefold. First, I wish to take another look at what can only be described as Father Mapple's manipulation of biblical discourse. The differences between the text of Jonah and Mapple's sermon have often been noted. Yet both those critics who see Mapple's emendations as Melville's utterly serious attempt to provide the reader with a moral yardstick to judge his characters, and those who believe that Melville ironically undercuts Mapple's sermonizing, have to a greater or lesser extent ignored the fact that the best commentary on Mapple's sermon is to be found in the Book of Jonah itself. Second, I would like to call attention to an aspect of the Book of Jonah that Girard's theories help to illuminate but that, somewhat surprisingly, he neglects to mention in his brief discussion of this biblical text. Finally, I want to argue that, by evaluating the understanding of scapegoating implicit in both texts, we may be in a better position to map out, on the one hand, Ahab's and his crew's relation to the White Whale, and, on the other, Ishmael's role in the overall narrative scheme of the novel.

In his *The Errant Art of Moby-Dick*, William Spanos (87–114) claims that the majority of Melville critics have avoided discussing Father Mapple's sermon because of the subversive implications of Ishmael's reading of it. However, Spanos's lengthy discussion of Mapple's sermon and its place within the overarching narrative of *Moby-Dick* is in several ways an elegant though perhaps predictable updating of "anti-biblical" interpretations of the sermon and Melville's mighty book first proposed by Lawrance Thompson in his 1952 book, *Melville's Quarrel with God*. Thompson took issue with the then-dominant "Christian" readings of Melville which, at least since Nathalia Wright's *Melville's Use of the Bible*, set out to prove that, even though in his sermon Mapple completely disregards the fourth and last chapter of Jonah—where the Lord shows His kindness and mercy by sparing the city of Nineveh—"the structure of *Moby-Dick*," as Wright asserted, "calls for the sermon and narrative to agree" (83–84). Thompson argued, instead, that Mapple's sermon "is ridiculed and burlesqued" by both Ishmael and Melville, and that, unlike Mapple's Jonah, the biblical prophet was a "headstrong, recalcitrant, God-challenging" figure who obeyed divine authority "only after God had scared poor Jonah witless" (Thompson 164). Yet Thompson's belief that Melville's texts nearly always call for anti-Christian, anti-biblical readings ignored the extent to which the story of Jonah, and especially the fourth chapter omitted by Mapple, is already implicitly and devastatingly critical of Mapple's sermon.

Mapple makes of Jonah a man who, in boarding the ship on which he wishes to run away from the Lord, is terrified of being "discovered" and treated as a criminal. "So disordered, self-condemning is his look, that had there been policemen in those days, Jonah, on the mere suspicion of something wrong, had been arrested ere he touched a deck" (49). This is a clear manipulation of the original text, where things stand in exactly the opposite way. In the Bible the narrator points out that "the men knew that he fled from the presence of the Lord, because he had told them" (1:10). Mapple adds that, once on the ship, Jonah fears that God will soon punish him. Yet in the Bible we read that, despite the agitation certainly caused by the "mighty tempest" sent by God, "Jonah was gone down into the sides of the ship; and he lay, and was fast asleep" (1:5). There is no indication, in other words, that Jonah is troubled by his conscience. Mapple goes on to argue that once Jonah is cast into the sea and swallowed by a "great fish" he "does not weep and wail for direct deliverance. He feels his dreadful punishment is just. . . . And here, shipmates, is true and faithful repentance; not clamorous for pardon, but grateful for punishment" (52). In the Bible, however, Jonah is not slow in invoking God's help—"out of the belly of hell cried I, and thou heardest my voice" (2:1)—and yet he can in no way be said to become "a model for repentance," as Mapple dubs him, because even once he finally agrees to preach to the Ninevites, he remains, in his own words, "angry, even unto death" (4:9) vis-à-vis God. Summing up, there can be little doubt that Melville's irony is not directed so much at the Bible as at the particular reading of the Book of Jonah offered by Mapple.

Spanos denounces Mapple's sermon as a perfect type of the Puritan jeremiad, "teleological and logocentric with a vengeance" (100), and proceeds to juxtapose Ishmael's befriending of the pagan Queequeg to Mapple's orthodoxy. Like Thompson, Spanos ignores that the biblical Jonah—far from being, as Mapple argues, grateful for being punished—is incensed by God's decision not to punish Nineveh; that is, Jonah can conceive of divine authority only in terms of sacred violence, thus joining hands with Mapple in praising a God chiefly known to him for His "rod." Yet the biblical narrator casts a critical light on Jonah's behavior by showing that Jonah fled from his mission not because, as Mapple maintains, he was "appalled at the hostility he should raise" (53) but because he suspected all along that the Lord would eventually forgive the Ninevites, thus undermining the continuum linking prophetic Truth and sacred violence. "Therefore I fled unto Tarshish: for I knew thou art a gracious God, and merciful, slow to anger, and of great kindness, and repentest thee of the evil" (4:2). The Bible makes clear beyond any shadow of doubt that Jonah has no fear whatsoever of the Ninevites—he is only afraid of God's mercy.[3]

Jay Holstein has rightly seen that the book of Jonah's "core teaching . . . [points to] the boundlessness of divine compassion even for pagan humanity" (19). Holstein, however, believes that Melville is out to attack such a teaching everywhere in *Moby-Dick* by affirming "a paganism which sees man at the mercy of powers either alien and malevolent (in the case of the white whale) or indifferent (in the case of the sea) to man" (20). Unlike Spanos and Holstein, I want to argue that Ishmael's "pagan" response to Mapple's sermon is not only cast in a strong biblical and Christian language but also in terms that clearly articulate some of the preoccupations of the biblical narrator of Jonah, beginning with his blurring the distinctions between "heathens" and "children of God," as well as his preference for a peaceful resolution of conflict contra Jonah's invocation of God's wrath.

In "A Bosom Friend," the chapter following Mapple's fiery sermon, we see the pagan Queequeg and the Christian Ishmael become "cronies . . . a cosy, loving pair" (57). It would be hard not to take Ishmael's words in this chapter as an explicit critique of Mapple's misreading of the Bible, especially when the issue of Queequeg's idolatry is discussed. Ishmael comically concludes that in order to be a good Christian by doing to his fellow man what he would have his fellow man do to him, he must turn idolater. Similarly, when Ishmael pleads with Bildad and Peleg to hire Queequeg, he mentions "the great and everlasting First Congregation of this whole worshipping world" as a community in which "we all join hands" (84) instead of fighting one another. In both cases Ishmael's rhetoric turns its irony not so much against Christian ethics as against those institutional forms that turn religion into unquestionable dogma, and in some sense, as highlighted by Peleg's words, Ishmael becomes a sort of anti-Mapple: "Young man, you'd better ship for a missionary, instead of a fore-mast hand; I never heard a better sermon. Deacon Deuteronomy—why Father Mapple himself couldn't beat it" (84). Yet Ishmael's language is anything but anti-Biblical: like the narrator of the Book of Jonah, Ishmael appeals to mercy for and tolerance of the Other and, most important, juxtaposes the violent mimicry of revenge, which would justify the destruction of Nineveh, with an ironic but thoroughly peaceful imitation of the idolater's behavior that is in some sense deeply Christian. Ishmael's sly critique of Mapple's sermonizing is by no means "pagan": instead, its logic is utterly dependent on the antisacrificial message at the center of the Book of Jonah, where God is shown not only as forgiving the Ninevites but also as repenting himself for having contemplated at some point the evil prospect of revenge.[4]

As I noted above, what is missing in Girard's brief reading of the Book of Jonah—which focuses exclusively on its first chapter—is this fundamental feature of the story—fundamental, that is, in terms of Girard's own scapegoat theory. The crew expels the victim chosen by Chance, thereby restoring order on the ship and placating Nature's fury, but the God unto whom Jonah is sacrificed does not kill him. The Book of Jonah can thus be seen as a nearly perfect illustration of that "revelation of the structuring power of victimage" ("Generative Scapegoating" 117), which Girard sees as first taking place in the Hebrew Bible, before reaching its climax in the Gospels. The Book of Jonah depicts a world in which men are still resorting to scapegoating, while the Lord not only spares Jonah's life but goes on to grant the salvation of Nineveh, thus severing the connection between violence and the sacred. The Lord of the Book of Jonah's is a largely peaceful and tolerant God—the God whom Ishmael seems implicitly to invoke, especially when describing his relationship with Queequeg. Indeed, just as the Bible shows that the "heathens" can be more God-fearing than the Hebrews, Ishmael juxtaposes his genuine friendship with the pagan Queequeg to contemporary Christians' "hollow courtesy." Yet *Moby-Dick* does not end in New England. While Ishmael at this stage in the novel appears to share the Biblical narrator's hope of overcoming the primitive equation between violence and the sacred, it remains to be seen whether the overall story he tells succeeds in doing so or whether, as I am afraid is the case, Ishmael's own rhetoric is ultimately imbricated in the victimage mechanism he appears to contest in the early part of the novel.

Monstrous Doubles

By analyzing Ahab's relation to the White Whale through Girard's interpretive lenses, one immediately realizes that it provides a perfect illustration of what Girard calls "mimetic desire," the perverse relation linking the desiring subject and his "monstrous double." According to Girard, desire is always mimetic and "triangular"—always directed toward an object that is desired by a model one feels compelled to imitate. In other words, there is no such thing as a "pure" or "spontaneous" desire: in Girard's view one desires something because someone else also wants it and, by so doing, ignites the spark of desire.[5] In our case, Ahab perceives the White Whale as the custodian of some awful secret that must be wrestled away from him, and Melville is careful to represent the struggle between the two as one in which the antagonists end up mirroring each other. Ahab famously declares that he sees in Moby Dick "outrageous strength, with an inscrutable malice sinewing it. That inscrutable thing is chiefly what I hate; and be the white whale agent, or be the white whale principal, I will wreak that hate upon him" (140). Notice that here Ahab identifies the whale's malice with a hateful "strength" that can hardly be distinguished from the hate *he* feels toward the whale. This equation between what Ahab hates and the force that makes him hate it is reinstated in the final pages of the novel, when Ahab defines as equally "inscrutable" and cruel the mysterious force that compels him to seek revenge (406). Ahab, therefore, learns his desire for revenge mimetically, by imitating his model Moby Dick; appropriately enough his wish is "to dismember my dismemberer" (143), to do to his rival what the latter has done to him. Ahab desires, that is, *to be like the whale*, to which he is often implicitly compared and which he resembles even in physical and symbolical details.[6]

The model of Ahab's desire thus becomes, literally, his "monstrous double." The "wall" that Ahab sees incarnated in Moby Dick, and which he wishes to dismantle, is a fit emblem of the Girardian *skandalon*: "the model exerting its special form of temptation, causing attraction to the extent that it is an obstacle and forming an obstacle to the extent that it can attract. The *skandalon* is the obstacle/model of mimetic rivalry; it is the model in so far as he works counter to the undertakings of the disciple and so becomes an inexhaustible source of morbid fascination" (Girard, *Things Hidden* 416).[7]

According to Girard, only "generative" or collective violence can transform the monstrous double into a savior and its killing into a sacrifice, and it is by appealing to the generative qualities of violence that Ahab justifies to the crew, and to himself, his revenge mission. Ahab himself sees the whale precisely as a scapegoat both in the sense that "all evil . . . [is] visibly personified, and made practically assailable in Moby Dick" and in that he "piled upon the whale's white hump the sum of all the general rage and hate felt by his whole race from Adam down" (156). Ahab here stands out as the typical Nietzschean man of resentment who, trapped in the "it was," "lives his past in the future . . . and can hope to will only by directing his power towards revenge."[8] His fixation with the past, however, transcends the temporal and spatial boundaries of his own person and is magnified into a collective rage that comes to include all Time and humanity. His hunt can thus be easily read as a classic attempt to rid a violent world through violent means. Indeed, Moby Dick's status as scapegoat in the Girardian sense goes a long way in explaining why the White Whale is perceived as both malicious and sacred: his nature is the ambivalent one of the sacrificial victim, who is said to be responsible for the violence at large in society but whose sacrifice will also grant the return to a state of peace. It is no accident that Ahab insists maniacally on the *ritual* aspect of the hunt for Moby Dick, which he distinguishes from the commercial goals of the *Pequod*, vainly invoked by Starbuck. Yet Melville's discourse, for all the emphasis it places on Moby Dick's monstrosity, is never simply mythical. As a whole, that is, the novel does not make of the White Whale a monster deserving punishment and annihilation. By repeatedly calling attention to the fact that the hunter and the monster are really one and the same being, Ishmael can be said to be following, at least up to a point, the example of the biblical narrator of Jonah and his attempt to unveil the paradoxical, circular logic of scapegoating.

Ahab's attempt to sacrifice Moby Dick fails. On the other hand, it can be said that the sacrificial crisis described in the novel is ultimately brought to a close by sacrificing—in a fascinating reversal of the traditional scapegoating mechanism requiring one victim to perish so that the rest of the community may be saved— both Ahab and his crew, minus Ishmael, to the captain's monstrous double. Obviously, the sacrificial outcome of the novel could be construed by the narrator as the consequence of a purely arbitrary chain of events—a fortuitous outcome of his adventure and nothing else. This, however, is not how Ishmael describes the climactic moments of his story. On the contrary, his rhetoric resurrects time and again throughout the novel, and especially in the end, the religious, sacrificial logic embodied in the sailors' behavior in the Book of Jonah. Even though in "The Mat-Maker" Ishmael identifies Chance as the force that "has the last featuring blow at events" (179), when it comes to describing Moby Dick's last blow at the *Pequod*, he sees it as the working of Fate—of a retributive Violence which, for all of its possibly nihilistic shadings, still obeys some mysterious, superhuman logic. As even a cursory glance at the language employed by Ishmael in the epilogue will show—from the Job epigraph to the evocation of what "the Fates ordained" and the mention of "unharming sharks" and sea-hawks "with sheathed beaks" (427)—the narrator strives to read some degree of logic and justice into the whale's "swift vengeance."

In this regard Priscilla Wald has rightly argued that "when Ishmael ends *Moby-Dick* with Rachel's searching for her children he paraphrases a gospel that itself repeats Jeremiah in fulfillment of the prophecy. Repetition, in Matthew, is authorizing and authenticating. But in *Moby-Dick* it is a reflection of Ishmael's internalization of Ahab, his need, that is, to find meaning in chance events, such as his survival."[9] Equally significant in Ishmael's search for meaning, and a further proof that his narrative cannot rid itself of a jeremiadic rhetoric ultimately akin to the one employed by Father Mapple, is Ishmael's choice of epigraph for his epilogue. The identical lines from Job—"And I only am escaped alone to tell thee" (1:14–19)—are to be found in the introductory paragraph of Mary Rowlandson's captivity narrative, one of the best examples of the Puritan jeremiad. If it is difficult to deny the critical and satirical dimension of several of Ishmael's narrations, it would be equally wrong to overlook the novel's continuity with those traditions Ishmael works hard to distance himself from but can never break away from completely. In this case, I can see no irony in Ishmael's use of the Job quotation. On the contrary, Ishmael, like Mary Rowlandson, is the sole survivor of a massacre through which a divine agency avenges itself. This is not to say that Ishmael is any less terrified as the witness of Moby Dick's revenge than Rowlandson is as the chronicler of the punishment dispensed by an angry God to His backsliding children: the violence through which the sacred makes itself known wears, like the Indian violence described by Rowlandson, a fearsome, diabolical mask. But just as Rowlandson's infernal Indians are ultimately a manifestation of God's wrath, also Moby Dick's "eternal malice" is, in Ishmael's rhetoric, a manifestation of the sacred.

A close reading of the "Chase" chapters will further sustain a skeptical approach to one of the strongest commonplaces of post–World War II Melvillean criticism, according to which the main action of the novel can be traced in Ishmael's progressive withdrawal from Ahab's deadly and fatalistic vision. If Ahab declares that "we are turned round and round in this world . . . and Fate is the handspike," and that he himself is "The Fates' lieutenant" (407, 418), when Ishmael notes that "the hand of Fate had snatched all their [the crew's] souls" (414), he places an equal emphasis on Fate as the ultimate cause of events. The world of the novel, as Ishmael describes it, is neither "alien and malevolent" nor simply "indifferent," as suggested by Holstein, but a world ruled by a Fate whose revenges and punishments are seen by the narrator not as gratuitous acts but as embodiments of a supernatural violence. In Moby Dick's furious aspect a moment before the final charge, Ishmael not only reads *the same hateful traits* always seen by Ahab but also the features of a being bent on taking revenge: "Retribution, swift vengeance, eternal malice were in his whole aspect" (425). As seen from the point of view of its ending—as all narratives must ultimately be seen—the universe of *Moby-Dick* is one in which a divine agency powerfully reasserts the connection between violence and the sacred *against* the theological outlook presented by the Book of Jonah. Ishmael's rhetoric makes of the White Whale's revenge against Ahab and his crew one of those "judgments of God" that—as seen in "The Town-Ho's Story"—are a prerogative of Moby Dick's. In the novel's apocalyptic ending "God's burning finger"—evoked by Ishmael in "The Candles"—touches once again the "fated" *Pequod*'s quarterdeck.

Ishmael, therefore, is far from resigning himself to seeing his adventure and his own salvation as utterly void of meaning, and, as narrator, he ends up in a position that the biblical Jonah would have certainly envied him for. Ishmael becomes a sort of "resurrected" Jonah who can tell the story of how a wicked leader and his community were eventually punished and annihilated. There is thus some degree of truth in Wai-chee Dimock's suggestion that Ahab is doomed from the start and set up by the novel's logic as the designated victim on whose shoulders all blame will have to fall.[10] Ahab is, after all, marked by moral and physical abnormalities, which, as Girard explains, have always been typical features of mythic victims, from so-called primitive mythologies all the way to Oedipus and beyond.[11] To the extent that Ishmael's narrative responds to Ahab's construction of Moby Dick as a scapegoat by casting Ahab in the role of the deserving victim, one can argue that Ishmael is writing what Girard calls a "text of persecution"—a text which, by blaming all violence on the victim, blinds us to our own participation in the violence of scapegoating.

What must be added, however, is that the novel's final act of victimization takes place only after the text has staged, and to a large extent demystified, the logic of scapegoating. The absurdity of revenge—on a "dumb brute," moreover—is highlighted at various points in the text, and yet by the end Ishmael seems incapable of letting go of the logic of revenge, and he conceives the whale's act as one of "divine retribution": the same divine retribution that is renounced in the Book of Jonah. The novel appears divided between, on the one hand, the critique of the victimary mechanism and its cathartic effects and, on the other, the need nevertheless to provide its readers with an obligatory scapegoat, which entails a recanting of the former critique. Thus Melville offers us an insight into the perverse contradiction that not only revenge but also the critique of revenge itself is always in danger of running into; he alerts us, that is, to the fact that, in Girard's own words, "the indignant or ironic denunciation of the hunt for scapegoats may constitute a new kind of scapegoating." It is perhaps no accident, then, that the very crowd that should have witnessed the execution of the White Whale is turned by the novel into the real victim of a "redoubled and inverted theater" (Girard, "Hamlet's Dull Revenge" 183)—of a blow-back in which the reader's complicity with Ishmael is predicated on a thinly disguised act of sacrificial violence. Those readers who, like Spanos, insist on seeing Ishmael as an uncomplicated, well-rounded, subversive character and focus on the "peaceful" resolution of the narrative, whereby even a symbol of death like Queequeg's coffin is turned into a life-buoy, seem to forget the bloodbath required by the novel's "redeeming" ending—a redeeming ending in which, if on the one hand what was originally singled out as the designated surrogate victim escapes alive from the hands of a barbaric crew equivalent to Girard's enraged mob, on the other hand an enraged Moby proceeds to annihilate his own antagonist and his associates.[12] The resolution of Melville's book is an inescapably violent one, utterly unlike the peaceful and jocose ending of the Book of Jonah.

The Primal Sacrifice

The sacrificial dimension of *Moby-Dick*'s ending may be further highlighted by showing the extent to which it amounts to a rewriting of what I take to be the primal scene of Melville's lifelong obsession with victims, scapegoats, and sacrifice: the ending of *Typee*. In order to understand the victimary mechanism displayed in the final pages of Melville's first novel, however, we must first take a close look at the third paragraph of its first chapter. There, I believe, we can find in a nutshell the theme to which Melville's narratives would return time and again. Tommo's first words in the novel describe the ship's microcosm in a state of crisis: there is virtually no food left on board and, as we learn in more detail in a subsequent chapter, the crew is composed "of a parcel of dastardly and mean-spirited wretches, divided among themselves, and only united in enduring without resistance the unmitigated tyranny of the captain" (21). Yet what prevents the social crisis from turning into a full-fledged sacrificial crisis is not only the fear inspired by the captain's absolute authority. As we learn in the novel's third paragraph, a more suitable scapegoat figure than the captain comes to the crew's rescue.

> There is but one solitary tenant in the chicken coop, once a gay and dapper young cock. . . . [T]here he stands, moping all the day long on that everlasting one leg of his. . . . He mourns, no doubt, his lost companions, literally snatched from him one

by one, and never seen again. But his days of mourning will be few; for Mungo, our black cook, told me yesterday that the word had at last gone forth, and poor Pedro's fate was sealed. His attenuated body will be laid out upon the captain's table next Sunday, and long before night will be buried with all the usual ceremonies beneath the worthy individual's vest. Who would believe that there could be anyone so cruel as to long for the decapitation of the luckless Pedro; yet the sailors pray every minute, selfish fellows, that the miserable fowl may be brought to his end. They say the captain will never point the ship for the land so long as he has in anticipation a mess of fresh meat. This unhappy bird can alone furnish it; and when he is once devoured, the captain will come to his senses. I wish thee no harm, Peter; but as thou art doomed, sooner or later, to meet the fate of thy race; and if putting a period to thy existence is to be the signal for our deliverance, why—truth to speak—I wish thy throat cut this very moment; for, oh! How I wish to see the living earth again! (4)

On a first reading the story of Pedro/Peter the cock would seem only a way to describe comically the desolation on board the *Dolly*, but if we reconsider this passage after reading the whole novel we cannot fail to realize that here the narrator is tracing the contours of the human drama running through the entire narrative. And at the heart of such drama stands not only the contradictory nature of human desire but also the function of violence within the network of human relations.

The narrator tells us that Pedro, the sole survivor of his tribe, walks on one leg as he awaits to be devoured by the captain: here there is an obvious foreshadowing of Tommo's predicament in the Typee valley. As we know, Tommo's injured leg hurts, especially when he is afraid he will be eaten up by the alleged cannibals. But Pedro is much more than a metaphor for Tommo's captive condition. We are told that the price to pay for the "deliverance" of the crew from both the misery and the tyranny on board the ship requires Pedro's sacrifice: only after eating the fowl will the captain agree to touch land. Even though the tone of the passage is comical, the sacrificial nature of the cock's "decapitation" is strongly underlined. The cock will be eaten on the Lord's day and then "buried" with all the proper rites. Even though he claims he has nothing against Pedro, when addressing the cock with the "thou" and "thy" reminiscent of the King James Bible, the narrator admits he would be willing to slit the cock's throat any time if that could convince the captain to put an end to the voyage. Pedro is therefore a typical sacrificial victim, a "scapecock" who, as the classical scapegoats studied by Girard, is both despised and revered. He is marked by a physical defect readable as the external sign of some mysterious sin (Pedro limps—like Oedipus and dozens of other designated victims, including of course Ahab), and he is also the convenient target of a hatred which, as it cannot be directed toward the one most directly responsible for the crew's sufferings, must be deflected on a substitute victim.

Melville's analysis of the nature of sacrifice, however, is intertwined with an important, though less explicit, commentary on Christian discourse. It is no accident that when Tommo addresses him directly, he turns the cock's name into the anglicized Peter, thus underlining its religious implications. To the extent that in Christian tradition Peter's crucifixion is a sort of mirror-like repetition—Peter was nailed to the cross upside down—of Christ's own crucifixion, the text seems to suggest that even such an apparently innocent killing as that of the last cock on board must be read as the attenuated or allegorical version of a more deadly serious sacrifice in which the target of communal resentment is not a fowl but a human being.[13] Moreover, once we are alerted to the Christian dimension of the narrator's language, we can hardly miss the reference to Peter's denial of Christ "before the cock crows." Peter is, in Girard's view, "the most spectacular example of mimetic contagion" in the whole Gospel narrative—a textbook demonstration of how irresistible is the mimetic desire to unite against the victim (*I See* 19). Even Peter, who has been up to this point the first of Christ's disciples, cannot resist the crowd's violent unanimity.

To arrive at an adequate understanding of why Melville brings up such an intricate knot of religious references, we must turn to the end of the novel. After three months on the island, Tommo feels every day more a captive than a guest of the Typees. Ironically, while at the beginning of the narrative his desire was to touch land, now he seems ready to do anything to sail again. If initially the ship was the prison and the island the object of his, and his companions,' desire, now things are reversed. Yet what remains unchanged is the way in which the fulfillment of desire and the road to "freedom" are paved with violence. The Typees do not want Tommo to leave, and when Tommo reaches the shore and jumps into the sea to board a nearby boat, the native Mow-Mow, along with other warriors, rush into the water in hot pursuit. It is at this point that Tommo performs his Peter-like betrayal. To prevent Mow-Mow from seizing one of the oars, Tommo grabs the boat hook and, "exerting all [his] strength," strikes Mow-Mow "just below the throat" (252). One can hardly fail to see the resemblance between this blow against the islander and the earlier one against Pedro the cock. Both Mow-Mow and Pedro are construed as the last obstacle between the narrator and his, albeit temporary, deliverance; both are marked by physical defects (the cock limps, Mow-Mow is one-eyed) that qualify them as scapegoat figures; both are the target of terrible blows "just below the throat" described as a regrettable but ultimately necessary form of violence.

We are now in a better position to understand the novel's initial references to sacrifice and the Scriptures. Notwithstanding the narrator's pose as a critic of colonialism and the white man's violence, as a whole the text presents Tommo as an individual ready to resort to violence whenever his desires meet with resistance.[14]

If at the beginning the only throat to be slit on the road to deliverance is that of Pedro the cock, by the end the throat to be struck is that of a human being whom Tommo needs to demonize in order to justify his own behavior. The reason the cock is named Peter is by now clear. Peter is not only the Christ-like victim of communal violence but also the disciple incapable of resisting the crowd of persecutors. At the end of the novel, by presenting himself as a potential victim of Typee violence, Tommo—like Peter—chooses the side of violence because he is afraid of becoming himself the target of violence. When Tommo tries to run away, the tribe is for the first time shaken by an eruption of internal violence: "a new contest arose between the two parties [those who wished Tommo to leave and those who wished him to stay] who had accompanied me to the shore; blows were struck, wounds were given, and blood flowed" (250). What we have here is a textbook sacrificial crisis: an explosion of violence that subsides only when Mow-Mow and his warriors run after Tommo.

It is no wonder that Tommo depicts his pursuers, and especially Mow-Mow, as bloodthirsty savages capable of swimming while holding a "tomahawk" between their teeth—a weapon, that is, which suddenly brings us back from Polynesia to America and its own savages and favorite scapegoat figures. In brief, Tommo gains his freedom only thanks to an intensification of the violence he originally needed to escape from the tyranny of the ship and, most important, by construing his act of violence as a necessary act of self-defense—as a form of "good," legitimate violence in opposition to the frenzy of a mob of hostile savages. Yet if we read carefully enough between Tommo's words, we can see that what he has actually done is select a scapegoat figure who—just like Pedro acting as the captain's surrogate—will turn the sacrificial crisis around and lend justification to the narrator's use of violence. Mow-Mow, in other words, provides Tommo with a mimetic model that allows him to mitigate the "horror" he feels at the moment he strikes the islander.

Sacrifice and Survival

After this detour through the South Seas and the early days of Melville's writing career, we should be able to appreciate the extent to which the ending of *Moby-Dick* is, structurally speaking, a rewriting of the victimizing scenario found in the last pages of *Typee*. As I mentioned above, for a student of sacrificial strategies what is striking about the ending of *Moby-Dick* is that, instead of witnessing the unanimous killing of a single, designated scapegoat (the Whale) and the deliverance of the entire community, it is the community that is sacrificed while a single individual survives. This is what Girard would call an "inverted mimetic crisis," examples of which are to be found in several mythologies.[15] A Biblical example is of course the story of Noah, a story evoked in fact by Ishmael when he writes that "the great shroud of the sea rolled on as it rolled five thousand years ago" (427), thereby reminding the reader that what he or she has just witnessed is a miniature reenactment of the Flood. Just as in the ending of *Typee* a band of savages is united in pursuing a human victim whose limping and marginal status as a foreigner make him a likely scapegoat, in the final pages of his major novel Melville sets up a situation in which a crew that has been repeatedly described as savage and barbaric directs its hate toward an animal victim. Yet in both cases the mimetic crisis is suddenly reversed as the would-be scapegoaters are turned into scapegoats themselves. Both Tommo and Moby Dick strike back against their pursuers. From this point of view it is significant that Ishmael directs his attention to Tashtego, the last visible crewmember of the sinking *Pequod*. Tashtego, an American Indian, is an updated version of Mow-Mow: a savage perceived as the member of a doomed race (like the Typees, and like Pedro the cock), represented as fierce as any one of Mrs. Rowlandson's Indians, and brandishing to the end his hammer (the whaling equivalent of Mow-Mow's tomahawk). Tashtego, in short, metonymically underlines the status of Ahab and the entire crew as appropriate victims of the Whale's revenge.

Once we have fully grasped the sacrificial dimension of this final scene, we are in a position to read Ishmael's deliverance through different lenses. Like Tommo—and unlike the Ishmael of the early chapters—Ishmael is saved only to the extent that he denies his former link with the "savage" world. The pagan harpooners have by the end become so many metaphors of the doomed, vanishing savages of America, "fixed by infatuation, or fidelity, or fate, to their once lofty perches" (426) as the *Pequod* is inexorably drawn into a deathly vortex. That Ishmael is saved by taking a hold of Queequeg's coffin-canoe is from this perspective deeply ironical, and it is quite telling that we have had to wait for an American Indian critic and novelist to point out that Ishmael's seizure of the coffin should be interpreted as an act of "white" appropriation of a formerly "red" space. As we are reminded by one of the Indian characters in Louis Owens's *The Sharpest Sight*, "When that white storyteller come bouncing up on the Indian's coffin, he killed off half of himself and he lost his power but didn't know it."[16] Even though Ishmael, unlike Tommo, does not seize a boat hook to kill off his "savage" half, there can be no doubt that the deaths of such figures as Tashtego and Queequeg are sacrificially necessary to the providential plot that leads to Ishmael's miraculous survival.

In the end the *Pequod*, which Ishmael in "The Try-Works" had already described as a ship "freighted with savages, and laden with fire . . . and plunging into that blackness of darkness" so as to seem "the material counterpart of her monomaniac commander's soul" (327), has become nothing less than an incarnation of Satan himself, sinking not to the bottom of the Ocean but to hell. The sacrificial scope of the last pages of the novel is thus properly underlined by Ishmael's religious rhetoric, which stages the scapegoating of the *Pequod* as a casting out of Satan. Yet this inevitably raises the issue of how an agent of "eternal malice" like the White Whale can accomplish the ritual expulsion of an equally malicious entity like that of Ahab and his crew (by the end, as Ishmael emphasizes more than once, they are hardly distinguishable). To borrow a phrase from "The Doubloon," "all are Ahab" (332). Here Ishmael's narrative amounts to an implicit, unwitting reply to one of the key questions raised by Jesus in the Gospels—a question to which Girard has devoted much attention: "How can Satan cast out Satan?" (Mark 3:23). Briefly, if we take Satan as another term for the violence of the mimetic crisis, to expel Satan through Satan means to expel violence through violence thanks to the sacrificial mechanism, that is, by turning the violence that threatens to destroy a community into the violence of all against a single victim. In the case of *Moby-Dick*, the novel literally ends with the satanic expulsion of Satan: with the *Pequod*, which, "like Satan," "sink[s] to hell," dragging along with her "a living part of heaven" (427)—the sea-hawk nailed to the mainmast by Tashtego's hammer, an emblematic portrait of the victimary mechanism itself. Yet the invaluable feature of Ishmael's narrative is that it sheds light on how the violent and vengeful world of the ship is brought to an end by a creature described as equally violent and vengeful: a virtual textbook illustration of Girard's notion that "the Satan who expels and reestablishes order is really identical to the Satan who foments disorder" (*I See* 44). Ishmael's story expels Ahab's violence only through a confirmation of that violent, revengeful, and "sacred" nature of Moby Dick on which Ahab's vision depends.

If one agrees that Ishmael's voice is ultimately intertwined with the rhetoric of the jeremiad and its victimizing ideology, what remains to be seen is what degree of distance from the narrator is granted to the reader by *Moby-Dick* as a whole. According to James Duban, Melville should be in no way confused with Ishmael. By arguing against those who wish to make of Ishmael a "cultural hero" who speaks for Melville as well as against those who impute to Melville himself the flawed vision of his narrator, Duban insists that Melville employs Ishmael in order to *critique* the latter's ideological assumptions. Analogously, Donald Pease (274–75) also wishes to exonerate Melville from Ishmael's blindness. He convincingly argues that Ishmael's discourse is implicated in Ahab's totalizing scenario but, like Duban, Pease refuses to see in the narrator's contradictions a reflection of the author's own impasse. Thus he resorts to Melville's correspondence with Hawthorne in order to find at least a modicum of the "genuine fellow feeling" lacking in the catastrophic world of the novel. But while in the letter that Pease quotes from, Melville does speak of the "infinite fraternity of feeling" that has overtaken him on account of his friend's understanding of *Moby-Dick*, in that same letter Melville also famously states: "I have written a wicked book, and feel spotless as the lamb."[17] These words—in a letter exceedingly rich with references to religion and sacrifice—strike me as a telling instance of that "new mood of harmony and peace"

(Girard, "Generative Scapegoating" 91) following a successful scapegoating—and the novel's scapegoat is of course, first and foremost, the would-be scapegoater himself, captain Ahab. Melville is staging in the letter what Walter Burkert, another student of ritual violence, calls a "comedy of innocence" (166): by expressing at once guilt (I have written a wicked book) and disclaiming his responsibility (I feel spotless as the lamb), Melville himself acknowledges his novel's participation in the logic of sacrifice.

Pease and Duban are to my mind right in underscoring a position already brilliantly argued for by Walter Bezanson nearly fifty years ago, thus reminding us of the dangers involved in any simplistic identification of Ishmael with Melville. It is hard, however, to believe that the author can transcend completely the merciless, revengeful world inhabited by Ishmael. It is certainly plausible, as Duban notes, that Melville created a narrator "whose assumptions, sincerely advanced, the reader is independently left to analyze, judge, and perhaps find inadequate" (365). But if the reader may—to confine ourselves to the theme at hand—see the limitations of Ishmael's sacrificial reading of the novel's ending, one can also argue that the ending that so readily lends itself to Ishmael's reading is the work of an author fully aware of its victimizing mechanism. To an extent, what allows Ishmael to tell the tale of sin and punishment denied to Jonah is the fact that Ahab, unlike the Ninevites, never repents, thus paving the way to his well-deserved condemnation.[18] In the second chapter of the Book of Jonah, however, we can see that the Lord is also willing to forgive those who, like Jonah himself, do not repent. In *Moby-Dick*, instead, there is neither repentance on Ahab's part nor forgiveness toward him, and this is due, I think, to both the sacrificial rhetoric embraced by Ishmael and Melville's own narrative choices.

My conclusion should not be taken as implying a moral condemnation of Melville. On the contrary, also on this score one must admire his "Shakespearean" stature: like the "divine William," Melville knew all too well how hard it was to conceive a tragic path that did not lead up to the cathartic effect granted by the victimage mechanism.[19] Just as Hamlet's drama is, in Girard's eyes, an attempt to highlight and subvert the logic of revenge tragedy without depriving the public of the customary sacrificial ending, *Moby-Dick* can be seen as the (inevitably flawed) critique Melville mounts against our victimizing propensities. *Moby-Dick* does not rest content in offering us one or more victims who receive the punishment they deserve. Instead, the novel tries hard to cast light on how any desire for revenge and any effort at solving contradictions by having recourse to violence can only reinstate Kenneth Burke's "cult of the kill." By offering us an anatomy of the contradictory and circular fascination that violence exerts upon the individual and society at large, the novel goes a long way in laying bare the sacrificial logic that underlies it.

Melville, as both Pease and Duban have rightly seen, cannot be identified wholesale with Ishmael, and the narrative does, to an extent, allow the reader to take an independent perspective toward the narrator. From the very beginning of the novel, it is quite clear that Ishmael's voice is fraught with tensions and contradictions. Far from being a narrator who talks to us from the heights of his accomplished redemption, Ishmael is someone who not even the cathartic ending of the adventure he is about to narrate has managed to gain a long-term psychological and existential balance. In the very first paragraph of his narrative, Ishmael declares:

> Whenever I find myself growing grim about the mouth; whenever it is a damp, drizzly November in my soul; whenever I find myself involuntarily pausing before coffin warehouses, and bringing up the rear of every funeral I meet; and especially whenever my hypos get such an upper hand of me, that it requires a strong moral principle to prevent me from deliberately stepping into the street, and methodically knocking people's hats off—then, I account it high time to get to sea as soon as I can. (18).

As the insistent use of "whenever" indicates, Ishmael's "hypos" is not an occasional but a recurrent condition, and since the Ishmael who talks to us here can only be the one who survived the *Pequod*'s disaster, it is clear that what he has gone through has not managed to permanently heal his soul. On the contrary, Ishmael seems condemned to go to sea any time his depression is so severe that he is tempted to find some relief in violence. The jovial tone of this opening chapter should not distract us from seeing that going to sea is Ishmael's only cure: the only way he has to find an outlet to a violent impulse he may direct toward others or himself: "This is my substitute for pistol and ball. With a philosophical flourish Cato throws himself upon his sword; I quietly take to the ship" (18). As an account of Ishmael's sea adventures, *Moby-Dick* is also therefore a "substitute for pistol and ball": an act of imaginative violence capable of healing to the extent that it can provide its narrative "pistol" with a legitimate target. The usefulness of the victimage mechanism is therefore theorized from the start of the novel.[20] But if on the one hand Melville grants Ishmael his "wicked book," on the other *Moby-Dick* does not hide the fact that "spotlessness" is often nothing but the paradoxical effect of our participation in the violence of sacrifice. From Ishmael's viewpoint his "mighty book" can indeed function as a means to exorcise the violence that surrounds him and, most important, to expel—for a time at least—the violence he harbors within himself. From the point of view of a reader able to distance himself or herself from the narrator, *Moby-Dick* is best compared to Queequeg's famous tomahawk-pipe, "which, it seemed, had in its two uses both brained his foes and soothed his soul" (92). By reminding us that what soothes our souls is all too often what hurts those we have chosen as our enemies, Melville, without transcending it, unveils the mis(t)ery of the victimage mechanism.

Read as a meditation on the war-or-peace theme, *Moby-Dick* may be considered an illustration of the appeal that the rhetoric of sacrifice holds out for both the pro-war and the anti-war camps. The novel, that is, not only shows how iron-fisted leaders can manipulate their audiences by pointing to a scapegoat as the cause of every conceivable evil, but it also emphasizes how easily the peace-seeker can be lured by the logic of victimage into believing that the achievement of peace requires the endorsement of war. Seen from this perspective, *Moby-Dick* stands out as much more than an—albeit significant—indictment of war and deserves to be considered as the first deliberate American exploration of the paradoxes and contradictions of the "anti-war" novel as well. Writing against war and violence always requires, to some degree, that what is perceived as the agent of violence be constructed as an enemy. The redemption of some seems to entail inevitably the condemnation of others. The lamb-and-wicked-book imagery Melville used to comment on his finished novel is in fact illuminating when applied to (anti-) war literature—a literature made of wicked books yet paradoxically hoping to promote lamb-like values. The ultimate irony of such imagery, of course, is that the lamb is not only a symbol of peace but, alas, a symbol of the sacrificial victim as well. The narrative logic highlighted by Melville is a zero-sum game in which the survivor's (and potential victim's) gain is another, actual victim's loss. No wonder Melville claimed that his book was broiled "in hell-fire," though the hell Melville referred to was mainly of a cultural, psychological, and spiritual category. The hell to which we turn in the next chapter is the actual one of war or, better, of the Great War, and of the poor devils lying physically mangled and mentally devastated in a field hospital near the front.

CHAPTER 6

"Curious Anesthetics"

Ellen La Motte and the Wounds of the Great War

The (American) Lady with the Lamp

In his poem "The Lady with the Lamp" (1857), Henry Wadsworth Longfellow had celebrated Florence Nightingale (1820–1910) as the bearer of the light of hope amid the darkness of military hospitals. Sixty year later, that proverbial definition provided the title for a review by G. W. Fuller appearing in *The Masses*, within the section "Books That Are Interesting," edited by Floyd Dell. The "lady" of the title was in this case the American Ellen Newbold La Motte (1873–1961), whose lamp, according to Fuller, burnt with an even brighter light than Nightingale's in *The Backwash of War*, a collection of thirteen stories based on her experience as a volunteer nurse in Belgium at a hospital behind the French lines between 1915 and 1916. Not only did Fuller describe La Motte's as "an immortal book," in a post scriptum, Floyd Dell himself, after choosing *The Backwash of War* as "the book of the month," added that it was "one of the best books written in the last ten years in the English language." Perhaps Fuller's and Dell's enthusiasm was in part due to their endorsement of the writer's anti-war position. Yet the work's originality and La Motte's considerable skills were underlined also by other contemporary reviews, including the less favorable, or even the hostile ones. The *New York Times Book Review*, for example, wrote that even though *The Backwash of War* was "revolting—even sickening at times," one should add that "Miss La Motte's book is evangelical. [. . .] It is interesting to note that when there is so much to tell 'literary style' is ignored, thus producing the greatest of 'styles'—Truth. 'The Backwash of War' literally breathes, or rather sobs, sincerity. It is, unconsciously, a stern, strong preachment against war." Even a decidedly critical piece, appearing in the *Independent* on November 13, 1916, and accusing the author of possessing "a mind which perceives nothing but what is debased in human weakness and suffering," admitted that La Motte had reached "the limit of realism," while the *Springfield Republican* praised La Motte for bringing to the forefront "the septic, gangrenous aspects of war, which are, after all, just as true as its inspiring, red-blooded side."

Considering that also those who disliked the book were forced to acknowledge its originality, it is surprising that *The Backwash of War* was quickly forgotten. This was partly due to contingent reasons. As soon as the United States entered the war, the text was censored and disappeared from bookstores. The American government could not tolerate any text that portrayed the war in Europe in a devastatingly negative light. In 1934 La Motte's volume was reprinted and, once again, critics could not fail to recognize its exceptional qualities. World War I had left behind a substantial quantity of war narratives, and reviewers were quick to insert *The Backwash of War* into a newly established tradition of "anti-war" literature. The *Saturday Review of Literature*, for example, thought La Motte's short stories worthy of comparison with Erich Maria Remarque's *All Quiet on the Western Front* (1931) since both texts insisted on the "bestiality of war." Analogously, the *New Republic* underlined the irony and the "naked realism" of the text by comparing it to another World War I classic, Henri Barbusse's *Le Fue* (1916).

Neither the 1934 reprint nor the praise it received, however, managed to rescue *The Backwash of War* from oblivion. Ellen La Motte continued to write, publishing not only articles in a number of important magazines and journals but also essays and stories; she received numerous awards (including a special medal from the Japanese Red Cross); she became directly involved in the fight against the opium trade, gaining from the Chinese government the Lin Tse Hsu Memorial Medal. All of this did not prevent her most important work from being forgotten. To the best of my knowledge, it was only in 1969 that La Motte's book resurfaced, in an article by Eric Solomon for *Texas Studies in Literature and Language*. In Solomon's view, *The Backwash of War* is one of the few texts anticipating the "anti-heroic," "anti-religious," "anti-humanistic" feelings so crucial in the great war novel that is the main focus of his article, Joseph Heller's *Catch-22*. Notwithstanding Solomon's concise but pointed remarks, it would be another thirty years before anyone would take notice of La Motte's book, and even today the genius of this writer awaits proper recognition. To this date, there is no single critical essay entirely devoted to *The Backwash of War*, with the partial exception of Margaret Higonnet's insightful introduction to *Nurses at the Front*, a volume in which, seventy years after the 1934 reprint, nine of the original thirteen stories have been republished.[1]

War and Gender

While Higonnet deserves praise for reprinting a generous selection of La Motte's volume, the rediscovery of the latter's work must be understood, more generally, as being yet another result of the important work done over the last few decades by feminist critics on the theme of "women and war." It is no exaggeration to say that feminist preoccupations of one sort or another lie behind most of the recent studies on war literature and the relations between war and literary representation. This is hardly surprising. Military culture has traditionally defined itself in juxtaposition to the female world, or, better, to its historically constructed image. All military conflicts require at some level a redefinition or renegotiation of gender lines.[2] The gendering of "war talk"—to quote an important critical collection (Cooke and Woollacott) published some years ago—is therefore crucial to any understanding of the cultures of war. War is always, among other things, a force engaged in redrawing, rethinking, or crossing the culturally constructed spaces of what is "male" and what is "female." Yet it is important to emphasize that feminist interest in war—an interest extending well beyond the domain of literary and cultural studies into the fields of history, philosophy, psychoanalysis, anthropology, and sociology—has comparatively little to do with a desire to attack masculine ideologies of war from the point of view of a supposedly peaceful or pacifist second nature of women.[3] What feminist critics are most interested to explore is the *gendered nature* of all wars and war-related practices. As the editors of *Behind the Lines: Gender and the Two World Wars* (Higonnet et al.) have said, "War must be understood as a gendering activity, one that ritually marks the gender of all members of a society, whether or not they are combatants" (4). On the basis of this fundamental insight one can reread canonical war literature with new eyes as well as call into question the notion that war should be understood as the exclusive province of soldier-writers engaged in the production of fictional, autobiographical, or semi-autobiographical texts.

"War," in other words, cannot be reduced to the experience of combat—an experience that some women have shared but from which (until recently) they have been traditionally for the most part excluded. To begin with, the effects of war extend well beyond the battlefield. Hunger, poverty, and deep social and cultural crises are all devastating byproducts of war. Moreover, in the twentieth century the confines of the so-called "battle front" have exponentially dilated both conceptually and practically. Beginning with the "total mobilizations" of World War I, civilians have become not only directly involved in the war effort but also the direct targets of military operations to the point that the distinction between combatant and noncombatant has increasingly broken down. In sum, the shape taken by war over the last hundred years or so has increasingly eroded the cultural (and patriarchal) prejudice according to which women are marginal figures in the discourses of and about war, as witness also the immense literary output of women's writings on war uncovered over the past thirty or so years.[4] It is worth keeping in mind that *The Backwash of War* is only one of the many texts on war by women that of late have been rediscovered, reprinted, and discussed. Just to stick to English-language texts authored by women who, like La Motte, worked as nurses near the front during the Great War, one should remember at least *The Forbidden Zone*, by U.S. writer Mary Borden, as well as the works of two British authors: Enid Bagnold's *A Diary without Dates* (1918) and Helena Zenna Smith's (pseudonym for Evadne Price) *Not So Quiet* … (1930). These texts are rich with observations as significant as the ones found in the novels, memoirs, and autobiographies of better-known male writers, but they are also interesting in terms of style and aesthetics.[5] Analogously, *The Backwash of War* deserves to be read not only as an interesting historical "document." La Motte's tales are extraordinary because they shed light on a hitherto overlooked side of war but also because—as Floyd Dell was the first to realize—La Motte created a style capable of representing without compromises a content that is not simply shocking but often—even by today's standards—outright nauseating. According to Dell, La Motte's writing functions as a kind of "curious anesthetics." This is not to say that her objective is to absorb the reader's shock. Quite the contrary. *The Backwash of War* "tells unsparingly all that there is to tell [. . .] with a quality of art which partly anaesthetizes some of the emotions and appeals directly to the mind—a tremendous artistic achievement." Without having recourse to sensationalism or sentimentalism, La Motte illustrates in detail the perverse mechanisms regulating the horrific world of military hospitals, and the "anesthetics" she employs, far from allaying the reader's disgust, allow her to come as close as possible to the wounds of the Great War.

The Backwash of War: An Anatomy of the Great War

> When he could stand it no more, he fired a revolver up through the roof of his mouth, but he made a mess of it. The ball tore out his left eye, and then lodged somewhere under his skull, so they bundled him into an ambulance and carried him, cursing and screaming, to the nearest field hospital. (*Backwash* 15)

This is the literally *fulminating* opening of "Heroes," the first story in La Motte's book. The brutality of the scene rests not simply with the anatomical details of the horror being described but also, most important, with the fact that the reader is offered no protective filter. We know nothing about either the narrator or the subject matter. We have no emotional or psychological reference point allowing us to deflect or interpret for us the torments thrust before our eyes. This is an excellent illustration of Floyd Dell's "anesthetic" style. La Motte's mode of presentation appeals more to the mind than to the emotions. Of course, a passage like this evokes horror, but it is a horror we cannot process with the heart, but only with our intelligence, by trying to understand why and what the unnamed protagonist "could not stand anymore." What can be so insufferable to push a man to put a gun in his mouth and "make a mess of it"? These questions are at least partially answered by the rest of the story, but La Motte's first preoccupation is to impress upon her reader what is "war in the concrete." As Elaine Scarry has shown, precisely because "the main purpose and outcome of war is injuring" (63) the structure of war requires that wounds be at least in part hidden from view through various rhetorical and manipulative strategies. La Motte's writing moves in the opposite yet complementary direction, so as to tirelessly bring to light the effects of violence on human bodies that are war's most intimate raison d'être. In her stories, without ever sounding morbid or naively sentimental, La Motte focuses on the wounds, the lacerated human flesh, the nauseating smell of putrefaction so as to remind us, "This is War."

The few critics who have written about La Motte have compared her style with that of important U.S. war writers such as Stephen Crane, Ambrose Bierce, and, of course, Ernest Hemingway, whom La Motte often resembles for her short sentences, her dry prose, and the laconic, indeed "anesthetized" tone of much of her writing. A comparative study of La Motte's work is long overdue and would help consolidate her critical reputation. Here I wish only to insist that if on the one hand her constant recourse to an ironic perspective, her compulsive focus on the horrors of war, and the rhythm of her prose suggest La Motte's closeness to Crane, Bierce, and Hemingway, then on the other, the author of *The Backwash of War* is animated by a sense of moral indignation that in these other writers is not always equally sustained and uncompromising. Even though she tries her best not to moralize, the political-ethical substance of her stories is unequivocal. The irony, the absurdity, the flashes of black humor are never added on to the narrative material: they emerge from war's most intimate structure and modus operandi. Half a century before Joseph Heller, La Motte had already realized that, when observed closely, the whole war was a Catch-22 writ large, where absurdity reigned supreme.

"Heroes" provides a perfect example of La Motte's anatomizing of war. The soldier who attempts suicide and is promptly hospitalized is "a deserter" and, "since he had failed in the job, his life must be saved, he must be nursed back to health, until he was well enough to be stood up against a wall and shot. This is War" (15). The military logic here illustrated is a fitting anticipation of the one Joseph Heller's Yossarian confronts in *Catch-22*.[6] A deserter must be executed—that is, he must be killed—but to try to kill oneself is a form of desertion and therefore the traitor must be first cured and then ritually shot by a firing squad because "discipline must be maintained" (15). It is to no avail for the clumsy would-be suicide to scream and struggle on the operation table, spraying blood all over the place. The soldier must be made to obey military reason, even at the cost of smashing two of his teeth "that added a little more blood to the blood already choking him" (18). The tragic irony of the situation is so plain that the narrator—who by now we know to be a nurse—can limit herself to a few terse, implacable reflections:

> He [the deserter] was so different from the other patients, who wanted to live. It was a joy to nurse them. This was the *Salle* of the *Grands Blessés*, those most seriously wounded. By expert surgery, by expert nursing, some of these were to be returned to their homes again, *réformés*, mutilated for life, a burden to themselves and to society; others were to be nursed back to health, to a point at which they could again shoulder eighty pounds of marching kit, and be torn to pieces again on the firing line. It was a pleasure to nurse such as these. It called forth all one's skill, all one's humanity. But to nurse back to health a man who was to be court-martialed and shot, truly that seemed a dead-end occupation. (19)

The irony is all in the facts, even though La Motte likes to underscore the absurdity of the situation by employing out-of-place terms like "joy" and "pleasure," and by punning on the mission of the military hospital, a "dead-end" pursuit not only because it serves no purpose (the *Grands Blessés* are not returned to life but, in the best of cases, to a condition of death-in-life) but also because its end is precisely death, the opposite of what we would expect from a hospital. For all their irony, the narrator's musings are also forcefully rational. Why should curing a soldier who will be later executed be less absurd than taking care of those injured ones who are anyway destined to be torn to pieces by the enemy's machine guns? By pretending to protest the "waste" of medicines on a deserter, the narrator actually delves deeper into the frightening folly of war. "All this waste for a man who was to be shot, as soon as he was well enough. How much better to expend this upon the hopeless cripples, or those who were to face death again in the trenches" (19–20).

The narrator's attempt to find a logic in military reason ends up highlighting its folly and is matched by the impossibility of tracing a clear line between the "cowardice" of the deserter and the "courage" of the supposed hospitalized "heroes":

> The night nurse was given to reflection. One night, about midnight, she took her candle and went down the ward, reflecting [. . .]. How pitiful they were, these little soldiers, asleep. How irritating they were, these little soldiers awake. Yet how sternly they contrasted with the man who had attempted suicide. Yet did they contrast, after all? Were they finer, nobler, than he? The night nurse, given to reflection, continued her rounds. (20)

As she continues her walk through the hospital wards the nurse looks closely at these soldiers and, rather than simply pitying them, she calls attention to their misery, their stupidity, their vulgarity—"How filthy they all were, when they talked with each other, shouting down the length of the ward" (22)—thus reaching the conclusion that these men are actually by no means better than the so-called traitor.

> Wherein lay the difference? Was it not all a dead-end occupation, nursing back to health men to be patched up and returned to the trenches, or a man to be patched up, court-martialed and shot? The difference lay in the Ideal. One had ideals. The other had ideals, and fought for them. Yet had they? [. . .] Courageous dreams of freedom and patriotism? Yet if so, how could such beliefs fail to influence their daily lives? [. . .] And suddenly she saw that these ideals were imposed from without—that they were compulsory. [. . .] Base metal, gilded. And they were all harnessed to a great car, a Juggernaut, ponderous and crushing, upon which was enthroned Mammon, or the Goddess of Liberty, or Reason, as you like. Nothing further was demanded of them than their collective physical strength [. . .]. Individual nobility was superfluous. All the Idealists demanded was physical endurance from the mass. (23–24)

This is one of the rare occasions in which the narrator indulges in general considerations about war, but her observations spring from a careful assessment of reality. To begin with, if La Motte tells us once again that the hospital's is a "dead-end occupation," regardless of the "ideals" nurtured by those cured (and it is worth noting that the narrator admits that even the suicide has an ideal, and therefore also from this perspective he is not unlike the "heroes" injured on the battlefield), the remark also implicitly calls into question the nobility and heroism *of her own work as a nurse*. In the passage quoted, as in the story as a whole, it is clearly implied that, like it or not, also the behavior of those who imagine themselves as untainted by war may actually contribute to its continuance.[7] Obviously, La Motte does not say it would be better to let the injured die. Hers is a bitter reflection on the difficulty of opposing the dynamics of total wars. Her political-philosophical ruminations on war as the ultimate byproduct of massive indoctrination show that, no matter what the "Ideal" one thinks to be fighting for, war's abstraction can sustain itself only by taking hold of the "physical force"—of the bodies—of the combatants. Such insistence on the materiality of the warrior ideal, besides emphasizing how abstraction and concreteness bleed into each other, has the effect of further highlighting the ironic status of the narrator, whose tending of human bodies can be easily read as a sign of her subordination to the Idol of War.

In this story, deserters and heroes are on the same plane. Without romanticizing the would-be suicide (after all, if his behavior is understandable, it is also part and parcel of the more general violence of war), the deconstruction of war's binary oppositions put forth by La Motte forces us to rethink war as a form of collective suicide rather than through the commonly invoked notions of "heroism," "patriotism," "progress," and "civilization." One of the hospitalized soldiers' words, which end the story, highlight the extent to which the nurse's nocturnal reflections are not so peculiar. "Dost thou know, *mon ami*, that when we captured that German battery a few days ago, we found the gunners chained to their guns?" (24). The power of the "great car" of war is not merely ideological. The German soldiers literally chained to their machine-guns provide a clear demonstration of the absolute power that, in time of war, the state exerts over its subjects. When the narrator insists that the "ideals" of the soldiers do not come from within themselves but are instead "compulsory," she is not only thinking of the effects of propaganda. War depends on coercion, and the image of soldiers shackled to their guns refers back to that of the soldiers tied to the great car of war. To quote the protagonist of the story "Pour la Patrie"—a mortally wounded soldier who receives a medal on his deathbed—"I was mobilized against my inclination. Now I have won the *Médaille Militaire*. My Captain won it for me. He made me brave. He had a revolver in his hand" (131).

As in "Heroes," in "Pour la Patrie" La Motte is both critical *and* self-critical. Once again, the violence of war, which has devastated the protagonist's abdomen, is matched by the equally brutal violence of his captain, who forced him to get out of his trench. In his hospital bed the poor man "cried out for mercy. But what mercy had we? We gave him morphia, but it did not help. So he continued to cry to us for mercy, he cried to us and to God. Between us, we let him suffer eight hours more like that, us and God" (127–28). Far from exalting her role as caretaker or dispenser of relief, the nurse underlines her impotence—a human impotence that appears to her as the counterpart of a wider divine impotence. Moreover, as an institution, religion connives with medicine in sustaining the war effort. Called upon to celebrate last rites, the military chaplain is described as a grotesque figure who, "holding a tray of Holy Oils in one hand, while with the other he emptied the basin containing black vomitus out the window," forces a dying soldier into uttering words against his will: "*Dites: 'Dieu je vous donne ma vie librement pour ma patrie* (God, I give you my life freely for my country). The priests usually say that to them, for death has more dignity that way. It is not in the ritual, but it makes a soldier's death more noble [. . .]. He was being forced into it. Forced into acceptance. Beaten into submission, beaten into resignation" (129–30). In order to underscore the obscene subjugation of the church to military logic, the narrator observes that, when finally the soldier utters the prescribed patriotic formula, "a *volley* of low toned Latin phrases, rattling in the stillness like the popping of a *mitrailleuse*" (130, emphasis added) is discharged by the mouth of the priest. By attending to his pastoral duties the reverend turns into a shooter: the "popping" of his sentences is metaphorically—and hence morally—indistinguishable from that of the machine guns. He is a minister of the God of war.

In the story "La Patrie Reconnoissante" the attack on the hypocrisy of the war machinery is delivered from the point of view of Marius, a former cab driver who, aware that he must die of gangrene, fearlessly inveighs against everyone. For starters, he vents his anger at the hospital personnel, formed by "*sales embusqués*"—that is, by shirkers who, thanks to special protections, have managed to avoid life in the trenches: "For ten hours have I laid there, waiting for you! And then you come to fetch me, only when it's safe!" Marius is equally furious at two American ambulance drivers: "'*Sales étrangers!*' He screamed. 'What are you here for? To see me, with my bowels running on the ground? Did you come for me ten hours ago, when I needed you?" (30). One more time, La Motte introduces a viewpoint calling into question her own position as an external observer and recorder of the events:

> "Strangers! Sightseers!" he sobbed in misery. "Driving a motor, when it is I who should drive the motor! Have I not conducted a Paris taxi for the past ten years? [. . .] What are they here for—France? No, only themselves! To write a book—to say what they have done—when it was safe! If it was France, there is the Foreign Legion [. . .] to stand in the trenches as I have done! But do they enlist? Ah no! It is not safe! (31)

Marius has also no faith in supposedly more genuine forms of patriotism. As his agony proceeds, the youth lying next to him, with a liver injury and an amputated hand, receives a *Croix de Guerre*. The boy has not performed any heroic gesture, but "all *mutilés* are given *the Croix de Guerre*, for they will recover and go back to Paris, and in walking about the streets of Paris, with one leg gone, or an arm gone, it is good for the *morale* of the country that they should have a *Croix de Guerre* pinned on their breasts" (33). The narrator's critique is complemented by Marius's bitter observations on the army's classist nature. Addressing "a little *joyeux*, that is to say, a soldier of the *Bataillon d'Afrique*" (34), Marius reminds him that he would never receive any medal, because *la patrie reconnoissante* foresees no honor for those who belong to a "criminal" regiment (the adjective "criminal" must have struck La Motte for its unwitting irony—can there be such a thing as a noncriminal war?).[8] The asphyxiating atmosphere of the hospital hall becomes the objective correlative of the moral and political rottenness of war. The story is one of the most shocking in the entire book. Over the course of the soldier's three days' agony, "the wound in his abdomen gave forth a terrible stench, filling the ward, for he had gas gangrene, the odor of which is abominable." Meanwhile, in the bed next to his, "lay a man with a fecal fistula, which smelled atrociously," while on the opposite side "lay a man who had been shot through the bladder, and the smell of urine was heavy in the air round about" (30–31). La Motte insists on the obscene, nauseating, revolting, insufferable connotations of these devastated bodies on the verge of decomposing—on the "filthy death" of "heroes" in a war that both sides had identified as an occasion for "purification." The words Marius shouts before dying, rather than paying homage to his "mother country," equate the latter's hypocrisy and obscenity to those of the enemy's "mother country": "'*Vive la Patrie Reconnoissante!*' he yelled. '*Hoch le Kaiser!*' Then he died" (41).

The "Awful Interval"

Marius is one of La Motte's typical characters. He voices many uncomfortable and irrefutable truths, yet he never rises to heroic proportions. His cynicism, his deliria, his shouting all make him insufferable to the other patients and (to an extent) even to the reader. La Motte is fascinated by Marius's subversive, at times outright nihilistic attitude. His tragic stature lies with his isolation: no one appears to grasp the "terrible truths" behind his "foul words" (40). As La Motte writes in her introduction, "Much ugliness is churned up in the wake of mighty, moving forces, and this is the backwash of war. Many little lives foam up in this backwash, loosened by the sleeping current, and detached from their environment. One catches a glimpse of them—often weak, hideous or repellent" (viii). As implied in the metaphor she uses, her interest focuses on these "repellent" creatures surfacing amid the foam of the backwash of war. These figures, whom La Motte's stories place in front of us in all their ugliness and misery (both social and moral), are synecdoches of the more general horror of war. Here is a passage from the chapter titled "The Interval," exemplary on both a stylistic and a conceptual level.

> There are three dying in the ward today. It will be better when they die. The German shells have made them ludicrous, repulsive. We see them in this awful interval, between life and death. This interval when they are gross, absurd, fantastic. Life is clean and death is clean, but this interval between the two is gross, absurd, fantastic. (94)

The war reconfigures the soldiers' bodies in a cruel, grotesque way. The sense of unreality and death-in-life, now a staple of the "modern memory" studied by Fussell, Leed, and others, surfaces already in the words used by La Motte to describe the "ludicrous, repulsive" (99) interval between life and death in which these survivors are forced to vegetate.

The soldiers' shattered bodies are by no means La Motte's exclusive source of horror. The wounded are often physically repellent; the officers visiting the hospital are morally disgusting. Take the two generals who distribute *Croix de Guerre* and *Médaille Militaire* to the most seriously wounded. The ceremony lasts a few minutes, and it takes place when the fate of the soldier has already been sealed so that, in one of war's further ironies, the granting of a medal is usually a sign of impending death (one of the generals is "encircled in a sweeping black cloak" [34]). The medical staff, too, is for the most part unsympathetically portrayed. Most of the nurses are, like Fouquet (the protagonist of "The Hole in the Hedge"), men who avoided the draft (*embusqués*) thanks to influential connections, and are, understandably, the target of the patients' rage. Yet the narrator refrains from easy moralizing. Fouquet foams at the mouth when showered with insults, but puts up with them because "anything is better than the front line trenches. Fouquet knew this, because the wounded men were so bitter at his not being there" (50). Here is another weak character whose victimization is described in "anesthetic" terms—not sentimentally, that is, but with a detachment meant to provoke the reader's response. The narrator observes that the soldiers hate Fouquet not because he is a coward but because they are "jealous" of him. "They very much envied him for escaping the trenches, and considered it very unjust that they knew no one with influence who could have protected them in the same way" (50). One more time, La Motte first juxtaposes two apparently opposite situations that, once they are analyzed closely, turn out to be very similar. The soldiers who vomit (at times literally) their resentment on Fouquet would like to be in his place; they aspire to be like him.

The world of the civilians surrounding the hospital is often equally squalid and morally corrupt. "A Belgian Civilian," for example, focuses on the agony of a Belgian ten-year-old hit in the abdomen "or thereabouts. And dying, obviously" (73). The child would like to have his mother assist him, but his lamentations do not meet with any sympathy on the part of the other patients: "The patients were greatly annoyed by this disturbance, and there was indignation that the welfare and comfort of useful soldiers should be interfered with by the whims of a futile and useless civilian, a Belgian child at that" (75). This is a rare case in which, albeit with a touch of irony, La Motte juxtaposes the "sentimental" disposition of both the ward's nurse (presumably La Motte herself) and the *Directrice*, to the insensitivity of the hospitalized "heroes." "The nurse of that ward also made a fool of herself over this civilian, giving him far more attention than she had ever bestowed upon a soldier. She was sentimental, and his little age appealed to her—her sense of proportion and standard of values were all wrong" (75). Maternal values have no place in war, not only metaphorically. When the mother of the child is finally found and taken to the hospital, her response is different from the expected one. "She had been dragged away from her husband, from her other children, and she seemed to have little interest in her son, the Belgian civilian, said to be dying" (76–77). The hospital's *Directrice* appears to cultivate more "maternal" feelings than the child's own mother. "The *Directrice* . . . seemed to feel that a mother's place was with her child, if that child was dying. . . . Which was a point of view opposed to that of this Belgian mother, who seemed to feel that her place was back in Ypres, in her home, with her husband and other children" (77). Though aware that her child may not survive the night, the woman wishes she could go home and decides to stay only to oblige the *Directrice*. Shortly before dawn the son dies and the mother, though "moved by the death of her son," immediately leaves for Ypres:

> "My husband," she explained, "has a little *estaminet*, just outside Ypres. We have been very fortunate. Only yesterday, of all the long days of the war, of the many

days of bombardment, did a shell fall into our kitchen, wounding our son, as you have seen. But we have other children to consider, to provide for. And my husband is making much money at present, selling drink to the English soldiers. I must return to assist him." (79)

The story underscores how the nefarious effects of war extend well beyond the trenches, perverting also those values we consider at the base of our civilization. The notion that war can turn out to be a source of income ("'These Belgians!' said a French soldier. 'How prosperous they will be after the war! How much money they will make from the Americans, and from the others who come to see the ruins!'" [80–81]) cannot but provoke the reader's indignation. However, La Motte's skill as a writer lies in her ability to complicate the story's moral understanding. The woman seems to be sincere about her duties toward the rest of the family. Her rationality may appear excessive and hard to forgive—how can a woman think of her *estaminet* while the son is dying amid atrocious pains?—but war is *also* this, an "awful" struggle for survival leaving little or no room for unproductive sentiments.

Medicine and Torture

One of the striking features of La Motte's book is the narrator's devastating irony toward the practice of medicine, something that has not been properly emphasized by the few who have written about her work. As mentioned earlier, La Motte targets her own narrator with some sharp critical barbs. More generally, the critique of medical practice—or of medicine's limits—is one of the recurring themes of the book. This is particularly noteworthy, considering La Motte was a professional nurse. For example, in "Alone," the soldier Rochard is suffering horribly from a "gas gangrene" (59). Massive doses of morphine cannot ease his pain. "Morphia, good as it is, is not as good as death. . . . Thus, the science of healing stood baffled before the science of destroying" (64–65). With this simple but effective sentence, La Motte calls attention not only to how the machinery of war appropriates science to its logic: she also registers the greater force of military "science." Medicine's lack of power vis-à-vis war is not a purely technical fact. As suggested by the story's title, Rochard's tragedy is that he dies "alone," "a stranger among strangers." The hospital guarantees a nurse "to wait upon him, but there was no one there to love him. . . . And it seemed as if the red, staring eye was looking for something the hospital could not give. And it seemed as if the white, lazed eye was indifferent to everything the hospital could give" (67–68). If medical science cannot repair the destructive consequences of war, human feelings also fail. By repeating that "there was nobody to love him, to forget about that smell" (68), the narrator records her own inability as a nurse to provide Rochard with the love he so desperately needs, as if the insufferable stench of his wound were an obstacle that neither science nor feeling can overcome.

While "Alone" is tinged with a pathetic tone, "A Surgical Triumph" privileges a satirical, grotesque register that eventually turns into black humor. Of all the stories in the volume, it is the one that best anticipates the representation of military medicine that would characterize, first, Dalton Trumbo's *Johnny Got His Gun* and, later, Heller's *Catch-22*. The story concerns the son of Antoine, a barber in the Latin Quarter, drafted at age eighteen and then seriously wounded. The "kind-hearted Red Cross ladies" who care for him write to Antoine, inviting him to send money for the son's cures—in particular for an artificial leg. Antoine, who limps himself, is resigned that his son "would be more hideously lame than he himself" (157–58). Shortly after the first round of bad news, Antoine receives a further request to provide for two artificial arms and eventually he is informed that "a marvelous operation had been performed upon the boy, known as plastic surgery, that is to say, the rebuilding, out of other parts of the body, of certain features of the face that are missing" (158). The young man's body—the "surgical triumph" of the title—is literally rebuilt by the surgeons, but the outcome is not the expected one—at least from the father's point of view.

> Antoine looked down upon the surgical triumph. This triumph was his son. The two were pretty well mixed up. A passion of love and a passion of furious resentment filled the breast of the little hairdresser. Two very expensive, very good artificial legs lay on the sofa beside the boy. They were nicely jointed and had cost several hundred francs. From the same firm it would also be possible to obtain two very nice artificial arms, light, easily adjustable, well hinged. A hideous, flabby heap, called a nose, fashioned by unique skill out of the flesh of his breast, replaced the little scrub nose that Antoine remembered. The mouth they had done little with. All the front teeth were gone, but these could doubtless be replaced, in time, by others. Across the lad's forehead was a black silk bandage, which could be removed later, and in his pocket there was an address from which artificial eyes might be purchased. (159–160)

In this case, "the science of healing" overlaps with (rather than opposes) the "science of destroying." Latter-day Frankensteins engaged in the construction of a completely "artificial" being, the doctors prolong war's destructive consequences without worrying that inside this "wreck" there is still a human being so desperate as to implore his father to kill him ("Kill me, Papa." [160]).[9] La Motte is clearly incensed by this monstrous side of medical practice, and she attacks it again in "A Citation," writing about a surgeon "bent on making a reputation for himself, and this consisted in trying to prolong the lives of wounded men who ought normally and naturally to have died" (172). Rather than being concerned with the welfare of his patient (a soldier with a typical wound in the abdomen), the doctor wishes to keep him alive, even though that means "prolonging his suffering over a considerable portion of time" (172). Like many of the physicians described by La Motte, this one as well cares only for his "reputation." What is even worse—especially in light of what would take place years later in the extermination camps—is that no one objects to these inhuman experiments because Grammont, the wounded soldier, is a so-called *apache*: a "criminal" forced into the army who "had no life to return to, that was the trouble" (174). Turned into a human guinea pig, Grammont is subjected to three months of cure that amount to "three months of torture" (176).

Women and Wives, Men and War

La Motte betrays no anxiety in treading upon a traditionally masculine territory. When she rounds off her description of "the backwash of war" with the statement "This is War," she rejects the position of the subject who is not supposed to know war, insisting that a woman is also capable of defining the substance of a supposedly exclusively masculine practice. La Motte does not excuse herself for entering a "forbidden zone." Right from the book's introduction, she claims to have an important alternative viewpoint on martial matters, arguing that in every war there are always two sides: the "noble," glamorous side offered by propaganda and patriotism, and the squalid, foul-smelling, revolting side she calls "the backwash of war." Until now, literature privileged the former; it is time to look more closely at the latter.

> There is a dirty sediment at the bottom of most souls. War, superb as it is, is not necessarily a filtering process, by which men and nations may be purified. Well, there are many people to write you of the noble side, the heroic side, the exalted side of war. I must write to you of what I have seen, the other side, the backwash. They are both true. (112)

It is probably no accident that this passage is part of "Women and Wives." This story occupies a central position in La Motte's volume not only structurally but also symbolically. In it La Motte sketches an analysis of war that moves from some fundamental intuitions regarding its classist as well as gendered nature. Unlike most of the other stories, "Women and Wives" does not focus on the soldiers' lacerated bodies but on the moral and material wounds inflicted by an aggressively patriarchal culture on women's minds and bodies. The story opens during a relatively quiet scene, when "one of the patients showed the nurse a photograph of his wife and child, and in a moment every man in the twenty beds was fishing back of his bed, in his musette, under his pillow, for photographs of his wife" (106). Also in this story La Motte looks at reality from multiple perspectives and suggests a number of erroneous interpretations that are eventually taken apart in the closing lines. Initially, the writer's tone is nearly pitiless:

> Pathetic little pictures they were, of common, working-class women, some fat and work-worn, some thin and work-worn, some with stodgy little children grouped about them, some without, but all were practically the same. They were the wives of these men in the beds here, working-class wives of working-class men—the soldiers of the trenches. Ah yes, France is democratic. It is the Nation's war and all the men of the nation, regardless of ranks, are serving. But some serve in better places than others. The trenches are mostly reserved for men of the working class, which is reasonable, as there are more of them. (106–7)

The point of view initially adopted by the narrator is an intentionally detached one. Aesthetically, the pictures of the soldiers' wives are all equally "pathetic." Yet the observation that the consumption of these women's bodies—whether thin or large—is caused by presumably backbreaking labor introduces a socially minded perspective. The sentence immediately following links the uniformity, both metaphorical and literal, of these proletarian wives to that of their husband-soldiers. In this way, the daily work of these women is equated to the literally body-breaking duties performed by uniform-wearing proletarians. War thus stands out not only, as we shall see in a moment, as a massacre of proletarian armies subjugated by opposing yet similar nationalistic ideologies but also as a veritable Clausewitzian prosecution of politics through other means—in this case, as the prosecution of a politics of brutal capitalist exploitation.

The passage ends with an ironic consideration of the "democratic" nature of the ongoing "Nation's war." The trenches are large and it is therefore "reasonable" that they should be filled with working-class people, since they make up the majority of the population. At the same time, however, the narrator tells us that there are "better" places where one can serve the motherland—places where the chances of surviving are much higher. The rhetorical strategy employed by La Motte, here as elsewhere, is typically Swiftian. By adopting a viewpoint foreign to the working class itself, the narrator allows language to betray its ideological bias. Why, if the nation is indeed democratic—and therefore must be governed by the majority's will—would millions of citizens willingly decide to fight in the trenches when there are less risky occupations? In a few sentences, La Motte effectively sketches the moral and political tragedy of the Great War. A democracy that is healthy (from both a mental and an institutional point of view) would never agree to an armed conflict of such proportions. If a "democracy" behaves so illogically, it is seriously ill, and the causes of this illness lie with a class dictatorship for which the "democratic" state functions as a mere cover-up.

La Motte's critique highlights how militarism mobilizes *both* gender *and* class discourses. As elsewhere, the narrator relies on sarcasm, by noting the wounded soldiers' pathetic, nostalgic attachment to their "little, ugly wives, the stupid, ordinary wives," who soon turn out to be metaphors for a longing to return to civilian life, so that "the words home and wife were interchangeable and stood for the same thing. And the glories and heroisms of war seemed of less interest, as a factor in life, than these stupid little wives" (107). Insignificant from a martial viewpoint, these "little, ugly wives" are in fact far more attractive to soldiers than the glory supposedly available on the battlefield. To the blind devotion to the motherland—often presented by propaganda either as a phallic mother calling her sons to martyrdom or as a figure charged with a destructive and vampire-like eroticism—these men prefer wives who may be lacking in sensuality but are inseparable from a domestic sphere that guarantees a "life" and a "home" impermeable to the lure of "heroism."[10]

The sympathy which, albeit silently, is extended to these "men without women"—in Hemingway's phrase—takes on vague sentimental contours when the narrator discovers that the chief orderly Armand is married, and the mail he always anxiously awaits is from his wife. Simon, the young surgeon, despite his Teutonic appearance ("six feet of blond brute," 108), also has "something finer, something tenderer, something nobler, to distinguish him from the brute." He often talks to the narrator affectionately about his three children and his wife, to whom he always remembers to send a "small surprise or present." Behind all this, as the narrator explains, lies the fact that while "on various pretexts" several women manage to enter the "War Zone," wives are never allowed to come near it.

> Wives, it appears, are bad for the morale of the Army. They come with their troubles, to talk of how business is failing, of how things are going to the bad at home, because of the war [. . .]. They establish the connecting link between the solider and his life at home, his life that he is compelled to resign. Letters can be censored and all disturbing items cut out, but if a wife is permitted to come to the War Zone, to see her husband, there is no censoring the things she may tell him. So she herself must be censored, not permitted to come. (110)

Even though the army undergoes long periods of "active inactivity," wives are victims of a "censorship" that is not concerned with *morals* but only with the soldiers' *morale*. Wives, in fact, "mean responsibility" (111) and must be kept at a distance from the troops. This is not to say that all women endanger the functioning of the war machinery. On the contrary, the narrator knows "there are plenty of women" around soldiers because while *their* wives are forbidden from entering the war zone, "*other people's* wives may come. It is not the woman but the wife that is objected to. There is a difference. In war, it is very great" (110, emphasis added).

From this point onward, the story's perspective changes radically. So far, the reader has been led to believe that men are the main victims of war. Suddenly, however, we realize that the soldiers' position—and in this case class differences appear less relevant than gender differences—is much more contradictory than we suspected, and the principal victims of army-sponsored sexual politics are those women who "mean distraction and amusement, just as food and wine. So wives are forbidden, because lowering to the morale, but women are winked at, because they cheer and refresh the troops" (111). The state of war is revealed as a carnivalesque suspension of everyday rules at the expense of a socially weaker subject.[11] Moreover, the exploitation of women within the military world lies on a continuum with their everyday-life oppression. "After the war, it is hoped that all unmarried soldiers will marry, but doubtless they will not marry these women who have served and cheered them in the War Zone. That, again, would be depressing to the country's morale" (111). The narrator unravels the "paradoxical" situation dialectically. Everything has two sides, like the one-franc coin with the Liberty-Equality-Fraternity writing on the one side, the much less promising image of the reaper on the other. Just as there is "a dirty sediment at the bottom of most souls" (112), there is also something rotten at the bottom of all ideals of "purity" and nobility mobilized in war. To this rotten core, as we have seen, La Motte gives the name of "the backwash of war," and it is worth noticing that, in the story under discussion, the abject part the martial ideology must repress takes the form of the woman's exploited body. "A rose is a fine rose because of the manure you put at its roots" (111). The romantic idealization of women (as "roses") sublimates and hides the ravaging of their bodies (as "manure"). The role a world at war assigns to women is not that of mothers (and wives) capable of generating new forms of life but that of "manure" of the nation. In this latter role, women are metaphorically associated with the millions of men killed in the Great War, whose bones would later be used literally as fertilizers. In one stroke, La Motte highlights the twin reification of men as cannon fodder and of women as flesh for entertainment.

Having exposed the duplicity of the military and patriarchal logic, the narrator takes a second look at the "tenderness" with which some of the men think of their distant wives. Though he anxiously awaits his wife's letters, Armand has no qualms about carrying on a relationship with a nearby village girl. Even Simon, the blond surgeon, has a young girl to entertain himself with. The narrator therefore wonders, "Why should we all be bored with tales of Simon's stupid wife, when that's all she means to him?" (113). Also, the hospital's *Gestionnaire* travels twelve miles every evening to meet up with a woman, and even the sixty-four-year-old doctor, with grandchildren and his Legion of Honor, has a fourteen-year-old lover. We are now in a better position to understand why the narrator chooses to describe the soldiers' wives as stupid and pathetic—by so doing she takes on the implicit point of view of the soldiers themselves, who value them so little and are ready to partake of other people's wives as if they were food or wine. As is the case with Simon, what La Motte finds shocking is that male hypocrisy is so ingrained that it may not even be perceived as such by the men. Like Simon, most soldiers are simply oblivious of the paradoxical, farcical, and crazed nature of their behavior.

In the last pages of the story, La Motte denounces how the moral duplicity of patriarchal discourse overlaps with that of nationalist propaganda. After observing how war ruins hundreds of girls who, before the war, were "decent girls," the narrator once again sarcastically dons the mask of the "respectable" outsider and explains how it is well-known that girls are easily seduced by men, especially men in uniforms, with their "gilt buttons and braid." "It's not the men's fault that most of the women in the War Zone are ruined. Have you ever watched the village girls when a regiment comes through [. . .]? Have you seen the girls make fools of themselves over the men?" (114). Here the narrator seems to blame women for being so foolish as to fall for the glamour of martial power. In fact, however, La Motte wishes to lay bare the true ideological nature of the warrior's appeal by juxtaposing the *romance* of the soldier-knight to the reality of sexism, and by attacking the double standard according to which women are first an object of desire and later no longer acceptable as wives. By arguing that if in that particular war zone the army has not resorted to the "professional prostitutes from Paris," it is only because of the availability of local girls, the story equates the two forms of sexual exploitations. Moreover, the narrator's considerations unambiguously clarify that while some girls may be so foolish as to fall for the glitter of the masculine symbols of power, ideological seduction is underpinned by a cynical and brutal system of coercion. Sticking to her ironic point of view, the narrative voice notes that, obviously, "across the lines, back of the German lines, in the invaded countries, it is different. The conquering armies just ruined all the women they could get hold of. Any one will tell you that. *Ces sales Bosches!* For it is inconceivable how any decent girl, even a Belgian, could give herself up voluntarily to a Hun! They used force those brutes!" (114–15). Here La Motte dissects the antinomy on which the patriarchal-nationalist ideology rests. In order not to contradict the idea that the Germans are merciless Huns, it is not possible to envision that some women may have willingly coupled with the invaders. However, while it is argued that "over there, in the invaded districts, the Germans forced those girls," on *our side* things are said to be different. "Here, on this side, the girls cajoled the men till they gave in. Can't you see? You must be pro-German!" (115). La Motte's strategy is quite clear. Either the Germans are not the rapist Huns described by the French propaganda, or "our" soldiers are in fact "brutes" whose treatment of women hardly differs from that characterizing their enemies. Once again, La Motte's rhetorical strategy must be understood as a political assault on the binary oppositions structuring the masculine logic of war. In this case La Motte—more explicitly than in most of her other stories—calls into question the opposition between the two enemy armies in order to attack their common brutality against women, who "are all ruined and not fit for any decent man to mate with, after the war" (115).

The concluding lines of this crucial story sum up what might be defined as a feminist reading of World War I. Some of these women appear particularly dangerous not because they may transmit to "our" soldiers some venereal disease but because they may work as spies for the enemy. The narrator relates the story of two very intelligent and beautiful girls who would entertain only officers, to whom they would pose many logistical questions. Since "when a man is excited will answer unsuspectingly any question put to him" (116), these young women gathered very useful information, which they later passed on to the enemy. The story thus far seems to confirm all the worst stereotypes about the unreliable, treacherous nature of women and the moral and political danger they incarnate. However, when the girls' spying is finally uncovered, we come to know that the young women's families were held hostage by the German army and that they were blackmailed "with threats of vile reprisals upon their families if they did not produce information of value" (117). The story provides an allegorical key to the entire narrative. The Germans realize that, because they are particularly attractive, these two girls would end up being reserved for the officers. What initially appears as female weakness vis-à-vis gallant men in uniforms turns out to be the product of a male violence always at hand whenever more "peaceful" means of seduction and subjugation fail. However, aware that this episode may in turn be decoded as a clichéd example of German cruelty, the narrator ends her tale with a penetrating observation. After ironically reiterating the viewpoint that situates all brutality in the enemy camp—"They are very vile themselves, these Germans"— she wonders about an aspect of the story she finds "curious" and surprising: "How well they understand how to bait a trap for their enemies. In spite of having nothing in common with them, how well they understand the nature of those who are fighting in the name of Justice, of Liberty and Civilization" (117–18). La Motte reminds us how fictitious the opposition between the two warring sides is, since it relies on the demonizing of an enemy whose barbarism is nothing but a mirror image of one's own violence. She also shows how such symbolic economy is based upon a campaign of systematic devastation of women's minds and bodies, especially of those in a socially and economic weaker position. Read from this perspective, war appears as an absurd context between two enemy camps marked by a common brutality quite evident in the treatment of women of all classes and nations. The war in the trenches thus stands out as a kind of smokescreen that hides from view the daily war that a multitude of brutal men—regardless of their nationality—conduct against women.

From the viewpoint of literary history "Women and Wives" may be read as a vigorous polemic against the notion that the Great War gave women an opportunity for emancipation that resulted from the upheavals caused by the mobilization of millions of men. If on the home front many women had a chance finally to join the work force and thus make significant gains on the social level, the fact remains that "the battlefront—preeminently a male domain—takes economic and cultural priority" (Higonnet et al. 6). This is why Margaret and Patrice Higonnet prefer to employ the metaphor of the "double helix" to describe the paradoxical condition of both "progress and regress" which, in their view, characterized the social as well as symbolic status of women during the two world wars. In a world at war, the material condition of women is always destined to change, but the relations of domination and subordination do not disappear. On the contrary, there are situations in which such relations are not only confirmed but actually reinforced by the martial logic. La Motte's story is particularly effective in that it sheds light on how the subjugation and sexual exploitation of women are part of a martial ideology that rests upon the demonization of the enemy. From the viewpoint of social realism, "Women and Wives" represents a specific condition experienced by women whose lives were directly and all too often brutally affected by military operations. On a symbolic plane, the story is fully consistent with the subversive project pursued by La Motte in her book as a whole. The distinction between "women" and "wives" showcased by the title turns out to be a fictitious one. From the point of view of the patriarchal ideology investigated by La Motte, the distinction between "good," pure, and idealized women, on the one hand, and "bad," polluted, and dangerous women, on the other, is merely a contingent one. If, on a material plane, the women closer to the front are the ones who suffer the most, on a symbolic and cultural level the distant wives—who may at first appear to occupy a privileged position—are equally subjugated. Ellen La Motte is capable of detecting in her personal experience as a nurse the signs of moral, social, and political problems of universal significance, as she deftly interweaves her stories with History. If it is unlikely that the Lamp lit by her writing may bring us any consolation, its light allows us to see the Great War and, more generally, the material and psychological wounds of "War" with a clarity that, while extraordinary in 1916, has not lost its force even today.

CHAPTER 7

Waging War on the Sacred

William Faulkner's *A Fable*

Who cares what the fact was, when we have made a constellation
of it to hang in heaven an immortal sign? [. . .]
"What is history," said Napoleon, "but a fable agreed upon?"
—Ralph Waldo Emerson

If God's on our side
He'll stop the next war
—Bob Dylan

Christ: Martyr or Rebel?

The July 1916 issue of *The Masses*—one of the most influential American left-wing periodicals of the time—featured a drawing by Boardman Robinson titled "The Deserter."[1] On its left side, enveloped in a white tunic, Jesus faces a firing squad comprising soldiers from all the belligerent armies taking part in the Great War. Many war propaganda posters featured Jesus in khaki sighting down a gun barrel (Ehrenreich 205). Robinson pictured Jesus as a war deserter. It is unlikely that William Faulkner had this illustration in mind when, decades later, he started thinking about *A Fable*. According to the book's acknowledgments page, the inspiration came from film director William Bacher and movie producer Henry Hathaway during one of Faulkner's Hollywood stints as screenwriter. Probably Faulkner drew also, in part, on Henry Cobb's *Paths of Glory* (1935), the World War I novel eventually rediscovered and made famous by Stanley Kubrick's 1957 movie.[2] Yet, though Faulkner is commonly considered a political moderate if not an outright conservative, his war novel shares the same key idea displayed in Robinson's drawing. Whoever

Boardman Robinson, "The Deserter." *The Masses*, July 1916.

opposes war imitates Christ, but those who imitate Christ are considered, by the powers that be, as nothing but deserters, and they must be put to death. Jesus returns, and the nations at war are quick to crucify him anew.

The recipient in 1955 of both the National Book Award and the Pulitzer Prize, *A Fable* is hardly a favorite among Faulkner critics. Many contemporary reviewers found both its Gospel analogies and its theology unsophisticated.[3] Later critics often concurred, arguing that the abundance of anti-realistic elements ultimately undermined Faulkner's project. Paradoxically, however, the more Faulkner moved away from verisimilitude, the more he got closer to the real. Notwithstanding the implausibility of the story, in which a *figura Christi* leads the mutiny of a French battalion, the allegory suggests an ethical and political moral that, in the eyes of many critics, makes the text cheaply didactic. It is probably no accident that what remains to this date the most detailed study of the novel—Keen Butterworth's *A Critical and Textual Study of Faulkner's* A Fable—is an attempt to show that, far from being an attack on war, *A Fable* actually offers a tragic portrait of the limits of idealism. In Butterworth's view, Faulkner's text is implicitly supporting rather than criticizing an authority figure like the Marshall, who is willing to sacrifice his son in order to "save civilization."

More recently, *A Fable* seems to have found a small but impressive group of admirers. Richard Godden, Noel Polk, and Joseph Urgo have contributed in decisive ways to a more adequate understanding of a novel that may well have its flaws but should neither be dismissed as a wooden allegory nor defended by jettisoning its political content.[4] In particular, there is much to learn from Urgo's reading, which sees *A Fable* as the major text of Faulkner's "apocrypha," a group of late works aiming—like the apocryphal Gospels—at contesting the "canonical" versions of reality. After noticing that criticism has generally attacked Faulkner for rewriting the Passion story under the guise of an episode from World War I, Urgo retorts that "the corporal in *A Fable* is not a *symbolic* Christ, nor is the story an *allegory* based in the life of the historical Jesus. The reason critics find that the symbolism does not work in *A Fable* is because there is very little symbolism in it. In the spirit of a gnostic gospel or other New Testament apocrypha, *A Fable is* Christ's life, not symbolically or allegorically, but apocryphally. . . . The corporal is not *like* Christ. . . . Rather, the corporal *is* Christ, and the story *is* the story of His last days on earth—not the historical Christ, but an apocryphal Christ" (95). I find this interpretation largely correct. If we return for a moment to Boardman's drawing, we immediately realize that its polemical sting lies precisely with the fact that the man dragged in front of the firing squad is not a figure that allegorically or symbolically reminds us of Christ, but is *Jesus himself.* The firing squad, which includes representatives from all the warring armies, is not about to shoot a man who is *similar* to Jesus but Jesus in flesh and blood. Boardman's Jesus—to remain within Urgo's terms—is therefore "apocryphal" as much as Faulkner's. And he, too, like Faulkner's Jesus, is offered to us "as a model of rebellion and insurrection against authority" (Urgo 104).

Though I agree that with *A Fable* Faulkner tries to renovate our faith in the Scriptures "by supplanting Christ as a figure of authoritarian control and by replacing the martyr with the rebel" (105), there is one problem with the interpretive key proposed by Urgo. The reason we recognize the figure of Jesus in Boardman's drawing is, quite simply, that it matches Christ's iconic traits as these have been preserved by cultural memory. If the deserter in front of the firing squad wore a regular uniform and short hair, who would be able to guess that the man is Jesus? Analogously, if we are able to read in a certain way what happens to Urgo's "apocryphal" Jesus, it is only because we are already familiar with an "official" story that inevitably guides our perception of the events. In other words, Faulkner's writing can be "apocryphal" only in a figurative sense because its aim is not so much that of offering us a different version of the life and preaching of the historical Jesus as that of rewriting in a *contemporary* setting the traditional story we already know. By rethinking the story of the Passion as a war story, the novel criticizes both the ideology of war and those readings of the Scriptures that sustain the theory and the practice of war. The two sides of Faulkner's literally *desecrating* critique run parallel to each other. The critique of war—at least in the "Christian" West—requires a critique of traditional reading protocols of the Gospels, and, conversely, only a radical critique of war and violence can inaugurate a truly "subversive" reading of Jesus' story.

To sum up: a certain "allegorical" dimension is intrinsic to the text because, in reimagining the Passion story as a World War I tale, Faulkner automatically reinterprets the canonical Gospels and, most important, calls into question the hegemonic readings of his time (and of our own time as well). His act of rewriting can only be an act of distancing, and hence an allegorizing, of the preexistent text. While Urgo's interpretation shows how a new way of looking at Jesus' story can provide the basis for a penetrating critique of war, it leaves in the background the reverse of such rhetorical strategy, in which a war story unmasks the readings of the Scriptures that have historically sustained the Western martial ideology. Boardman's drawing not only denounces the bloodthirsty and anti-Christian spirit of the "Christianized" West; it does so by resorting to a polemical use of the central figure whom belligerent armies prayed to in order to be blessed with victory and protection. Similarly, *A Fable* does not simply fuse together an "apocryphal" tale and a war story but forces the reader to rethink the Gospels of tradition from the point of view of the critique of war and violence, thereby making possible a counterreading of Jesus' story. In particular, as Urgo argues, mainly through the words of Marthe, the corporal's sister, Faulkner poses the crucial question of what kind of God may require the death of His son as an instrument of salvation, as well as "what kind of God would also destroy the Son to preserve the Father's authority" (121–22). By building on this fundamental insight, the present chapter investigates the sacrificial logic of historical Christianity unveiled by Faulkner's novel. By staging the Passion story within a theater of war, Faulkner not only voices his anxiety vis-à-vis a world devastated by two global conflicts and, after Hiroshima, technically capable of self-destruction, but, perhaps most important, he also shows that in order to abolish war one must first confront the intrinsically violent nature of the sacred.

Since my thesis is that the novel underscores the equivalence between violence and the sacred by juxtaposing to a sacrificial reading of the Gospels an anti-sacrificial interpretation, it will be necessary to explain briefly the meaning and interpretive significance of these two terms. The idea that the story of the Passion culminates in the "sacrifice" of Jesus is a largely accepted one, but the extent to which the human sacrifice described in the Gospels can be distinguished from the ones central to pagan rituals and mythologies is much debated. According to René Girard's well-known thesis, all sacrifices ultimately spring from the scapegoat mechanism, thanks to which human communities keep under control the risk of internal turmoil that periodically threatens to tear them apart. Once a victim whose social marginality underscores its "monstrous" features has been selected, the community can redirect its violence on this "legitimate" target, and the social crisis is overcome in a display of the violence of all against one. In Girard's view, myths, rituals, and all religious thought spring from this "generative violence." Burdened with all the sins of the community, the designated victim is later transformed into a savior and his death hailed as a sacrifice—that is, as an act that literally (*sacer + facere*, "to make sacred") brings into existence the sphere of the sacred, whose objective is to shield the community from further outbreaks of violence. Here it is not important to discuss up to which point this theory may be universally valid, as Girard would have it, nor need we examine the many objections raised against it.[5] What is worth emphasizing is that such violent origins seem to be shared by Christianity given that, as acknowledged by Girard himself, the story of Jesus bears a striking resemblance to those narrated in several pre-Christian mythologies. There is, however, a crucial difference separating the latter from the Gospel story. Whereas the scope of mythology is to highlight both the guilty and redeeming nature of the victim, whose persecution is seen as just, the Gospels are written from a completely different point of view. Jesus is *not* guilty, and the story is not told from the perspective of his persecutors, as is the norm in classical myths. On the contrary, the Gospels proclaim the innocence of the victim and therefore, according to Girard, nothing would be more wrong than calling the crucifixion of Christ a "sacrifice." "There is nothing in the Gospels to suggest that the death of Jesus is a sacrifice, whatever definition (expiation, substitution, etc.) we may give for that sacrifice. . . . The passages that are invoked to justify a sacrificial conception of the Passion both can and should be interpreted with no reference to sacrifice in any of the accepted meanings" (*Things Hidden* 180).[6]

Girard's claim that *nothing* in the Scriptures sustains a sacrificial reading is controversial. The theologian Walter Wink notes that "the idea of the sacrificial, expiatory death of Jesus is far more pervasive in the New Testament than Girard acknowledges." Moreover, the apostle Paul "betrays a certain ambivalence toward the sacrifice of Christ. Girard has stressed one side of that ambivalence, his critics the other. For Paul, Christ is the *end* of sacrificing and the revelation of the scapegoat mechanism. . . . But by depicting him as sacrifice, Paul also gives credence to the notion that God caused Jesus to be a *final* 'sacrifice of atonement by his blood' (Romans 3:25)" (Wink 153). This "confusion" on Paul's part, according to Wink, has unfortunately brought much support to the sacrificial reading of the Passion. Girard himself has at least in part conceded this point, writing that "it is possible to demonstrate that historical Christianity took on a persecutory character as a result of the sacrificial reading of the Passion and the Redemption. . . . Because Christians have been incapable of understanding the relationship of Christ to his own death, they have followed the Epistle to the Hebrews and taken up the term 'sacrifice.' They have only seen the structural analogy between the Passion and the sacrifices of the Old Law, and in doing so they have failed to take into account an incompatibility" (*Things Hidden* 225). Whether one agrees with Girard that the Scriptures have been misread, or else traces the ambiguity within the texts themselves, one fundamental fact remains. All reactionary visions of Christianity are rooted in a sacrificial reading of the Passion. Consequently, no liberating, nonviolent reading of the Gospels is possible unless we insist on the nonsacrificial character of Jesus' death.

A "Pacifist" Novel?

Before analyzing how Faulkner's text concretely stages the clash between the sacrificial and the anti-sacrificial readings of the Passion, it is necessary to confront a preliminary objection. Some readers believe that any reading of *A Fable* as an anti-war novel would run counter to what the author himself wrote in a preface, which, even though it was suppressed by the editor, cannot be dismissed. That Faulkner felt the need to provide his readers with an interpretive key, "as though he feared the text of the novel might not have made his point clear enough" (Blotner, *Biography* 2:1493), is certainly noteworthy. Yet even Faulkner's own words of advice may be read in different ways. Usually, much emphasis is placed on the preface's first sentence—"This is not a pacifist book"—as if to exorcize the thought that a modernist writer par excellence like Faulkner would suddenly decide to write an openly political book. If we read the preface's entire first paragraph, however, it becomes unequivocally clear that if the novel does not amount to a "pacifist" apologue, it is simply because what at the time was commonly identified as "pacifism" struck Faulkner as not being anti-war and anti-military enough.

> This is not a pacifist book. On the contrary, this writer holds almost as short a brief for pacifism as for war itself, for the reason that pacifism does not work, cannot cope with the forces which produce the wars. In fact, if this book had any aim or moral (which it did not have, I mean deliberately, in its conception, since as far as I knew or intended, it was simply an attempt to show man, human beings, in conflict with their own hearts and compulsions and beliefs and the hard and durable insentient earth-stage on which their griefs and hopes must anguish), it was to show by poetic analogy, allegory, that pacifism does not work; that to put an end to war, man must either find or invent something more powerful than war and man's aptitude for belligerence and his thirst for power at any cost, or use the fire itself to fight and destroy the fire with; that man may finally have to mobilize himself and arm himself with the implements of war to put an end to war; that the mistake we have constantly made is setting nation against nation or political ideology against ideology to stop war; that the men who do not want war may have to arm themselves as for war, and defeat by the methods of war the alliances of power which hold to the obsolete belief in the validity of war: who (the above alliances) must be

taught to abhor war not for moral or economic reasons, or even for simple shame, but because they are afraid of it, dare not risk it since they know that in war they themselves—not as nations or governments or ideologies, but as simple human beings vulnerable to death and injury—will be the first to be destroyed. (Quoted in Blotner, *Biography* 1494)

Whatever one wishes to say about this passage, there can be no doubts concerning Faulkner's staunch antimilitarist position. Whether *A Fable* actually conveys his utter dislike of war is, of course, open to question. However, there is no textual basis whatsoever to argue that this paragraph expresses Faulkner's resignation toward the inevitability of war "as long as man remains man," even providing a rationale for the casting of the Marshall as "moral center" of the novel (Butterworth 16). Faulkner states unambiguously that those who see any validity in war hold on to an "obsolete belief," and he attacks those "alliances of power" (perfectly embodied by the Marshall) that insist in seeing war as a way to solve conflicts between peoples, nations, and ideologies. Therefore, what about Faulkner's critique of "pacifism?" Whereas a couple of years later, in his address to the leaders of the civil rights movement, Faulkner stressed the virtue of patience and non-violence, in the preface under discussion the writer sees "pacifism" as unable to deliver any significant political changes.[7] Yet if Faulkner dislikes "pacifism," it is not because he does not desire peace but because "it does not work"—it is no match for the powers that conduct wars. The objection is far from new in its understanding of pacifism as a form of "passivism."[8] The "pacifism" Faulkner criticizes has little or nothing to do with the active and courageous anti-war attitude advocated by the likes of Jane Addams, Tolstoy, Gandhi, and many, many others (see chapters 2 and 3). Moreover, Faulkner's preface explicitly criticizes the Wilsonian idea of "a war to end all wars" when it insists that the notion of "setting nation against nation or political ideology against ideology to stop war" is nothing but a "mistake." Faulkner thus objects to the commonplace idea that it is only thanks to war that human communities get to enjoy peace. But if neither war nor pacifism can "put an end to war," what kind of anti-war strategy does he advocate?

The author mentions two alternatives. Either human beings will prove capable of "invent[ing] something more powerful than war," or else they will have "to arm themselves as for war, and defeat by the methods of war the alliances of power which hold to the obsolete belief in the validity of war." The choice is between, on the one hand, the advent of something like Gandhian non-violence as "the mightiest force in the world" (*Non-Violence* 1:167) and, on the other, a soldiers' armed rebellion against their military commanders. The fact that Faulkner liquidates in one sentence the idea of a force unlike that of war seems to suggest that Gandhi's non-violence (which he claimed to admire) was all right for blacks in the South but not a sufficient power to fight against military elites. A certain deliberate vagueness characterizes also the phrasing of the second resistance strategy. The invitation to soldiers to arm themselves *as for war* and to make use of "the implements of war" in order to abolish war is in contradiction with the refusal of war as an instrument for settling differences among competing nations or ideologies. Also, what does the author have in mind when he refers to the "implements of war"—is Faulkner inciting soldiers to threaten their commanders with cannons, tanks, and grenades? If that is so, then what is it that on a moral as well as a practical plane would distinguish this kind of "war" from War as such?[9]

It would be silly to expect from such a brief text the analytic detail of a full-fledged argument on as complex a relationship as that between peace and war. Faulkner faces the dilemma that all individuals wishing to take a stance *against* war have to confront. To wage war on war, as Faulkner wishes to do, requires one *not* to give up a conflictual position and therefore the rejection of what he identifies as "pacifism." Yet conflict may always slide closer to a form of war. Notice that the writer invites soldiers to mobilize *as for war*—that "as" appears to carry a metaphorical implication and may be seen as an attempt at distancing war without renouncing the right to rebellion. Similarly, with the idea of "fighting fire with fire": Faulkner invokes a homeopathic strategy by resorting to an unmistakable Gospel allusion ("I have come to bring fire on the earth, and how I wish it were already kindled!" Luke 12:49) that may be applied both to war's destructiveness and to the idea of purification. Finally, the term *implements* may also refer to both a martial context and the world of labor. Since an implement is "a means of achieving an end" (*American Heritage Dictionary*) it is not just a synonym for "weapon." A regiment, for example, is as much an "implement of war" as a tank, and Faulkner's address to soldiers could be read as a call to fight against the military from within and therefore by holding fast to the courage and determination we usually associate with the figure of the soldier.

Even if one agrees that the discarded preface is meant to evoke a force capable of transcending both war and resignation, couldn't Faulkner's intention to show "by poetic analogy, allegory, that pacifism does not work," be interpreted as a not-so-thinly veiled reference to the final defeat met by the corporal's rebellion? The preface would thus serve to highlight the distance between the author's philosophy and his central character's strategy. However, though this strikes the military commanders as a "monstrous and incredible" fact, the corporal and his twelve disciples manage to disseminate their anti-war message and, albeit temporarily, they not only stop an attack but they bring the entire front to a standstill. The corporal's "pacifism" is no passivism and, at least for a time, it "works." Moreover, it also inspires the Runner—the character in the second paragraph of the discarded preface whom Faulkner describes as the one who, confronted with the evil that is in the world, does not simply take notice and despair, he decides "to do something about it" (Blotner, *Biography* 1495). In other words, it is by no means clear that the ineffectual "pacifism" stigmatized by Faulkner should be identified with the corporal. On the contrary, as mentioned in one of his letters, the writer equates Jesus to "some movement in mankind which wished to stop war forever," identifying Christ with a radical impulse that is far from being acquiescent.

Violence and the Sacred

Not only does Faulkner de facto agree with Boardman Robinson's thesis that if Jesus were to return in a world at war he would necessarily be a deserter. In the Scriptures, Christ is crucified by a *pagan* imperial authority. In *A Fable*, the corporal is sentenced to death by the representatives of a self-proclaimed *Christian* civilization. From this perspective the new crucifixion is more scandalous than the original one, as it registers the failure of the historical mission of Western Christianity. As illustrated by Robinson's drawing in *The Masses*, World War I was a betrayal of the so-called "Christian roots" of European culture. Notwithstanding the minority voices of Christian pacifists, all the National Catholic Churches of Europe as well as the Protestant ones, rather than trying to halt what Pope Benedict XV himself described as a "useless slaughter," rallied to the support of their respective national governments, blessed the troops, and reminded citizens of their "sacred" patriotic duties.[10] The novel's antireligious polemic does not invest only the priest who visits the corporal on the night before the corporal's execution and whose words underscore the Church's support of the violence of the state. *A Fable* goes beyond the targeting of specific religious institutions by suggesting that, as Walter Wink has said, "All war is metaphysical; one can only go to war religiously" (26). A sacred dimension is always present at the heart of any war and this is why Faulkner's decision to rewrite the story of Jesus as a war story is so important and worth attending to.[11]

The mythical aura enveloping many of the stories of the Great War—from the diaries of participants to newspaper accounts and propaganda to "literature" proper—may be seen as springing from the intrinsically religious nature of the martial experience. As Fussell notes, legends like the ones on the "Angel of Mons" appearing in the sky to protect the British retreat in August 1914 are examples of a military folklore trying to assign meaning to a chaotic and terrible experience while also invoking a supernatural protection. What needs emphasizing here is the constant recourse to what Fussell describes as "the sacrificial theme, in which each soldier becomes a type of the crucified Christ" (119), a theme central, for example, in innumerable poems on the Great War. "The image of crucifixion was always accessible at . . . the French and Belgian crossroads, many of them named Crucifix Corner. . . . Reminded of the Crucifixion all the time by the ubiquitous foreign calvaries and by the spectacle of uniformed miscreants immobilized and shamed with their arms extended, the troops readily embraced the image as quintessentially symbolic of their own suffering and 'sacrifice'" (118). Bearing in mind both Fussell's observations and the intimate connection between war (both ancient and modern) and sacrifice, the objections often raised against Faulkner for having arbitrarily superimposed an extraneous allegorical framework on the matter of the Great War appear absolutely off the mark. On the contrary, the choice of the Passion as backdrop of the Great War is consistent both with the religious, often specifically Christian discourses circulating among the trenches and with the direction followed by the many scholars who have emphasized the "obscene fascination" of war by focusing on its special relation to the sacred.[12] Finally, as Jonathan Vincent has shown, mobilization in the United States was assisted by the spectacular growth of a body of pro-war literature that not only insisted on the need to sacrifice one's life for the good of the nation but did so in specifically Christian terms, by depicting "soldiers' deaths as splendid reenactments of Christ's crucifixion" (557). Passion imagery was explicitly invoked in tracts and novels like Coningsby Dawson's *The Glory of the Trenches* (1917), where self-sacrifice was seen as the key to national and spiritual regeneration (Vincent, especially 557–64). If we read *A Fable* against this background of sacrificial literature, it becomes difficult to miss the compelling war-resisting reasons behind Faulkner's choice to read the Passion story as delivering a lesson utterly opposite to the one that warmongers found in the Gospels.

In Faulkner's novel, the imbrication of the martial universe with the religious sphere is underlined on various occasions. Take, for example, the emblematic final pages, describing the old Marshal's funeral:

> [F]irst behind the caisson walked . . . the aged batman who had outlived him . . . carrying before him on a black velvet cushion the sheathed sabre, his head bowed a little over it like an aged acolyte with a fragment of the Cross or the ashes of a saint. Then came . . . the unrankable black-banded uniforms of the generals and the robes and mitres and monstrances of the Church . . . in pagan and martial retinue and rite . . . the crowd dividing and humbly behind it to flow away on either side until it had surrounded and enclosed the sacred and dedicated monument. (367)

The comparison of the sword to "a fragment of the Cross" is deeply ironic not only because the participants to the ceremony venerate a weapon as if it were a holy relic but also because, far from being the crucified, the Marshall is the crucifier. The Marshall is the father who puts his deserter son to death. If the cross is the symbol of the victim, the sword—whose shape resembles that of a cross—stands metaphorically for the violence of war and sacrifice. Yet Faulkner does more than highlight the superimposition of a symbol of peace on an icon of war. The funeral scene underscores how the sacred is crucial to the *memory* of war—to its transformation into an object of *devotion*. A religion originating in the identification with the victim and the refusal of violence is disfigured and re-deployed to invoke further sacrifices.[13]

Besides showing the incongruence between militarism and Christian symbology, Faulkner's novel highlights the complete *fusion* of war and the sacred. This is nowhere better seen than in the long passage in which the Marshall, looking out of his window above the city, mentally reviews the world he faces by ordering it hierarchically. I quote only a few key passages of a "catalogue" almost four pages long.

> First and topmost were the three flags and the three supreme generals who served them: a triumvirate consecrated and anointed, a constellation remote as planets in their immutability, powerful as archbishops in their trinity, splendid as cardinals in their retinues and myriad as Brahmins in their blind followers; next were the three thousand lesser generals who were their deacons and priests and the hierarchate of their households, their acolytes and bearers of monstrance and host and censer . . . then the civilians; Antipas his friends and their friends, merchant and prince and bishop, administrator clacquer and absolver to ministrate the attempt and applaud the intention and absolve the failed result, and all the nephews and godsons of Tiberius in far Rome and their friends and the friends of the wives and the husbands of their friends come to dine with the generals and sell to the generals' governments the shells and guns and aircraft and beef and shoes for the generals to expend against the enemy . . . and then and last even anonymity's absolute whose nameless faceless mass cluttered old Jerusalem and old Rome too while from time to time governor and caesar flung them bread or a circus as in the old snowy pantomime the fleeing shepherd casts back to the pursuing wolves fragments of his lunch, a garment, and as a last resort the lamb itself. . . . Out of that enduring and anguished dust it rose, out of the dark Gothic dream, carrying the Gothic dream, arch- and buttress-winged, by knight and bishop, angels and saints and cherubim groined and pilastered upward into soaring spire and pinnacle where goblin and demon, gryphon and gargoyle and hermaphrodite yelped in icy soundless stone against the fading zenith. (202–04)

As Noel Polk has noted, in making military power virtually identical to that of religion, the Marshall takes for granted that "God is as much responsible for the one as for the other: *this is the way things are*"—things are immutable because they reflect a God-created human "nature" (Polk, "Roland Barthes" 111–12). But if the military world and that of the Church mirror each other, the point being made is not simply ideological but political and theological as well. The reference to the figure of Herod Antipas—the one who, according to tradition, had John the Baptist beheaded and who sent Jesus back to Pilate—is from this point of view revealing. The General's world is peopled by the "nephews and godsons of Tiberius" and by a network of merchants and politicians whose progenitor is a vassal of Roman power like Antipas. Contemporary military power is continuous with the imperial power of Rome *at the time of Antipas and Tiberius*—the time, that is, of Jesus' crucifixion. In the Marshall's view, contemporary civilization descends from a society founded on sacrifice and, "blind" to the reasons of the victim, founds its "dark Gothic dream" on a grotesque marriage between "gryphon," "demons," and "knights," on the one hand, and "angels and saints and cherubim" on the other. The references to the "circus" and the lamb left prey to the wolves remind us of the link between power and the sacrificial mechanism, while also confirming that historical Christianity—as the priest will later explain to the corporal—had to ally itself with "Rome" against Jesus, a figure who in the Marshall's vision can only be the designated victim.

It is not enough, however, to insist on the hypocrisy of a power surrounding itself with Christian symbols, even though it must actually trace its origin back to those authorities who crucified Christ. Military violence, like sacrificial violence, presents itself as "sacred" to the extent that it acts as the lance and shield of the community, protecting the community from the chaos of undifferentiated violence. In the words of General "Mama Bidet": "It wasn't we who invented war. . . . It was war which created us. From the loins of man's furious ineradicable greed sprang the captains and the colonels to his necessity. We are his responsibility" (*Fable* 45). Bidet's reasoning sounds like a baroque version of Heraclitus's aphorism—"War is the father of all things, of all things it is king"—and its aim is to turn a man-made phenomenon into a superhuman, divine agency to whom all must submit. Soldiers do not make wars. Wars make soldiers. Paradoxically, though he evokes the notion of "responsibility," Bidet's scope is to deny that human beings can be held responsible for their destiny. As he makes clear in discussing the mutiny with general Gragnon, "We can permit even our own rank and file to let us down on occasion. . . . They may even stop the wars . . . ours merely to guard them from the knowledge that it was actually they who accomplished that act" (65). Bidet's argument is in line with his previous considerations on the "invention" of war. To argue that war originates from an "ineradicable greed" at once internal (it is born of the "loins" of man) and external (it is structured as a superior force to be obeyed at all costs) means exactly to protect men from the knowledge that the cause of war is not Nature or the sacred but man himself.

It is mainly in the characterization of the Marshall—of the figure cast as "God" by the novel's allegorical scheme—that it is possible to detect the exemplary union of war and the divine. Dinnah Pladott is right in observing that, surprisingly, only a few critics "acknowledged the discrepancy between the Scriptural representation of a divine Parent who sends his only begotten Son to redeem the world as a mark of love, and Faulkner's portrayal of a supreme leader who is willing to execute his only son in order to defend an inhuman and authoritarian bureaucracy" (80). If, however, as I have so far argued, Faulkner's intent is to denounce how a sacrificial vision of Christianity is functional to the acceptance of the inevitability of war, Faulkner's choice is absolutely consistent. The sacrificial reading of the Passion, in fact, though granting of course Jesus' innocence, continues to cast him as a scapegoat figure whose task is to redeem the sins of humankind since Adam's fall. This makes of God a divinity whose wrath is placated only thanks to yet another human sacrifice. Consequently, Faulkner makes of "God" a General lording over other generals. If "Christian" Europe was capable of plunging its peoples into a hell like that of the Great War, it could only believe in a God of violence, in a God like the Marshall.[14]

War and Sacrifice

Besides the millennia-old connection between war and sacrifice, Faulkner—who wrote about the Great War just after the end of World War II—could have invoked some significant historical precedents for his allegorical choices. Marshall Pétain, who had already been canonized as the "savior of Verdun" during the Great War, was elevated by some leaders of the Catholic Church to the rank of "savior" of his homeland after the Nazi occupation of France. As Omer Bartov has noted, "The ecclesiastical adulation of 'le Maréchal-Christ' peaked with the German invasion of the Soviet Union in 1941, described by Cardinal Baudrillat as a 'noble common enterprise'" (61). Whether Faulkner was aware of the "divine" title attributed to Pétain, he was certainly conscious of how the language of war was saturated with religious imagery and, more specifically, of how it juxtaposed semi-divine heroes to scapegoat figures. The French cardinals who kneeled in front of the Marshall-Christ (and let me note in passing that I know of no popular blasphemy that can match this Church-sponsored one) were the same ones who continued to evoke, along with the specter of communism, the perennial anxieties of the "Jewish problem" (Bartov 60–63). In *A Fable*, however, the Christ and the Marshall are *not* one. On the contrary, in Faulkner's view the historical mission of Jesus was that of rebelling *against* sacrificial reason.

In *A Fable*, the term *sacrifice* recurs often, and the narrative's intent is always that of unveiling its violent, immoral, and manipulative character. For example, the attack that General Gragnon is supposed to carry out, which fails when his men refuse to leave the trenches, is described in sacrificial terms: "The attack was already doomed in its embryo, and whoever commanded it, delivered it, along with it. . . . [Gragnon] saw at once that this particular attack was intended to fail: a sacrifice already planned and doomed in some vaster scheme, in which it would not matter either way, whether the attack failed or no" (19). In this case, however, the soldiers escape their predestined scapegoat role, which is shifted to Gragnon, "a man who had neither friends nor influence to make people with five stars on the General Staff, or civilians with red rosettes in the Quai d'Orsay, squirm" (19). Gragnon, who would like to put all his mutinous men in front of a firing squad, is aware that he is himself destined to be sacrificed on the altar of his superior Bidet's promotion, due to his socially marginal position. Gragnon's reflections are figuratively and ironically continuous with the very first description the novel gives of the soldiers who led the mutiny:

> They were . . . chained to one another and to the lorry itself like wild beasts, so that at first glance they looked not merely like foreigners but like creatures of another race, another species; alien, bizarre, and strange. . . . Then you saw that four of the thirteen were really foreigners [. . . and] now the crowd itself had discovered that the fourth one was alien still somehow to the other three, if only in being the object of its vituperation and terror and fury. Because it was to—against—this one man that the crowd was raising its voices and its clenched hands, having barely glanced at the other twelve. (13)

The scene is drenched in sacrificial imagery. On the one hand, there is a crowd that is quickly transformed from a "tongueless brotherhood of dread and anxiety" into a furious mob ready to discharge its pent-up resentment on a figure marked, like all scapegoats, by a profound alterity. If all the participants in the mutiny appear so "strange" as to belong to a different race altogether, the corporal stands out as the strangest among the strange and therefore as the obvious target of a mob who deems him responsible for the retribution likely to be visited upon husbands, sons, and brothers. It is significant that Faulkner chose to begin his novel with this scene. The corporal is the man who has done more than anybody else to save the soldiers' lives. Yet as he is dragged in front of a military court, the crowd sees the pacifist corporal as the cause of the violence likely to invest the entire battalion.[15]

Even though Faulkner sets an angry crowd against an innocent scapegoat, he does not paint the former in purely negative terms. If, left to itself, the crowd appears ready to "crucify a bastard the army's going to fix anyway" (186)—a fact well testified by the lynching attempt on the corporal's sisters and wife—Faulkner reminds his readers that the women and the men of the crowd are themselves victims of an analogous, perhaps greater, violence. The citizens advancing toward the *Place de Ville* are a mass "carrying its fragile bones and flesh into the iron orbit of the hooves and sabres with an almost inattentive, a humbly and passively contemptuous disregard, like martyrs entering an arena of lions" (4–5). This passage is noteworthy, especially given the critical tendency to see Faulkner as a writer who feared and despised crowds and masses. Vis-à-vis an ironclad army, the crowd is transfigured from an angry mob into a community of martyrs—of potential sacrificial victims. The irony of the situation derives from the crowd's inability to become conscious of its own victimhood. The people, rather than supporting the corporal's rebellion, prefer to vent their rage against the sacrificial lamb offered to them by the military, who thus keep under control what could become a socially explosive situation. Faulkner's diagnosis goes therefore well beyond an instinctive and ultimately reactionary fear of crowds by casting light on the power elite's ability to exploit to its own advantage an archetypal human attraction to scapegoating.[16]

From this viewpoint an episode of the Marshall's African experience, occurring years before the Great War, is especially significant. In charge of a desert garrison, the supreme commander-to-be must confront a military and diplomatic crisis. One of his men has raped and killed a woman of a neighboring tribe. The Riff's village chief asks for the life of the offender. If the French refuse to meet his request, on the following day the tribe will attack the fort. The Marshall at this point wily asks for a volunteer who, at night, would sneak out of the garrison and look for reinforcements. As expected, the guilty soldier is the one who comes forward, unaware that the Marshall's plan, explicitly labeled a "sacrifice" (226), is to deliver him into the hands of the Riff warriors, who torture him to death. The Marshall acquires the reputation of a wise commander who saved many human lives by sending only one man to his death. To quote his long-time friend, the captain, "The siege, the investment was lifted: the enemy retired and that sunset the commandant buried its lone casualty [. . .] with a bugle and a firing squad [. . .] and he departed [. . .] leaving nothing behind him but that little corner of France which he saved, to be mausoleum and cenotaph of the man whom he tricked into saving it" (226). The captain's interlocutor objects that the Marshall has nevertheless de facto killed a man, a "human being." The captain retorts that the man in question was nothing but a "murderer" (226). The moral nature of the sacrificed man, however, is not the point. The man is an unrepentant killer, and he is directly responsible for the ensuing crisis. From a juridical point of view, he is anything but innocent. Yet his innocent or guilty status in the case at hand is irrelevant. What counts is that, on a functional plane, the man plays the role of the scapegoat providing the solution to a social crisis and, paradoxically, is transformed from a criminal into the "savior" of that corner of the "motherland." His death is *literally* a sacrifice: an event that makes "sacred"—by turning it into a "mausoleum"—that portion of colonial land.

To many this African episode proves that the Marshall is a man ready to take on terribly difficult tasks. His "trick" is a small masterpiece of realpolitik diplomacy, which though debatable at the level of moral absolutes, prevents a war. The episode, however, also shows that among the "qualities" of the Marshall one that stands out is his ability to deceive and manipulate human instincts. The scapegoat is objectively guilty, yet this can hardly justify the fact that he is sent to his horrible execution unawares. The Marshall's plan foresees that the man responsible for the rape will be the one volunteering for the mission. This, however, is at best an educated guess. Another soldier could very well have stepped forward, and in terms of the Marshall's scheme, it would have made no difference whatsoever. Moreover, the Marshall apparently does not consider the possibility of following standard military procedures, by proposing to the Riff's tribe that he himself find and condemn the offender to death. Instead, he immediately opts for a more brutal form of sacrifice that satisfies the needs of both "civilized" and more "primitive" communities. The soldier's atrocious death is thus the collaborative result of two groups who make peace thanks to the immolation of a designated victim. That the Marshall will follow an analogous strategy with the corporal's rebellion should make us pause. From the point of view of martial rule, the corporal is unquestionably guilty of mutiny. Hence, his execution is justified. Similarly, on a functional level, not only does his death put an end to the rebellion; it also prevents other executions, including that of his own disciples. The analogies between the two episodes are meant, I think, to remind us that notions of "guilt" and "innocence" must always be contextualized and that all sacrifices can always be constructed as pragmatically and even humanely justifiable. On the other hand, the corporal's execution shows how the "peace" gained by sacrificing a scapegoat can only be the prelude to a resumption of war. In Africa, the peace the Marshall safeguards is that of colonial occupation and European imperialism, setting the ground for the enrollment of thousands of African soldiers sent to meet their fate on the battlefields of Europe.[17] Analogously, once the situation on the western front is pacified thanks to the corporal's execution, the war can resume its inexorable course.

"Man's Immortality: His Deathless Folly"

The last part of the novel is the one richest in those allegorical references to the Gospels that have displeased critics. The corporal and his disciples consume a last supper; one of the disciples betrays the corporal; first the Marshall and later a priest try to lead him into the temptation of renouncing his convictions in exchange for his life; finally, the deserter is shot along with two thieves and, as he falls against a fence, his head is enveloped in barbed wire, the modern equivalent of Christ's crown of thorns.[18] His body is then collected by his two sisters and his wife and buried on a farm near the front. An enemy bombardment destroys the tomb and the corporal's body "vanishes"—only to be interred, due to a set of chance events, in the monument to the Unknown Soldier. Five years later, that same "sacred and dedicated monument" (367) becomes the burial ground of the Marshall as well. Even such a shorthand summary should suggest that, though Faulkner bases his story on that of the Passion, the differences between his novel and the Gospels are no less significant.[19] Faulkner's intent is not so much to rewrite the Passion story as to re-imagine the timeless archetype in such a way that it would force us to reconsider its original meaning. From this point of view, the confrontation between the Marshall and his corporal son is of utmost significance. What Faulkner stages is the clash between two irreconcilable, diametrically opposed views of Christianity. One, articulated by the Marshall's words, frames the Gospel story into a sacrificial pattern. The other, embodied in the corporal's stance, insists instead that love and solidarity, not blind obedience to sacred idols, is what Christianity is—or should be—all about.

The supreme General knows he must dish out a scapegoat to both the army and the civilian population. The corporal is the ideal candidate. As his father says, "You caused them to fear and suffer, but tomorrow you will have discharged them of both and they will only hate you: once for the rage they owe you for giving them the terror, once for the gratitude they will owe you for taking it away, and once for the fact that you are beyond the range of either" (290). The Marshall understands the regulative and expiatory function of the sacrifice he is about to perform. The violence generated among civilians by the fear of seeing their dear ones shot for mutiny would find an outlet in his son's execution. This, however, would not extinguish the people's hatred for the corporal, who would continue to be loathed for having first brought terror amid the citizenry and then having saved them from the state's violent reaction. By agitating the specter of a *damnatio memoriae*, the father tries to convince the son to repudiate the reasons for his mutiny. In exchange, the father will not only sacrifice another man in his place, but he will also reward the corporal with limitless freedom and power. Here the confrontation between the two takes on contours that have long perplexed critics. The figure to whom the narrative logic assigns the role of "God" turns suddenly into the Satan tempting Jesus in the desert. The Marshall first offers his son "the earth" by providing him with a car and an official safe conduct. Then he promises his son power "matchless and immeasurable" (295) to the extent that the corporal will one day be even more powerful than his own father. Finally, the old General offers his son life, described as the supreme good whose loss cannot be compensated by any "heaven, salvation, immortal soul." Faulkner's "apocryphal" imagination does not rest content in representing the God embraced by historical Christianity as a Commander-in-Chief and goes as far as to suggest that this divinity is in the end hard to distinguish from the figure commonly reputed to be his ultimate enemy. "God" and the devil appear to be in cahoots like the belligerent armies, whose main worry in Faulkner's novel is not how to defeat one another but how to put down any resistance against war.

More than likely, Faulkner drew his inspiration for this "temptation" scene not only from religious sources but—as Cleanth Brooks (231–32) suggested many years ago—from the famous "Legend of the Grand Inquisitor" featured in the fifth book of *The Brothers Karamazov*. The story that Ivan tells his brother Alëša starts from a premise similar to that of *A Fable*—Christ comes back to earth only to be repudiated by "his" Church—and the charges that the Grand Inquisitor lays at the feet of Jesus are analogous to the ones voiced by both the Marshall and the priest sent to tempt the corporal one last time. The Inquisitor attacks Jesus for his foolish desire of donating freedom to men, praising instead the Church for having "improved upon [His] creation and founded it instead on *miracle, mystery* and *authority*. And men were delighted that once more they were led like sheep, and that that terrible gift which had brought them so much suffering was lifted from their hearts at last" (322, original emphasis). The diagnosis of the human condition traced by the Marshall is nearly identical: he accuses the corporal of having brought "terror" rather than reassurance to the citizens of Chaulnesmont, thereby ignoring that human beings must be ruled by a power ready to exploit their "deathless folly." Moreover, just as Jesus replies with silence to the Grand Inquisitor's allegations, so too does corporal speak only a few words, leaving the stage to the Marshall, who, like Dostoyevsky's Cardinal, praises the institution he represents (and that is founded, like the Inquisition, on the systemic use of violence) for having given the world the only shape it may reasonably take. In particular, in Dostoyevsky's novel the Inquisitor rails at Jesus for not having accepted "the world and Caesar's purple" (323), unlike the Church, which realistically chose to forge a foundational alliance between "Rome and the sword of Caesar" (322). "We ceased to be with You and went over to him a long time ago, already eight centuries ago. . . . We have taken the sword of Caesar, and in taking it, of course, have rejected You and followed *him*" (343–44). *Him* is, of course, the Satan who tempts Christ in the desert. Faulkner thus follows Dostoyevsky's idea about the Church's compromise with the powers that be and, specifically, with violence (Caesar's sword), but Faulkner ups the ante by suggesting that it is the image of God himself that is grotesquely disfigured when Christianity chooses to brandish the sword.[20]

The priest sent to tempt the corporal one more time rehearses the theme of the scandalous alliance between religion and political/military power, so central in Ivan Karamazov's tale:

It wasn't He [Jesus] with His humility and pity and sacrifice that converted the world; it was pagan and bloody Rome which did it with His martyrdom; furious and intractable dreamers had been bringing that same dream out of Asia Minor for three hundred years until at last one found a caesar foolish enough to crucify him. . . . Because only Rome could have done it, accomplished it, and even He . . . knew it, felt and sensed this, furious and intractable dreamer though He was. . . . It was Paul, who was a Roman first and then a man and only then a dreamer and so of all of them was able to read the dream correctly and to realize that, to endure, it could not be a nebulous and airy faith but instead it must a *church*, an *establishment*, a morality of behavior inside which man could exercise his right and duty for free will and decision, not for a reward resembling the bedtime tale which soothes the child into darkness, but the reward of being able to cope peacefully, to hold his own, with the hard durable world in which . . . he found himself. (307–8)

Faith is ridiculed as a "nebulous" and "airy" affair, useful to keep people "dreaming" but utterly useless in a "hard durable," real world that human beings cannot change but only accept as is.[21] Paradoxically, therefore, Christianity spreads in the world thanks only to the means provided by the political and military power of a "Rome" both "pagan and bloody." Yet the priest will show that he himself does not fully believe in his own rationalizations. In a later scene he throws himself at the feet of the condemned man, imploring to be "saved." The priest somehow grasps the truth, though he is incapable of transcending a culture of violence and sacrifice, so that—even after he has admonished the corporal not to be so "proud" as to compare himself with Christ—he will kill himself with a bayonet while thinking of the spear that pierced Christ's flank.

The lengthiest assault on the corporal's "baseless" revolutionary dream comes from the Marshall himself. What makes such attack openly and unmistakably "ideological" is the fact that it is justified as a defense of "man":

"I know that he has that in him which will enable him to outlast last even his wars; that in him more durable than all his vices, even that last and most fearsome one; to outlast even this next avatar of his servitude which he now faces: his enslavement to the demonic progeny of his own mechanical curiosity from which he will emancipate himself by that one ancient tried-and-true method by which slaves have always freed themselves: by inculcating their masters with the slaves' own vices—in this case the vice of war and that other one which is no vice at all but instead is the quality-mark and warrant of man's immortality: his invincible and deathless folly. . . . [Y]ou with your youth could . . . see the day when he will have invented his own private climate and moved it stove bathroom bed clothing kitchen and all into his automobile . . . the entire earth one unbroken machined de-mountained dis-rivered expanse of concrete paving protuberanceless by tree or bush or house or anything which might constitute a corner or a threat to visibility. . . . [B]y that time his wars will have dispossessed him by simple out-distance; his simple frail physique will be no longer able to keep up, bear them, attend them, be present. . . . Then that will be gone too; years, decades then centuries will have elapsed since it last answered his voice . . . when he will crawl shivering out of his cooling burrow to crouch among the delicate stalks of his dead antennae like a fairy geometry, beneath a clangorous rain of dials and meters and switches and bloodless fragments of metal epidermis, to watch the final two of them engaged in the last gigantic wrestling against the final and dying sky robbed even of darkness and filled with the inflectionless uproar of the two mechanical voices bellowing at each other polysyllabic and verbless patriotic nonsense. Oh yes, he will survive it because he has that in him which will endure even beyond the ultimate worthless tideless rock freezing slowly in the last red and heatless sunset, because already the next star in the blue immensity of space will be already clamorous with the uproar of his debarkation, his puny and inexhaustible and immortal voice still talking, still planning; and there too after the last ding dong of doom had rung and died there will still be one sound more: his voice, planning still to build something higher and faster and louder; more efficient and louder and faster than ever before, yet it too inherent with the same old primordial fault since it too in the end will fail to eradicate him from the earth. I don't fear man. I do better: I respect and admire him. And pride: I am ten times prouder of that immortality which he does possess than ever he of that heavenly one of his delusion. Because man and his folly—"

"Will endure," the corporal said.

"They will do more," the old general said proudly. "They will prevail." (298–300)[22]

Can we call "man" the human being destined to "prevail" in the dystopic future sketched by the Marshall? Reduced to mechanical insects enveloped in "armored bodies" worthy of comparison with those Ernst Jünger wrote about in the aftermath of the Great War, these "men" are capable of "prevailing" only by infusing in the machines that have enslaved them the very same "vice," the same "primordial error" afflicting societies since the dawn of humankind.[23] The vice, that is, of war, whose "folly" alone can guarantee men an "immortality" of sorts. As the Marshall has previously stated, "The phenomenon of war is its hermaphroditism: the principles of victory and of defeat inhabit the same body and the necessary opponent, enemy, is merely the bed they self-exhaust each other on. . . . A vice so long ingrained in man as to have become an honorable tenet of his behavior and the national altar for his love of bloodshed and glorious sacrifice" (291). Paradoxically enough, it is the throat-grappling impulse, along with the desire to lord over one's fellow humans that make possible the survival of a "man" ready, when the sun will burn out, to export its madness to some other solar system. War, in the old General's vision, has the same function of Girard's sacred, given that "if it is true that the community has everything to fear from the sacred, it is equally true that the community owes its existence to the sacred" (*Violence and the Sacred* 267). Humankind, as the General admits, is plagued by a "vice" that can be cured only if it is raised to the status of religion. War is nothing but the external "monster" with which man keeps at bay "the very monster which he inhabits."

The "national altar" requires sacrificial victims but the General would prefer to see the corporal renounce his faith rather than execute him. Thus, he proposes a deal to his son, prompted by a logic homologous to the one that in Africa spared him a clash with the Riff tribe. The corporal has been betrayed by a Polcheck (a latter-day Judas), and his father will blame the mutiny on the traducer: "I will take Polcheck tomorrow, execute him with rote and fanfare; you will not only have your revenge . . . you will repossess the opprobrium from all that voice down there which cannot go to bed because of the frantic need to anathemise you. Give me Polcheck, and take freedom" (292–93). The old General is incapable of imagining an order founded on something other than sacralized violence. It is no accident that, in evoking the biblical precedent of Abraham and Isaac ("You even have a substitute to your need as on that afternoon God produced the lamb which saved Isaac" [292]), he does not point to it as an example of how the Lord contains the violence of human sacrifice by accepting the slaughter of an animal. On the contrary, he evokes it to reiterate the image of a violent, bloody God, as shown by a small but crucial textual detail. As Faulkner could not fail to remember, Abraham sacrifices a ram, *not* a lamb. The word "lamb," in the Bible, is used by Abraham to refer implicitly to Isaac. When the son asks the patriarch where the lamb is they must sacrifice, Abraham answers that God himself will provide the offering. By confounding the ram with the lamb—a term which in the biblical story is a stand-in for human sacrifice—the Marshall replicates the logic that leads him to suggest that Polcheck take the place of the corporal, thereby completely overturning the inspiration of the Scriptures where, in however ambivalent a fashion, the sacrificial reason of archaic Judaism is called into question.[24]

The reference to the lamb as the providential victim that "saves" Isaac also foreshadows the sacrificial interpretation of the Passion that Faulkner dismantles. The corporal says explicitly that he does not wish to die (384) and rejects the father's offer not because he is morbidly attracted to the idea of his immolation but because that would entail the betrayal of his disciples. To each of the father's temptations he always responds by mentioning those "ten" who continue, against all odds, to believe in a common cause. They are ten because Polcheck-Judas has betrayed him and Piotr-Peter has temporarily denied him. Piotr's story can be seen as a further proof that Faulkner refused to inscribe his story of the Passion within a sacrificial framework. When the mutineers are first identified, one of them claims to be Pierre Bouc, and since he is not on the sergeant's list, he is temporarily released. Now, *Bouc* in French means "goat," and *le bouc emissaire* is precisely the French term for scapegoat. When the other mutineers are questioned, they claim not to know any Pierre Bouc, as if to figuratively repudiate the role of the sacrificial victim the military hierarchies wish to assign to them. Later, however, we come to learn that the man who has deceivingly taken up this name is not only one of the corporal's followers and fellow countryman, he is the allegorical reincarnation of Peter. Like Peter, this man also repents for having denied his teacher and asks to be jailed again with his comrades: "My name is not Pierre Bouc. I am Piotr—" (300). Also Piotr, therefore, when he is about to rejoin his companions, rejects the role of sacrificial victim symbolically assigned to him by a mistaken surname, printed on his official army documents.

The Scar That Will Not Heal

If war is right, then God is might
And every prayer is vain:
Look not for Christ upon the hills—
He lies among the slain.

—Parke Farley (1914)

While the munity led by the corporal is successful and brings to a temporary halt all military operations on the western front, the Runner's rebellion meets with tragedy from the very start. The elites of the warring armies have secretly met in order to squash by common accord any further mutiny. Thus, when both the allied troops and the German soldiers ignore the attack orders and run toward one another empty-handed, the artillery from both sides mercilessly fires on them. The logic of sacrifice is here applied on a vast scale, to wipe out the dangerous idea that peace may be reached not through war but through a sort of war-strike: "They can't afford to let it stop like this. I mean, let us stop it. . . . If they ever let us find out that we can stop a war as simply as men tired of digging a ditch decide calmly and quietly to stop digging the ditch—" (263). The image of unarmed soldiers who, moving from opposite trenches, come so close as to clearly see their faces and discover they all had "one face, one expression," only to be annihilated by "friendly" fire, would appear to seal the utter defeat of a strategy of non-violent resistance to war. There is no doubt that, after the failure of the Runner-led rebellion and the execution of the corporal, the novel takes on a decidedly somber tone. Yet Faulkner continued to denounce the violence at the heart of the sacred. Let us go back to the concluding scene mentioned earlier. Six years have passed since the end of the Great War, and the Marshall's coffin is about to be interred in the same monument to the Unknown Soldier where, by accident, the corporal's "nameless bones" have ended. Only the readers know that those bones belong to a deserter and hence that "sacred and dedicated monument" is marked by a twofold irony. On the one hand, the body of the soldier who should represent the martial ideals of the nation belongs to the one who has fought strongly against them; on the other, the scene as a whole suggests that the protocols and institutions of official memory are able to cannibalize any challenge brought to the status quo. The corporal's body is indistinguishable from that of millions of other dead soldiers. But to the extent that the body of the corporal is, allegorically speaking, the body of Christ, his being interred in a *military* monument provides a perfect illustration of the argument Faulkner struggles to make throughout the entire novel. The civilization of the "Christian" West not only de facto crucifies Jesus at any new war but also proactively neutralizes his rebellious message by worshipping him in the name of the violence he rejected. In other words, the clash between a sacrificial and an anti-sacrificial reading of the Gospels that is one of the novel's major themes is perfectly summed up in the ironic nature of the Parisian mausoleum to the Unknown Soldier.[25]

A Fable's chilling final pages are shattered by the intrusion of a man or, better, "not a man but a mobile and upright scar, on crutches, he had one arm and one leg, one entire side of his hatless head was one hairless eyeless and earless sear . . ." (368). The Runner, though disfigured by war, has not lost his faith in the corporal's principles and is still capable of uttering his cry of indignation.

> "Listen to me too, Marshall! This is yours: take it!" and snatched, ripped from his filthy jacket the medal which was the talisman of his sanctuary and swung his arm up and back to throw it [. . .]. "You too helped carry the torch of man into that twilight where he shall be no more: these are his epitaphs: They shall not pass. My country right or wrong. Here is a spot which is forever England—"
>
> Then they had him. He vanished as though beneath a wave, a tide of heads and shoulders above which one of the crutches appeared suddenly in a hand which seemed to be striking down at him with it until the converging police [. . .] jerked it away . . . (369)

This scene brings us back to the novel's opening. Once again, an angry mob turns violent against one who has dared to oppose a meaningless war. The Runner is a living scar, and yet the crowd, rather than turning its eyes to the still bleeding wounds of the soldiers, prefers to assault a conveniently marginal and hideous scapegoat, thereby exorcising the violence that has devastated the entire continent.

The Runner's grotesque figure, mutilated by war into a fragment of the human body, may be read as Faulkner's allegorical reply to the "culture of remembrance," which, in the aftermath of World War I, struggled to find a meaning in war's devastations and provide some consolation to the survivors. As Martin Jay argues, one of the great merits of Walter Benjamin was to invoke, against such a mythicization of war, the intransigent use of allegory as a rhetorical figure that "refused to sublimate and transfigure a blasted landscape like that of the war into a locus of beauty, a forest of symbolic correspondences" (227). Benjamin harshly criticizes the consolatory use of religious images by attacking in particular the recourse to the theme of Resurrection, whose aim was to overcome the trauma of war by providing an illusory hope of reconciliation. For Benjamin the dead *should not* rest in peace, "at least as long as they remained in false graves" (Jay 230).[26] In the final scene of *A Fable*, Faulkner counters the "symbolic correspondences" evoked by the commemoration of the Marshall with an allegorical creation analogous to the one discussed in a well-known passage of Benjamin's book on German tragic drama. "Whereas in the symbol destruction is idealized and the transfigured face of nature is fleetingly revealed in the light of redemption, in allegory the observer is confronted with the *facies hippocratica* of history as a petrified, primordial landscape. Everything about history that, from the very beginning, has been untimely, sorrowful, unsuccessful, is expressed in a face—or rather in death's head" (*Origin* 166). The Runner is the Faulknerian equivalent of Benjamin's *facies hippocratica*: a figure destined to remind us not only of the horrors of the Great War but of all wars, and Faulkner is quite right in having him shout, "Tremble. I'm not going to die. Never" (370). As an allegory of all the scars of war, the Runner is destined to live on forever. Analogously, the corporal, himself interred in a tomb that is doubly "false," will not and should not rest in peace. Only his restlessness will keep alive the hope of "a true awakening from the spell of myth and mystification that produced the conditions that led to the war in the first place" (Jay 235).

Against any consolatory transcendence, Faulkner evokes the "immortal" immanence of the mangled human body—an immanence implicit in the word most often applied to the novel's "Christ": *corporal*. While no wholesale escape from the sacrificial culture of war nurtured by the state is possible, a focus on the scars that will not heal may keep alive the spirit of rebellion and nurture a countermemory that may resist the official narratives of war. Against the celebration of victory, the novel points to a counterhistory of defeat shared by all victims of war, regardless of their national belonging. There is no guarantee this resistant narrative may bear fruit. The ending of the novel is bleak, and in calling attention to the state's capacity to feed its sacrificial logic on what should be a quintessential symbol of peace, it may be said to call into question its own status as an imaginary assault on war. If Faulkner's Jesus does embody a resistant spirit, his non-violent tactics work only for a short while and are in the end crushed by the superior force of the state. However, to read the novel as an allegory of the limits of civil disobedience in times of war is to miss its main point. War resistance may take many paths, but to be successful it must come to terms with war's most intimate nature, which is not only political but also—perhaps mostly—theological. War depends on a sacrificial ideology, and we may hope to resist the former only by dismantling the latter. *That* is the novel's most precious insight—an insight we cannot afford to ignore, given that "sacrifice functions as the hinge between religion, war-culture and national self-identity" (Denton-Borhaug 130).

CHAPTER 8

War, Fiction, and Truth

Tim O'Brien's "How to Tell a True War Story"

> A thing may be incredible and still be true:
> sometimes it is incredible because it is true.
> —Herman Melville, *Mardi*

A Postmodern War?

Ever since Fredric Jameson referred to the Vietnam War as "this first terrible postmodernist war," the notion of a special connection between the conflict in Indochina and the rise of both postmodern theory and postmodernity itself has become commonplace.[1] Introducing a collection of essays on this topic, Michael Bibby observes that "the blossoming of postmodern studies occurred in the shadow of that moment when the last Huey lifted off from the U.S. embassy in Saigon, bringing to an ignominious close one of the most heinous chapters in twentieth-century history" (ix). If we shift our perspective from the United States to Europe, we could also notice that all the founders of postmodern theory—from Jacques Derrida and Michel Foucault to Jean Baudrillard and François Lyotard—published their most original works between the arrival in Vietnam of the first American Hueys and the lift-off of the last one on April 29, 1975. This is not to say there is any direct correlation between these two events, as if Parisian intellectuals were storming master narratives and logocentrism in a sympathetic response to Vietcong guerrilla activities in the jungles of the former French colony. As Bibby notes, "the historical and theoretical relationships of postmodernity and the war" are complex and hotly debated. In his own contribution, for example, Bibby takes issue with Jameson's interpretation of the Vietnam War as an expression of postmodernity, arguing instead that, "given that an organized discourse on postmodernism was not widely available until after the war, it seems more historically accurate to read postmodernity as an expression of a post-Vietnam condition rather than the other way around" (xiv). In its suggestion that we see postmodernity as a specifically "post-Vietnam" condition, this view may be a touch too U.S.-centered. It would be hard to maintain that in Western Europe there was no "organized discourse on postmodernism" until the end of the Vietnam War. What can be conceded is that most cultural readings of the Vietnam War and its aftermath are heavily indebted to postmodern theory. The implication seems to be that the reality of a war in which—to quote from the author discussed in this chapter—"the only certainty is overwhelming ambiguity" (O'Brien, *Things They Carried* 88) can be properly told only by resorting to a narrative style cultivating uncertainty, skepticism, and what Jameson describes (in reference to Michael Herr's *Dispatches*) as "a whole new reflexivity" (45).

There is certainly a danger in placing too much emphasis on the notion of Vietnam as a "postmodern war." To quote the Italian critic Stefano Rosso, while Jameson (and many others) may be right in suggesting that postmodernist literary techniques are especially appropriate for representing "a conflict lacking a visible center," "for the most part, even in quite recent works, this 'terrible war' is represented precisely 'in the traditional paradigms of the war novel or movie' and, with very few exceptions, it does not open up 'a whole new reflexivity'" (27–28, 29).[2] As Rosso has shown in his study of Vietnam War narratives, the number of texts marked by "linguistic innovations" is very small. Out of a corpus of literally hundreds of novels and films, only a few can be labeled as postmodern works. By concentrating in this chapter on Tim O'Brien's "How to Tell a True War Story"—a piece from *The Things They Carried* that would at first seem to confirm the existence of a strong correlation between the war in Vietnam and literary postmodernism—I do not wish to discount other representational strategies. However, if we accept Robert Wright's notion that "no other conflict in U.S. history has been burdened so overwhelmingly by the tension between fact and fiction, truth and deception" (303), then "How to Tell a True War Story" may be said to provide us with a wealth of stimulating reflections on that overwhelming tension.[3]

According to Wright, "It is precisely the belief that the *truth* of the Vietnam War is accessible to the powers of rational historical analysis which many literary artists have found to be not only erroneous but contemptible" (215). Yet the title of O'Brien's story suggests that while he too may wonder what kind of "truth" can emerge from the "ineffable, indescribable, finally unrepresentable nature" (Clark 5) of the Vietnam War, he may not find the notion of truth contemptible. His story— which may also be better defined as a mix between a collage of very short stories or vignettes, and an extended metafictional meditation—occupies an uncomfortable position between a postmodernist uneasiness with "truth," on the one hand, and a rational commitment to rules for distinguishing between truth and falsehood, on the other. No matter how skeptical he may be regarding the possibility of delivering through his stories some kind of "truth," O'Brien is equally resistant to postmodernist ideas regarding the alleged fictive nature of the real itself.

In certain respects, as we shall see, the story here analyzed may be seen as embodying some of the philosophical features of postmodernity criticized by Christopher Norris in his well-known polemic against Baudrillard's provocative statement that the (first) Gulf War would not, and had not, taken place. I do not believe, however, that O'Brien thoroughly embraces the most "radical," and to me irrational, positions of postmodern ideology. It is symptomatic, I think, that even Jim Neilson (192–209), who accuses O'Brien of having irresponsibly turned his back on historical reality in order to accept a depoliticized notion of the imagination, agrees with many of O'Brien's admirers in describing him as a postmodern writer. In Neilson's view, however, O'Brien's postmodern aesthetics does not deserve praise for its capacity to bear witness to the "unrepresentability" of war. Neilson sees O'Brien as a writer who, in opposing a "totalizing" account of war, only ends up privileging his personal experience of Vietnam, thereby discounting the conflict's historical and political substance. As I argue in the following pages, even though there are some ideological blindspots in O'Brien's attempt to come up with a definition of a "true" war narrative, "How to Tell a True War Story" is by no means a demonstration of how, for O'Brien, "imagination is virtually the only reality" (as Neilson suggests). No matter how much the writer may insist on the contingent status of truth, his "postmodern" outlook coexists with a vision that is in many respects "Transcendentalist" and as such typical of an important U.S. literary-philosophical tradition that—at least in O'Brien's case—elicits a firm ethical position. The complex and "plural" nature of truth, in other words, does *not* become an excuse for bypassing the moral dilemmas of the Vietnam War.

A True War Story Is Never Moral / All Stories Have a Moral Function

It is not easy to summarize "How to Tell a True War Story," a mosaic of miniature short stories providing O'Brien with points of departure (or arrival) for his theorizing on the art of storytelling.[4] Even though O'Brien conducts his discussion with a certain dose of irony, his overall tone is serious. There can be no question that, his indulging in paradoxes and contradictions notwithstanding, he never forgets the ethical as well as cognitive urgency of the theme he has chosen to investigate. From this viewpoint, it is no sheer coincidence that the story's title carries two different meanings. On the one hand "How to Tell a True War Story" may be paraphrased as "how to narrate a true war story," a title emphasizing the mode in which a responsible and committed storyteller should deliver his or her tale

so as not to contaminate its truth. The title, however, can also be glossed as saying "how to recognize a true, as opposed to a false, war story," and in this case,
its warning would be addressed to the reader not as a potential narrator but as a
listener of war stories. By oscillating between these two meanings, as Rosemary
King has observed, the title invites the reader to take on both roles and therefore
to participate directly in the entangling of "the relationship between fact and fiction" (182). At the same time, O'Brien's word play affects the meaning of "true,"
"a word he uses alternately throughout the story to mean either factually accurate,
or something higher and nobler" (R. King 182). In brief, beginning with the very
title of his story, O'Brien foregrounds the tension between a "strong" and to some
extent transcendental notion of truth and a more conventional, commonsensical
view of what makes a story true.

O'Brien begins with private Rat Kiley's story. After losing a friend who stepped
on a landmine, Kiley writes a letter to his friend's sister—a "very personal and
touching letter" from his heart (75). Rat feels sure he has managed to express his
innermost feelings, but, two months later, he admits being deeply irritated because
"the dumb cooze never writes back" (76). This episode calls the reader's attention to
the communication problems arising between those who experience war firsthand
and those who do not, as well as to the more general problem of what may be the
right way to write a war story—O'Brien's primary focus. His first reflections are
formulated as advice to readers and, implicitly, also to writers and tellers of "true"
war stories. According to O'Brien,

> A true war story is never moral. It does not instruct, nor encourage virtue, nor
> suggest models of proper human behavior, nor restrain men from doing the things
> men have always done. If a story seems moral, do not believe it. If at the end of a
> war story you feel uplifted, or if you feel that some small bit of rectitude has been
> salvaged from the larger waste, then you have been made the victim of a very old
> and terrible lie. There is no rectitude whatsoever. There is no virtue. As a first rule of
> thumb, therefore, you can tell a true war story by its absolute and uncompromising
> allegiance to obscenity and evil. (76)

This passage raises significant interpretive problems. To begin with, it states that
in order to be true, a war story must absolutely restrain from preaching a moral.
The implication here is that, by so doing, it would inevitably aim at transcending
both the logic and the language of war itself. As O'Brien makes clear later on in
his text, while a story has no obligation to realism and verisimilitude, its relation
with war should be rigorously mimetic, though the truth mirrored by a true story
should not be confused with the facts of battles or military strategies. The fundamental truth that literary fiction should register is war's absolute, unredeemable
evil. Any concession on this front would make the reader "the victim of a very old

and terrible lie," as if from war's destruction something good may ultimately arise. This would turn readers into targets of a moralizing ideology, subservient to the logic of those who promote wars.

O'Brien thus sheds light on one of the most insidious and most seductive intellectual lures for readers and writers of war stories alike: that of transforming the text from an attack on war into an implicit justification for it. If, as Ward Just (215) has noted, one writes about war also to exorcize it and to learn to accept that something as terrible as war may indeed exist, war stories in the end would not so much express a hatred of war as something very close to its polar opposite. War stories would be ways to rationalize war's "meaningless" violence. Against such consoling rationalizations, O'Brien invokes a pure, dirty, merciless truth.

My reading of O'Brien's passage stands opposed to his refusal to inscribe a moral within his war stories. My point is that war stories characterized by "an uncompromising allegiance to obscenity and evil" *do intend* to impart a moral lesson to the reader. That lesson may not be self-evident, but, unless a text goes unread, it can never escape interpretation and thus being to a greater or lesser extent domesticated by whatever "moral" the reader will detect in it. However, O'Brien's argument is saturated with moral preoccupations even when considered from the writer's own perspective. It would be hard to imagine a war story with a higher moral and instructive function than one perfectly capable of showing that war can never teach us anything.

It is thus hardly surprising that, in an interview with Brian McNerney, O'Brien develops an argument that turns upside down the one he makes in "How to Tell" regarding the absence of morality in "a true war story." Asked about the effects his war stories are supposed to have on his readers, O'Brien does not deny the moral scope of his storytelling, even though he does specify that the moral dimension or *function* of a war story should never amount to *one* moral. "All stories have at their heart an essential moral function, which isn't only to put yourself into someone's shoes but to go beyond that and put yourself into someone else's moral framework. How would *you* behave in that world? What was the moral thing to do and not to do?" (McNerney 10). To O'Brien the moral scope of any story cannot be traced back to *one* specific message encoded in the text akin to Henry James's legendary "figure in the carpet." The morality of a story lies with its ability to force the reader to meet face to face the moral dilemma(s) of a specific character. In the same interview, O'Brien adds that "fiction in general, and war stories in particular, serve a moral function, but not to give you lessons, not to tell you how to act. Rather, they present you with philosophical problems, then ask you to try to adjudicate in some way or another" (10). A true war story, therefore, though it should not preach a moral, must *be* moral in its substance. Thus while O'Brien emphasizes that his stories are no moral allegories, his desire not to instruct readers is itself a form of instruction. Here, as elsewhere, O'Brien proposes a radical narrative strategy that is inevitably destined to a logical short-circuit. The need to escape from obeying a moral imperative becomes itself a new moral imperative.[5]

A Plural Truth

So far, I have mentioned the main structural weakness of O'Brien's narrative utopia. There is, however, a further contradictory element in his manifesto. Even assuming that a war story could be as "true" as he would like it to be—and therefore treat us to an altogether obscene, undiluted representation of evil—it would be perceived as such only by someone endowed with some notion of goodness. In other words, the elimination of all goodness inside the narrative cannot (and should not!) be matched by its erasure outside the text because, if that were the case, the reader would have no way to judge war as pure evil. To have a thoroughly evil war, you need a reader capable of discriminating between good and evil, regardless of what a true story actually tells. There is, therefore, a serious danger built into O'Brien's storytelling project. If war stories were simply to insist obsessively on the sheer horror of war, they would open an unbridgeable gap between a "sane" reader and the madness that is war. They would turn war into pure Otherness, something incomprehensible or "sublime" in the postmodern, Lyotardan sense of the term stigmatized by Norris in his *Uncritical Theory* (73–81).

Robert Stone, another war writer, comments on the moral complications of this kind of narrative strategy when he observes that "we cannot make it [the evil of war] stop by saying, 'This is not us. This is them. This is him, this is someone else.' No, this is me, this is me. This is my head that's filled with murderousness" (233). Like O'Brien, Stone wants writers to emphasize the "depravity and craziness and weirdness and murderousness" (233) of war, but he also wants them to remind readers that they too are complicit with its horrors. The implications of this point of view are illustrated by the words of Vietnam veteran Ron Faust in a letter to *The Nation* of several years ago. Faust believes that veterans cannot return home "as long as the rest of this country refuses to *let* us come home; that is, not until it faces up to what *we* did as a nation in Vietnam. We will 'finally come home' on the day we can look other Americans in the eye and see there the confession: 'Yes, we did this terrible thing *together*'" (quoted in Clark 5). In short, the representation of war as Other would seriously clash with the therapeutic function of storytelling so dear to O'Brien, and which asks for the reader's imaginative participation in the suffering and devastations of war.

Whether O'Brien realizes these moral dangers, consistent with his belief that "you can tell a true war story by the way it seems to never end" (83) he goes on to refine, complicate, but also outright contradict his original set of rules. "In any war story, but especially a true one, it's difficult to separate what happened from what seemed to happen," he writes. "What seems to happen becomes its own happening and has to be told that way. The angles of vision are skewed" (78). True war stories, then, have no secrets to tell. They offer no path to some hidden truth, and "in many cases a true war story cannot be believed. If you believe it, be skeptical. . . . In other cases you can't even tell a true war story. Sometimes it's just beyond telling" (79). That no language may be adequate to render the monstrosity of war is of course one of the oldest topoi of war literature and one we have discussed at various points in this book. O'Brien, however, considers the problem from the point of view of both the writer and the reader. By calling attention to the fact that a story is always a *production* of the real, not its neutral mirroring, the narrator undermines the reader's confidence in the factual accuracy of the text. If in war many things are almost beyond telling, then we as readers must be skeptical of whatever writers tell us, especially when what they tell us appears to be believable.

In her brilliant critical reading of Michael Herr's *Dispatches*, Evelyn Cobley argues that the novelty of this text lies in Herr's awareness "that facts can never speak for themselves because they are always already somebody's interpretation. . . . Herr cannot trust his eyes. For him meaning does not wait passively to be uncovered; it must be constructed on the same slippery foundations of all fiction-making" (100, 101). O'Brien shares Herr's vision and preoccupations. He insists that war stories, if they wish to be true, must work against our confidence in the notion of objectivity. "For the common soldier, at least, war has the feel—the spiritual texture—of a great ghostly fog, thick and permanent. There is no clarity. Everything swirls. . . . In war you lose your sense of the definite, hence your sense of truth itself, and therefore it's safe to say that in a true war story nothing is ever absolutely true" (88). Moreover, as O'Brien notes a page later, "Absolute occurrence is irrelevant. A thing may happen and be a total lie; another thing may not happen and be truer than the truth" (89).

Puzzled by arguments of this kind, Jim Neilson has accused O'Brien not only of being indifferent to the historical truth of the Vietnamese conflict but also of encouraging a skeptical attitude precluding any possibility of formulating true statements on the nature and causes of the war. If O'Brien is interested in truth, how can he state that the mark of a true war story lies paradoxically in the story's refusal to embrace any absolute truth? To argue that a true war story should reproduce the sense of confusion felt by the "common soldier" in the field, is it not a way to give up preemptively on the possible construction of "an explanatory framework that can choose between competing truth claims" (Neilson 192)? For Neilson, O'Brien's storytelling displays a distrust in the possibility of representing the real analogous to the one Christopher Norris criticizes in Baudrillard's vision of the Gulf War as a hyperreal event. Even though O'Brien does not take as extreme a position as Baudrillard, in Neilson's view *The Things They Carried* fails to provide its readers with a critical perspective on the Vietnam War. O'Brien does not attempt, Neilson says, "to identify those truths about the war that have been obscured by nationalist myth and capitalist hegemony, focusing instead on the processive and paradoxical nature of all truths" (193).

Some of O'Brien's ruminations do echo—whether intentionally or not—arguments made by contemporary postmodernist and deconstructive philosophies. His insistence on the textual nature of any representation could be seen as inspired by Paul de Man's arguments concerning the impossibility of a nonrhetorical construction of truth or by Hayden White's skepticism toward the existence of clear-cut, "strong" distinctions between historiographic and fictional accounts of reality. O'Brien argues not only that we, as readers of war stories, should be satisfied with an indirect knowledge of war given that all most of us can know about war comes from reading or listening to war stories; he adds also that *first-person witnesses* of war, too, can never have access to an unmediated, direct view of what takes place around them. Notice that the term chosen by O'Brien to describe "the great ghostly fog" separating the soldier from the surrounding world is "spiritual *texture*" (88, emphasis added). There is always a text(ure) between the subject and the object, which is why "something can happen and be a total lie" (89). Truth cannot be reduced to objectivity. On the contrary, objective data may at times be deceptive and prevent us from reaching the truth.

All of this is not to say that Neilson is right in condemning O'Brien's allegedly postmodern aesthetics as intellectually paralyzing because, by endlessly multiplying the potential truths of war, it nihilistically relativizes the notion of truth itself. If it can be conceded that for O'Brien there can be no truth without a story, I don't think he wishes to argue that there is no truth except that of the imagination. To repeat what Fredric Jameson wrote twenty or so years ago, it is one thing to acknowledge "that history is inaccessible to us except in textual form" (*Political Unconscious* 35) and another to argue that, since history can be approached only through its prior contextualization, then history as such does not exist. O'Brien insists that reality is usually so complex and multifaceted that it may be amenable to different textual reconstructions; in addition, he realizes that "sometimes it's just beyond telling" (79)—that, in other words, sometimes the gap between the resources of language and a reality that is rigorously nontextual (otherwise it could not be "beyond telling") is too wide. Take, for example, a miniature story inserted in "How to Tell" that narrates the incredible mission of a six-men platoon sent "into the mountains on a basic listening-post operation. The idea's to spend a week up there, just lie low and listen for enemy movement" (79). As the days go by, the soldiers begin to hear a strange music, "like the mountains are tuned in to Radio fucking Hanoi" (80). The longer the platoon is in the jungle, the more intense and unbelievable the noise becomes, until "one night they start hearing voices. Like at a cocktail party. . . . It's crazy, I know, but they hear the champagne corks. They hear the actual martini glasses" (81). On the verge of going crazy, the platoon asks the air force to intervene, and the whole area is flooded with bombs and napalm. The morning after there is a total silence, "not a single sound, except they still *hear* it" (82). At this point the platoon gives up and decides to return to base, and when the soldiers are questioned by a colonel anxious to know what happened, what is that they "heard" up there, "they just look at him for a while, sort of funny like, sort of amazed, and the whole war is right there in that stare. It says everything you can't ever say" (82). The platoon's experience is incommunicable, and it is to some extent enveloped in mystery even for the soldiers who live through it. The exact nature of whatever they heard is simply impenetrable. The noise (or the noisy silence) at the heart of private Sanders's story is the expression of an "absent cause." It defies credibility that in the jungle there may be a cocktail party in progress, and yet that is what the soldiers believe they have heard. Even though O'Brien considers it ungraspable, he by no means erases the referent. Like a famous haiku story in Herr's *Dispatches*—"Patrol went up the mountain. One man came back. He died before he could tell us what happened" (6)—Sanders's story also is meant to call our attention to the limit of what we may be able to know, without, however, arguing that what we cannot understand is therefore nonexistent.

There is a further, perhaps more significant difference between O'Brien's insistence on the textual nature of all truths and what Cobley describes as the "fact/ fiction opposition" (111).[6] As a fiction writer—unlike Herr, whose primary intent is to offer at least in part a journalistic account of the war—O'Brien has no real responsibility to the factual truth of his narration. He may well be skeptical about the existence of some fact and yet continue to believe in a higher truth somewhat independent of factual reality. The story under consideration, after all, is titled "How to Tell a True War Story," and not, say, "True War Stories Can't Be Told" or "No War Stories Can Ever Be True." The story's emphasis would make no sense unless a distinction between truth and falsehood is maintained. In O'Brien's case the impossibility of reaching a final truth does not translate into nihilistic desperation but stimulates a series of endless attempts at storytelling. As he writes on the last page of the story under discussion, "You can tell a true war story if you just keep on telling it" (91). O'Brien, in short, does not argue that his stories are beyond truth and falsehood; if anything, his opposition to any positivist realism and his subsequent choice of the imagination as a privileged tool for communicating truth has more in common with what Alessandro Portelli has described as "the sense of fluidity, of unfinishedness, of an inexhaustible work in progress, which is inherent to the fascination and frustration of oral history" (vii) than with the contemporary glorification of the ontological indeterminacy of the linguistic sign.

In "How to Tell a True War Story," as in most other stories included in *The Things They Carried*, O'Brien raises metanarrative questions either in the first-person or through characters who tell or listen to stories; or—by way of contrast—by focusing on a veteran like Norman Bowker, who is incapable of turning his experience into narrative form (nobody seems interested in listening to him) and ends up committing suicide. In "Notes" O'Brien writes, "By telling stories, you objectify your experience. You separate it from yourself. You pin down certain truths. You make up others. You start sometimes with an incident that truly happened [. . .] and you carry it forward by inventing incidents that did not in fact occur but that nonetheless help to clarify and explain" (180). This is obviously music to the ears of oral historians, whose task is to attend both to real facts and to how those facts are transformed by "the activity of memory and imagination" (Portelli 15).

O'Brien's narratives, however, are written, not oral, and his desire to continue telling a story forever must remain a utopian wish. While an oral historian must always be faithful to a "double truth"—the truth of facts and the truth of their more or less imaginative description—O'Brien can candidly admit that for him "story-truth is *truer* sometimes than happening-truth" (*Things They Carried* 203, emphasis added). The subjective feel of a given experience *may be* superior to what stands out as the objective truth of the situation. Let's take for example two opposite statements that Neilson considers as exemplary illustrations of O'Brien's embrace of postmodern relativism, found in a dialogue that "Tim" has with his daughter Kathleen years after the war:

> "Daddy, tell the truth," Kathleen can say, "did you ever kill anybody [in Vietnam]"?
> I can say honestly, "Of course not."
> Or I can say, honestly, "Yes." (204)

The narrator's answer may at first appear not only utterly indifferent to factual reality but also a way to evade the moral (as well as political) urgency of the question. And yet if we contextualize the dialogue between the narrator and Kathleen, we should be able to see that O'Brien's words are by no means an attempt to occupy a space beyond truth and falsehood. First, we should note that the passage just quoted brings to an end the short chapter "Good Form," wherein the narrator tells us that although he actually served in the province of Quand Ngai, everything he has written so far is made up, including the chapter "The Man I Killed." "I did not kill him. But I was present, and my presence was guilt enough." But a few lines below he deprives the reader also of this certainty: "But listen. Even *that* story is made up" (203). Here O'Brien finally decides to distinguish between "happening-truth" and "story-truth" by placing the two truths next to each other, showing us that "Tim" has killed the young Vietnamese mentioned in "The Man I Killed" only in his imagination. O'Brien, however, has already stated that "story-truth is *truer* sometimes than happening-truth" (203)—his presence in Vietnam is enough to make him a killer, or an accomplice of killers, whether he has actually killed someone or not. It is therefore simply not true that for O'Brien the two truths with which "Tim" replies to his daughter Kathleen are the same. In this chapter, O'Brien provides us with all we need to distinguish between different truth claims. From this viewpoint, it is clear that the meaning of the adverb "honestly," found in both answers, must be understood in relation to the two truths to which it refers. The apparent "honesty" of the first answer relies on the opportunistic, somewhat hypocritical use of what seems to be a hard fact. Many U.S. soldiers in Vietnam may never have directly killed an enemy. Moral honesty, however, should take precedence over "the facts," and it is perhaps no accident that this chapter ends with a clear, "Yes." Far from trying to suggest that both answers are true, O'Brien's story demonstrates not only that it is possible to distinguish between different types and degrees of truth, but also that this interpretive operation is intrinsically *political*.[7]

War with a Thousand Faces

One of the most glaring paradoxes of "How to Tell a True War Story" concerns the recurrent oscillation between the idea of war as an indescribable phenomenon and a vision of war as the nearly inexhaustible source of endless meanings.

> War is hell, but that's not the half of it, because war is also mystery and terror and adventure and courage and discovery and holiness and pity and despair and longing and love. War is nasty; war is fun. War is thrilling; war is drudgery. War makes you a man; war makes you dead. The truths are contradictory. It can be argued, for instance, that war is grotesque. But in truth war is also beauty. For all its horror, you can't help but gape at the awful majesty of combat. (86–87)

It should be superfluous to notice how this passage outright contradicts the one on the total obscenity of war, quoted at the beginning of this chapter. Now the aim of a true war story is no longer that of displaying its absolute evil; on the contrary, "any battle or bombing raid or artillery barrage has the aesthetic purity of absolute moral indifference—a powerful, implacable beauty—and a true war story will tell the truth about this, though the truth is ugly" (87). Even though O'Brien continues to refer to war as morally "ugly," by imagining war as a polysemous reality of which nearly everything might be said, he could be accused of fueling the "absolute moral indifference" attached to the "aesthetic purity" of combat actions. O'Brien's Whitmanian catalogue, in which many incompatible "truths" converge, could be constructed as a way to confuse the reader, who is left without the cognitive tools required to operate rational distinctions.

Before analyzing this problem in some detail, I would like to emphasize that O'Brien deserves praise for his honesty. The narrator frankly admits that it should not be surprising if war, despite its horrible, nasty side, remains a source of excitement and fascination. Though O'Brien himself has privately stated that he does not share "Tim's" appraisal of the "beauty" of war, he has also added that he understands why some people insist on describing war as an attractive experience. The historical record is full of firsthand witnesses—both male and female—waxing lyrical about the strong, intense bonds that wars create among those who take part in them, as well as about the sublime spectacle of destruction offered by many military operations. O'Brien is thus aware that no serious war writer can choose to ignore the disturbing though well-documented aesthetic and emotional appeal of war. As noted by Jean Elshtain, "To turn a blind eye to expressions of love *and* hate for war, wartime, and army life voiced by combatants and noncombatants alike means that, by definition, one will fall short in one's understanding of 'why war?'" (11). There are literally thousands of examples one could give of the emotional intensity that war is capable of inducing.[8] Here I would like to quote the words of a female nurse who served in Vietnam and who emphasized that there is an exciting side of war that has little to do with machismo or bloodthirstiness: "I think about Vietnam often and I find myself wishing I was back there. Life over there was so real and in some ways so much easier. There was no such thing as black or white, male or female. We dealt with each other as human beings, as friends. We worked hard, partied hard, we were a unit. A lot of us, when we left, wished we didn't have to come home" (quoted in Elshtain 10).[9] O'Brien is fully aware that true war stories cannot ignore this utopian side of the war experience. What remains to be understood is whether the narrator's honesty may not turn out to be a way to give war once again an air of, albeit only aesthetical, respectability, which the notion of war as sheer evil endorsed at the outset of the story seemed to have disposed of.

This question may be considered as connected to the notion of war as a supremely contradictory reality. How can a "true" war story communicate to its readers the horror of a war that is at one and the same time sublime? Is it enough to signal that even when "it's astonishing" and "fills the eye" ("How to Tell" 87), war is nevertheless *ugly*? By posing the question in these terms, doesn't O'Brien run the risk of making the "ugliness" of war an empty moral category that is, indeed, at odds with his desire not to preach any moral, but, more than that, also functions as a way to accommodate the chaotic proliferation of an array of apparently irreconcilable meanings? The catalogue quoted above would seem in fact to encourage a morally dangerous skepticism. Take, for example, the two statements "war makes you a man" and "war makes you dead." Set next to each other, the two phrases would both seem to be objectively true. As far as the first is concerned, the experience of war, no matter how devastating, does not exclude in principle the possibility of individual growth. The fact that so many war stories, novels, and memoirs employ, though often in an ironic register, the narrative paradigm of the *Bildungsroman* is an eloquent illustration of this. "A man" is such a generic signifier that could be applied both to the Rambo-type soldier, whose wars never end, and to the veteran who comes to reject war and turns into a committed pacifist. On the contrary, the second statement has a higher degree of objectivity. To quote the historian Giovanni De Luna, "In death we have the defining essence of war" (xvi). Of course to insist on this aspect of war as opposed to, say, its "higher" scopes is to make a political and ethical choice, and therefore the phrase "war makes you dead" also cannot be considered as ideologically neutral. However, unless we are provided with an unequivocal indication of how to interpret the word "man" in the first sentence, one could suspect that the substantial objectivity of the second sentence has the scope of covering the ideological ambiguity of the preceding one. By moving rapidly from one definition of the signifier "war" to the following one, the passage produces upon the reader an effect that, to borrow a term from Giovanni Bottiroli's *Retorica*, one would be tempted to classify as "confusive." In a "confusive regime" (*regime confusivo*), Bottiroli writes, "no opposing relation, no *negation* is possible" (178). A confusive rhetoric is therefore analogous to the rhetoric of the Freudian unconscious, where "there is no, no," and different registers of articulation are lacking.

That the language of a "true" war story might, or perhaps *must*, draw its inspiration from the language of dreams, folly, and destruction is hardly surprising. If, however, such language were to occupy a *dominant* position, then Neilson's strictures on O'Brien's narrative style would be justified. The war described by O'Brien would amount to a sort of mythological marshland, the timeless vortex lyrically analyzed by James Hillman's controversial *A Terrible Love of War*. But are we sure that O'Brien's passage is ruled by a "confusive regime" and that such regime is granted a hegemonic status in both the story under scrutiny and the book as a whole?[10]

We may begin by noting that the passage under examination is preceded by one of the miniature stories told in "How to Tell," prefaced in its own turn by a synthetic metanarrative reflection:

> True war stories do not generalize. They do not indulge in abstraction or analysis.
>
> For example: War is hell. As a moral declaration the old truism seems perfectly true, and yet because it abstracts, it generalizes, I can't believe it with my stomach. Nothing turns inside.
>
> It comes down to gut instinct. A true war story, if truly told, makes the stomach believe. (84)

O'Brien's catalogue is meant to oppose the simplifications, the commonplaces, the worn-out definitions of war. But there is more to it, perhaps. The man who made immortal the slogan "War is hell" is no other than William Tecumseh Sherman, the Union general who ordered the burning of Atlanta: a man who knew the extreme cruelty of war but did not do much to mitigate its fury.[11] The rejection of a "catachresized figure" belonging to the "separative regime"—that is, to "the institutional uses of a language, those that are either prescribed or foreseen (or easily foreseeable) by its codes" (Bottiroli 166)—is also an attempt to display the political-moral ambiguity of a clichéd description that is only superficially anti-war.

The seemingly chaotic list of war's definitions offered by the narrator, rather than reaffirming war's undefinability, complicates a narrative and linguistic domain often drenched with trite formulas. As opposed to a concession to the postmodernist "drifting of meaning," the evocation of the different and contradictory faces of war should be read as an attempt to outline that alternative, third "meaning regime" that Bottiroli describes as "distinctive" (*distintivo*) (169, 171, 211). The various definitions of the war experience given by the narrator are neither mutually exclusive nor simply marked by the "figural anarchy" that is a distinguishing trait of the confusive regime. Instead, they intend to affect each other's meaning, and thus ask the reader to imagine a world where horror and beauty, under certain circumstances, may coexist.

Why War?

I will return in a moment to the contrast between "abstraction" and "gut instinct" that stands as a corollary to the refusal of sealing war into some moralizing formula. First, however, I would like to consider what Neilson describes as a (postmodern) "rapid-fire succession" of questions without answers on the causes of the war whose effect, in his view, is to undermine any ability to reach a rational understanding of history. In the story "On the Rainy River," for example, the narrator asks himself:

> Was it a civil war? A war of national liberation or simple aggression? Who started it, and when, and why? What really happened to the USS *Maddox* on that dark night in the Gulf of Tonkin? Was Ho Chi Minh a Communist stooge, or a nationalist savior, or both, or neither? What about the Geneva Accords? What about SEATO and the Cold War? What about dominoes? (O'Brien, *Things They Carried* 44)

I agree with Neilson on one point: compared to the nearly obsessive attention he devotes to the complex and contradictory status of truth in war stories, as well as to the role that memory and the imagination play in reshaping experience, the space O'Brien reserves for a different though certainly no less important question is quite limited. However, it is also fair to say that if the causes of war are, obviously, one of the main concerns of historical inquiry, they cannot be equally central—for understandable reasons—in literary approaches to war. To some, a question like "why war?" falls completely outside the genre of the war narrative. See, for example, what Samuel Hynes has written in this regard in his influential *The Soldier's Tale*:

> [W]ar narratives are not quite autobiographical. They're not quite history either. Historians tell the big stories, of campaigns and battles, of the great victories and the disastrous defeats [. . .]. The men who were there tell a different story, one that is often quite ahistorical, even antihistorical. Their narratives are indifferent to the exact location of events in time [. . .]. Most of all, they are not concerned with *why*. War narratives are experience books; they are about what happened, and how it felt. *Why* is not a soldier's question [. . .]. *Why* is the momentum behind the narratives; but it isn't the story. (11–12)

According to Hynes, there should be a clear-cut division of labor. A direct witness of war need only be faithful to his or her own personal experience: to the sensations and emotions felt at a particular moment. The soldier's tale should not dwell on the reasons for war, which are the historian's field of inquiry. In other words, O'Brien is only doing his job, thereby wisely ignoring questions that fall outside his direct experience of Vietnam.

To an extent, Hynes's observations are sound ones. How can we ask a fiction writer, who is by definition free to fluctuate between fantasy and reality, to face problems that require a different methodological approach and a different use of historical and archival sources? However, Hynes's position strikes me as excessively antihistorical. It may well be the case that traditionally war narratives do not raise questions as to why wars are fought, or that, even though they may ask "Why war?" they quickly reach the conclusion that no definitive answer may be found. Yet since in war a man must disobey the key commandment of civilized life (thou shall not kill), wondering why that may be the case would seem a rather legitimate question to raise for a war writer. Obviously, such a question can be tackled in an infinite variety of ways, and there is no doubt that O'Brien is scarcely interested, as seen in the previously quoted passage, in discerning among the various interpretations of the causes of the Vietnam War. Yet the writer does have something important to say on the problems of *guilt* and *responsibility*, which are two crucial ethical and political articulations of the "Why war?" question.

In order to emphasize O'Brien's substantially *irresponsible* writing technique, Neilson quotes the following passage from "In the Field," another story from *The Things They Carried*:

> When a man died, there had to be blame. [. . .] You could blame the war. You could blame the idiots who made the war. You could blame Kiowa for going to it. You could blame the rain. You could blame the river. You could blame the field, the mud, the climate. You could blame the enemy. You could blame the mortar rounds. You could blame people who were too lazy to read a newspaper, who were bored by the daily body counts, who switched channels at the mention of politics. You could blame whole nations. You could blame God. You could blame the munitions makers or Karl Marx or a trick of fate or an old man in Omaha who forgot to vote.

> In the field, though, the causes were immediate. A moment of carelessness or
> bad judgment or plain stupidity carried consequences that lasted forever. (198–99)

Here, O'Brien would be guilty of refusing to place in some hierarchical order the
various forms of blame he mentions. Thus, a man who forgets to vote would stand
as guilty as the generals who directly orchestrate wars, or as the military indus-
tries manufacturing deadly weapons, or, worse yet, as those natural forces (mud,
rain, climate) that have nothing to do with war. This rhetorical choice would lead
O'Brien to privileging the more direct and brutal cause-and-effect mechanism
dominating the battlefield. Neilson is right, I think, to consider the opening sentence of the passage as ideologically suspect, but he seems to forget an important
detail. Even though we may be right in assuming a loose continuity between the
textual "Tim" and the autobiographical voice of O'Brien's, we must note that the
considerations quoted *cannot* be attributed to the narrator. "Tim" is recording the
thoughts of Lieutenant Jimmy Cross, and he does that from a clearly ironic perspective. Cross multiplies in a disorderly fashion the people or agencies to blame
in an attempt to alleviate *his own* guilty feelings for having chosen to make camp
with his soldiers in an "indefensible" spot and thus for having laid in a major way
the ground for Kiowa's death. At the end of his effort to extend the number of those
who may be blamed for the incident, however, Cross seems to realize that "in the
field" there is an "immediacy" that does not grant him any relief. The lieutenant
has a direct responsibility for what took place and, therefore, referring to the "immediate" causes of what happens during a military confrontation does not so much
erase the more general and greater causes that have led to the war as it shows that
Cross is somehow beginning to realize how much *he* is to blame.[12] Unlike Christ,
ironically evoked by both the JC initials and his last name, lieutenant Jimmy Cross
is incapable of granting his disciples any salvation. Whether his decision is defined
as "a moment of carelessness," "bad judgment," or "plain stupidity" (198–99), the
fact remains that Cross is in several ways responsible for dragging his unit into a
hellish situation.

One may accept my reading of this passage and still legitimately object that
O'Brien seems to show little interest in a serious discussion of the political and
historical causes of the Vietnam conflict. However, the reason behind his reluctance
to play the historian's role has little to do with an alleged desire to evade the (un)
ethical dimension of war in order to seek refuge in the precinct of the imagination.
As shown by the episode in which private Kiowa loses his life, O'Brien prefers to
focus on the direct responsibilities of his characters rather than the larger ones of
more distant forces. After all, it would be a lot easier to blame some more or less
abstract entity (the government, imperialism, the Cold War) than to highlight the
guilt of single, seemingly insignificant individuals. "Jimmy Cross did not want the
responsibility of leading these men. He had never wanted it. In his sophomore

year at Mount Sebastian college he had signed up for the Reserve Officer Training Corps without much thought. An automatic thing: because his friends had joined, and because it was worth a few credits, and because it was preferable to letting the draft take him" (190). *That* is Jimmy's original sin: his conformism—the "automatic" response that would lead him to roam the Indochinese jungles with an "automatic thing" in his hands. And, as we shall see in a moment, this is also "Tim's" original sin, highlighted by O'Brien in one of the narrative's most intense and memorable moments.

The story "On the Rainy River" is devoted to the summer when the narrator must decide whether to go to Vietnam or else opt for an alternative that if, on the one hand, would allow him to follow his conscience and refuse the draft, on the other would certainly expose him to his community's disapproval.

> My conscience told me to run, but some irrational and powerful force was resisting, like a weight pushing me toward the war. What it came down to, stupidly, was a sense of shame. Hot, stupid shame. I did not want people to think badly of me. Not my parents, not my brother and sister, not even the folks down at the Gobbler Café. […] I was ashamed of my conscience, ashamed to be doing the right thing. […]
>
> The day was cloudy. I passed through towns with familiar names, through the pine forests and down to the prairie, and then to Vietnam, where I was a soldier, and then home again. I survived, but it's not a happy ending. I was a coward. I went to the war. (54–55, 63).

As I anticipated in the ending of this book's second chapter, I take this to be a particularly strong "Emersonian" moment in O'Brien's writing. Here, with an argument that closely parallels that of Emerson's essay "War," the conventional definition of what makes a given behavior "cowardly" or "heroic" is completely undermined. O'Brien's use of irony in this passage is much stronger than, say, that of Stephen Crane in *The Red Badge of Courage*. Also in Crane's novel the notion of "heroism" is in various ways called into question. The protagonist, Henry Fleming, is seen by his comrades as a "hero," but no careful reader can afford to ignore that just as Henry was earlier on a victim of his own "real or imagined" fears, his "heroic" exploits are also by and large instinctive responses. His "brave" charge against the enemy is as casual as his panicky flight from the battlefield. Yet Crane's attack on heroism still relies on a rather traditional definition of what in war counts as an act of cowardice, and Henry's flawed conduct evokes by contrast the very notion of "heroism" that the narrative criticizes.[13] O'Brien goes much further because he redefines cowardice as the attitude displayed by those *who go to war*. Just as Emerson had insisted that "the cause of peace is not the cause of cowardice" and explained that a noble cause like that of non-violence could be defended only by someone *greater* than a "hero"—by someone ready "to be hanged at his own gate rather than consent to any compromise of his freedom"—"Tim" realizes there is nothing admirable and heroic in going to war, a decision precipitated by the *fear* of being criticized and ostracized. This is what leads "Tim" to compromise his own freedom of judgment, thus choosing what for Emerson is the worst kind of cowardice—the cowardice of those who fear to trust their own inner convictions.

Though O'Brien may devote scant attention to the causes of American involvement in Vietnam, the narrator is crystal clear concerning who is to "blame" for his participation in the war. "Tim" is to blame—his anti-Emersonian inability to listen carefully to the voice of his conscience leads him to follow cowardly the majority opinion. "Tim's" conformism seems almost literally to embody the Emersonian maxim that "imitation is suicide" ("Self-Reliance" 259), except for the fact that in the case of war a conformist attitude should be seen not just as a form of potential "suicide": its meaning should be expanded to take on homicide as well. O'Brien's formula—"I was a coward. I went to the war"—sounds like a confirmation, 150 years later, of Emerson's insight that one needs more courage and sangfroid to reject war than to take part in it.

A True War Story Is Never about War

I would like to conclude by returning to the juxtaposition between stories that make use of generalizations and abstractions, and "true" stories that follow the "gut instinct." This opposition between two narrative modalities serves as an introduction to another miniature story in "How to Tell," where we are informed of a bizarrely cruel episode that takes place after private Kurt Lemon's death. Emotionally devastated by the loss of his friend, Rat Kiley vents his rage in a series of machine-gun outbursts against a baby water buffalo. Rat's destructive fury is chilling, but with a move that at first leaves the reader confused, the narrator goes on to clarify that this story, which certainly has much to do with "guts," should not be read as a further demonstration of the horror and folly of war. On the contrary, Rat's story is—like many great war stories—a story of *love*. O'Brien intends of course to draw our attention to the fact that Rat's love, deprived of its natural object—his friend Lemon—turns into blind fury, a barbarous desire for annihilation. The body of the baby buffalo functions as a surrogate of the obvious target on which Rat would have discharged his rage: the body of the enemy. The very short story of Rat and the buffalo is thus a rewriting of another, archetypal story of furious love: that in which Achilles drags in the dust the slain body of Hector, in a futile attempt to fill the void left by the death of his friend Patroclus with the relentless devastation of the enemy's body.[14] It is in this contradictory, visceral nexus of love and hatred, destruction and will-to-redemption, that the narrator locates the deepest mark of a "true" war story. "Tim" thus reaches the paradoxical, provocative conclusion that a true war story is never about war. It's about sunlight. It's about the special way that dawn spreads out on a river when you know you must cross the river and march into the mountains and do things you are afraid to do. It's about love and memory. It's about sorrow. It's about sisters who never write back and people who never listen. (91)

It is virtually impossible to miss how this last definition of a true war story is quite distant from the notion that a war story should distinguish itself by its "absolute and uncompromising allegiance to obscenity and evil." There is plenty of obscenity and evil, of course, in Rat Kiley's desperate attempt to come to terms with his loss. Yet at this final juncture of his story, O'Brien provides the reader with an exit strategy from the concept of war as pure, unmitigated evil. His point is not to rehabilitate the experience of war as such but to show the reader how a "true" war story must be capable of showing also *the obverse side* of war. As he bitterly considers the fact that whenever he tells Rat Kiley's story in public, he has to face an audience that does not seem to grasp its deeper meaning, "Tim" snaps, "It *wasn't* a war story. It was a *love* story" (90). A "true" war story, the narrator implies, is the one in which we are allowed to catch a glimpse of the distortion or aberration of love—a tale which, as Kenneth Burke would have put it, encourages us to think of war as a "a special case of peace" where feelings of love are often visible only through their perversion.[15] A "true" war story is a story that manages at the same time to narrate war and to trope it into something else so that in the end, paradoxically, there is a sense in which "a true war story is never about war."

In an insightful comparison between Hemingway's and O'Brian's war narratives, Alex Vernon has written that "*The Things They Carried* very much renders love and war inseparable, each constituting and constitutive of the other." Indeed, for Vernon, "The essential subject of all of O'Brien's work is the exploration of the relationship between war and love" (198). In the instance under consideration, however, the love story is very different from the one that, in *A Farewell to Arms*, "masks" the violence and guilt inherent in the war story, thus setting up a pattern repeated by O'Brien's John Wade, who, in the novel *In the Lake of the Woods*, uses "his love story to foster his denial of his own war violence and lies" (Vernon 194). The kind of love story hidden in Rat Kiley's furious response to Lemon's death belongs to the "immense love" that soldiers have repeatedly declared feeling for their fellow combatants, and that Joanna Bourke has eloquently written about in her *Intimate History of Killing*. "Whether called 'mateship,' 'the buddy system,' or 'homo-erotic relationships,' the power of love and friendship in enticing men to kill has been widely commented upon. Although frequently exaggerated [. . .] combatants reported that they were able to kill because of the love they felt for their comrades" (129–30). Keeping this in mind, one may wish to argue that, in our case, rather than a war story masquerading as a love story (in order to cover up the horrors of war), what we have is a love story disguising itself as a war story, so as to please an audience more interested in the thrills of war than in the complexities of love. Yet O'Brien's war story does not cover up a straightforward love story: the "love" we detect at the bottom of this, as of many other war stories, is a love that can never be completely separated from hate and rage. It is a love that kills. "Tim's" remark may sound rather sentimental in its evocation of "love," but once we situate his statement within the context of the story he has just told, we immediately realize that this is not the kind of love-making that will bring war to an end.

"How to Tell a True War Story" is a compelling, insightful meditation on the moral perils and conceptual paradoxes any serious war writer must come to terms with. By encouraging the reader's distrust in any representation of war, O'Brien provides us with a powerful critique of any war story's attempt to salvage some goodness from the wreckage of war. Yet what O'Brien also shows—against his initial intentions—is that even the most self-deconstructive of war narratives can never completely do away with a kernel of positivity and "goodness." As he writes in a revealing passage, "Proximity to death brings with it proximity to life. After a firefight there is always the immense pleasure of aliveness. . . . You feel an intense, out-of-the-skin awareness of your living self—your truest self, the human being you want to be and then become by the force of wanting it. In the midst of evil you want to be a good man" (88). Goodness may blossom even in the "garden of Evil" (86); love sometimes is intertwined with horror; *peace* is distorted by war into monstrous forms without, however, being altogether erased from its texture. A "true" war story must remain faithful to these paradoxes. Even though, when read superficially, they may appear to cultivate a postmodern distrust in "truth," O'Brien's narratives do not abolish reality in order to chase the ghosts of a solipsistic, incorporeal imagination. On the contrary, O'Brien's imagination is a *cognitive* resource and, therefore, ultimately a *political* tool capable of unveiling the cowardice hidden behind what many call heroism, as well as the way even love can feed the monster of war.

CHAPTER 9

Beyond the Semantic Netherworld

Literature and the Iraq War

Orwell 2.0

It's Orwellian the way
Everyone claims Orwell for their side—these days
Everyone is fighting on behalf of Orwell and God.

—Eliot Katz, "Can We Have Some Peace and Quiet Please?"

In the opening paragraph of *The American Way of War*, Tom Engelhardt writes: "'War is Peace' was one of the memorable slogans on the façade of the Ministry of Truth, or Minitrue, in 'Newspeak,' the language invented in 1948 by George Orwell for his dystopian novel *1984*. Some sixty years later, a quarter century after Orwell's imagined future bit the dust, the phrase is, in a number of ways, eerily applicable to the United States" (1). As Engelhardt goes on to argue, "Because the United States does not look like a militarized country, it's hard for Americans to grasp that Washington is a war capital, that the United States is a war state, that it garrisons much of the planet, and that the norm for us is to be at war somewhere (usually, in fact, in many places) at any moment" (2–3). Despite the official withdrawal of American troops from both Afghanistan and Iraq, American military presence in the region remains significant. Moreover, as the situation in the Middle East deteriorates and the United States has found a new enemy in the Islamic State of Iraq and Syria (ISIS), it appears that the same president who was supposed to pull the United States out of the Iraq quagmire is committing the country to a "war on terror" that, as he himself has acknowledged, may go on indefinitely. This is hardly surprising, considering that it was Obama himself who launched a "drones war" along the Afghanistan-Pakistan border that has resulted in a long list of civilian casualties. Whatever his initial "uneasiness" at these "signature strikes," we have now learned that every week the president pores over "the equivalent of terrorist baseball cards, deciding who on a 'kill list' would be targeted for elimination by drone attack" (vanden Heuvel). Perhaps nothing more than these "video games made real" can erase the border between "peace" and "war." Controlled from comfortable locations thousands of miles away, such aerial weapons carry out the main business of war—that is, killing—as their "pilots" sit in front of a computer screen, perhaps sipping on their morning coffee. Once their shift is over, they get in their cars and drive back home to their spouses and kids. They have been "at war" all day, and yet their "peaceful" lives go on, at least ostensibly, without any traumatic interruption.[1] This chilling scenario must be compounded with the staggering military budget of the United States, a country that, even at a time of worldwide economic crisis, continues to invest in weaponry and the military roughly half of what the entire world spends for the killing business. Mindful of what William James wrote more than a century ago concerning "the intensely sharp *preparation for war*" being "the *real war*," it would be hard to disagree with him when he noted, "Every up-to-date dictionary should say that 'peace' and 'war' mean the same thing, now *in posse*, now *in actu*" (1283). It is no exaggeration to argue that the gargantuan outlays the U.S. government invests in the military-industrial complex amount to a war against its own people. "Every gun that is made, every warship launched, every rocket fired signifies, in the final sense, a theft from those who hunger and are not fed, those who are cold and not clothed. This world in arms is not spending money alone. It is spending the sweat of its laborers, the genius of its scientists, the hopes of its children. This is not a way of life at all in any true sense. Under the cloud of threatening war, it is humanity hanging from a cross of iron."[2] These words were not uttered by Noam Chomsky or Arundhati Roy, but by Dwight Eisenhower, and their urgency remains intact today when, as Engelhardt notes, "Of the nearly trillion dollars the U.S. invests in war and war-related activities, nothing goes to peace. No money, no effort, no thought. The very idea that there might be peaceful alternatives to endless war is so discredited that it's left to utopians, bleeding hearts, and feathered doves. As in Orwell's Newspeak, while peace remains with us, it's largely been shorn of its possibilities. No longer the opposite of war, it's just a rhetorical flourish embedded, like one of our reporters, in Warspeak" (7).

This book, however, has insisted that on both conceptual and pragmatic grounds war and peace are indeed part of a continuum, so that to construct them as absolute opposites may turn out to be, paradoxically, not a way to put an end to war but to make war perpetually available. Hence, as my epigraph suggests, what is Orwellian about the contemporary political and rhetorical scene is that while pacifists accuse war supporters of resorting to Newspeak in order to pass war as peace, advocates of military interventions attack pacifists by claiming that the peace they defend would allow terrorism to spread unchecked. Pacifists, too, would be guilty of employing their own Newspeak in order to hide how their position makes light of those plotting "evil" in various parts of the world. One way to counter this accusation is of course to show that most pacifists by no means ignore the violence that is endemic in many societies and conflict situations. Their alternative is not simply to say no to war but to say yes to other social and political means to pursue the objective of peace. As the title of a famous book by Johan Galtung has it, the pacifists' objective is to achieve peace by peaceful means.[3]

Maxine Hong Kingston in Search of the Lost Peace

As we have seen in the preceding pages, literature has always struggled with its own version of this dilemma. Since World War I, the "great" literature of war has been almost by default "anti-war," and yet it has rarely been able to construct peace as something other than the end of a horrible state of war. This paradox lying at the heart of modern war literature has been rarely investigated. Whatever else one might think of Maxine Hong Kingston's *The Fifth Book of Peace*, it is a work that deserves credit for doing exactly that. At a time when our neo-Orwellian moment was reaching its zenith as Gulf War I paved the way to Gulf War II, Kingston set on a personal and collective journey for the meaning of peace—a journey that took her through wars, of course, but that did not stop there. The book baffled many reviewers, who, expecting another work along the lines of *The Woman Warrior* and *Tripmaster Monkey*, complained about the text's "weirdness," its formal heterogeneity, its "utopianism," its moralistic preaching.[4] Today, however, Kingston's work seems to have met with some appreciation, at least among academic critics. In particular, three recent essays by Te-Hsing Shan, E. San Juan Jr., and Hsu Shounan have produced interesting readings of the text as, respectively, an example of "life writing" combining personal and political stories; as an important anti-imperialist intervention allegorically emphasizing the significance "of the communal production of meaning"; and as "a book on peace and the way to find peace" that can be profitably explored through French philosopher Alain Badiou's notion of the "event."

By following the leads provided by these critics, in what follows I call attention to some of the ways *The Fifth Book of Peace* stages a meta-literary reflection on how a literature of peace may differ from a literature of war. This theme may be seen as running counter to the direction advocated by the text itself since, as Kingston writes, "Things that fiction can't solve must be worked out in life" (241). However, by suggesting that the text interrogates the limits of war resistance not only in practice but also, and perhaps mostly, in literature, I am not trying to contain Kingston's political intervention within a merely aesthetic sphere. On the contrary, my point is that her thoughts on the literature of peace and war are an inseparable part of her pacifist politics.

The Fifth Book of Peace is divided into four parts (titled "Fire," "Paper," "Water," and "Earth") followed by a short epilogue. In the opening section, we learn about the 1991 Oakland-Berkeley fire that destroyed not only the author's house but also the 156-page manuscript of her novel-in-progress, "The Fourth Book of Peace." The fire is also associated with both the first Gulf War ("I know why this fire. God is showing us Iraq. It is wrong to kill, and to refuse to look at what we've done" [13]) and her father's envy of her work as a writer (Kingston's father's funeral took place the very day of the fire). In the "Paper" section, the author shifts to her search for the Three Chinese Lost Books of Peace, which may actually have been many more ("Three is a symbolic number. It just means there were a lot, more than one" [53]). Perhaps, as one of the learned men whom she consults tells her, "You yourself imagined Books of Peace. And since you made them up, you are free to write whatever you like. You write them yourself" (52). The book's third part, "Water," offers us a revised version of the burnt manuscript narrating the flight to Hawai'i of *Tripmaster Monkey*'s Wittman Ah Sing, his wife Taña, and their son Mario at the time of the Vietnam War. There the Wittmans continue their non-violent anti-war campaign by participating in the local Sanctuary movement, welcoming war deserters and draft dodgers. As Kingston informs us in the opening paragraph of the book's final "Earth" section, "There! That's what I wrote during two years of living at friends' houses after the fire. . . . I wrote past the place where the burned book left off. But found no happy ending. The War in Viet Nam won't come to a happy ending" (241). Here the author tells her readers she is done with fiction—in the remainder of her book she will focus on "life." The fourth part is thus devoted to Kingston's activity as an organizer of war veterans' writing workshops. These meetings, and the writing that takes place there, signal a turn from a self-centered artistic practice toward a communal perspective and a collective praxis. The many war stories composing this section are the work of many writers, or "peace warriors," who try—through storytelling—to heal themselves, thereby setting an anti-war model for the generations to come. These war stories do not produce *one* final idea of peace but chart the manifold ways peace may be both imagined and lived. In the epilogue the author, after mentioning her participation in the peace movement as the Bush administration was preparing its attack on Iraq, draws her (necessarily provisional) conclusion: "Children, everybody, here's what to do during war. In a time of destruction, create something. A poem. A parade. A community. A school. A vow. A moral principle. One peaceful moment" (402).

The upbeat tone of this ending notwithstanding, one could gloss *The Fifth Book of Peace* with terms similar to the ones Kingston herself employs in reference to her "restored" Fourth Book. Her fiction can offer hope but cannot stop the Iraq War, another devastation that, like the Vietnam War, "won't come to a happy ending." Kingston must acknowledge that, no matter how much one wishes to fashion a literature of peace, war is hard to defeat. Kingston mentions "the spirit of Yin—a feeling of peace and love" suffusing the most successful anti-war rallies, but though this makes for an extraordinary experience of non-violence, it is not enough to prevent the war. This reading, however, while not entirely wrong—it registers the unpleasant facts of history the book must contend with—could be turned on its head. War wins but not by a margin wide enough to crush all peace activism, which does not amount only to feeling good or "at peace" with one's conscience. Peace does not stop the war, but that is not to say it produces no concrete effects on the world. The world as we know it is a world at war, and the peace we desire must be wrested from *this* world. There is, therefore, an analogy between the peace activist operating in a world where war rules and the reader who wishes to read a true book of peace but (like the author herself) keeps running into war books. Kingston's solution is that since we do not have books of peace, we must make them up ourselves. One way to do that is to read against the grain of the texts of war—"to create something" truly new out of them just like the pacifist militant tries to turn a world of violence into a peaceful or at least a less violent environment.

The problem of how to turn war literature into peace literature runs like a red thread through the entire narrative. All sections are interspersed with comments on books or stories about war. In the "Paper" section, for example, Kingston writes, "In Chinatowns everywhere in the world, there are statues of Gwang Goong, god of war and literature" (48). He is often depicted reading a book, and Kingston finds out the book is Sun Tzu's *The Art of War*. Some scholars now argue that the book is actually not about war but about how to prevent war, as Sun Tzu's highest value was peace. Yet she is skeptical of this interpretation. After observing that the book is read in military academies as well as in business schools and is filled with directions on how to destroy, burn down cities, and so forth, she observes, "If the *Art of War* is such a good book, why isn't it called the *Art of Peace*?" Creative reading has its limitations, but for Kingston, this is not equivalent to saying that nothing good can come out of war and war stories. If anything, under certain circumstances "war causes peace" (227). Taken out of context this sounds Orwellian enough, but what Kingston actually means is that "the most unambiguous source of antiwar sentiments" is to be found among soldiers who have experienced (and come to despise) war. This is the crucial lesson the Wittmans learn from the Sanctuary movement in Hawai'i. "What became apparent to us [. . .] who got to know the GIs as persons was that most of the men became conscientious objectors BECAUSE of their military experience" (227). This provides Kingston's book with a nice transition to the "Earth" section, where she opens her first writing workshop by inviting war veterans "to gather the smithereens, and narrate them into story. We'll put that war into words, and through language make sense, meaning, art of it, make something beautiful. Something good" (260). Here Kingston is obviously not suggesting that war stories should make *war* beautiful. Instead, she implies that storytelling, while preserving a sense of the brutishness of war, must transcend its ugliness, thus allowing the veterans (mostly Vietnam War veterans) to "return home."

As the workshop takes place twenty years after the Vietnam War and is about "homecoming," Kingston refers to Odysseus as a sort of archetypal veteran, a man who also "took twenty years to get to and from the Trojan War" (260). As Jonathan Shay has shown in his *Odysseus in America: Combat Trauma and the Trials of Homecoming*, published one year before Kingston's novel, the Greek hero's troubled route back to Ithaca can shed light on the problems faced by former combatants as they, too, try to return to a civilian life. Anyone who has read the *Odyssey*, however, must find Kingston's evocation of Odysseus in a pacifist context somewhat puzzling. True, Odysseus wants to leave the Trojan War behind but, even brushing aside the numerous acts of violence he commits in his ten years of voyaging before reaching Ithaca, when he returns home he finds himself embroiled in a further war to regain possession of his estate. If Sun Tzu's *Art of War* is no *Art of Peace*, neither is the *Odyssey* an anti-war epic. Though Kingston makes no mention of this in her workshop-opening remarks, she does address the problem in the climactic, concluding paragraphs of the "Earth" section, where she compares the Odysseus story to her own retelling of the Chinese story of Fa Mook Lan. She now correctly observes that, "after twenty years of traveling to the war, fighting the war, destroying the other's city, and traveling home, Odysseus could not stop warring. He killed the men who had taken over his house; he killed a dozen women servants" (392). No matter how tired of war he may be, Odysseus is incapable, on his own, of embracing peace. Peace is a gift that comes from outside. As the violence is raging,

> suddenly a beautiful woman appears. She is Athena, the Hope of Soldiers. "Now, hold!" she shouts. "Break off this bitter skirmish; end your bloodshed, Ithakans, and make peace. Odysseus, master of land ways and sea ways, command yourself. Call off this battle now." At her words, the warriors on all sides lay their weapons down. Their hearts are glad, and together they vow peace. (392)

Even this rewriting, however, is problematic. Athena is an armed goddess—I see her domineering statue with helm, shield, and spear whenever I enter the "Sapienza" University of Rome campus. She was a goddess of war. Yes, she embodied the "human face" of war, leaving its most destructive, bloodthirsty side to Ares. She was also *Athena Ergane*, the patron of artisans, as well as the inventor of the female art of weaving, but it is a bit of a stretch to see her mainly as a peacemaker.[5] Athena is a fighting deity (*Athena Promachos*), and the peace she stands for is exactly the one Kingston mentions in her rewriting of the *Odyssey*—the peace that comes *after* war. Athena calls off the battle only after Odysseus has taken back his reign by force. In order to read the last book of Homer's narrative as a Book of Peace, therefore, Kingston must significantly edit the text. She must have it say something it does not quite say, but which is important if we wish to envision a different ethical foundation for our literary tradition.

Kingston's revision of Homer is offered after she has sketched out a rewriting of her own major literary accomplishment, *The Woman Warrior*. A key story in that book is the one of Fa Mook Lan, "who disguised herself as a man and who fought against the Tartars. I have told her story as a women's liberation story, and as a war story. But I now understand, it is a homecoming story. Fa Mook Lan leads her army home away from war. She shows the troops herself changing back from a man to a woman, and gives them a vision of the Feminine. It is possible for a soldier to become feminine. Veterans can return to civil society; they don't have to be homeless" (390). Even leaving aside that here Kingston risks conforming to a dubious Western tradition that has assumed "an affinity between women and peace, between men and war" (Elshtain 4)—also Fa Mook Lan invokes peace only *after* winning the war. Like Athena, she is a female figure who prefers peace to war, but she can hardly be considered an example of non-violence the way, say, Kingston's own source of inspiration in real life, the Vietnamese Buddhist monk Thich Na Than, can. Moreover, while she mentions Fa Mook Lan's and Odysseus's homecomings as models the veterans can follow in taking leave of the Vietnam War, she passes over the not-insignificant detail that the United States *lost* that war. Moreover, for the Americans the Vietnam War was not a people's war to take back one's country or defend it from a foreign invasion—it was, as Kingston obviously knows, a war of aggression.

Kingston's refusal to propose an authoritative definition of peace, valid for all times and places, is in many ways understandable and praiseworthy, but it also leaves the door open to definitions of peace both logically and ethically incompatible with one another. In rightfully lauding the work done by Thich Nhat Hanh and his Plum Village (France) community to bring about reconciliation between the former enemies of the Vietnam War, she observes, "A city of peace has resulted from war" (390). The peace mentioned here is of a very different nature from the one she eulogizes in her rewritings of both Homer's and her own work. The latter is a peace, like it or not, won *thanks* to war. The former is a peace that descends from an "antiwar sentiment," a peace born of the fight *against* war. The peace earned by Fa Mook Lan and Odysseus comes out of military victory. The peace embraced by war deserters, or by Kingston herself and her fellow Code Pink sisters, entails, on the contrary, accepting with no regrets (to quote the title of another book by Tom Engelhardt) the end of victory culture.

A more detailed reading of *The Fifth Book of Peace* would bring to light further definitions of peace given at various points in the narrative as well as provide better descriptions of the ones I have singled out. This would be in keeping with the spirit of the book, whose penultimate paragraph reads, "The images of peace are ephemeral. The language of peace is subtle. The reasons for peace, the definitions of peace, the very idea of peace have to be invented, and invented again" (402). With Melville's Ishmael, we might say that Kingston's book of peace is "but the draft of a draft," a book ever in the making. Yet, as Hsu Shounan has astutely observed, Kingston's "belief in the irrepresentable idea of peace must be an obstacle when she wants other people, or the government, to accept her idea of peace, or to negotiate with her peace-makers. The common ground between an irrepresentable idea of peace and a represented one is not easy to see. In fact, there might be no such common ground" (122). Perhaps Kingston does not so much insist on the notion of peace's irrepresentability as on the fact that all representations are, and should be, provisional. Still, this cannot absolve us from the duty of criticizing those instances where the concept of peace is deployed to justify war rather than to prevent it or end it. This is, indeed, one of the major impulses behind Kingston's writing, as we learn when she notes with regret that her own *Woman Warrior* "is being used as a text at the United States Air Force Academy in Colorado Springs. 'It gives a mythos to the women military students,' says instructor James Aubrey. I have to make up for that" (49). The way Kingston tries to make amends for that, as we have seen, is by rewriting *The Woman Warrior*'s central mythos in order to make it even more a peace story than it originally was intended to be. Yet even the new version of the story may not resist being read as a war story rather than as a peace story or, if you prefer, as a peace story that is actually a story about the need for war in order to achieve peace.

All this is not to suggest that, in the end, *The Fifth Book of Peace* falls apart because of its internal contradictions. If anything, the book forces the reader to interrogate himself or herself on the different versions of peace outlined by Kingston and to realize that the same term may be constructed in a variety of diverse ways, depending on the context and the intentions of those who employ it. Yet I think there can be no doubt that, in an age of preemptive war, preemptive peace is the one Kingston most forcefully argues for:

> If the world, time and space, and cause-and-effect accord with my mother's teachings—her Tao—then we have stopped wars years hence. We made myriads of nonwars. We have ended wars a hundred years from now. The war against Iraq, which began the same year as the Oakland-Berkeley fire, is still occurring. But the peace we make also continues, and fans, and lives on and on. (398)

This, far from being a lapse into idealism, is an important political statement meant to sustain a peace that would not be the ancillary of war. Peace here is conceived as a *force* that produces real effects on the world. As we fight for justice, equality, and against war, we make "myriads of nonwars." These nonwars may at times lack the massive strength required to prevent a huge tragedy like the Iraq War from taking place, but they plant the seeds of future conditions in which peace may blossom. The wars of tomorrow must be stopped today, not through a war-to-end-war, as in Odysseus's and Fa Mook Lan's cases, but by waging peace, as Kingston herself does, both in real life and in the imagination.

Brian Turner's Cosmopolitan Poetry

Kingston's search for peace takes place on a global level. Her narrative stretches from the continental United States to Hawai'i, China, France, and Vietnam, and it may thus be taken as representative of the "transnational" scope of much current American literary and critical writing. An analogous effort to push against the narrowness of national boundaries and identities animates the work of one of the most accomplished soldier-writers to have emerged from the so-called "war on Terror," the poet Brian Turner. Described in a recent article as "a rock star" of contemporary poetry circles, Turner has also enjoyed considerable media exposure, and his first collection, *Here, Bullet* (2005), has sold more than twenty-five thousand copies, with his second volume, *Phantom Noise* (2010), doing equally well. Most reviews have been favorable, even enthusiastic (see Bishop 300), and his work has been compared to that of celebrated war poets like Wilfred Owen, Randall Jarrell, Yusef Komunyakaa, and Bruce Weigl. Turner's texts do belong in many ways to the soldier-poet tradition: he is a direct witness of war's horrors and of soldiers' remarkable spirit of sacrifice. Yet the main reason Turner's poetry interests me lies with its sincere desire to produce a record of events open to the viewpoints, the culture, and the history of the people of Iraq.[6] This is why I think Turner's outlook deserves to be identified as cosmopolitan, at least if by that term we mean, as Bruce Robbins has suggested, not an impossibly "neutral" outlook above the fray but, more realistically, "a striving to transcend partiality that is itself partial, but no more so than similar cognitive strivings of many diverse peoples" ("Comparative Cosmopolitanism" 181). The kind of cosmopolitanism Robbins advocates is one that, "by suggesting that there is no uniquely correct place to stand, it can take some of the moralism out of our politics" (183). Or, as he has written more recently, cosmopolitanism may be an indispensable intellectual and political resource in confronting "the indifference, the ignorance, the lazy habits of backing one's own and of not thinking too much about the other side that maintain a sort of perpetual rehearsal for future military interventions while they also legitimate and enable ongoing ones" (*Perpetual War* 6). If that is what we mean by cosmopolitanism, Turner's poetry is a passionate and valuable effort to turn it into a poetic practice.

Turner's poetry, however, not only strives to achieve that epic balance between opposed combatants that, at least in Simone Weil's view, characterized Homer's

Iliad, but also may be said to extend its cosmopolitanism from space to *time*. In a number of poems, Turner claims his closeness to the people and the landscape of contemporary Iraq and to figures and moments from the distant Middle Eastern past as well. By contextualizing the U.S. invasion of Iraq within a much-expanded historical, even prehistorical framework, Turner outright rejects the official war narrative constructed by the media, the generals, and the politicians. This feature of some of his most valuable texts is interesting in its own right, yet it further intersects a critical discussion around the concept of "deep time" to which both comparatists like Robbins and Americanists like Wai-chee Dimock have variously contributed. In particular, here I would like to consider the critique of "deep time" Robbins has advanced in an essay included in *The Routledge Companion to World Literature*, where he highlights what are to him some of the unacknowledged ethical and political complications marring Dimock's book *Through Other Continents: American Literature across Deep Time* (2006). As I hope to show, this discussion is relevant to a better understanding of the strengths and of the limitations of Turner's poetics. On the one hand, Turner calls for an expansion of the Iraq war experience in geographical scale by focusing on the way the war veterans' traumatic memories bring the war home to America as well as by imagining the war as taking place on a transnational terrain where Americans and Iraqis are both at home and exiled. On the other hand, the rejection of linear time allows Turner to expand greatly the temporal scale of his war stories in ways that are as stimulating and problematic as are the uses of deep time in literary history.

Robbins's reservations about deep time revolve around a passage in Dimock's book that is of special significance to the present context. In her introduction to *Through Other Continents*, Dimock refers to the April 14, 2003, burning to the ground of the Iraqi National Library and the Islamic library as an easily foreseeable consequence of the U.S. Army's failure to protect those historical buildings. Among the documents housed in the libraries were some of the oldest extant copies of the Qu'ran, unique historical records dating back several centuries, and invaluable Arabic linguistic treatises. Dimock attributes the American Army's lack of interest in guarding these sites not only to the diktats of "a military timetable" but also to its operating "under the short chronology of a young nation . . . largely indifferent to the history of the world."

> For the archives of Baghdad had in fact been destroyed once before. In 1258, the Mongols, led by Genghis Khan's grandson Hulegu, had sacked the city and emptied the contents of its libraries into the Tigris River, so much so that the water turned black. Modern Iraqis see the actions of the United States as yet another installment of that long-running saga: "The Modern Mongols, the new Mongols did that. The Americans did that." All this made no sense to the marines. The year 1258 was long

ago and far away. It is separated by 745 years from 2003. The United States has nothing to do with it. (*Through Other Continents* 2)

Robbins's objection to Dimock's erasure of the 745-year gap separating the Mongol from the American invasion is that it builds on the idea of the "essential sameness" of the two events, thus dispensing us from a closer historical analysis of what is seen as simply yet another bloody turn of the screw. One might say, in Dimock's defense, that by making Americans modern Mongols, she undercuts the former's civilizing pretense, but Robbins's point is that such identification "oddly retains the normal, uncritical use of the Mongols to signify atrocious and inexplicable barbarism" (387).

To this I would add a different though related objection. I agree with Dimock that once its frame of reference is enlarged to other continents and to the millennia preceding it, "American literature emerges with a much longer history than one might think" (*Through Other Continents* 4), but I strongly doubt that any knowledge on the marines' part of what happened in Baghdad in 1285 would have led them to act differently. Can we really believe that a more robust knowledge of Middle Eastern history and of the many sackings of Baghdad besides the Mongol one would have had any effect on the U.S. Army's behavior in Iraq? Would not the army have flatly rejected any allegation of being a conquering force, retorting that they were there to "free" the country from a brutal dictatorship? Moreover, it seems disingenuous to isolate as an example of "barbarism" the burning and looting of the National Library, which, for all we know, was carried out by Iraqis. While it is true that the ultimate legal, political, and moral responsibility for this historic crime lies with the invading army, to equate the Mongol intentional devastation of the library with the American failure to guard it and preserve its treasures seems forced at best. While I by no means wish to deny that, as Djelal Kadir has written, "there is a direct line between the textual after-effects of the siege of 1258 and the siege of 2003" (*Memos* 42), I would agree with Robbins that if presentism is a danger, so also is what he calls "pastism." Do we really want—he rhetorically asks—"a fetishizing of everything from the past simply because it is past . . . that is likely to paralyze any action to change the present and, indeed, any proper allocation of praise and blame in any of the texts we examine, wherever they are located?" (390–91).

Before offering a reading of some of Turner's lines that display a cosmopolitanism that unfolds on both a geographical and temporal plane, let me dwell a moment on the different literary-critical framing of the 2003 siege of Baghdad offered by Kadir. After enumerating in detail the many sieges and devastations suffered by Madinat as-Salam—the "City of Peace," as its Abassid founder called it—Kadir writes that "this litany of calamity . . . is now an unavoidable part of the repertoire of anyone wishing to be a scholar of America with any degree of authority. . . . The Baghdadization of America has become as undeniable as the Americanization of Baghdad" (57). Kadir is of course well aware of what he himself identifies as "the asymmetry of power, the unevenness of the playing field, the discrepancy between conqueror and vanquished," but, mindful of how Baghdad, "has always consumed and transformed its besiegers" (43), he concludes, "there is a direct ratio in the intensity of this inexorable compensatory interchange. The more vehement, the more profound, the more protracted the siege and the more egregious its effects, proportionally greater will be the countereffects that define the besieging power" (57). Whereas for Dimock America's flaw lies with its "indifference" to the *longue durée* of planetary history, Kadir argues that no matter how stubbornly the invaders might wish to distance themselves from the invaded and construct their conduct as "exceptional," all imperial conquerors have ended up being affected "in incalculable ways" by the conquered. When it comes to evaluating how the war's "countereffects" are inscribed in the American literary response to the Iraq War, however, we must discern between texts that recoil from conceiving of America—as Kadir provokingly writes—"as a Middle Eastern country" (57), and those—like Turner's—who see "their" history intertwined with "ours," thereby promoting an ethical relation to the victims of Empire.

There are two poems in *Phantom Noise* wherein Turner explicitly refers to what happened in Baghdad in 1285. In "Al-A'imma Bridge," the poet writes about a tragic event occurring in August 2005 that cost the lives of nearly one thousand people. As we read in one of the endnotes appended to the volume, "Not one shot was fired—someone in the crowd of worshippers was said to have claimed a suicide bomber was among them, and panic ensued."

> They fall from the bridge into the Tigris—
>   they fall from railings or tumble down, shoved by panic,
>   by those in the crushing weight behind them,
>   mothers with children, seventy-year old men
>   clawing at the blue and empty sky, which is too beautiful (32)

Turner knows that when describing death en masse, one always risks losing touch with the immensity of the event. Thus, he tries to give us a sense of these people as separate individuals, with their own personal histories, memories, dreams, and specific sensibilities ("and Shatha, who feels the river's cold hands / pulling her under, remembers once loving / the orange flowers on the hillsides / of Mosul, how she lay under slow clouds / drifting in history's bright catalogue"). Turner situates these individual falls in deep time by seeing them as the latest episode in an endless "falling" of civilization and human decency that brings to mind T. S. Eliot's description of cultural collapse in *The Waste Land* and extends over millennia:

> they fall with 500 pound bombs and mortars,
>> laser-guided munitions directing the German Luftwaffe
>>> from 1941, Iraqi jets and soldiers from the Six-Day War,
>> the Battle of Karbala, the one million who died fighting Iran;
>
> and Alexander the Great falls, and King Faisal,
>>> and the Israel F-16s that bombed the reactor in '81,
>> and the Stele of the Vultures comes crumbling,
>>> the Tower of Samarra, the walled ruins of Nineveh (*Phantom Noise* 33)

Shifting within a few lines from the times of "the Babylonians and Sumerians and Assyrians" to landmark years of the past century ("the year 1956 slides under, along with '49 and '31 and '17"), Turner's poem stands opposed to a notion of time as (to quote from Dimock) made of "fixed segments, fixed unit lengths" (*Through Other Continents* 2). Most important, the year 1258 is positioned within a constellation that belongs in the Iraqi as well as the American historical landscape.

> Years unravel like filaments of straw, bleached gold
>> And given to the water, 1967 and 1972, 2001 and 2002:
>>> What will we remember? What will we say of these?
> it awakens the dead from the year 1258
>
>> who cannot believe what is happening here, Not a shot fired—
>>> our internalized panic deeply set by years of warfare,
>> the siege and adrenaline always at the surface, prepared;
>
> the dead from the year 1258 read from ancient scrolls
>>> cast into the river from the House of Wisdom,
>> the eulogies of nations given water's swift erasure;
> and the dead watch as they are swept downstream—(*Phantom Noise* 33)

As the use of the pronoun "we" and the adjective "ours" implies, the events described are no longer part of "their" history alone. The "internalized panic" is something shared as "we" contemplate the human falls into the Tigris of 2005 as well as those from the unmentioned but implicitly evoked Twin Towers in 2001. Turner stops short of drawing an explicit parallel between the U.S. invasion of 2003 and the Mongol invasion of 1285, but he connects the 1285 event as well as other moments in Iraqi history to a present shaped by American acts of war and the locals' response to them:

> And the Tigris is filling with the dead, filling
>> with bricks from Abu Ghraib, burning vehicles
>>> pushed from Highway 1 with rebar, stone, metal,
>> with rubble from the Mosque bombed in Samarra,

> guard towers and razor wire imprisoning Tikrit,
> it fills with the pipelines of money;
>
> marketplace bombs, roadside bombs, vehicle-driven
>   bombs, and the bombs people make of themselves (*Phantom Noise* 34)

All these lost lives may be "unwritten history, forgotten in American hallways," but the poet asks us to consider these people as *our* people and invites us to imaginatively

> give them flowers from the hills, flowers from the Shanidar cave,
>   where mourning has a long history, where someone in the last Ice Age
>   gathered a bouquet—give daisies and hyacinths
>   to this impossible moment, flowers to stand for the lips
>   unable to kiss them, each in their own bright beauty, flowers
>   that may light the darkness, as they march deeper into the earth. (*Phantom Noise* 35)

In this, as well as in several other poems, Turner situates his war stories not only within a much longer chronology than the standard one covered in soldier-writers' either autobiographical or fictional accounts. In fact, he projects his personal experience, to quote Dimock again, "against the history and habitat of the human species, against the 'deep time' of the planet Earth" (*Through Other Continents* 6). The Shanidar Cave is an archeological site in the Kurdistan region of Iraq where the first adult Neanderthal skeletons (dating between sixty-five thousand and thirty-five thousand years ago) have been located. Interestingly enough, for a poem intent on showing that Iraq and the United States are connected in many more ways than we might think at first, the skeletons were discovered by Smithsonian anthropologist Ralph Solecki, working with a team from Columbia University and Kurdish workers. It was Solecki who first suggested "that flowers had been buried with the Neanderthal dead," and, moreover, that "skeletons showed evidence of injuries tended and healed—indications that the sick and wounded had been cared for" (Edwards). Solecki's findings were extensively reported in his book *Shanidar: The First Flower People*, published in 1971. The "flower power" evoked by Turner as the source that may shed some light of compassion and tenderness on the ravages of wars both present and past suggests a history of healing and caring that predates by millennia the American countercultural scene, with its sometimes confused though generous calls to make love and not war. Yet as the title of Solecki's book suggests, our approach to those events buried in "deep time" are inevitably colored and filtered by the present moment. To place the invasion of Iraq within a larger spatial and chronological frame does not mean to recover an all-encompassing "planetarity," which, as Dimock herself must acknowledge, can only be "a never-to-be-realized horizon."[7] It does, however, mean to recover a multilayered and rich history of transcultural relations that undermines any attempt to contain the attack on Iraq within the "clash of civilizations" paradigm underlying the "War on Terror."

The 1258 Mongol devastation of Baghdad is the main subject of "Madinat As-Salam." In this case, Turner restrains from even an oblique comparison between this episode and the current "allied" invasion of Iraq. However, after describing how "After 50 days of siege and 40 days of plunder / 800,000 lay dead in the streets, beheaded / by Mongols, many bodies thrown to the river," the poem poses a question meant to draw its readers closer to this apparently remote event:

> And if we could stand among them,
> as bodies blacken in flame, plume upward,
> smoke flattening against heaven—if we could stand
> in the House of Wisdom as the invaders
>
> darken the river with texts and scrolls,
> the old stories burning around us,
> the very frame itself catching fire—
> what would we have to say of loss?
>
> Maybe we'd begin to question the word
> *beauty*, no matter what form it is recorded in—
> cuneiform, papyrus, stone. (*Phantom Noise* 54).

There is irony in the request that we stand in the ancient library—one of the most important centers of learning in the history of Islamic civilization—"as the invaders" wreak havoc all around. Turner, for one, knows something about invasions, like the rest of the U.S. soldiers deployed to Iraq. Yet Turner restrains from drawing an explicit comparison between the 1258 burning of the House of Wisdom and the 2003 devastation of the Iraqi National Library and the Islamic library for which the U.S.-led coalition army must ultimately be held responsible. In light of what we noted earlier, this might not be a bad thing, though one might still wonder why, after telling in painful detail about the pillage of Baghdad and the appalling slaughter of thousands of human beings, the poem shifts its conceptual gears to the rarified sphere of the aesthetic. What does *beauty* have to do with cruelty, devastation, and generalized massacre? That may be precisely the point. The poem on the surface laments, along with the loss of human life and decency, the loss of cultural treasures and the records of civilization. And of course, somewhat predictably, it calls attention to poetry's inability to make sense of violence on such a massive scale. Yet at a deeper level the text raises questions concerning the relationship between beauty and horror, or—as Walter Benjamin ("Theses" 256) famously put it—between civilization and barbarism. Regardless of the form it is recorded in ("cuneiform, papyrus, stone"), the word *beauty* itself is not easily removable from the acts of human violence marking the march of civilization. Rather than detecting some immortal, transhistorical virtue in the concept of literacy—the way Dimock does, according to Robbins, in her search for a standard "that would permit atrocities to be named as atrocities" (389)—Turner acknowledges the difficulty of transcending that unending record of brutality and conquest that is human history. No matter how much we might wish for beauty to save us, the aesthetic is no pass to a less violent world.

In "Gilgamesh, in Fossil Relief" (from his first collection, *Here, Bullet*), Turner describes a poet chiseling the old Sumerian epic into stone tablets and a contemporary archeologist reading those ancient markings, only to conclude,

> History is a cloudy mirror made of dirt
> and bone and ruin. And love? Loss?
> These are the questions we must answer
> by war and famine and pestilence, and again
> by touch and kiss, because each age must learn
> *This is the path of the sun's journey by night.* (60)

These lines see human societies as caught in an endless cycle of death and rebirth, darkness and light, corruption and tenderness, apparently destined to repeat the same mistakes. In Michael Rotenberg-Schwartz's view, what Turner describes in this poem "is history writ large, and faced with it poetry can do nothing but document the repetitive cycles of love and war that must be lived to be understood. Though it sounds like a grand gesture of defeat, in fact it stubbornly sets in place a narrative of history, the rise and fall of empires, at least as old as the Enlightenment" (paragraph 7). One might note that, however clichéd, this vision of history stands opposed to the imperial logic underwriting the attack on Iraq and, more generally, the whole War on Terror. In Turner's poetry, the American Empire's raiders are often invited—whether explicitly or not—to be mindful of the vanished conquerors of old, whose only surviving traces are "dirt and bone and ruin." Still, we must seriously ask whether poems like "Gilgamesh, in Fossil Relief" may not provide an illustration of what, according to Robbins, is "the threat of deep time"—namely, "to display wave upon wave upon wave of conquest, with nothing to distinguish one conqueror from the last" (389). I will not deny that, here and elsewhere, Turner may fall into the trap of collapsing history into archetype, but I would emphasize that the poem also undercuts what, in a reference to George Santayana, Kadir calls "the illusion that remembering [is] tantamount to self-redemption . . . that any necessary correlation exists between knowledge and wisdom, memory and redemption" (*Memos* 55). Each generation must travel through its "night journey" and learn lessons that most likely will be lost on its descendants. Yet Turner also sees in each generation a resource of human feelings ("touch and kiss") that may ward off war and malady. We know this is not exactly true. Humans make their history in conditions that are only in part shaped by them. The possibility of choosing love over war is not given to each generation in the same degree. It is worth noting, however, the poem's juxtaposition of concrete terms like "touch and kiss" (with their openness to an ethical relation to the Other) to abstract nouns like "war" and "famine." It is as if the poem were telling us that the past we should keep fresh and alive is that of love rather than that of stale ancestral hatreds.

Turner imagines an even more direct participation in Iraqi history and culture in "The Martyrs Brigade," a poem showing how the Iraqi struggle for freedom has been going on long before the U.S.-led coalition claimed to have "liberated" the country. The poet here reverses his role as a member of an occupying army and takes part in the rebellion against the British colonizers:

> The poets eat kahi and drink cardamom tea
> in Baghdad, and it could be 1948
> or 2004, and it could be British bombers
> overhead, or the 173rd Airborne
> parachuting down from a metal-blue sky,
> but these poets will soon be dead,
> and bridges will be blown all over Iraq,
> verses I cannot even translate
> will be lost forever, lost the way bodies
> carry their bullets to the grave,
> their wounds closed only by the earth
> thrown over, shovel by shovel,
> the burial of the 1920 Revolution Brigade
> to be repeated again in '48
> with the Wathbah uprising, and again
> it must seem, with the fighters
> in Tikrit, in Samarra, in Basra and Fallouja,
> *Jisr Al-Shuhada* they cry,
> for *The Martyr's Brigade* they would die,
> life is given purpose in struggle,
> at least for the young, and the passionate,
> for those who discover in fire
> an echo of the searing heat of their own veins,
> and if I could, I'd be there
> on the bridge with Al-Jawahiri in 1948,
> with government bullets in the air,
> my friend's brother dying in his arms even now,

and I would hold back the blood
with my own hands, if only to be there
and to ask them both before dying,
Is it worth it? And can there be no other way? (*Here, Bullet* 38)

Here the connection between an older British colonialism and the contemporary Anglo-American attack is explicit. Moreover, the current struggle against invasion is not written off as Islamic terrorism but as the prosecution of a resistance movement with deep roots in the country's past. Reviewers have praised Turner for presenting us with both the Iraqi and the American points of view—though of course "Iraqi" and "American" are simplifications, as each individual has a unique point of view on what happens around him or her. In this text, however, the speaker seems to identify completely with the Iraqi side, as he imagines marching next to the great Iraqi poet and freedom fighter Al-Jawahiri (the poet calls him "my friend"), whose brother was mortally wounded by British bullets during the 1948 anticolonial uprising and died in the poet's arms (see Ali 27). This happened more than half a century ago, but, as Turner writes, Al-Jawahiri's brother is "dying in his arms *even now*" (emphasis added). The speaker sees himself as a target of the "government bullets," but this identification does not prevent him from posing a complex question regarding the intricate relations between the struggle for freedom, death, and violence: "*Is it worth it? And can there be no other way?*" The question is of course left unanswered, and some may feel that, no matter how sympathetic to the Iraqi cause Turner may be, here he comes dangerously close to shifting the responsibility for bloodshed on to those who have been the target of colonial violence. I think such an accusation would be unfair to what Turner is trying to do here. He imagines that, had he been an Iraqi, he would have fought (then and now) against the colonizers; but as a soldier who bears daily witness to the devastation of war, he dreams also of a resistance, of an *other way*, that may spare the freedom fighters themselves further pain and loss. Yet he only wonders whether such other way exists or not. Turner registers the urgency of the question while also showing he has no answer to offer. This tension is inscribed in the poem's epigraph, in which yet another Iraqi poet meditates on the relation between, on the one hand, words, violence, and the desire not to forget and give up the fight, and, on the other, the wish to be healed. "*I hide a disaster behind the mask of words; I say to my wound: / 'Don't heal,' and to my grief: 'Don't abate'; / and to lovers I say: 'Wash in my blood.'*"

The final question posed by the poem provides, I think, a useful example of how, rather than fetishizing the past, Turner interrogates it and renegotiates his relation to it. Turner asks himself, and asks us to ask ourselves, whether a total fidelity to the past may not result in a repetition of its mistakes. Maybe, even in a past as glorious as that of the Martyrs' Brigade there is something we must let go.

Maybe there are other ways from the standard ones to keep alive the struggle for freedom. Of course, these are questions at once historical and political that make Turner's work, to quote Robbins again, "ethically riskier as well as more difficult" (389) than a complacent dive into an undifferentiated deep time. Personally, I think we should be grateful to him for taking such risks as well as for showing us that temporal cosmopolitanism can be as discerning and ethically sound, if not easier to practice, than cosmopolitanism in space.

The Disobedient Guardian Angel

Along with his respect and interest for the "enemy" and its culture, literature, and history, the most notable achievement of Turner's poetry lies with its insistence on the fact that the peace America should reasonably hope for must always begin by acknowledging and "working through" the wreckage of war. This is a point Turner has often made, as for example, in a piece written in response to Kathrin Bigelow's Academy Award–winning film *The Hurt Locker* (which is, incidentally, also the title of one of Turner's most popular poems):

> The last image of "The Hurt Locker" expresses a theme I've often tried to articulate. In the film, the main character cannot completely return to America, to the norm of a life back home. In a sense, he's in Iraq whether he's physically in a supermarket in the States, or in a bomb suit walking into the hurt locker.
>
> That image rings true to me, but I'd take it a step further: I'd say that we, as a nation, now contain this explosive ordnance within us. Within our national psyche. We have generations of combat veterans and military family members woven throughout the fabric of our entire culture. Some of us have to walk down those dusty streets. We have to approach that which might tear us apart. We have to try to defuse what is explosive within. ("Bomb within Us")

One of the ways the explosives that the people and the nation as a whole carry within themselves may be "defused" is by defusing the language of war itself. One way of doing that is illustrated in the prose poetry of "Last Night's Dream" (*Here, Bullet* 65), where the fantasy of making love to an Iraqi woman consciously rejects the idea of love and war as mutually exclusive. In the poem it would seem that to make love *is* in a sense to make war, but since the reverse is also true, the possibility remains open that the nation the orgasm "destroys" is neither Iraq or the United States but the *idea* of the nation as a bounded, garrisoned community.

Another way to defuse the incendiary language of war is by confronting the rage and the hatred that soldiers carry with them. My favorite example of this strategy is "Guarding the Bomber," a poem where Turner combines his humanizing of the enemy with his idea of poetry as a form of healing that requires a constant reassessment of the past, and of past wrongs in particular. As Turner himself explains, this poem originates with something he witnessed in Mosul. "An Iraqi man (who had accidentally blown himself up while trying to create a roadside bomb) was placed in a room on the base, with a guard to watch over him (even though his arms and legs had been blown off), while he 'recuperated.' I tried to write this poem first from that guard's point of view, but the poem didn't work because the medic and the guard had two very different stories to tell" ("Verses in Wartime"). Except for some objective details regarding how the medic attends to the mutilated patient, the poem takes place entirely within the patient's imagination—or better, within the patient's imagination as it is imagined by the medic. In the first part, the medic imagines the bomber "lying in debris / and settling dust" right after setting off the explosive. In the second half, the poem—in the draft originally published by Turner in one of his "Home Fires" articles for the *New York Times*—outlines what the medic imagines his Iraqi patient is thinking:

> much of his body unable to sweat, working here
> beyond me and my thoughts of his Paradise,
> wondering if the virgins will care for him
> as I do, changing his bedpan, bathing him
> with sponges and reassurances in English—
> a language he hates, its vowels
> a smooth sheen of oil on steel—no,
> he's far beyond my rifle and desert fatigues,
> his ghost limbs dextrous and agile—he's connecting
> the many wires he sees within me, searching
> for any flash of brilliance sealed within.

Before I say anything about these lines, let me quote Turner's own commentary on them:

> In the Quran, there is one section which discusses how there are a number of angels which must guard the pit of Hell so that those trapped within it cannot escape. What a horrible task something like that might be. . . . Many who read this [poem] might be offended or disturbed by this line of thinking—caring for those who would kill us—and I fully understand why this may well seem impossible and reprehensible. And I respect that fact. Still, the angels at the edge of the abyss—wouldn't they want, at some point, to lift those trapped in Hell; to try, if in only the smallest of ways, to offer an alternative to pain and suffering; to try to influence the perceptions of those who would do us harm by showing kindness? If we can never forgive, if we forever guard the pit and lift no one out from the flames, what might that say about us? I'm not saying I've been able to do this—the poem is simply considering the idea. ("Bomb within Us")

The poem, then, is in Turner's intentions an exploration of the possibility and limits of forgiveness. Originally, the poem should have told two stories—the guard's and the medic's. By erasing the guard's perspective, and yet titling the poem "Guarding the Bomber," Turner appears to have fused the two figures together, thereby suggesting that the medic may be thought of as a secular version of the angels guarding the pit of Hell. This would make for a Manichean scenario, with a demonic Islamic bomber in the fiery pit, on the one side, and an angelic and caring U.S. medic, on the other. Yet if we read carefully Turner's description of the angels guarding the abyss, we may conclude that these hell's angels' duty is not so angelic after all. Theirs is a "horrible task," requiring them to repress precisely those angelic, humane feelings Turner wishes to reactivate in his poem. If the medic guarding the bomber is a "guardian angel," in other words, he may also be an angel trying to lift a soul from hell, thus transgressing orders from above.

However, in following Turner's hint that "Guarding the Bomber" is a poem about forgiveness, we must register the rather surprising absence of the bomber's point of view, which the text offers only as refracted through the speaker's own imagination. We have no evidence, that is, of what—as Hannah Arendt and others have argued—is usually the prerequisite for initiating forgiveness: the wrongdoer's admission of the reprehensible nature of his past behavior. So the question considered by the poem is not only how do we forgive but how do we forgive someone who is not asking us to be forgiven. Rigorously applied, Christian ethics calls for unconditional forgiveness, whether the wrongdoer asks to be forgiven or not. Yet to some forgiving certain crimes seems not only almost humanly impossible but also ethically problematic. If we forgive a particularly heinous criminal, aren't we at risk of extending our forgiveness to the crime as well? In the present case, however, as the speaker's reference to his rifle and desert fatigues makes clear, it must be kept in mind that the bomber's crime was committed in the context of war—a war that Turner knows was initiated by the Americans, not by the Iraqis. Taken individually, the medic may be angelic, but as the member of an invading army who started an illegal war of aggression, even he may need to ask for forgiveness, especially when one keeps in mind the enormous difference in war-related deaths between Americans and Iraqis.

The question posed by the poem could be easily turned around, and one could wonder how the Iraqis can forgive the U.S.-led bombers that have turned their cities into rubble, destroyed their hospitals, schools, and Mosques, their water pipelines, their electrical plants, their sewage systems, not to mention the overall dismantling of social structures caused by the war. One must give Turner credit for leaving the question of forgiveness unspecified in his commentary on the poem: he never states that the problem of "caring for those who would kill us" is an exclusively *American* problem. Nor is he suggesting that "defusing" the explosives of war would be equivalent to forgetting. As Robin Barklis explains in an invaluable analysis of Arendt's notion of forgiveness, "Because our orientations toward the future are, for Arendt, always embedded in memory, future-directed action cannot completely destroy the past, because to do so would be to destroy its own condition of possibility."[8] As our discussion of Turner's poetry should have made clear, not only does he believe that forgetting his (and his nation's) war past would be impossible—he also insists that it would amount to an immoral, irresponsible act. Turner would also seem to share another of Arendt's beliefs. As Barklis explains, far from "liquidating past memory," we can forgive by "*increasing* the scope of our historical narratives. . . . [F]orgiveness, as opposed to forgetting, addresses past wrongs by recomposing our stories about them into narratives that allow for the separation of the forgiven actor and the action for which she is being forgiven, representing the action as nonessential to the actor's broader identity. This type of forgiveness recreates the identity of the forgiven by telling a new, fuller story about how they relate to past actions, but does not destroy the memory of those actions."

This is an apt description of what Turner's poem tries to do: it separates the bomber from the action he has performed by focusing on how the latter has redefined his bodily identity. The presumed intention of the bomber was that of inflicting damage upon those who are now taking care of him. His wrongdoing—as reframed by the medic's narrative—has literally backfired. By telling the bomber's story the way he does, the medic condemns the bomber's violent action and yet elicits the reader's compassion for the devastated attacker. If his were a revenge narrative, the poem's speaker would have called attention to the evil the bomber has done to his enemies, something that would retrospectively justify the misery he must now endure. Instead, the medic not only concentrates on the ghostly figure the bomber now makes—he also tries to imagine what the man must have felt as he came to realize his body was no longer whole. Yet, even though now the bomber seems to inhabit a spectral space, in the speaker's imagination he continues to perform some kind of work: "he's connecting / the many wires he sees within me, searching / for any flash of brilliance sealed within." How are we to understand these lines? Are they telling us that the bomber is still pursuing his destructive project by trying to locate a point of ignition within his caretaker's body? Or, on the contrary, are these lines meant to suggest that "the flash of brilliance" the patient is searching for is of a completely different kind? "Brilliance" is a word covering a wide semantic field, and we might conclude that, in his effort to forgive the bomber, the medic imagines his enemy's deadly work now "defused" into something altogether different—into a search for the "brilliance," the genius, the wisdom, the intelligence of a fellow human being. Whether the bomber is actually engaged in such a redeeming search for a "connection" with his caretaker, or not, the medic imagines he is. This would seem to be a prerequisite for the care he shows to his patient.

What remains somewhat obscure in this original version of the poem, however, is the question of what compels the medic to humanize, and therefore forgive, the bomber. An answer can be found, I think, in the revised version of the poem's ending—the one Turner actually published in *Phantom Noise*:

> no,
> he's far beyond my rifle and desert fatigues,
> his dexterous ghost limbs tending the fire,
> and whether I want to admit it or not
> the explosives continue around him, his arms
> elbow-deep in the blue flame and heat,
> reaching in to save me. (37)

Now the bomber is no longer searching for "a flash of brilliance" but "tending the fire," an odd phrase since, even assuming he wishes to light the bomb's fuse, he would strike a match or a lighter, not "tend" a fire. The tending of a fire is a continued act of "caring for" that does not describe an activity associated with bombing. Even more puzzling are the lines of the revised poem in which the speaker confesses that, though he may be reluctant to admit this much, he now imagines the bomber with "his arms / elbow-deep in the blue flame and heat, / reaching in to save me." Until now we have heard of the medic's effort to care for an enemy who does not seem to have changed his mind about the Americans (he still hates their language). However, no longer being a legitimate military target, the Iraqi can now be the object of the medic's compassion (but, perhaps, of the medic's prejudices as well, as the reference to a stereotyped image of the Islamic Paradise would seem to imply). The last thing we would come to expect is to see the bomber engaged in the act of "saving" the medic. Isn't it the other way around? Isn't it the medic who is trying to save whatever life is left of the bomber? It bears repeating that the bomber is operating with "his dexterous ghost limbs"—with the imaginary arms the speaker's imagination is providing for him. While we can never know the bomber's own thoughts, the medic's fantasy assigns agency—and a benefic one, at that—to the bomber. This enemy, who was most likely seeking to blow up an American convoy, is now imagined as trying to rescue the medic from the fire. I have to admit that if one ignores the Quran's passage that triggered Turner's imagination, this point may be a bit difficult to grasp. Even so, it should be clear that, by the end of the poem, the medic has come to realize that whatever compassion he shows the mutilated bomber is a way for him to recognize not only his enemy's status as a human being but *his own humanity* as well. Just as to dehumanize your enemy is ultimately to dehumanize yourself, to see the enemy as human is to save your own humanity—to reject falling into the pattern of eternal hatred and vengeance that (as we have seen at numerous points in this book) is the inexorable logic underlying all wars.

A knowledge of the story about the angels guarding the fiery pit provides an even richer, theological more than metaphysical context for these surprising closing lines. "The blue flame and heat" the medic mentions is, I submit, that of the abyss of hell: that is, in fact, the fire the bomber is now "tending." As Turner tells the story of the poem's origin, the angel showing pity for the condemned would necessarily be the American medic, and it should be *he*, not the bomber, the one who, "elbow-deep in the blue flame and heat," reaches in. What saves the poem is precisely the fact that it completely overturns Turner's original idea by showing that the medic is as much in need of a spiritual rescue as anyone else is. He may perhaps think of himself as an angel kinder than the fabled virgins of Paradise, but the final lines suggest that he could actually end up keeping company with the devil were it not for the angel pulling him out of the flames. And that angel is the bomber—the bomber, to go back to Arendt's idea of forgiveness, not as such, but as a fellow victim of war whose predicament reactivates what is human in the medic, thus literally "saving" him from the hell of war and eternal revenge. This larger context also shows how dangerous certain literal readings of the Holy Scriptures—whether these Scriptures be from the Bible or the Qu'ran is indifferent—may turn out to be. By imagining the bomber as a disobedient angel—as an angel who cannot accept that God may wish to punish some souls eternally, no matter how great the crimes they may have committed—the poem delivers a poignant "anti-war" message valid for all times and places. The disobedient angel is the disobedient soldier, the bomber who turns into a medic himself, as well as the medic who resists the impulse to take revenge. True, all this happens in the imagination, but that is where poets (including war poets) must operate.[9]

Turner's poetry is an effort to articulate a cosmopolitan perspective eschewing the friend-enemy binary on which, like all wars, the Iraq War also depends. One could object that Turner's cosmopolitanism is too firmly rooted in his condition as an American soldier to reach a truly universalist viewpoint. Yet the problem might not be so much that he is ostensibly more concerned with the American rather than the Iraqi side of the war, as the fact that, by often viewing occupiers and occupied as equally victimized by the senseless violence of war, his cosmopolitanism runs the risk of downplaying the "coalition" forces' status as original aggressors. However, this is definitely not the case with "The Discotheque," a poem from *Phantom Noise* dedicated to Tony Lagouranis, the author of *Fear Up Harsh: An Army Interrogator's Dark Journey through Iraq*. Turner confesses that it was only by reading this book that he realized he "was one of the infantry soldiers handing over captured detainees (prisoners) to the military police unit (MPs) in Mosul (who would in turn hand over the prisoners and my paperwork dispositions to men and women like Tony)" (*Phantom Noise* 62). This feeling of not knowing what you are actually doing borders of course with the cognate feeling of *not wanting* to know—a point effectively captured in the poem:

> I held a 9 mm pistol in my hand, watched
> How the prisoners' heads slumped in resignation,
> One of them mumbling a slow rocking of prayer.
>
> And I didn't feel a thing. I just wanted to sleep,
> To wake and find myself in California—
> *anywhere else* but here.

The poem is an explicit act of self-blaming. There is not so much self-pity as rage in Turner's acknowledgment that

> From that metal box shrouded in a camouflage netting
> I never heard the screaming. I never heard the breaking of men.
> I heard only music—guitars from distorted speakers. (62)

Here the poet may well be telling the truth—he did not know about the torturing and the violence—but he hardly takes this to be an extenuating circumstance. There is just too much irony in mistaking a torture chamber "for an on-base club"! No wonder the poem singles out "Sgt. Turner" as someone fully deserving to be blamed:

> Farid, Hasan, Mohamed, Abdullah, Jafar.
> How many have heard my words spoken in court?
> The Accuser. The Professor. Sgt Turner. (63)

Turner, "the Accuser"—and as we know the Accuser is Satan's other name—here stands accused: for not knowing or caring to know, and for acting the way he did. As in "Guarding the Bomber," where the would-be angel needs himself to be rescued from hell's fire, in "The Discothèque" the roles are reversed and "the Professor" is the one who is only now slowly beginning to learn.

The "Private Wars" of Women Soldiers

In poems like "The Discothèque," or the one I am about to mention, Turner breaks away from the temptation to eulogize the American soldiers as a bunch of decent guys caught in the wrong place at the wrong time. This is obviously not to say that many American or British soldiers deployed in Iraq were not "normal" people forced to do what they were told and who in many instances quickly realized the wrongheadedness of the whole enterprise. Neither should one deny that "coalition" soldiers would at times care for civilians and show sympathy for their plight.

Yet by emphasizing the goodness of particular individuals, one might lose sight of the army *as a system*, as a machinery of destruction guided by a specific politics. Moreover, in the case of the Iraq War, the U.S. Army's "band of brothers" mystique often hides its treatment of women soldiers, the theme of Turner's "Insignia," a poem with a very explicit epigraph: "One in three female soldiers will experience / sexual assault while serving in the military" (*Phantom Noise* 58). The poem unveils the paradoxical situation many women soldiers had to face in both Iraq and Afghanistan, where their most vicious enemies were their fellow male soldiers:

> It's you she's dreaming of, Sergeant—she'll dream of you
> for years to come. If she makes it out of this country alive,
> which she probably will. You will be the fire and the hovering
> breath. Not the sniper. Not the bomber in the streets. You. (58)

The same concept is expressed by one of the women interviewed by novelist and Columbia University professor of journalism Helen Benedict for her book *The Lonely Soldier: The Private War of Women Serving in Iraq*. "I wasn't carrying the knife for the enemy, I was carrying it for the guys on my own side" (163). The book painfully documents the horrors so many women soldiers in Afghanistan and Iraq had to endure at the hands of the men they served with. Though women had been directly involved in war-making well before the First Gulf War, "more American women have fought and died in Iraq than in any war since World War II. Over 191,500 women have served in the Middle East since March 2003, most of them in Iraq, which is nearly five times more than in the 1991 Gulf War and twenty-six times more than in Vietnam. And by September 2008, 592 American female soldiers had been wounded in action and 102 had died in Iraq, more than in the Korean, Vietnam, First Gulf and Afghanistan Wars combined" (3). The higher casualties of the Iraq War are a consequence not only of the greater number of women serving but of the fact that while in theory women were still barred from ground combat, the tasks often assigned to them were such that their participation in war was virtually no different from that of men. This, however, seems to have had little effect on their everyday army life. Whether because, as Benedict speculates, military culture has generally seen women "as sexual prey rather than as responsible adults" (4), or because "men resent women for usurping the masculine role of warrior" (5), "the military is still permeated with stereotypes of women as weak, passive sex objects who have no business fighting and cannot be relied upon in battle" (5). Unfortunately, these prejudices do not just make for a harrowing working environment; such sexist perceptions are the breeding ground of the shocking violence male soldiers direct against their women colleagues. Reliable studies conducted on female veterans from the Vietnam War and the First Gulf War, referred to by Benedict in her book, have established that one out of three women soldiers has been actually raped, while two-thirds have been sexually assaulted, and nearly 90 percent subjected to some form of sexual harassment. Exact figures are hard to obtain, as many women do not report the attacks they must endure out of fear of getting into trouble, of being called a snitch, of seeing their career ruined, or, sadly, because they know it is unlikely offenders will be prosecuted. The record shows that most sexual assailants get away with insignificant punishment. As Benedict notes, this is by no means to say that all male soldiers are rapists or that all women are unhappy about their experience with the U.S. Army. Yet male violence against women is so widespread in the military as to make this fact—at least from an American point of view—one of the most significant traits of the Iraq and Afghanistan Wars. The frequency with which the women whose stories Benedict relates reiterate the notion that their worst enemy was within their own units is revealing. "My company," explains a woman soldier serving in Iraq from 2005 to 2006, "consisted of fifteen hundred men . . . and under eighteen women. I was fresh meat to hungry men. The mortar rounds that came in daily did less damage to me than the men with whom I shared my food" (4). An Air Force sergeant deployed in Iraq in 2003 and again in 2006 uses similar words: "I ended up waging my own war against an enemy dressed in the same uniform as mine" (47).

As Benedict explains in her acknowledgments page, much of the material for her novel *Sand Queen* "was culled from the research I did for my nonfiction book, *The Lonely Soldier: The Private War of Women Serving in Iraq*. Although this is fiction, I have been helped and inspired by my interviews with more than forty veterans of the Iraq War, several of whom served at Camp Bucca and many of whom survived combat and mortar attacks. . . . Without their courage and honesty, and their willingness to tell me their stories, I could never have written about Kate Brady's experiences of war" (313). Reading the two books together, one can easily see the great extent to which *Sand Queen*'s main character goes through many of the same ordeals confronted in real life by the women interviewed in *The Lonely Soldier*. The novel, however, does more than simply condense into fewer figures and a more gripping narrative the same tragic scenario offered in the earlier book. *Sand Queen* is in large part devoted to main character Kate Brady's story. However, the novel introduces another important voice, that of Naema, an Iraqi woman who is the book's other narrator and whose sufferings both parallel and diverge in important ways from Kate's. The novel's double narrative, existential theme, and political focus explain the inclusion of *Sand Queen* in this chapter. Like Turner's, Benedict's literary perspective may also be described as cosmopolitan. Her characters' experiences, of course, are rooted in their specific individual, social, and historical circumstances. Occasionally, they do try to look at the world with the Other's eyes, but for the most part the pressures they experience are too great for any meaningful communication to take place. The reader, however, occupies a position allowing him or her to sympathize with the human plight of both Kate and Naema, as well as that of other characters, but also to be suspicious of any justification for the war. Like Turner, Benedict insists that the violence of war sweeps away everyone and turns today's victimizers into tomorrow's victims, yet she is careful to take into account issues of scale and political responsibility. Naema's perspective is therefore crucial. It prevents readers from forgetting the extent of the devastation visited by the "coalition" forces on Iraq, and it shows that while each individual life lost or damaged on both sides is an unacceptable tragedy, one cannot approach events from a "neutral" perspective. It is surely no accident that issues of responsibility, guilt, and blame are central to the novel's unfolding.

As already mentioned, though *Sand Queen* devotes more space to Kate Brady's story, it alternates her voice with that of Naema. I should now add that brief chapters told by a third-person narrator also punctuate the text. These chapters are devoted to Kate's experience in a VA hospital, and, late in the story, to her ambivalent reunion with Jimmy, the wartime fellow soldier she has fallen in love with. By showing proleptically that Kate's fate as a psychologically damaged war veteran is sealed, Benedict not only undercuts any hope for a happy ending, she also invites readers to pay attention to the various steps through which Kate's descent into her personal hell takes place. This is what makes of Kate a more narratively interesting character than Naema. Though Naema has a broader understanding of war, she has, when we first meet her, already experienced much of its horrors. Her destiny, as the destiny of her family, is even more tragic than Kate's, but Naema cannot blame herself for it. Kate, on the other hand, cannot escape blaming herself, even though for the most part she is just another victim of a cruel, senseless war, made even more terrible by the oppressive, tyrannical functioning of the very army that, ironically enough, was sent to bring democracy to Iraq.

Forced to share her sleeping quarters with "thirty-six snoring, farting members of the male sex" (7) and only two fellow women soldiers, Kate is singled out as a "sand queen," that is, as "an ugly-ass chick who's being treated like a queen by the hundreds of horny guys around her because there's such a shortage of females. But she grows so swellheaded over their attention that she lets herself be passed around like a whore at a frat party, never realizing that back home those same guys wouldn't look at her twice" (105). Kate is, of course, no whore, and though she is constantly insulted and harassed, she tries to be tough and handle the situation on her own as best she can. Similarly, when she stands all day long on a turret overseeing the Iraqi prisoners' camp, and some of them throw rocks, scorpions, and snakes at her, jeer and masturbate under her eyes, she says to herself, "I'll handle it, pray when I need to, suck it up like the soldier I am" (98). She is even capable of showing some understanding for the "enemy." "I don't really blame the prisoners for being angry. I mean, look at the poor fuckers, stuck in overcrowded, stinking hot tents for reasons they probably don't understand. I know most of them are innocent because we've been told as much. . . . . Some are real bad guys, of course, Saddam loyalists or insurgents. But most are just ordinary people who got caught by mistake" (98). Two such innocent people are Naema's little brother, and her father, who after being jailed and tortured by Saddam's police years before, is now re-experiencing brutality at the hands of the "liberators."

One morning Naema meets Kate in front of Camp Bucca, where, along with many other Iraqi women and elders, she walks every morning to inquire about her imprisoned relatives. Since Naema speaks English, she is able to communicate with Kate, who sympathizes with the woman's plight and tries to find out what happened to her father and brother. Yet there is never any hope that these two women may ever become friends. The novel shows that, in spite of all the empty rhetoric about being there to help the Iraqis build a democratic society, the local population can hardly be expected to have faith in those who, as Kate puts it, have "pulverized their towns, locked up their men and killed their kids" (8). Analogously, to the occupiers, the Iraqis "are capable of anything, or so we've been told: using babies as shields, smuggling weapons under pregnant women's dresses. And the worst thing is we can't tell from looking at them whether they're innocent civilians or bad guys" (37). Kate's good intentions notwithstanding, she is in no position to offer Naema any real help, and she ends up, by mistake, giving Naema's prisoner-father a savage beating.

The novel traces Kate's descent from decency into rage, desperation, and near madness, as one victimization leads inexorably to the next. First, she is sexually assaulted by her commanding officer, Kormick, and his sidekick, PFC "Boner." Saved from rape by Jimmy Donnell and Derek Johnson ("DJ"), Kate could press charges against the two assaulters, but she is afraid to be ostracized by her fellow soldiers even more. Besides, she has (correctly, as it turns out) no faith in the system. After the incident, however, the prisoners' jeering and obscenities become less and less endurable, especially after a rock hits Kate during a prison riot. She tells Jimmy she would like to beat up one of those lechers, and soon enough she gets to enact her revenge, except that she mistakes Naema's father for the "jerk-off." Once she realizes her mistake, Kate's guilty feelings prevent her from trusting the love she feels for Jimmy. Guilt is also the reason, after "Third Eye," one of the two other women in the unit, is raped, Kate does what seems to be the right thing. Thinking that if she had acted earlier she might have prevented her comrade's rape, she reports Kormick's and Boner's assault against her. After being led to believe the army will investigate the problem, Kate and Yvette (the third woman) are sent out on a dangerous, punitive mission. They will be escorting a convoy along the infamous Highway of Death. At the end of the outward journey, during a mortar attack against the compound, Yvette is killed and Kate, once again, feels she is at least in part to blame. She has now reached a sort of emotional dead-end. "I feel hard and tough and cold inside. I feel like a solider now. A real robot soldier. I know who I hate and I know who I want to kill. All the rest is bullshit" (283).

But does Kate really "know"? And assuming she does, can she act on what she knows? The first logical target of her rage should be someone like Henley, the lieutenant who sided with rapist Kormick and was responsible for sending her and Yvette on a very dangerous mission. It turns out, however, that once again Kate chooses to vent her rage against a more easily available target, by shooting in the groin the jerk-off she had intended to beat up all along. She avoids court martial only because, after shooting the prisoner, she falls from the guard-tower and is injured. Her career, however, is over—she is discharged for "failure to adjust" (132). At this point the short VA hospital chapters catch up with the main narrative, which ends with her flight from the hospital and her reunion with Jimmy, who now has a partner but allows Kate to stay in his house "for as long as [she] want[s]" (304). Benedict has announced her intention to write a sequel to *Sand Queen*, where presumably we may learn what subsequently happens to Kate. As it stands, Kate's story ends bleakly. One feels that the memories of war will forever haunt her: "Blood is in my eyes and my soul. Yvette's blood, Zaki's blood, the jerk-off's blood, the blood of the Iraqi worker I let die in the mortar attack. The blood of that little boy's donkey. Naema's dad covered in it as I ground his face into the sand" (299).

Haunting Comparisons

Naema's story, too, ends on a desperate note. When we last see her, she is about to discover what the reader already knows—that her brother and father have both been killed, and all her efforts to care for them have been as ineffectual as, for the most part, her attempts to cure the wounded in the Umm Qasr hospital (Naema is a medical student). The hospital scenes are indeed some of the most powerful in the whole book.

> The hospital corridors are swarming with people! A few blood-splattered nurses are trying to restore order, but the place is more like an overcrowded refugee camp than a house of rest and healing. And it is filthy! Beside us stand a sink full of bloody test tubes waiting to be washed. A tiny child lies alone screaming on a urine-stained gurney, its face and body so blistered with burns I cannot tell its sex. A boy is carried past with a metal shard impaled in his skull, his eyes rolling in agony. In one corner a cluster of people is drinking out of an oil drum, but when I draw near I see that the water is covered with slimy, gray scum. (250)

Naema's main role is to bear witness to the war from the point of view of an Iraqi civilian who, like many of her fellow citizens, suffered under Saddam but is hit even harder by a war whose first victims are innocent civilians. Her narrative may sound almost didactic at points, but it is in large part her eyewitness accounts that prevent the novel from turning into yet another narrative about American innocence lost in a useless, immoral war. Thanks to her, we learn the consequences of the invaders' "shock and awe" strategy: the looting, the crimes, the rapes, the lack of water, food, shelter, and health care. Moreover, we learn from her voice that Iraqi women—who under the 1959 Family Code enjoyed more freedom than Muslim women anywhere in the Middle East outside of Turkey—see many of their rights taken away. By showing the living conditions of the very population the war was supposed to set free, Benedict demonstrates that while the madness of war affects both occupiers and occupied, there is no question as to which side must bear the most suffering. I think it is no accident that although *Sand Queen* is mostly Kate's novel, the last chapter is left to Naema, and her very last words offer no consolation whatsoever.

> I cannot think of Khalil [her fiancé] and whether he is safe, of my future or of home. I cannot even whip up my habitual anger against the Americans and their senseless war. For all I can hear, echoing relentlessly in my head, are the words of mourning Mama spoke over Granny Maryam's body as she wrapped her in that shroud. Words that seem determined to extinguish, one by one, each tender flame of my hope.
> *I am the house of remoteness.*
> *I am the house of loneliness.*
> *I am the house of soil.*
> *I am the house of worms.* (310)

By the novel's end, both women are described as emotionally and spiritually destitute, and both may be seen as casualties of a war they were forced to endure. Yet whereas Naema has little to blame herself for, Kate's last words are an eloquent reprisal of her main psychological and moral problem: "'I didn't protect her ["Third Eye," who kills herself after returning home], Jimmy,' I whisper as the tears come. 'I didn't protect Yvette, either, or Naema's dad or her little brother. I've killed so many of them. Oh God, when will it stop?'" (305). Thus, while the war is not over when the novel ends—and it may well never be over for people who, like Naema and Kate, have gone through so much—it is only Kate who needs to be forgiven. This is not to say the novel suggests *all* Iraqis are innocent in the same way. Benedict does not romanticize the Other, and it is certainly no accident that Kate is sexually harassed, though in different ways, by both Iraqi and American men. Moreover, Naema is aware of the fact that cruelty and the defiance of international laws are not an exclusively American prerogative: "I cannot think of cluster bombs without outrage. . . . What sort of a demon invented a weapon like this? And what sort of a population allows its armies to use it? But then, what did we do when Saddam gassed the Kurds with his own demonic weapons? And what did we do when we slaughtered the Shia, my mother's people, stole their water, dried up their fields and destroyed their livelihoods? We, too, can be sheep" (114–15). Though Naema's narrative makes clear that her own family suffered during Saddam Hussein's rule, the "we" she uses in this passage implies that she cannot claim to be totally innocent of the crimes he committed to the extent that she, like the rest of the people, were "sheepishly" afraid to protest those terrible practices.

Naema's considerations should not be seen only as an example of how, through her words, the novel rejects the idea of the absolute innocence of the Other. Naema's words are also an illustration of comparative thinking. She begins by literally demonizing the enemy who would use such terrible and illegal weapons as cluster bombs, only to conclude that—"too" is the crucial word here—to the extent that she wishes to indict *all* Americans for the horrors of the Iraq War, she would have to do the same with her own people. Americans, Britons, and Iraqi all share sheepish streaks. This is not to say that the passage is supporting a kind of "chickens coming home to roost" philosophy. Indeed, the considerable accomplishment of this passage is that, while aiming at a critical analysis of her own nation's history along the lines of "we've been just as bad as the Americans or the Brits," Naema delivers *also* a sharp critique of the "coalition" countries. No careful reader can ignore that Naema's reasoning may be easily turned around, thereby forcing us to acknowledge that our side is behaving no better than the hateful, bloody dictator we claimed to be morally superior to. Yet Naema's most biting critique may not be the one implied in the virtual equivalence between Saddam's and the "allies'" way of war, as the one implicitly delivered when she says to herself, "We, too, can be sheep." The troubling point here, for Western readers, is not simply that they are guilty of failing to stop a war waged in their name. The more polemical point lies with the fact that even people who can claim to enjoy all the benefits of democracy in the end turn out to be as powerless as the "sheep" crushed by the iron heel of a ruthless dictatorship.

Understandably, much attention has been paid to *Sand Queen* as a continuation by novelistic means of Benedict's effort to expose the horrible conditions of so many women soldiers in the U.S. Army. Yet this is not its only important theme, and though *Sand Queen* has been predictably labeled an "anti-war" book, what would make it so, according to the reviewers, is the frank depiction of the horrors of warfare and the indictment of the U.S. Army's misogynist policies. These are certainly important aspects of the novel, but when reviews describe both Kate and Naema as each in her own way a victim of war, what goes nearly unmentioned is the fact that Kate is largely a victim whose problem is that she does not so much feel she is a victim but a victimizer. Kate believes she is to blame on a number of counts, and she cannot forgive herself. The question here is how should the reader regard Kate? With pity? With compassion? Well, yes, this is probably one way to respond to her personal tragedy. The reader knows (and this much Kate knows as well) that she has been victimized by the vast majority of her male comrades, who want to exploit her sexually as a woman and at the same time complain she is not enough of a "man." She is thus put in a no-win situation: no matter how much she tries "to suck up like a soldier" whatever happens to her in the hope that she will be seen as equal to the rest of the men, she is not a man, as her tormentor Kormick kindly reminds her: "You wish you had a cock, Brady? . . . A real cock like a man, so you can piss like a man? Nobody'd have to see your little pink ass, then, would they?" (46).

By blaming the victim, the institution of the army generates the psychological mechanism destined to plague Kate for the rest of her novelistic life. Kate, like so many victims of rape, is tortured by doubts that she may have in some way caused the violence she was subjected to ("While I go through everything that's happened—Boner punching me, Kormick attacking me in the shack—I keep thinking. *You could've fought back harder. You could've been tougher. You gave the wrong signals, admit it. What kind of a soldier are you anyway?*" [226]). The same is true when she blames herself for the deaths of Yvette, Zaki, and Naema's father. From the reader's viewpoint, Kate is not guilty of any of these deaths. True, Yvette is sent on a dangerous mission because she presses charges against Kormick along with Kate, but Yvette is actually the one who insists Kate report the assault. As for Zaki, all we know is that he died trying to escape—true or not, Kate has nothing to do with it. The only thing she can blame herself for with some justification is the beating of Naema's father: though she beat him by mistake, she may feel shame for wanting to revenge herself on a prisoner to begin with. Along the same lines, she may feel guilty for shooting the other prisoner in the groin, as well as for killing a donkey walked by a child, on her way back from Baghdad after Yvette's death. This does not mean the reader is invited to feel that Kate dug her own grave. On the other hand, can we really expect Kate to be coolly rational and forgive herself because not all the terrible things she was involved in are directly her fault? Are we sure this is what the novel is asking us to do—to feel that we know better than Kate, and so she should just snap out of her PTSD? Wouldn't this be like asking the reader to behave, more or less, like Kate's parents, or her former boyfriend Tyler, or even the nurses and doctors in the VA hospital—people who feel that, whatever horrors she may have witnessed or taken part in, Kate should go back to a "normal" life? Would not this be an easy—indeed, a cheap—way out of war?

Fortunately, this is not what *Sand Queen* is asking from its readers. Lacking what Benedict herself calls a "comforting ending" (Interview), the novel confronts the reader with one of the key dilemmas that are the legacy of all wars. If in a broad sense all soldiers may be considered as "victims" of war, then Kate is ten times more a victim because of her condition as a woman within an aggressively male-chauvinist army. Yet there is no question that even Kate—or, for that matter, even as sensitive, intelligent, and cultured a soldier as Brian Turner—cannot ignore the fact that they were sent to war in order to kill, to destroy, to victimize other people. And, if we are mindful of Naema's words, they were not ordered to do so by a tyrannical dictator: they were sent to war by a nation that prides itself as being the world's greatest democracy. It would be very unwise, therefore, to dismiss Kate's self-blaming as a simple misreading of her war experience. The point is not so much that she has nothing to do with the murders of Zaki and his father, or that it is simply untrue that Yvette's death was her fault. The point is that the guilt she feels cannot be washed away by invoking her naiveté about "traveling the world and keeping the peace" (42), her basic "goodness," or even her mistreatment by her male companions. Kate's guilt, like the trauma of Vietnam veteran Ron Faust mentioned in the previous chapter, could be dealt with only if the national community responsible for launching the war were to acknowledge its mistakes and share with its soldiers the consequences of its fateful decisions. This, however, hardly ever happens. Nations traditionally deal with postwar collective and individual traumas by offering survivors sacrificial narratives that sanctify the deaths and sufferings of their side as the "necessary price" to be paid for the survival and well-being of the community. This kind of national "healing" is predicated on forgetting, rather than the working through, the causes of war, and, needless to say, it rests on a Manichaean distinction between lives whose loss is grievable (those of our side) and lives whose destruction we are allowed to forget (those of "the enemy") (see Butler, *Frames of War* 1–32). That is why the kind of alternative work done by activists like Maxine Hong Kingston in the "coming home" workshops we discussed earlier is so important. If a returning soldier cannot be embraced by the nation as a whole, she should at least be able to communicate her feelings, her memories, and her shame to people who—rather than excusing "the violence of war as a regrettable but unavoidable exchange demanded by the needs of security" (Denton-Borhaug 226)—would help her assess her personal trauma as intimately connected to a machinery of destruction that, though to different degrees, we all have contributed in setting up.

Another way of saying all of the above would be to suggest that rather than insisting on reading Kate, we as readers should let Kate read *us*. How does her counternarrative, so different from the official histories of the war, interrogate us? How can we help the veterans as well as those distant people whose lives were permanently damaged by a war that was waged, like it or not, in our name? The novel offers virtually no hope that the lives of its two main characters may intersect in any meaningful way: Kate's and Naema's tragedies follow their separate courses, as if to say that the U.S. veterans' troubles and those of the Iraqis, though obviously related, are of a different nature. It would be hard to disagree with this. Yet, as witness the need of many Vietnam veterans to return to Vietnam, or Turner's own desire to go back one day to Iraq as a civilian, many veterans may find some peace only by reconnecting with the country where they fought, and with its people. To come home, they may also need to *leave* home, that is.[10] *Sand Queen* does not tell us how to achieve a reconciliation between the United States and Iraq, but it surely evokes a need for it. Like much of Turner's poetry, it is a novel that goes beyond the mere humanizing of the enemy and strives to teach readers something about the history, the people, and the culture of the country the United States spent trillions of dollars to bomb into the Stone Age. I am tempted to write that, works like the ones discussed in this final chapter, in their deft deployment of counternarratives that stubbornly refuse to be woven into a sacrificial history, are, for the most part, free of the contradictions and incongruity haunting all the "anti-war" texts analyzed in this book. A quick search on the Internet, however, informs me that Turner's poems, as well as passages from O'Brien's *The Things They Carried*, are read in a Connecticut high school on Memorial Day to celebrate "the sacrifices" of American soldiers who died for their country.[11] In his poem "Night in Blue," Turner writes, "What do I know / of redemption or sacrifice, what will I have / to say of the dead—that it was worth it, / that any of it made sense?" (*Here, Bullet* 70). This sounds to me to be the expression of a clear reluctance to participate in any sacrificial narrative, but, like Kingston, Turner, too, has no control over the use of his texts. As I have insisted throughout this book, the "anti-war" credentials of any poem or story are always debatable, as they depend to no small extent on the critical discourses we bring to bear on them. On another, deeper level, however, all war writing is to an extent mesmerized by its horribly fascinating subject matter. The spell may be broken, but only provisionally. That step beyond the hero Emerson invoked is as difficult to take in literature as in life.

Notes

Chapter 1. Anti-War?

1. "To prevent or at least control war are worthy aims, but attempts to circumscribe it often founder—and fortunately so, if the view is taken that rendering something comprehensible is a step towards rendering it acceptable. But, at the very least, the record can be kept" (McLoughlin, "War and Words" 19).

2. I deal more specifically with this problem in chapter 3. Two important studies on the ethical and aesthetical dilemmas connected to the notions of the "unspeakable" and the "unrepresentable" are Rothberg and Mandel.

3. When asked whether his is an "anti-war book," the narrator replies with a tentative, "Yes [. . .], I *guess*" (3, emphasis added).

4. Even Jason and Graves's *Encyclopedia of American War Literature* has no entry for "anti-war literature," though quite a few of the texts discussed are identified as being "antiwar." On his part, Samuel Hymes, in his bestselling *The Soldier's Tale*, speaks of anti-war journalism and protests but does not apply the label to literary works.

5. As far as cinema goes, Michael Cimino is on record for stating that "any good war movie" cannot but be an "antiwar movie" (as quoted in Joanna Burke 6), while Steven Spielberg has gone as far as stating, "Of course every war movie, good or bad, is an anti-war movie" (66). For the opposite view, see the comment attributed to François Truffaut: "There could be never an anti-war film, as the violence in such film would inevitably excite the viewer to the point of siding with one group over the other" (as quoted in Trafton 122). For a thoughtful reflection on the difficulty of identifying an anti-war cinema see Soltysik.

6. On the analogies between Vietnam narratives and classical Greek literature see also Trittle.

7. Simone Weil, "Ne recommençons pas la guerre de Troie," *Les nouveaux cahiers* 1: 2–3 (April 1–15, 1937).

8. On the concept of "refunctioning" (*Umfunktionierung*) see Benjamin, "Author as Producer."

9. The classic studies of the cultural impact of World War I are Fussel and Leed. See also Eksteins and Sherry.

10. For a recent, nearly antithetical discussion of nineteenth-century American literature's attitudes toward war and violence, see Reynolds. Rather than emphasizing his writers' resistance to violence, Reynolds sees their views as at best ambivalent.

11. As Danilo Zolo notes in his preface to a collection of Schmitt's writings, the German theorist's thesis relies heavily on the letter of the *Jus Publicum Europeaum* and much less on any empirical verification of the extent to which the juridical "shaping" of war was actually able to contain violence. The key text where Schmitt discusses the "bracketing" of war achieved by the *Jus Publicum Europeanum* is *Der Nomos der Erde* (1950).

12. To the best of my knowledge, there are no extensive critical discussions of how a "pacifist" novel may differ from an "anti-war" one. Often the terms are used interchangeably. One could apply to literature the political distinctions philosopher Duane Cady has made along the "moral continuum" beginning with "warism" at one end and reaching "pacifism" at the other, after encountering the "war realism," "just-warism," and "anti-war" positions. (Similar categories have been invoked more recently by Ceadel.) Yet such fine distinctions are not easily applicable to novels or poems.

13. On war's "morphogenetic" power see also Curi 13+.

14. Augustine of Hippo, letter to Bonifacius, in *Epistulae*, as quoted in Fumagalli Beonio Brocchieri 20.

15. However, by uncovering traces of war nearly everywhere, Lerner's version of Peace Studies would seem to confirm the anthropologically and linguistically foundational nature of war, rather than highlight the workings of peace.

16. "Just as 'peace' is more complex than the absence of war, so attitudes towards peace should be placed on a much wider range than is allowed by the simple label of 'pacifism' regularly applied to those opposed to war" (Gittings 3).

17. According to Curi (62), the first to theorize a difference between peace as an autonomous virtue and peace as the mere absence of war was Baruch Spinoza in his *Tractatus theologico-politicus* (1670).

18. Twain wrote elsewhere that "to trust the God of the Bible is to trust an irascible, vindictive, fierce and ever fickle and changeful master." To this unappealing figure he juxtaposed "the true God . . . a Being who has uttered no promises, but whose beneficent, exact, and changeless ordering of the machinery of His colossal universe is proof that He is at least steadfast to His purposes; whose unwritten laws, so far as they affect man, being equal and impartial, show that he is just and fair" (Baetzhold and McCullough 337).

19. I must thank Donatella Izzo for this observation.

Chapter 2. *Ad Bellum Purificandum*

1. Udall's, Kammen's, and Dykstra's endorsements all appeared on the dust jacket of the book.

2. The relevant material on the "Bellesiles affair" is easily accessible on the web. A good place to start is the Wikipedia article on Bellesiles: http://en.wikipedia.org/wiki/Bellesiles.

3. Report of the Investigative Committee in the matter of Professor Michael Bellesiles, http:// www.news. emory.edu/Releases/Final_Report.pdf.

4. The best defense of Bellesiles is Wiener 73–93.

5. For an attack on Bellesiles's work as an example of "postmodern critical theory," see Sherman.

6. I wish to thank Marilyn Young for directing me to Robin's essay.

7. Available at http://www.brothersjudd.com/index.cfm/fuseaction/reviews.detail/book_id/36/Arming%20Ameri.htm (accessed October 2006).

8. I am referring to Wolfe's "Anti-American Studies."

9. On the "nonviolence tradition" in the United States, see also Chernus. On the antebellum American peace movement, see Ziegler.

10. "The vision of freedom animating the founders of seventeenth-century Anglo-America and of the eighteenth-century American republic distinguished their purpose from that of the Old World, constantly embroiled in bloody disputes over privilege and power.... Military power was poison—one not without its occasional utility, but a poison all the same and never to be regarded otherwise" (Bacevich 32–33). Bacevich's scathing analysis of the "new American militarism" is proof that there are, after all, intelligent conservative minds who disagree with archetypal readings of the American soul as essentially bloodthirsty. A conservative Catholic, as he describes himself, Bacevich writes that even though today "Americans have come to define the nation's strength and well-being in terms of military preparedness, military action, and the fostering (or nostalgia for) military ideals," this is "to a degree without precedent in U.S. history" (2).

11. In early nineteenth-century culture, "the word *damnable* still meant 'capable of damning one to an eternity in Hell'" and Cooper understands that "the conquering of the wilderness forces New World Christians to act like Old World pagans" (McWilliams, *Last* 119–20).

12. See Foucault, *"Society Must Be Defended"* and *Power/Knowledge*. I discuss his views in the next chapter.

13. Of course, discourses of peace are not expressed only in the language of war. Peace-building is an everyday activity taking place in civil society and involving especially the spheres of education and mass communication (see Brock-Utne). But to the extent that the conquest of peace entails a simultaneous "conquest of violence," "active" peace, conceived as the practice of nonviolence, will always be conflictual (see my discussion of Maxine Hong Kingston's *The Fifth Book of Peace* in the final chapter).

14. Friedrich's volume is a shocking collection of World War I photographs, prefaced by a trilingual (German, English, and French) call to fight those who make wars possible. It

was republished in the United States as *War against War*, with an introduction by Douglas Kellner (Seattle: Real Comet, 1987). For Jean Paul's "Kriegserklärung gegen den Kriegsee," see his *Samtliche Werke: Historisch-kritische Ausgabe*, vol. 14, *Politische Schriften* (1939), 79–98.

15. Two notable examples of politico-ideological critiques of Emerson are Newfield, and Rowe 1–41. There are, however, important studies of Emerson that stand outside these two "schools" of Emerson criticism. Among these see Buell, Cadava, Cavell, Patterson, and Voelz.

16. Along with Stack and Lopez, see the essays collected by Lopez in a special "Emerson/Nietzsche" issue of *ESQ: A Journal of the American Renaissance* 43 (1997).

17. Another essay on this theme is Stessel's "The Soldier and the Scholar."

18. The recasting of peace as a form of cultural and moral conflict destined to replace physical and armed struggle should be read as an early translation of peace as nonviolence, even though the latter, Gandhian term came to the English language only in the 1920s.

19. For Gandhi's comments on the *Bhagavad Gita* see *Non-Violence* 2:17–18. Nikhil Bilwakesh has shown that Emerson also was drawn to the *Gita* (which he read in Charles Wilkins's 1785 English translation) at a time when he shifted from a passive condemnation of slavery to an active participation in the abolitionist movement. While Gandhi read Arjuna's decision to fight, following his debate with Krishna, allegorically, and thus as not inconsistent with non-violence, Emerson was drawn to the *Gita* because it offered him an example spurring his social activism. As for Thoreau, according to Reynolds (112–19), the *Gita* "provided the religious rationale for the deep-seated violent impulses he periodically felt" (114).

20. As Manara (280n) reports, in Gandhi's complete writings we find one hundred occurrences of the phrase "non-violent resistance," eighteen occurrences of the phrases "non-violent fight" or "non-violent sanction," fifty-seven occurrences of "non-violent struggle," twenty-five occurrences of "non-violent war," and, finally, forty-one cases where the expression "non-violent army" is employed.

21. *Satyāgraha* is translated by Gandhi himself as "Truth-force."

22. "In characterizing the institution of slavery as a form of war . . . Emerson appropriates and exploits the abolitionist rhetoric of [Wendell] Phillips, who in February 1861 declared that 'Slavery is a form of perpetual war'" (Cadava 34).

23. Though often ignored, Huggard's study remains to this day useful and instructive.

24. From a speech delivered at the Central Meeting Hall in Chicago on April 30, 1899, and quoted in Davis 142. Addams gave a talk on "A Moral Substitute for War" at the Ethical Culture Society in Chicago in the spring of 1903, prior to the publication of William James's famous essay. See also Randolph Bourne's 1916 "A Moral Equivalent for Universal Military Service," where he replaces James's national army with "a national service for education" (144).

25. Gregg was "the first American to develop a substantial theory of nonviolent resistance" (Kosek 1318). Two other important U.S. thinkers on these matters are Rollo May and Joel Kovel. In *Power and Innocence* May insists that we are mistaken when we think of love and power "as opposites of each other," describing non-violence as a form of "integra-

tive power" (113). In *Against the State of Nuclear Terror* Kovel sees "nonviolent practice [as] a titanic struggle" to overcome "the paranoid mechanisms" lying at the heart of violence. Kovel acknowledges that when historically "the conditions for nonviolent development are absent and a people is subjected to the rule of murderous gangsters, then armed struggle is the only recourse of dignity" (163), but he adds that "unless nonviolence is held forth as the paramount goal of struggle, and . . . made to condition the present, then it loses all its moral force, and the cycle of domination will be ever renewed" (164). I am grateful to Gordon Hutner for directing me to these sources.

26. This is the key "feedback loop" Joshua Goldstein identifies in his *War and Gender*. A nice study of the connections between war, gender, and literary representation is Phillips's *Manipulating Masculinity*.

27. Ambrose Bierce, "Peace," *The Devil's Dictionary* (in Winter, "Laughing Dove" 251).

28. See also the perhaps involuntarily ironic title of Gittings's book, a celebration of "the glorious arts of peace" *from the Iliad to Iraq*.

29. From a letter to Garrison, quoted in Ziegler 134.

30. On *Indian Killer* see Mariani, "Negotiating."

31. Butler's meditations on violence and non-violence (see "Claim of Non-Violence," *Precarious Life*, and "Critique") may well be seen as the latest expression of the militant non-violent U.S. intellectual tradition sketched in this chapter. An excellent intervention on Butler's work and many of the issues discussed in this chapter is Critchley 207–45. As he writes,

> "History is a seemingly unending cycle of violence and counterviolence, and to refuse its overwhelming evidence in the name of some a priori conception of nonviolence is to disavow history in the name of an abstraction that, in the final analysis, is ideological. There are contexts where a tenacious politics of nonviolence . . . can be highly effective. There are contexts where a mimesis of Gandhi's tactics might also prove successful, as was the case for several years in the civil rights movement in the United States in the 1960s and in the words and deeds of Martin Luther King. . . . There are contexts where a difficult pacifism that negotiates the limits of violence might be enough. But . . . there are also contexts, multiple contexts, too depressingly many to mention, where nonviolent resistance is simply crushed by the forces of the state, the police, and the military. In such contexts, the line separating nonviolent warfare and violent action has to be crossed. Politics is always a question of local conditions, of local struggles and local victories. To judge the multiplicity of such struggles on the basis of an abstract conception of nonviolence is to risk dogmatic blindness" (239).

I completely agree with Critchley.

32. Mandela and the leaders of the ANC deserve immense credit for making possible a peaceful transition to a free, post-apartheid South Africa. The work done by the Truth and Reconciliation Commission—whatever its limitations—was crucial to this end. However, the choice of renouncing violence and not seeking revenge was made possible by the dismantling of apartheid. Until that happened, Mandela maintained that armed struggle could not be ruled out as an option.

33. "U.S. Has Mandela on Terrorist List." *USA Today*, April 30, 2008, available at http://www.usatoday. com/news/world/2008-04-30-watchlist_N.htm (accessed March 10, 2015).

34. Many of the passages by Gandhi and King I quote herewith are taken from Losurdo's book. My interpretation, however, does not always follow Losurdo. While I agree with his critical analysis of the "mythological" elements of non-violence, Losurdo at times downplays its ethical significance. Moreover, as Enzo Traverso notes in his perceptive review, the author has regrettably chosen not to perform an equally rigorous critical analysis of the revolutionary "myth of violence."

35. http://en.wikiquote.org/wiki/Mohandas_Karamchand_Gandhi#To_Every_Briton _.281940.29.

36. http://astheysawit.com/2142-1944-india.html.

37. "The Casualties of the War in Vietnam." Speech delivered at The Nation Institute, Los Angeles, February 25, 1967. Available at http://www.aavw.org/special_features/speeches_speech_king02.html.

38. I wish to thank Ferdinando Fasce for directing me to Dudziak's text.

39. Ritter's brilliant, short book is a further reminder of the extent to which the peace and justice movement has no choice but dwell in a "war imaginary" (my term). As Ritter convincingly argues, the peace movement takes part in a conflict and its aim is to win—with bloodless means, but *to win* nonetheless.

Chapter 3. The Rhetorical Equivalent of War

1. The larger point of de Lauretis's essay is that both positions are based on a particular representation/repression of sexual difference.

2. One must note, however, that in his later work Derrida has elaborated different, more nuanced views of the force/language, war/peace connections.

3. A well-known 2001 study by the International Committee of the Red Cross sets the ratio at 10:1. These figures have been disputed, so I stick to the more conservative estimates in Kaldor (8).

4. There are of course an International Criminal Tribunal and the United Nations Human Rights Council, which have the power to investigate and, in some cases, to bring to trial "war criminals." Yet it would be intellectually dishonest to think of these bodies as the international equivalent of the judiciary of a democratic country, not to mention that countries like Russia and the United States have never ratified the founding treaty of the ICC, and China has never even signed it. So far the only criminals who have been tried belong to "politically weak nations." Despite their moral authority, the Geneva Conventions have a limited impact on what actually takes place in the world.

5. Here, as elsewhere in the essay, James's argument echoes the one made by Emerson in his essay, "War." James shared with Emerson a belief in the pedagogical function of war but could not, understandably, share the optimism on war's demise of the early Emerson, who argued that "war is on its last legs; and a universal peace is as sure as is the prevalence of civilization over barbarism, of liberal governments over feudal forms. The question for us is only *How soon?*" ("War" 161). I must note that, as Professor Gregg

Crane kindly informed me in a March 25, 2012, email, the William James Collection at Harvard's Houghton Library does not include any volume with Emerson's "War" essay. This does not rule out the possibility that James may have come across the essay anyway, considering how much Emerson he read. Moreover, some ideas introduced in "War" run through other writings of Emerson. I am grateful to Prof. Crane for taking the time to share with me this information, and to Ross Posnock for putting me in touch with him.

6. From a political viewpoint, Burke's project may be described as preferring a moderate, social-democratic approach to one calling for a revolutionary dismantling of society. Two useful discussions of Burke's methodology from both a literary-critical and cultural-political perspective are Lentricchia, *Criticism and Social Change*, and Jameson, "Symbolic Interference." While Lentricchia sees Burke as a kind of heterodox Marxist, worthy of being compared to the likes of Gramsci and Adorno, Jameson argues that though Burke stresses the historical dimension of any symbolic act, he appears resistant to expanding his work in a more properly political direction.

7. However, as Burke knew well, even the language of the Gospels is not entirely free of war imagery, with the passage in Matthew 10:34 ("Do not think that I came to bring peace on Earth; I did not come to bring peace, but a sword") being perhaps the most famous example of the rather agonistic notion of Peace often espoused by Jesus. Also, it is surprising that Burke would not mention Gandhi, whose non-violent philosophy and practices were leading India toward independence. Moreover, certain forms of Hinduism or Buddhism may more rigorously identify Peace and Non-Violence with Being, given their refusal to harm also nonhuman life.

8. According to Foucault, "'Dialectic' is a way of evading the always open and hazardous reality of conflict by reducing it to a Hegelian skeleton, and 'semiology' is a way of avoiding its violent, bloody, and lethal character by reducing it to the calm Platonic form of language and dialogue" (*Power/Knowledge* 115). If Burke's approach is unquestionably dialectical and his "semiological" practice is certainly dedicated to the purification of the violent side of reality, it cannot stand accused of turning a blind eye to the reality of human conflicts. For Burke no peace or dialogue would be capable of abolishing conflicts altogether.

9. See Scarry, especially 81–91 and, more generally, 60–157. Though Scarry compares war to a series of bloodless competitions, she emphasizes that "the severe discrepancy in the scale of consequence makes the comparison of war and gaming nearly obscene, the analogy either trivializing the one, or, conversely, attributing to the other a weight of motive and consequence it cannot bear" (83).

10. Limon's notion of metonymic retreat resembles what McLoughlin identifies as "not-writing" directly about war, which she sees as a rhetorical equivalent of "military diversion tactics: attention is diverted away from the main action, but with the inevitable result that the true target eventually becomes clear" (*Authoring War* 139). After the semiotics of C. S. Pierce, McLoughlin sees war writing as often privileging an "indexical" modality over an "iconic" one: rather than trying to describe war (or a battle) as a whole, the war writer focuses on one of war's consequences (140). That is what Crane at least in part does in this story: he announces in the title itself that he will focus on a "detail"

of the battle, though it is unclear whether this "detail" may be seen as either iconic or indexical—that is, as war itself or as an episode that points to war.

11. "His companions . . . *perhaps* had forced him into this affair. . . . He had blindly been led by quaint emotions, and laid himself under an obligation to walk squarely up to the face of death. *But he was not sure that he wished to make a retraction, even if he could do so without shame.* As a matter of truth, he was sure of very little. He was mainly surprised" (627, 628; emphasis added).

12. In a different, perhaps even opposite key, one could read in the decision taken by a "dreaming," "dazed," "surprised" Collins the expression of an unconscious death wish not unusual in the proximity of war. Collins's expedition would thus be an anticipation of the Russian roulette in Michael Cimino's *The Deerhunter* (1978), another example of how the "games" that war inspires are potentially lethal ones. On the importance of play in the work of Stephen Crane, especially in the guise of commercial "amusement," see Brown, *Material Unconscious*.

13. See Shaw, who insists in particular on the story's satirical dimension; Dooley 86–88; Nagel; and, in part, Halliburton 147–51, the only one to take into account the failure of Collins's act, a detail that is instead crucial in Monteiro. More on this below.

14. I draw here on Richard Middleton Kaplan's "Facing the Face of the Enemy."

15. Levinas, *Difficult Freedom: Essays on Judaism*, quoted in Kaplan, "Facing the Face of the Enemy" 75.

16. "The empty bucket suggests the emptiness of his heroism" (Stallman 335).

17. "For we must needs die, and *are* as water spilt on the ground, which cannot be gathered up again" (2 Samuel 14:14).

18. I am here echoing Burke's use of these terms in "War" 250.

Chapter 4. An American Counter-Epic?

1. For an analysis of the U.S. Enlightenment that is in some respects parallel to Tosel's, see Gourgouris.

2. This paradox is of course much older than Kant. What is new is that Kant sees it as a moral as well as a political problem for democracies.

3. The extent to which revolutionary rhetoric was imbued with religious and millennial elements is a debated issue among historians. Melvin B. Endy, for example, disagrees with the idea that the American Revolution was perceived as a kind of holy war.

4. In Washington Irving's 1820 tale, Rip Van Winkle falls asleep on the eve of the revolution and reawakens only twenty years later, when the traumatic rupture with the motherland has been consummated.

5. Also, Edward Larkin writes that "American Revolutionary War writing only rarely addresses the violence and bloodshed of the conflict with Britain" (126–27). For an extended discussion of the repression-of-the-revolution motif, see Proietti, especially chapter 1.

6. The rhetorical operation performed by Arendt on the American Revolution is analogous to the one Esposito (51–59) sees her performing in her conceptualization of the

founding of Rome. Following Virgil, Arendt sees the foundation of Rome as a posthumous reparation for the destruction of Troy, and thus as a repudiation of the violence of beginnings.

7. See especially Dowling. Other works consulted include Ford, Tichi (114–50), and Elliott (92–127).

8. Dowling takes the phrase "retrospective radicalism" from Raymond Williams.

9. *The Vision of Columbus* was republished in a new edition in 1793. A second edition of *The Columbiad* came out in 1808, followed by a third one in 1813, and by a fourth and final edition in 1825. On the differences between *The Vision* and *The Columbiad*, see Ford 74–84 and Bernstein 185–90.

10. I have learned a great deal on the American quest for an epic from McWilliams's excellent study and also from Enrico Botta's invaluable Ph.D. dissertation, "La letteratura epica statunitense tra la Dichiarazione d'Indipendenza e il Centenario," Università dell'Aquila, 2011.

11. This final section of *The Columbiad* anticipates by thirty years the more widely known vision of "the Parliament of Man, the Federation of the World," offered by Alfred Tennyson's "Locksley Hall."

12. For a discussion of Indian figures in Barlow's work, see Conger as well as Blakemore 44–50.

13. To be precise, Barlow does have something to say, as when in Book 5 he juxtaposes the peaceful English settlers to the merciless, bestial Indians. The latter, moreover, are presented as the original "invaders" (!): "Gay villas smile . . . Till war invades . . . with files of savage foes" (5.44, 47, 48).

14. See Lepore xiv. A further proof of Barlow's acceptance of some of the worst stereotypes concerning the barbarian nature of the Indians is the scene where Lucinda, in her attempt to reach her Tory lover, is slain by two Mohawks. Barlow commissioned the painter John Vanderlyn to furnish an illustration of this scene for the first edition of *The Columbiad*. Titled *Death of Jane McCrea* in honor of the historical figure after which Barlow fashioned his Lucinda, Vanderlyn's painting is an eloquent example of that vision of the Indian as bloodthirsty savage that would dominate the literature and iconography of the United States for at least two centuries. See Sheardy.

15. While blind to white violence against the Indians, Barlow, to his credit, forcefully criticizes slavery in Book 8. There, Atlas, the guardian spirit of Africa, condemns the hypocrisy of those who fought a revolution in the name of liberty, only later to deny freedom to African peoples.

16. *In the Beginning There Was Joy* is the title of Fox's "primer for children of all ages" but also the title of the Italian translation (*In principio era la gioia*) of his much longer and richer *Original Blessing*.

17. Quoted in Tosel 17. For the original, see Kant 168.

18. What Seelye argues apropos an earlier imagining of peace—Philip Freneau's and Hugh Henry Brackenridge's *The Rising Glory of America* (1771)—may be repeated about *The Columbiad*, a text that prefers to emphasize "future harmonies not past conflicts" (202).

Chapter 5. "Cain's Ring"

1. On *Moby-Dick*'s global reach, see Moretti, *Modern Epic*, and Kaplan, "Transnational Melville."

2. Here and elsewhere all scriptural quotations are from the King James Bible, the one Melville read.

3. Biblical scholars have often commented on the ironic and satirical elements of the Jonah story. For a reading of the story as an example of classical satire, see Ackerman.

4. Also Elisa New (293–94) has detected a "sacrificial imperative" at the heart of Mapple's sermon. New, however, fails to see that even such a champion of what she calls "Hebraic prolixity" as Ishmael is ultimately implicated in a sacrificial rhetoric.

5. Even though Girard emphasizes the dangers of mimetic desire as the breeding ground of the sacrificial crisis, he acknowledges (see especially *Origine*) that humanity's imitative propensities can often have positive effects.

6. Both Ahab and Moby Dick are marked by a "wrinkled brow"; the whiteness of the whale is matched by Ahab's "white hair," his "white mark," and his "barbaric white leg" (made of whale-bone, of course); both are marked with scars and wounds; both are compared to a pyramid, and both Ahab and Moby Dick are called "King of the sea." Moreover, even the *Pequod* is compared by Ishmael to a whale. The idea that Ahab and Moby Dick are "doubles" is not a new one: see, for example, Slotkin, *Regeneration through Violence* 545.

7. As Moby Dick's double, Ahab shares the whale's scandalous nature. And interestingly enough, as Girard reminds us, "the Greek word *skandalizein* comes from a verb that means 'to limp.' What does a lame person resemble? To someone following a person limping it appears that the person continually collides with his or her own shadow." (*I See* 19). This etymology is of course interesting also in connection to Tommo's limping in *Typee*.

8. "The greatest danger to the self is the past, for disappointment may transform the will to power into the desire for revenge. The will does not learn easily to forget or to pass by. 'This indeed this alone,' Zarathustra concludes, 'is what revenge is: the will's ill will against time and its 'it was'" (Siebers, *Ethics or Criticism* 138).

9. "Ishmael, traditionally considered a foil for Ahab's megalomaniacal acts of interpretation, is in fact finally, although subtly, seduced by Ahab's point of view; his mirroring ultimately submits, to a large extent, to a reflection of rather than on Ahab" (125).

10. Dimock, *Empire for Liberty* 109–39. Dimock argues that "Ahab can have only one narrative, not a narrative of vengeance, but a narrative of doom," but it seems to me that his narrative is one of doom (like that of a Macbeth or a Hamlet) precisely *because* it is a narrative of vengeance. In fact, the man who is scapegoated by the novel is himself a great would-be scapegoater. What the narrative does to him is no more and no less what he would have done to the White Whale.

11. As in the case of the White Whale, Ahab's scapegoat status helps to explain his ambivalent characterization. As an embodiment of the "sacred" he is both revered and loathed. He can be represented as a Christ figure metaphorically wearing the Crown of Lombardy and yet also as an ally of the satanic Fedallah.

12. For one of the best arguments in defense of Ishmael as "redeemed hero," see Sten. We know that Melville drew on the legendary tales of "Mocha Dick; or, The White Whale of the Pacific." However, we do not know what prompted Melville to choose the name "Moby"

for his whale. If we keep in mind the whale's magnitude as well as how Moby Dick "tasks" and "heaps" Ahab, it is perhaps not farfetched to imagine that Melville wanted to exploit the semantic value of both the noun "mob" and the verb "to mob." Along these lines it is worth noting that during "The Chase—Second Day" Starbuck yells at Ahab that "all good angels [are] *mobbing* thee with warnings" (418, emphasis added). Simply put, the angels' "mobbing" of Ahab cannot outweigh the perverse attraction of Moby Dick's mobbing.

13. After describing the situation on board the *Dolly* and mentioning that the ship is heading toward the Marquesas, the narrator immediately thinks of "*heathenish rites and human sacrifices*" (5, original emphasis). In a sense, that is what he has been talking about from the beginning.

14. Here D. H. Lawrence's comments are still valuable: "So Melville escaped, and threw a boat-hook full in the throat of one of his dearest savage friends, and sank him, because that savage was swimming in pursuit. That's how he felt about the savages when they wanted to detain him. He'd have murdered them one and all, vividly, rather than be kept from escaping" (128).

15. On this see *Origine* 176–77. Girard does not explain in detail how to interpret such inversions of the mimetic crisis. Yet the Boroboro myth from Levi-Strauss's *The Raw and the Cooked* to which he refers bears a striking resemblance to the ending of *Moby-Dick*. After a deluge the earth's population is growing too fast and Meri, the sun, orders the entire population to cross a river by walking over a tree trunk. Under such great weight the trunk collapses, and all the people perish except one Akaruio Bokodori, who was lagging behind because of his deformed legs. Akaruio, however, will resurrect everyone, thanks to his drum and his magic. Akaruio is obviously a scapegoat figure—deformed, endowed with unusual powers, at some distance from his community. He is therefore an embodiment of the sacred, the one capable of restoring harmony to a community plagued by a "crisis of indifferentiation" (that is, a mimetic crisis in which social differences disintegrate and the group is ridden with violence) represented by the two consecutive floods. In the case of *Moby-Dick*, the reversal of the mimetic crisis results, on the one hand, in the confirmation of the "sacred" status of the whale, and, on the other, in the miraculous survival of Ishmael who is himself, like Akaruio, an outcast, the "orphan" picked up by the *Rachel*. Obviously, as Ishmael ultimately inhabits a novelistic rather than a mythic universe, his "resurrection" of the community can only be a purely narrative feat.

16. "But you know, it was a white man's book. There was a Indian man in it who smoked the pipe with the storyteller. . . . At the end, the white-man storyteller come bouncing up to the surface of the ocean on that Indian's coffin. You know grandson, us Choctaws signed nine treaties with the government, smoking the pipe nine times, and everytime it's like this book. The white man comes riding to the surface on a Indian's coffin" (Owens 90–91).

17. The Melville letter to Hawthorne is the famous one dated November 17[?], 1851. (See Melville, *Correspondence* 212.)

18. Interestingly enough, Ahab tells Captain Gardiner: "May I forgive myself, but I must go" (398). In his monomaniacal, self-referential logic, Ahab conceives forgiveness as something coming not from the Other but from himself.

19. Shakespeare's influence on *Moby-Dick* has been one of the traditional themes of Melvillean studies at least since Charles Olson's and F. O. Matthiessen's investigations.

Yet, though Matthiessen titled his *American Renaissance* chapter on *Moby-Dick* "The Revenger's Tragedy," the sacrificial dimension of Ahab's revenge has gone largely unnoticed.

20. Also the early scenes of *Moby-Dick*, that is, are structurally similar to the opening of *Typee,* just as the ironic, circular nature of Ishmael's desire to go to sea is a recasting of Tommo's longing for adventure, first, and for "Home" and "Mother," later.

Chapter 6. "Curious Anesthetics"

1. Higonnet, *Nurses at the Front* vii–xxxviii. The volume includes also a selection of stories from Mary Borden's *The Forbidden Zone* (1929); Borden was director of the hospital where La Motte worked. Higonnet had previously written about La Motte in "Not So Quiet." For evidence that scholars continue to ignore *The Backwash of War* see the *Encyclopedia of American War Literature* (Jason and Graves), a thick volume with no mention whatsoever of La Motte.

2. Here is a drastically abridged list of English-language works in which this thesis has been amply illustrated and supported: Cooke and Woollacott; Cooper, Munich, and Squier; Higonnet et al.; Huston, "Tales," and "Matrix"; Lassner; Marcus, "Asylums"; Tylee; Plain; Schneider. Among the many studies concentrating specifically on the construction of masculinity in war discourse and literature, see Phillips and also Adams. For a comprehensive, multidisciplinary analysis of war and gender, see Goldstein.

3. For a critique of the woman-peace equation, see Elshtain.

4. McLoughlin coins the term *parapolemics* to identify war writing (such as hospital accounts) focusing on "the temporal and spatial borders of war" (*Martha Gellhorn* 105).

5. On these and other works, see Marcus's "Corpus," an indispensable afterword to Helen Zenna Smith's novel.

6. This story also anticipates one of the italicized passages ("Chapter V") in Hemingway's *In Our Time* (51), where a sick man cannot stand up in front of the firing squad in charge of his execution. I thank Donatella Izzo for this observation.

7. Similar observations characterize a story—tellingly titled "Conspiracy"—in Mary Borden's *The Forbidden Zone*. By resorting to the female metaphor of "mending," Borden underscores how her work as a nurse hardly escapes the functioning of the war machine. "It is all carefully arranged. Everything is arranged. It is arranged that men should be broken and that they should be mended [. . .]. You send your socks and your shirts again and again to the laundry, and you sew up the tears and clip the ravelled edges again and again just as many times as they will stand it. [. . .] And we send our men to the war again and again, just as long as they will stand it" (124). The nurses that "mend" the soldiers' bodies participate in the "conspiracy" against them, bending their "domestic" skills to the necessities of war. A similarly disenchanted conclusion is reached by the protagonist of Helen Zenna Smith's *Not So Quiet . . .,* once she realizes that though her tasks may be peaceful, they are still part of the operations of war.

8. "There is no war that fails to commit a crime against humanity. . . . In other words, wars become permissible forms of criminality, but they are never non-criminal" (Butler, *Frames or War* xviii). This echoes a famous line from Hemingway: "Never think that war, no matter how necessary, nor how justified, is not a crime" ("Foreword" xv).

9. One wonders whether Dalton Trumbo knew this story: the similarities between *Johnny Got His Gun* and La Motte's "Surgical Triumph" are striking. In both narratives

medicine is largely an instrument of torture rather than cure, and the human body is bit-by-bit replaced by artificial parts, with Trumbo going one step further than La Motte, as his Johnny has also lost his mouth and cannot even speak.

10. As Jane Marcus, among others, has shown (see "Corpus" and especially "Asylums") apropos British state propaganda, wartime posters featured "enormous matriarchs and fearfully forbidding phallic mothers and stern young wives pointing equally phallic fingers, urging men to go and fight." These images "cannot in any sense be seen as women's images of themselves but rather as such effective patriarchal projections that ordinary soldiers and university-educated poets could blame the women at home for the deaths of their comrades" ("Asylums" 67–68). The women created by war-state propaganda thus complemented the vision held by many male writers, who saw "women as bloodthirsty vampires who gloat over men's death and derive pleasure and profit from war" (54). When placed against this background, La Motte's ordinary, "little stupid wives" acquire an almost subversive character.

11. As Stallybrass and White note, the subversive charge of the Bakhtinian carnival may also take the form of *displaced abjection*, "the process whereby 'low' social groups turn their figurative and actual power, not against those in authority, but against those who are even 'lower' (women, Jews, animals, particularly cats and pigs)" (53).

Chapter 7. Waging War on the Sacred

1. Boardman Robinson (1876–1952) was a highly respected artist and illustrator. His work appeared in the *New York Times*, the *New York Tribune*, and in socialist magazines like *The Masses* and *The Liberator*. After the United States entered the war, Robinson, through his pacifist drawings, was accused of violating the Espionage Act. Boardman often couched his anti-war messages in Gospel imagery. See, for example, his "Last Supper" (*The Masses*, January 1917) and his drawing of Christ dragged to the war front (*The Masses*, June 1917).

2. On the novel's genesis, see Butterworth 1–10. On the similarities with *Paths of Glory*, see Julian Smith.

3. For an overview of critical responses to *A Fable*, see Butterworth 10–16 and 85–89.

4. See Godden; Polk, *Children* (196–218) and "Scar"; Urgo 84–125.

5. For a critical discussion of Girard's theories, see the essays collected in Dumochel, especially Lucien Scubla's contribution.

6. Paul Ricoeur, in his late *Vivant jusqu'à la mort*, also argues that the Passion should not be read as a form of sacrifice (Kearney 77–78). Ricoeur's reading of the Passion—which underlines the notion of "dying unto oneself and serving the other" (91), celebrated in the Last Supper—is consistent with Faulkner's insistence on the Corporal's devotion to the fellow rebels who will survive him (on this, see below). For an excellent critical examination of the connections between U.S. war culture and Christian sacrifice see Denton-Boraugh.

7. In 1956, in *Ebony*, Faulkner invited black leaders to "go slow," adding that they should display an "inflexible and non-violent flexibility"—an expression so tortuous that it shows how difficult it was for Faulkner to formulate a clear position on the issue (Williamson 308).

8. On conflating pacifism with passivism, see Cady 24–28.

9. Here Faulkner echoes the ending of Dalton Trumbo's *Johnny Got His Gun*, in which the novel's mutilated, mute, and hospital-ridden protagonist has a vision of himself "as a new kind of Christ" and defiantly asserts, "We are men of peace we are men who work and we want no quarrel. But if you destroy our peace . . . [w]e will use the guns you force upon us. . . . You plan the wars you masters of men plan the wars and point the way and we will point the gun" (242–43).

10. Pope Benedict XV defined the war an *inutile strage* in a public appeal to all belligerent countries on August 1, 1917. See http://it.wikipedia.org/wiki/Papa_Benedetto_XV.

11. A nearly identical view is expressed by the dissenting Catholic theologian Ernesto Balducci: "The end of the sacred is the end of the culture of war [. . .] unless the sacred is disposed of, there can be no culture of peace" (as quoted in Mazzi, *Ernesto Balducci* 89).

12. On the relation of war and the sacred, see not only Caillois, Girard, and Ehrenreich, but also Fornari, Hillman, LeShan, Kilani, and (perhaps most important) Kahn, whose work is a sobering reminder of how sacrifice continues to provide the basis for many contemporary "liberal" notions of sovereignty.

13. "The crucifix, as it is unconsciously exhibited and perceived, is the icon of the basic justification, century after century, for acquiescing to the existence of violence and war. It is an invitation to recline one's head and be resigned" (Mazzi, *Cristianesimo* 186). Both the bowed head of the batman and the oppressive silence finally broken by the Runner's shout of rebellion are objective correlatives of the acquiescence to violence. Mazzi's reflections have been invaluable in helping me to understand the relation between violence and the sacred.

14. The figure of the Marshall also embodies Faulkner's anxieties vis-à-vis an Atomic Age marked by a "nuclear rationality" that goes hand in hand with a "sense of the sacred with neo-pagan roots" (Zizola 130).

15. Godden (38) notes that, in keeping with the novel's Christian allegory, the alien corporal can only be a figurative Jew, and perhaps even a real one—*the* Jew, the Other, the scapegoat.

16. On Faulkner's crowds in *A Fable* see Nicolaisen.

17. The novel refers to the presence of colonial troops in the Allies' ranks. "It's like another front, manned by all the troops in the three forces who cant speak the language belonging to the coat they came up from under the equator and half around the world to die in, in the cold and the wet—Senegalese and Moroccans and Kurds and Chinese and Malays and Indians—Polynesian Melanesian Mongol and Negro" (268).

18. In light of what Olivier Rozac has written on barbed wire as an "implement of power" and an instrument of control typical of the modern era, Faulkner's choice seems altogether appropriate.

19. See Ficken and Magee.

20. For Butterworth it is simply "ridiculous" to see the Marshall as an impersonation of God, the devil, Caesar, or Pilate, given that even though Faulkner "alludes" to all these figures, he is describing a character of his novel—a mortal human being—not a transcendent figure. Of course, the General is a human being. If, however, Faulkner wanted such character to allude to several figures at odds with one another, this must affect not only the way we interpret this particular character but also the way in which the character encourages us to reread the theological and evangelical references he evokes.

21. As Terry Eagleton (*Reason, Faith, and Revolution*) has noted, atheism can bear a striking resemblance to religious fundamentalism.

22. Some of the Marshall's lines were repeated by Faulkner in his Nobel Prize speech. This has led some critics to conclude that the writer was sympathetic to the old General's worldview and in particular to his confidence in man's ability to "endure." My impression, on the contrary, is that also in his Nobel Prize speech Faulkner marks his distance from his character's views. Here is the crucial passage: "I decline to accept the end of man. It is easy enough to say that man is immortal simply because he will endure: that when the last dingdong of doom has clanged and faded from the last worthless rock hanging tideless in the last red and dying evening, that even then there will still be one more sound: that of his puny inexhaustible voice, still talking. *I refuse to accept this.* I believe that man will not merely endure: he will prevail. He is immortal, *not because he alone among creatures has an inexhaustible voice, but because he has a soul, a spirit capable of compassion and sacrifice and endurance.* The poet's, the writer's, duty is to write about these things. It is his privilege to help man endure by lifting his heart, by reminding him of the courage and honor and hope and pride and compassion and pity and sacrifice which have been the glory of his past" (Banquet Speech). The parts of Faulkner's speech I have italicized represent a clear critique of the notion of "enduring and prevailing" as constructed by the Marshall. Moreover, while in the novel the Marshall links man's survival to that of his "deathless folly," in the Nobel Prize speech there is no reference to the latter.

23. See Jünger, and, for an important critique, Huyssen. This extraordinary passage seems to foresee the current Revolution in Military Affairs (RMA), based on "the gradual reduction, if not elimination, of the element of the human combatant" (Dal Lago 17–18).

24. Wilfred Owen's 1918 poem "The Parable of the Old Man and the Young" features a version of the Abraham-and-Isaac story in which the patriarch does not hear the angel's call and "slew his son / And half the seed of Europe, one by one" (quoted in Tate). Whether Faulkner knew this poem or not, both his and Owen's texts rewrite the biblical story as an archetype of the sacrificial logic underlying the Great War.

25. As described by Faulkner, the monument to the Unknown Soldier provides a textbook illustration of what George Mosse has called "the Myth of the War Experience," "which looked back upon the war as a meaningful and even *sacred* event. . . . The memory of war was refashioned into a *sacred* experience which provided the nation with *a new depth of religious feeling, putting at its disposal ever-present saints and martyrs, places of worship, and a heritage to emulate. . . . The cult of the fallen soldier became a centerpiece of the religion of nationalism. . . .*" (7, emphasis added).

26. This notion also informs Abel Gance's film, *J'accuse* (1919, silent; 1939, sound), "where the protagonist Jean Diaz, in a feverish hallucination and apocalypse, witnesses the masses of dead soldiers rise from the Verdun battlefield so that their sacrifice not be forgotten by civilians" (Kelly, "Ambiguity" 7).

Chapter 8. War, Fiction, and Truth

1. Jameson, *Postmodernism* 44–45.

2. See also Vernon (7–18), who writes, "The myth that links combat in Vietnam with postmodern literature implies that the postmodern condition created the battlefield

tactics rather than the battlefield itself. . . . The jungle, not the culture of late capitalism, made Vietnam into the fragmented, chaotic mess of small combat units" (12). For a different view, see Carpenter.

3. It is no accident that Herr's *Dispatches* is considered as one of the best American testimonies on the Vietnam experience. Neither a novel nor an objective reportage, *Dispatches* is driven by the belief that, as Ward Just has written, "the writer comes close to the heart of the war, its infinitely still center, when he begins to invent Vietnam" (215).

4. Throughout this chapter, I identify O'Brien with the story's narrator. The reason for this is simply that "Tim" is the first-person narrator of the whole book. Of course, this "Tim" is O'Brien's fictional projection, which implies that in the story under consideration the narrator is also a fictional stand-in for the author, who may not necessarily agree with all he says. I am aware of this, and the reader should understand that when I write O'Brien, I mean "O'Brien." However, since the textual O'Brien is the only one we have access to, the "true" O'Brien can but hover on the margins of his stories as a sort of ghostly, ultimately ungraspable presence.

5. O'Brien's position closely parallels the "methodological cul-de-sac" (143) on which, according to Paul Jay, hinges a certain U.S. philosophical tradition. Thinkers like Richard Rorty and Stanley Fish, on the one hand, subvert the absolute pretenses of traditional philosophy; on the other hand, they make an absolute of their own critical position.

6. James Wilson develops a very different reading of Herr's text by arguing, among other things, that *Dispatches* "fails to transcend the limits of its self-reflexive stance" (45). His conclusion is that "if external reality depends on who perceives it, history comes to no more than a figment of a writer's imagination" (51).

7. As Stefano Rosso reminded me, the problematic nature of O'Brien's answer is further complicated—for those who know the writer's biography—by the fact that at the time he wrote *The Things They Carried*, O'Brien had no children.

8. Many studies have been devoted to the obscene appeal of violence and war. See, for example, Joanna Burke, Chris Hedges, and James Hillman, though perhaps the best account is still Glenn Gray's *The Warriors*.

9. No wonder Jean-Paul Sartre once remarked, "War is a form of socialism" (91).

10. Note in this regard that, as Bottiroli argues, "No artistic text can, *strictu sensu*, be confusive, because that would deprive it of the ground that makes it visible to its public" (169). The utopia of a purely confusive war story would therefore automatically revert into a dystopia.

11. The so-called "War is Hell speech" was delivered by Sherman on July 19, 1879, to a graduating class of the Michigan Military Academy. The phrase reoccurs in an April 11, 1890, speech, as Sherman addressed a crowd of more than ten thousand people in Columbus, Ohio: "There is many a boy here today who looks on war as all glory, but, boys, it is all hell." See "William Tecumseh Sherman," http://en.wikipedia.org/wiki/General _Sherman.

12. A careful reading of the story shows that on the battlefield even direct causality may need to be relativized. Cross is not solely responsible—other concurring causes are at least the "young soldier" who turns on a torchlight, thereby signaling to the enemy the

platoon's position, as well as the incessant rain, without which the ground would not turn into the river of mud in which Kiowa drowns.

13. For a more detailed discussion of this unsolved tension in Crane's novel, see my *Spectacular Narratives* 139–71.

14. Rat's furious behavior also echoes Ajax's slaughter of a herd of sheep after he is denied the right to inherit the armor of the dead Achilles.

15. See chapter 3 herewith.

Chapter 9. Beyond the Semantic Netherworld

1. The blurring of confines between the home front and the battlefield is one of the staple features of many recent films on the United States' "Arab wars." See Stewart.

2. From a speech before the American Society of Newspaper Editors, April 16, 1953, http://www.quotationspage.com/quote/9556.html.

3. See *Peace by Peaceful Means: Peace and Conflict, Development and Civilization*.

4. The quotations from negative reviews of Kingston's book come from Shan.

5. On Athena's doubleness, see Elshtain 51n. In the last book of Homer's epic, only a few lines before the ones quoted by Kingston, Athena asks her father Zeus whether he wishes the war to continue or not. His answer is revealing: "Why this formality of inquiry? / Did you not plan that action by yourself—/see to it that Odysseus, on his homecoming, / should have their blood? Conclude it as you will" (*The Odyssey*, translated by Robert Fitzgerald [New York: Doubleday, 1963], p. 459, XXIV, 527–32).

6. For thoughtful readings of Turner's work, see Peebles (118–34) and Najmi. This is not to say Turner's poetry has not been criticized. Sinan Antoon, for example, has singled out *Here, Bullet* as a case of "embedded poetry," while Elliot Colla sees Turner's work as an expression of the war's "Military-Literary Complex." While I do agree with some of these critics' strictures, I also believe that, more so than most other Iraq war writers, Turner makes in his poetry a sincere effort to consider the "enemy's" perspective.

7. *Through Other Continents* 6, quoting Spivak 101.

8. I wish to thank Professor Barklis for permission to quote from a paper she delivered at the Western Political Science Association Annual Meeting, Portland, Oregon, March 22, 2012.

9. Richard Kearney's interpretation of the biblical episode of Jacob's fight with the stranger resonates with what I am trying to get at here. In Kearney's view, Jacob fights the whole night against "someone . . . he perceives to be a threatening adversary, until he finally opens himself to the Other. . . . Jacob ultimately opts for peace, ultimately acknowledging 'the face of God' in the visage of his mortal enemy" (20).

10. "I'm home, but the house is gone" (48) is the opening sentence of Tim O'Brien's memoir, "The Vietnam in Me." "Home" is, of course, Vietnam.

11. "Poetry Friday: 'Here, Bullet,' for Memorial Day." Available at http://usedbooksin-class.com/2013/05/23/poetry-friday-here-bullet-for-memorial-day (accessed June 28, 2014).

Works Cited

Ackerman, James S. "Jonah." In *The Literary Guide to the Bible*, edited by Robert Alter and Frank Kermode, 234–43. Cambridge, Mass.: Harvard University Press, 1987.

Adams, Jon Robert. *Male Armor: The Soldier-Hero in Contemporary American Culture*. Cultural Frames, Framing Culture. Charlottesville: University of Virginia Press, 2008.

Addams, Jane. *Newer Ideals of Peace*. New York: MacMillan, 1907.

Adler, Joyce Sparer. *War in Melville's Imagination*. New York: New York University Press, 1981.

Alexie, Sherman. *The Lone Ranger and Tonto Fistfight in Heaven*. New York: Atlantic, 1993.

Ali, Tariq. *Bush in Babylon: The Recolonisation of Iraq*. London: Verso, 2004.

Antoon, Sinan. "Embedded Poetry: Iraq; Through a Soldier's Binoculars." *Jadaliyya*, available at http://www.jadaliyya.com/pages/index/18082/embedded-poetry_iraq;-through-a-soldiers-binocular.

Arendt, Hannah. *Between Past and Future*. Harmondsworth: Penguin, 1993.

———. *On Revolution*. New York: Penguin, 1990.

———. "Reflections on Little Rock." *Dissent*, Winter 1959: 47–58.

Armstrong, Nancy, and Leonard Tennenhouse. "Introduction: Representing Violence; Or 'How the West Was Won.'" In *The Violence of Representation: Literature and the History of Violence*, edited by Nancy Armstrong and Leonard Tennenhouse. London: Routledge, 1989.

Bacevich, Andrew J. *The New American Militarism: How Americans Are Seduced by War*. New York: Oxford University Press, 2005.

Baetzhold, Howard G., and Joseph B. McCullough, eds. *The Bible According to Mark Twain: Irreverent Writings on Eden, Heaven, and the Flood by America's Master Satirist*. New York: Touchstone, 1996.

Bagnold, Enid. *A Diary without Dates*. London: Virago, 1978.

Bakhtin, Mikhail. *The Dialogic Imagination*. Edited by Michael Holquist. Translated by Caryl Emerson and Michael Holquist. Austin: University of Texas Press, 1981.

Barklis, Robin. "Arendt on Forgiveness and Identity Formation." Paper delivered at the Western Political Science Association Annual Meeting, Portland, Oregon, March 22, 2012. By permission of the author.

Barlow, Joel. *Poetry: The Works of Joel Barlow*. Edited by William K. Bottorff and Arthur L. Ford. Vol. 2. Gainesville, Fla.: Scholars' Facsimiles and Reprints, 1970.

Bartov, Omer. *Mirrors of Destruction: War, Genocide, and Modern History*. New York: Oxford University Press, 2000.

Bellamy, Edward. *Looking Backward, 2000–1887*. New York: Penguin, 1982.

Bellesiles, Michael A. *Arming America: The Origins of a National Gun Culture*. New York: Knopf, 2000.

Benedict, Helen. Interview by Anne Strainchamps. "Writing War Fiction: Helen Benedict on *Sand Queen*." *To the Best of Our Knowledge*. National Public Radio, October 16, 2011.

——. *The Lonely Soldier: The Private War of Women Serving in Iraq*. Boston: Beacon, 2009.

——. *Sand Queen*. New York: Soho, 2011.

Benjamin, Walter. "The Author as Producer." In *Understanding Brecht*, 85–104. Translated by Anna Bostock. London: NLB, 1977.

——. "Critique of Violence." In *Reflections: Essays, Aphorisms, Autobiographical Writings*, edited by Peter Demetz, 277–300. New York: Schocken, 1978.

——. *The Origin of German Tragic Drama*. Translated by John Osborne. Radical Thinkers. London: Verso, 2003.

——. "The Storyteller." In *Illuminations: Essays and Reflections*, edited by Hannah Arendt, 83–109. New York: Schocken, 1968.

——. "Theses on the Philosophy of History." In *Illuminations: Essays and Reflections*, edited by Hannah Arendt, 253–64. New York: Schocken, 1968.

Bercovitch, Sacvan. *The Rites of Assent: Transformations in the Symbolic Construction of America*. New York: Routledge, 2000.

Bernstein, Samuel. *Joel Barlow: A Connecticut Yankee in an Age of Revolution*. Cliff Island, Minn.: Ultima Thule, 1985.

Bezanson, Walter E. "*Moby-Dick*: Work of Art." In *Moby-Dick: Centennial Essays*, edited by Tyrus Hillway and Luther S. Mansfield, 31–58. Dallas: Southern Methodist University Press, 1953.

Bibby, Michael. "Introduction." In *The Vietnam War and Postmodernity*, edited by Michael Bibby. Boston: University of Massachusetts Press, 1999.

Bilwakesh, Nikhil. "Emerson, John Brown, and Arjuna: Translating the *Bhagavad Gita* in a Time of War." *ESQ: A Journal of the American Renaissance* 55.1 (2009): 27–58.

Bishop, James Gleason. "'We Should Know These People We Bury in the Earth': Brian Turner's Radical Message." In *War, Literature, and the Arts: An International Journal of the Humanities* 22.1 (2010): 299–306.

Blakemore, Steven. *Joel Barlow's* Columbiad: *A Bicentennial Reading*. Knoxville: University of Tennessee Press, 2007.

Blotner, Joseph. *Faulkner: A Biography*. Vol. 2. New York: Random House, 1974.

——, ed. *Selected Letters of William Faulkner*. New York: Random House, 1977.

Blum, Edward J. "God's Imperialism: Mark Twain and the Religious War between Imperialists and Anti-Imperialists." *Journal of Transnational American Studies*. 1.1 (2009): 35–8. Web.

Bogel, Fredric. *The Difference Satire Makes: Rhetoric and Reading from Jonson to Byron*. Ithaca, N.Y.: Cornell University Press, 2000.

Bondurant, Joan V. *Conquest of Violence: The Gandhian Philosophy of Conflict*. Berkeley: University of California Press, 1967.

Borden, Mary. *The Forbidden Zone*. New York: Doubleday, 1929.

Borman, William. *Gandhi and Non-Violence*. SUNY Series in Transpersonal and Humanistic Psychology. Albany: State University of New York Press, 1986.

Bottiroli, Giovanni. *Retorica: L'intelligenza figurale nell'arte e nella filosofia*. Turin: Bollati Boringhieri, 1993.

Bourke, Joanna. *An Intimate History of Killing: Face-to-Face Killing in Twentieth-Century Warfare*. New York: Basic, 1999.

Bourne, Randolph. "A Moral Equivalent for Universal Military Service." In *War and the Intellectuals: Essays by Randolph Bourne, 1915–1919*, edited by Carl Reek, 142–47. New York: Harper, 1964.

Brocchieri, Mariateresa Fumagalli Beonio. *Cristiani in armi: Da Sant'Agostino a papa Wojtila*. Bari: Laterza, 2006.

Brock, Peter. *Pacifism in the United States: From the Colonial Era to the First World War*. Princeton, N.J.: Princeton University Press, 1968.

Brock-Utne, Birgit. *Feminist Perspectives on Peace and Peace Education*. Oxford: Pergamon, 1989.

Brooks, Cleanth. *Toward Yoknapatawpha and Beyond*. New Haven, Conn.: Yale University Press, 1978.

Brown, Bill. *The Material Unconscious: American Amusement, Stephen Crane, and the Economies of Play*. Cambridge, Mass.: Harvard University Press, 1994.

Brown, Richard Maxwell. "Overview of Violence in the United States." In *Violence in America: An Encyclopedia*, edited by Ronald Gottesman, 1:1–20. New York: Scribner's, 1999.

Buell, Lawrence. *Emerson*. Cambridge, Mass.: Harvard University Press, 2003.

Burke, Kenneth. *Attitudes toward History*. Berkeley: University of California Press, 1984.

———. *A Grammar of Motives*. Berkeley: University of California Press, 1969.

———. "Literature as an Equipment for Living." In *The Philosophy of Literary Form: Studies in Symbolic Action*, 293–304. Berkeley: University of California Press, 1973.

———. *A Rhetoric of Motives*. Berkeley: University of California Press, 1969.

———. "War, Response, and Contradiction." In *The Philosophy of Literary Form: Studies in Symbolic Action*, 234–57. Berkeley: University of California Press, 1973.

Burkert, Walter. "The Problem of Ritual Killing." In *Violent Origins: Walter Burkert, René Girard, and Jonathan Z. Smith on Ritual Killing and Cultural Formation*, 149–76. Edited by Robert G. Hamerton-Kelly. Stanford, Calif.: Stanford University Press, 1987.

Butler, Judith. "The Claim of Non-Violence." In *Frames of War*, 165–84.

———. "Critique, Coercion, and Sacred Life in Benjamin's 'Critique of Violence.'" In *Political Theologies: Public Religions in a Post-Secular World*, edited by Hent de Vries and Lawrence E. Sullivan, 201–19. New York: Fordham University Press, 2006.

———. *Frames of War: When is Life Grievable?* London: Verso, 2009.

———. *Precarious Life: The Powers of Mourning and Violence.* London: Verso, 2004.

Butterworth, Keen. *A Critical and Textual Study of Faulkner's* A Fable. Ann Arbor: University of Michigan Research Press, 1978.

Cadava, Eduardo. *Emerson and the Climates of History.* Stanford, Calif.: Stanford University Press, 1997.

Cady, Duane L. *From Warism to Pacifism: A Moral Continuum.* Philadelphia: Temple University Press, 2010.

Caillois, Roger. *La vertigine della guerra.* Translated by Mauro Pennasilico. Rome: Edizioni Lavoro, 1990. Originally published as *Le vertige de la guerre* (1950).

Camfield, Gregg. "Joel Barlow's Dialectic of Progress." *Early American Literature* 21.2 (1986): 131–43.

Carpenter, Lucas. "'It Don't Mean Nothin': Vietnam War Fiction and Postmodernism." *College Literature* 30 (2003): 30–50.

Casadei, Alberto. *La guerra.* Bari: Laterza, 1999.

———. *Romanzi di Finisterre: Narrazione della guerra e problemi del realismo.* Rome: Carocci, 2000.

Case, Clarence Marsh. *Non-Violent Coercion: A Study in Methods of Social Pressure.* New York: Century, 1923.

Cavell, Stanley. *Emerson's Transcendental Etudes.* Edited by David Justin Hodge. Stanford, Calif.: Stanford University Press, 2003.

Ceadel, Martin. "Pacifism and Pacificism." *The Cambridge History of Twentieth-Century Political Thought.* Vol. 6 of the Cambridge History of Political Thought. Edited by Terence Ball and Richard Bellamy, 473–92. Cambridge: Cambridge University Press, 2003.

Chernus, Ira. *American Nonviolence: The History of an Idea.* Maryknoll, N.Y.: Orbis, 2004.

Clark, Michael. "Vietnam: Representations of Self and War." *Wide Angle* 7 (1985): 5–11.

Cobley, Evelyn. "Narrating the Facts of War: New Journalism in Herr's *Dispatches* and Documentary Realism in First World War Novels." *Journal of Narrative Technique* 16.2 (1986): 97–116.

Cockburn, Alexander. "The Year of the Yellow Notepad." *CounterPunch,* March 24–30, 2002. Available at http://www.counterpunch.org/2002/03/23/year-of-the-yellow -notepad (accessed March 3, 2015).

Colla, Elliott. "Still in Bed." *Jadaliyya,* available at http://reviews.jadaliyya.com/pages/ index/18113/still-in-bed (accessed March 3, 2015).

Conger, Danielle E. "Toward a Native American Nationalism: Joel Barlow's *The Vision of Columbus.*" *New England Quarterly* 72.4 (1999): 558–76.

Cooke, Miriam, and Angela Woollacott. *Gendering War Talk.* Princeton, N.J.: Princeton University Press, 1993.

Cooper, Helen, Adrienne Munich, and Susan Merrill Squier, eds. *Arms and the Woman: War, Gender, and Literary Representation.* Chapel Hill: University of North Carolina Press, 1989.

Cooper, James Fenimore. *The Last of the Mohicans.* Introduction by Richard Slotkin. Harmondsworth: Penguin, 1986.

Cramer, Clayton. "Shots in the Dark." *National Review Online,* September 23–24, 2000 (accessed January 15, 2008).

Crane, Stephen. *Prose and Poetry*. New York: Library of America, 1984.

Critchley, Simon. "Nonviolent Violence." *The Faith of the Faithless: Experiments in Political Theology*, 207–45. London: Verso, 2012.

Crosby, Ernest. *Swords and Plowshares*. New York: Funk and Wagnalls, 1902.

Curi, Umberto. *Pensare la guerra: L'Europa e il destino della politica*. Bari: Dedalo, 1999.

Dal Lago, Alessandro. "The Global State of War." *Ephemera: Theory and Politics in Organization* 6.1 (2006): 9–26.

Davis, Allen F. *American Heroine: The Life and Legend of Jane Addams*. New York: Oxford University Press, 1973.

Dawes, James. *The Language of War: Literature and Culture in the U.S. from the Civil War through World War II*. Cambridge, Mass.: Harvard University Press, 2002.

Dawson, Conigsby. *The Glory of the Trenches: An Interpretation*. New York: Grosset and Dunlap, 1918.

Deer, Patrick. "Introduction: The Ends of War and the Limits of Culture." *Social Text* 91 (2007): 1–11.

de Lauretis, Teresa. "The Violence of Rhetoric: Considerations on Representation and Gender." In Armstrong and Tennenhouse, *The Violence of Representation*, 239–58.

Dell, Floyd. "The Book of the Month." *The Masses*, January 1917: 30.

De Luna, Giovanni. *Il corpo del nemico ucciso: Violenza e morte nel mondo contemporaneo*. Turin: Einaudi, 2006.

Denton-Borhaug, Kelly. *U.S. War-Culture, Sacrifice and Salvation*. Oakville, Conn.: Equinox, 2011.

Derrida, Jacques *Negotiations: Interventions and Interviews, 1971–2001*. Edited, translated, and with an introduction by Elizabeth Rossenberg. Stanford, Calif.: Stanford University Press, 2002.

———. *Of Grammatology*. Translated by Gayatri Chakravorty Spivak. Baltimore, Md.: Johns Hopkins University Press, 1974.

———. *Writing and Difference*. Translated by Alan Bass. Chicago: University of Chicago Press, 1978.

Dimock, Wai-chee. *Empire for Liberty: Melville and the Poetics of Individualism*. Princeton, N.J.: Princeton University Press, 1989.

———. *Through Other Continents: American Literature across Deep Time*. Princeton, N.J.: Princeton University Press, 2006.

Dooley, Patrick. *The Pluralistic Philosophy of Stephen Crane*. Urbana: University of Illinois Press, 1993.

Dos Passos, John. *Three Soldiers*. Introduction by Townsend Ludington. Harmondsworth: Penguin, 1997.

Dostoyevsky, Fyodor. *The Brothers Karamazov*. Translated by Ignat Avsey. Oxford: Oxford University Press, 1999.

Douglass, Mary. *Purity and Danger: An Analysis of Concepts of Pollution and Taboo*. London: Routledge, 1966.

Dowling, William. *Poetry and Ideology in Revolutionary Connecticut*. Athens: University of Georgia Press, 1990.

Duban, James. "Chipping with a Chisel: The Ideology of Melville's Narrators." *Texas Studies in Language and Literature* 31 (1989): 341–85.

Dudziak, Mary L. *Cold War, Civil Rights: Race and the Image of American Democracy*. Politics and Society in Twentieth-Century America. Princeton, N.J.: Princeton University Press, 2011.

Dumouchel, Paul, ed. *Violence and Truth: On the Work of René Girard*. Stanford, Calif.: Stanford University Press, 1988.

Eagleton, Terry. *Reason, Faith, and Revolution: Reflections on the God Debate*. Terry Lecture Series. New Haven, Conn.: Yale University Press, 2009.

Edwards, Owen. "The Skeletons of Shanidar Cave." *Smithsonian*, March 2010.

Ehrenreich, Barbara. *Blood Rites: Origins and History of the Passions of War*. New York: Holt, 1997.

Eksteins, Modris. *Rites of Spring: The Great War and the Birth of the Modern Age*. Boston: Houghton Mifflin, 1989.

Elliott, Emory. *Revolutionary Writers: Literature and Authority in the Early Republic, 1725–1810*. New York: Oxford University Press, 1982.

Elshtain, Jean Bethke. *Women and War*. New York: Basic, 1987.

Emerson, Ralph Waldo. "Heroism." In *Essays and Poems*, edited by Joel Porte, 369–81. New York: Library of America, 1996.

———. "Self-Reliance." In *Essays and Poems*, edited by Joel Porte, 257–82. New York: Library of America, 1996.

———. "War." In *The Complete Works of Ralph Waldo Emerson*, 11:151–76. Boston: Houghton Mifflin, 1904.

Endy, Melvin B. "Just War, Holy War, and Millennialism in Revolutionary America." *William and Mary Quarterly* 42.1 (1985): 3–25.

Engelhardt, Tom. *The American Way of War: How Bush's Wars Became Obama's*. Chicago: Haymarket, 2010.

———. *The End of Victory Culture: Cold War America and the Disillusioning of a Generation*. New York: Basic, 1995

Esposito, Roberto. *L'origine della politica: Hannah Arendt o Simone Weil?* Rome: Donzelli, 1996.

Eutsey, Dwayne. "'From the Throne': What the Stranger in 'The War-Prayer' Says about Mark Twain's Theology." *Journal of Transnational American Studies* 1.1 (2009): 50–54.

Faulkner, William. Banquet speech. Available at http://www.nobelprize.org/nobel_prizes/literature/laureates/1949/faulkner-speech.html (accessed November 2, 2012).

———. *A Fable*. New York: Vintage, 1977.

Ferguson, Robert. "'What is Enlightenment?' Some American Answers." *American Literary History* 1 (1989): 245–72.

Ficken, Carl. "The Christ Story in *A Fable*." *Mississippi Quarterly* 23 (1970): 251–64.

Fiedler, Leslie. "The Antiwar Novel and the Good Soldier Schweik." Foreword to *The Good Soldier Schweik*, by Jaroslav Hašek, v–xiv. New York: New American Library, 1963.

Ford, Arthur L. *Joel Barlow*. Boston: Twayne, 1971.

Fornari, Franco. *Psicanalisi della Guerra* (1966). *The Psychoanalysis of War*. Translated by Alenka Pfeifer. Bloomington: Indiana University Press, 1975.

Foucault, Michel. *Power/Knowledge: Selected Interviews and Other Writings, 1972–1977*. Edited by Colin Gordon. New York: Vintage, 1980.

———. *"Society Must Be Defended": Lectures at the Collége de France, 1975–1976*. Edited by Mauro Bertani and Alessandro Fontana. Translated by David Macey. New York: Picador, 2003.

Fox, Matthew. *In the Beginning There Was Joy*. New York: Crossroad, 1995.

———. *Original Blessing*. New York: Tarcher/Putnam, 2000.

Fuller, W. G. "The Lady with the Lamp." *The Masses*, January 1917: 29–30.

Fussell, Paul. *The Great War and Modern Memory*. New York: Oxford University Press, 1975.

Gallie, Walter Bryce. *Philosophers of Peace and War: Kant, Clausewitz, Marx, Engles, Tolstoy*. The Wiles Lectures. Cambridge: Cambridge University Press, 1978.

Galtung, Johan. *Peace by Peaceful Means: Peace and Conflict, Development and Civilization*. London: Sage, 1996.

———. *Peace: Research, Education, Action*. Essays in Peace Research. Vol. 1. Copenhagen: Ejlers, 1975.

Gandhi, Mohandas K. *An Autobiography; or, The Story of My Experiments with Truth*. Edited by Mahadev H. Desai. Ahmedabad: Navajivan, 1996.

———. *Non-Violence in Peace and War*. 2 vols. Ahmedabad: Navajivan, 1948.

Girard, René. "Generative Scapegoating." In *Violent Origins: Ritual Killing and Cultural Formation*, edited by Robert G. Hamerton-Kelly, 73–105. Stanford, Calif.: Stanford University Press, 1987.

———. "Hamlet's Dull Revenge." *Stanford Literary Review* 1–2 (1984–85): 159–200.

———. *I See Satan Fall Like Lightning*. Translated and with a foreword by James G. Williams. Maryknoll, New York: Orbis, 1999.

———. *Origine della cultura e fine della storia: Dialoghi con Pierpaolo Antonelli and João Cezar de Castro Rocha*. Milan: Cortina, 2003.

———. *Things Hidden since the Foundation of the World*. Translated by Stephen Bann and Michael Metteer. Stanford, Calif.: Stanford University Press, 1987.

———. *Violence and the Sacred*. Baltimore, Md.: Johns Hopkins University Press, 1977.

Gittings, John. *The Glorious Art of Peace: From the Iliad to Iraq*. Oxford: Oxford University Press, 2012.

Godden, Richard. "*A Fable* . . . Whispering about the Wars," *Faulkner Journal* 17 (Spring 2002): 25–88.

Goldstein, Joshua. *War and Gender: How Gender Shapes the War System and Vice Versa*. Cambridge: Cambridge University Press, 2001.

Gourgouris, Stathis. "Enlightenment and *Paronomia*." In *Violence, Identity, and Self-Determination*, edited by Hent de Vries and Samuel Weber, 119–49. Stanford, Calif.: Stanford University Press, 1997.

Gray, J. Glenn. *The Warriors: Reflections on Men in Battle*. New York: Bison, 1989.

Gregg, Richard Bartlett. *The Power of Non-Violence*. Philadelphia: Lippincott, 1935.

Gruesser, John. "'Sivil' Disobedience: America's Greatest Contribution to World Peace." In *American Studies and Peace*. Proceedings of the 25th AAAS Conference, edited by Dorothea Steiner and Thomas Hartl, 173–81. Frankfurt: Peter Lang, 1999.

Guelzo, Allen C. *Lincoln's Emancipation Proclamation: The End of Slavery in America*. New York: Simon and Schuster, 2004.

Halliburton, Richard. *The Color of the Sky: A Study of Stephen Crane*. Cambridge Studies in American Literature and Culture. New York: Cambridge University Press, 1989.

Hanley, Lynne. *Writing War: Fiction, Gender, and Memory*. Amherst: University of Massachusetts Press, 1991.

Hanssen, Beatrice. *Critique of Violence: Between Poststructuralism and Critical Theory*. Warwick Studies in European Philosophy. London: Routledge, 2000.

Hedges, Chris. *War Is a Force That Gives Us Meaning*. New York: Random House, 2002.

Hemingway, Ernest. *A Farewell to Arms*. Harmondsworth: Penguin, 1972.

———. "Foreword." In *Treasury for the Free World*, by Ben Raeburn. New York: Arco, 1946.

———. *In Our Time*. New York: Scribner's, 1970.

Herr, Michael. *Dispatches*. New York: Avon, 1978.

Higonnet, Margaret. "Not So Quiet in No-Woman's Land." In Cooke and Woollacott, *Gendering War Talk*, 205–26.

———, ed. *Nurses at the Front: Writing the Wounds of the Great War*. Boston: Northeastern University Press, 2001.

Higonnet, Margaret, and Patrice Higonnet. "The Double Helix." In Higonnet, Jenson, Michel, and Weitz, *Behind the Lines*, 31–50.

Higonnet, Margaret, Jane Jenson, Sonya Michel, and Margaret Collins Weitz, eds. *Behind the Lines: Gender and the Two World Wars*. New Haven, Conn.: Yale University Press, 1987.

Hillman, James. *A Terrible Love of War*. New York: Penguin, 2004.

Holmes, Robert L. *On War and Morality*. Studies in Moral, Political, and Legal Philosophy. Princeton, N.J.: Princeton University Press, 1989.

Holstein, Jay. "Melville's Inversion of Jonah in *Moby-Dick*." *Iliff Review* 42 (1985): 13–20.

Horsburgh, H. J. N. *Non-Violence and Aggression: A Study of Gandhi's Moral Equivalent of War*. New York: Oxford University Press, 1968.

Huggard, William Allen. *Emerson and the Problem of War and Peace*. Iowa City: University of Iowa Press, 1938.

Huston, Nancy. "The Matrix of War: Mothers and Heroes." In *The Female Body in Western Culture: Contemporary Perspectives*, edited by Susan Rubin Suleiman, 119–36. Cambridge, Mass.: Harvard University Press, 1986.

———. "Tales of War and Tears of Women." *Women's Studies International Forum* 5.3–4 (1982): 271–82.

Huyssen, Andreas. "Fortifying the Heart—Totally: Ernst Jünger's Armored Texts." *New German Critique* 59 (1993): 3–21.

Hynes, Samuel. *The Soldier's Tale: Bearing Witness to Modern War*. New York: Penguin, 1997.

Independent. Unsigned review of *The Backwash of War*, by Ellen N. La Motte. November 13, 1916: 284.

James, William. "The Moral Equivalent of War." In *Writings, 1902–1910*, edited by Bruce Kuklick. New York: Library of America, 1987.

Jameson, Fredric. *The Political Unconscious: Narrative as a Socially Symbolic Act*. Ithaca, N.Y.: Cornell University Press, 1981.

———. *Postmodernism; or, The Cultural Logic of Late Capitalism*. Post-Contemporary Interventions. Durham. N.C.: Duke University Press, 1991.

———. "Symbolic Inference; or, Kenneth Burke and Ideological Analysis." In *The Ideologies of Theory: Essays 1971–1986*, 1: 137–52. London: Routledge, 1988.

Jason, Philip K., and Mark A. Graves, eds. *Encyclopedia of American War Literature*. Westport, Conn.: Greenwood, 2001.

Jay, Martin. "Against Consolation: Walter Benjamin and the Refusal to Mourn." In *War and Remembrance in the Twentieth Century*, edited by Jay Winter and Emmanuel Sivan, 221–39. Studies in the Social and Cultural History of Modern Warfare, vol. 5. Cambridge: Cambridge University Press, 1999.

Jay, Paul. *Contingency Blues: The Search for Foundations in American Criticism*. Wisconsin Project on American Writers. Madison: University of Wisconsin Press, 1997.

Jones, Peter G. *War and the Novelist: Appraising the American War Novel*. Columbia: University of Missouri Press, 1976.

Jünger, Ernst. *The Storm of Steel*. London: Chatto and Windus, 1929.

Just, Ward. "Vietnam—Fiction and Fact." *Triquarterly* 65 (Winter 1986): 215–28.

Kadir, Djelal. "Defending America against Its Devotees." *Comparative American Studies* 2.2 (2004): 133–52.

——. *Memos from the Besieged City: Lifelines for Cultural Sustainability*. Cultural Memory in the Present. Stanford, Calif.: Stanford University Press, 2011.

Kahn, Paul. *Sacred Violence: Torture, Terror, and Sovereignty*. Law, Meaning, and Violence. Ann Arbor: University of Michigan Press: 2008.

Kaldor, Mary. *New and Old Wars: Organized Violence in a Global Era*. Cambridge: Polity, 1999.

Kammen, Michael. *A Season of Youth: The American Revolution and the Historical Imagination*. New York: Knopf, 1978.

Kant, Immanuel. *Perpetual Peace: A Philosophical Essay*. Translated and with an introduction and notes by M. Campbell Smith. Preface by L. Latta. London: Allen and Unwin, 1917.

Kaplan, Amy. "Transnational Melville." *Leviathan* 12.1 (March 2010): 42–52.

Kaplan, Richard Middleton. "Facing the Face of the Enemy: Levinasian Moments in *All Quiet on the Western Front* and the Literature of War." *Modern Fiction Studies* 54.1 (Spring 2008): 72–90.

Kearney, Richard. *Anatheism: Returning to God after God*. Insurrections: Critical Studies in Religion, Politics, and Culture. New York: Columbia University Press, 2010.

Kelly, Van. "The Ambiguity of Individual Gestures: Revisions of World War I in Abel Gance's *J'accuse*, Alain's *Mars ou Laguerre jugee*, and Bertrand Tavernier's *La vie et rien d'autre*." *South Central Review* 17.3 (2000): 7–34.

Kilani, Mondher. *Guerre et sacrifce: La violence extrême* (2006). Translated by V. Carrassi. *Guerra e sacrificio*. Bari: Dedalo, 2008.

King, Martin Luther, Jr. *The Autobiography of Martin Luther King, Jr.* Edited by Clayborne Carson. New York: Warner, 1998.

King, Rosemary. "O'Brien's 'How to Tell a True War Story.'" *Explicator* 57.3 (1999): 182–83.

Kingston, Maxine Hong. *The Fifth Book of Peace*. New York: Vintage, 2004.

Kosek, Joseph Kip. "Richard Gregg, Mohandas Gandhi, and the Strategy of Nonviolence." *Journal of American History* 91.4 (2005): 1318–48.

Kovel, Joel. *Against the State of Nuclear Terror*. Boston: South End, 1983.

Lagouranis, Tony, and Allen Mikaelian. *Fear Up Harsh: An Army Interrogator's Dark Journey through Iraq*. New York: New American Library, 2007.

La Motte, Ellen N. *The Backwash of War*. New York: Putnam, 1934.

Larkin, Edward. "American Revolutionary War Writing." In *The Cambridge Companion to*

War Writing, edited by K. McLoughlin, 126–34. Cambridge Companions to Literature. Cambridge: Cambridge University Press, 2009.

Lassner, Phyllis. *British Women Writers of World War II: Battlegrounds of Their Own*. London: Palgrave Macmillan, 1998.

Lawrence, D. H. *Studies in Classic American Literature*. Cambridge Edition of the Letters and Works of D. H. Lawrence. Edited by Ezra Greenspan, Lindeth Vasey, and John Worthen. Cambridge: Cambridge University Press, 2003.

Lears, T. J. Jackson. *No Place of Grace: Antimodernism and the Transformation of American Culture, 1880–1920*. New York: Pantheon, 1981.

Leed, Eric J. *No Man's Land: Combat and Identity in World War I*. Cambridge: Cambridge University Press, 1979.

Lentricchia, Frank. *Criticism and Social Change*. Chicago: University of Chicago Press, 1983.

Lepore, Jill. *The Name of War: King Philip's War and the Origins of American Identity*. New York: Vintage, 1998.

Lerner, Laurence. "Peace Studies: A Proposal." *New Literary History* 26.3 (1995):641–65.

LeShan, Lawrence. *The Psychology of War: Comprehending Its Mystique and Its Madness*. Chicago: Noble, 1992.

Limon, John. *Writing after War: American War Fiction from Realism to Postmodernism*. New York: Oxford University Press, 1994.

Lindgren, James. "Fall from Grace: *Arming America* and the Bellesiles Scandal." *Yale Law Journal* 111.8 (2002): 2195–249.

Lindgren, James, and Justin L. Heather. "Counting Guns in Early America." *William and Mary Law Review* 43 (April 2002): 1777–842.

Lopez, Michael. *Emerson and Power: Creative Antagonism in the Nineteenth Century*. DeKalb: Northern Illinois University Press, 1996.

Losurdo, Domenico. *La non-violenza: Una storia fuori dal mito*. Bari: Laterza, 2010.

Lynd, Staughton, and Alice Lynd. "Introduction." In *Nonviolence in America: A Documentary History*. Revised edition. Edited by Staughton Lynd and Alice Lynd, xi–xlvi. Maryknoll, N.Y.: Orbis, 1996.

Magee, Rosemary. "*A Fable* and the Gospels: A Study in Contrasts." *Research Studies* 47.2 (1979): 98–107.

Manara, Fulvio Cesare. *Una forza che dà vita: Ricominciare con Gandhi in un'età di terrorismi*. Milan: Unicopli, 2006.

Mandel, Naomi. *Against the Unspeakable: Complicity, the Holocaust, and Slavery in America*. Cultural Frames, Framing Culture. Charlottesville: University of Virginia Press, 2006.

Mansfield, Nick. *Theorizing War: From Hobbes to Badiou*. Basingstoke: Palgrave, 2008.

Marcus, Jane. "The Asylums of Antaeus: Women, War and Madness; Is There a Feminist Fetishism?" In *The Difference Within: Feminism and Critical Theory*, edited by Elizabeth A. Meese and Alice A. Parker, 49–83. Amsterdam: Benjamins, 1989.

———. "Corpus/Corpse/Corps: Writing the Body in/at War." Afterword in Smith, *Not So Quiet*... 241–300.

Mariani, Giorgio. "Negotiating Violence and Identity in Sherman Alexie's *Indian Killer*." *FIAR: Forum for Inter-American Research* 4.2 (November 2011).

———. *Spectacular Narratives: Representations of Class and War in Stephen Crane and the American 1890s*. American University Study Series 24, American Literature (Book 37). New York: Lang, 1992.

Mariani, Giorgio, and Alessandro Portelli. "Mythic Pro-Americanism: An Italian Odyssey." In *Americas' Worlds and the World's Americas / Les mondes des Amériques et les Amériques du monde*, edited by Amaryll Chanady, George Handley, and Patrick Imbert, 85–94. Ottawa: Legas, 2006.

May, Rollo. *Power and Innocence: A Search for the Sources of Violence*. New York: Norton, 1972.

Mazzi, Enzo. *Cristianesimo ribelle*. Rome: Manifestolibri, 2008.

———. *Ernesto Balducci e il dissenso creativo*. Rome: Manifestolibri, 2002.

McLoughlin, Kate. *Authoring War: The Literary Representation of War from the* Iliad *to* Iraq. Cambridge: Cambridge University Press, 2011.

———. *Martha Gellhorn: The War Writer in the Field and in the Text*. Manchester: Manchester University Press, 2007.

———. "War and Words." In *The Cambridge Companion to War Writing*, edited by K. McLoughlin, 15–24. Cambridge Companions to Literature. Cambridge: Cambridge University Press, 2009.

McNerney, Brian C. "Responsibly Inventing History: An Interview with Tim O'Brien." *War, Literature, and the Arts* 6.2 (1994): 1–26.

McWilliams, John P., Jr. *The American Epic: Transforming a Genre, 1770–1860*. Cambridge Studies in American Literature and Culture. Cambridge: Cambridge University Press, 1989.

———. The Last of the Mohicans: *Civil Savagery and Savage Civility*. Twayne's Masterworks Studies, vol. 143. New York: Twayne, 1995.

Melville, Herman. *Correspondence*. Edited by Harrison Hayford, Hershel Parker, and G. Thomas Tanselle. Evanston: Northwestern University Press, 1993.

———. *Israel Potter: His Fifty Years of Exile*. Edited by Harrison Hayford, Hershel Parker, and G. Thomas Tanselle. Evanston: Northwestern University Press, 1982.

———. *Moby-Dick*. Edited by Hershel Parker and Harrison Hayford. New York: Norton, 2002.

———. *Typee*. Edited by Harrison Hayford, Hershel Parker, and G. Thomas Tanselle. Evanston: Northwestern University Press, 1968.

Metres, Philip. *Behind the Lines: War Resistance Poetry on the American Homefront since 1941*. Contemporary North American Poetry Series. Iowa City: University of Iowa Press, 2007.

Monnet, Agnieszka Soltysik. "Is There Such a Thing as an Anti-War Film?" *The Wiley-Blackwell Companion to the War Film*, edited by Douglas A. Cunningham. Forthcoming.

Monteiro, George. "After the *Red Badge*: Mysteries of Heroism, Death, and Burial in Stephen Crane's Fiction." *American Literary Realism, 1870–1910* 28.1 (1995): 66–79.

Moretti, Franco. *Modern Epic: The World System from Goethe to García Marquez*. London: Verso, 1995.

Mosse, George L. *Fallen Soldiers: Reshaping the Memory of the World Wars*. New York: Oxford University Press, 1990.

Nagel, James. "Stephen Crane's Stories of War: A Study of Art and Theme." *North Dakota Quarterly* 43.1 (1975): 5–19.

Nagler, Michael. *Is There No Other Way? The Search for a Nonviolent Future*. Berkeley: Berkeley Hills, 2001.

Najmi, Samina. "The Whiteness of the Soldier-Speaker in Brian Turner's *Here, Bullet*." *Rocky Mountain Review* (Spring 2011): 56–78.

Neilson, Jim. *Warring Fictions: Cultural Politics and the Vietnam War Narrative*. Jackson: University of Mississippi Press, 1998.

New, Elisa. "Bible Leaves! Bible Leaves! Hellenism and Hebraism in Melville's Moby-Dick." *Poetics Today* 19.2 (1998): 281–303.

Newfield, Christopher. *The Emerson Effect: Individualism and Submission in America*. Princeton, N.J.: Princeton University Press, 1996.

New Republic. Unsigned review of *The Backwash of War*, by Ellen N. La Motte. *New Republic* November 7, 1934: 374.

New York Times Book Review. Unsigned review of *The Backwash of War*, by Ellen N. La Motte. October 15, 1916: 432.

Nicolaisen, Peter. "Collective Experience and Questions of Genre in *A Fable*." In *The Artist and His Masks: William Faulkner's Metafiction,* edited by Agostino Lombardo, 397–414. Rome: Bulzoni, 1991.

Norris, Christopher. *Uncritical Theory: Postmodernism, Intellectual, and the Gulf War*. Amherst: University of Massachusetts Press, 1992.

Norris, Margot. *Writing War in the Twentieth Century*. Charlottesville: University of Virginia Press, 2000.

O'Brien, Tim. *If I Die in a Combat Zone, Box Me Up and Ship Me Home*. New York: Broadway, 1999.

———. *The Things They Carried*. Boston: Houghton Mifflin/Seymour Lawrence, 1990.

———. "The Vietnam in Me." *New York Times Magazine*, October 2, 1994: 48–57.

Owens, Louis. *The Sharpest Sight*. Norman: University of Oklahoma Press, 1992.

Patterson, Anita Haya. *From Emerson to King: Democracy, Race, and the Politics of Protest*. W. E. B. Du Bois Institute. New York: Oxford University Press, 1997.

Pearce, Roy Harvey. *The Continuity of American Poetry*. Princeton, N.J.: Princeton University Press, 1961.

Pease, Donald. *Visionary Compacts: American Renaissance Writings in Cultural Context*. Wisconsin Project on American Writers. Madison: University of Wisconsin Press, 1987.

Peebles, Stacey. *Welcome to the Suck: Narrating the American Soldier's Experience in Iraq*. Ithaca, N.Y.: Cornell University Press, 2011.

Perret, Geoffrey. *A Country Made by War: From the Revolution to Vietnam; The Story of America's Rise to Power*. New York: Vintage, 1990.

Perretta, Vanda. "Marte non ha bisogno di avvocati." In *Ideologia della guerra*, edited by Ferruccio Masini, 77–97. Naples: Bibliopolis, 1987.

Phillips, Kathy J. *Manipulating Masculinity: War and Gender in Modern British and American Literature*. New York: Palgrave Macmillan, 2006.

Pladott, Dinnah. "Faulkner's *A Fable*: A Heresy or a Declaration of Faith?" *Journal of Narrative Technique* 12.2 (1982): 73–94.

Plain, Gill. *Women's Fiction of the Second World War: Gender, Power, and Resistance*. New York: St. Martin's, 1996.

Poirier, Richard. *Poetry and Pragmatism*. Convergences. Cambridge, Mass.: Harvard University Press, 1992.

———. *The Renewal of Literature: Emersonian Reflections*. New Haven, Conn.: Yale University Press, 1987.

Polk, Noel. *Children of the Dark House: Text and Context in Faulkner*. Jackson: University Press of Mississippi, 1998.

———. "Roland Barthes Reads *A Fable*." In *Faulkner's Discourse. An International Symposium*, edited by Lothar Hönninghausen, 109–16. Tübingen: Niemeyer, 1989.

———. "Scar." In *Faulkner and War*, edited by Noel Polk and Ann J. Abadie, 128–59. Faulkner and Yoknapatawpha, 2001. Jackson: University Press of Mississippi, 2004.

Ponzio, Augusto. "Presentazione." In *Mondo di guerra*, edited by Andrea Catone and Augusto Ponzio. Rome: Meltemi, 2005.

Portelli, Alessandro. *The Death of Luigi Trastulli and Other Stories: Form and Meanings of Oral History*. SUNY Series in Oral and Public History. Albany: State University of New York Press, 1991.

Pratt, Mary Louise. "Harm's Way: Language and the Contemporary Arts of War." *PMLA* 124.5 (2009): 1515–31.

Proietti, Salvatore. *Storie di fondazione: Letteratura e nazione negli Stati Uniti post-rivoluzionari*. Rome: Bulzoni, 2002.

Quint, David. *Epic and Empire: Politics and Generic Form from Virgil to Milton*. Literature in History. Princeton, N.J.: Princeton University Press, 1992.

Reynolds, Larry. *Righteous Violence: Revolution, Slavery, and the American Renaissance*. Athens: University of Georgia Press, 2011.

Richmond, Oliver. *The Transformation of Peace*. Rethinking Peace and Conflict Studies. Basingstoke: Palgrave, 2005.

Ricoeur, Paul. *Vivant jusqu'à la mort*. Paris: Seuil, 2007.

Ritter, Scott. *Waging Peace: The Art of War for the Antiwar Movement*. New York: Nation, 2007.

Robbins, Bruce. "Comparative Cosmopolitanism." *Social Text* 31/32 (1992): 169–86.

———. *Perpetual War: Cosmopolitanism from the Viewpoint of Violence*. Durham, N.C.: Duke University Press, 2012.

———. "Uses of World Literature." In *The Routledge Companion to World Literature*, edited by Theo D'haen, David Damrosch, and Djelal Kadir, 383–92. Routledge Literature Companions. New York: Routledge, 2012.

Robin, Corey. "Remembrance of Empires Past: 9/11 and the End of the Cold War." In *Cold War Triumphalism: The Misuse of History after the Fall of Communism*, edited by Ellen Schrecker, 274–97. New York: Norton, 2004.

Rorty, Richard. *Achieving Our Country: Leftist Thought in Twentieth-Century America*. William E. Massey Sr. Lectures in the History of American Civilization (1997). Cambridge, Mass.: Harvard University Press, 1999.

Rosso, Stefano. *Musi gialli e berretti Verdi: Narrazioni Usa sulla Guerra del Vietnam*. Bergamo: Bergamo University Press-Edizioni Sestante, 2003.

Rotenberg-Schwartz, Michael. "On the Use of Diffusion in War Poetry: A Reading of David Harsent's *Legion* and Brian Turner's *Here, Bullet*." *Arabesques: Cultures and Dialogues*. Available at http://www.arabesques-editions.com/journal/michael_schwartz/1565515.html (accessed March 10, 2015).

Rothberg, Michael. *Traumatic Realism: The Demands of Holocaust Representations*. Minneapolis: University of Minnesota Press, 2000.

Rowe, John Carlos. *At Emerson's Tomb: The Politics of Classic American Literature*. New York: Columbia University Press, 1997.

Roy, Arundhati. "War is Peace." In Zinn, *Power of Nonviolence*, 182–92.

Rozac, Olivier. *Storia politica del filo spinato*. Verona: Ombre corte, 2001.

San Juan, E., Jr. "Dialectics of Aesthetics and Politics in Maxine Hong Kingston's *The Fifth Book of Peace*." *Criticism* 51.2 (2009): 181–209.

Sartre, Jean-Paul. "War Diary." Translated by David Fernbach. *New Left Review* 59 (2009): 89–120.

Saturday Review of Literature. Unsigned review of *The Backwash of War*, by Ellen N. La Motte. September 22, 1934: 134.

Scarry, Elaine. *The Body in Pain: The Making and Unmaking of the World*. New York: Oxford University Press, 1985.

Schmitt, Carl. *The Concept of the Political*. Translated by George Schwab. Chicago: University of Chicago Press, 2007.

———. *Der Nomos der Erde* (1950). *The* Nomos *of the Earth in the International Law of the* Jus Publicum Europaeum. Translated by G. L. Ulmen. New York: Telos, 2006.

Schneider, Karen. Loving Arms: *British Women Writing the Second World War*. Lexington: University Press of Kentucky, 1997.

Schwetman, John D. "Violence." In *Encyclopedia of American Studies*, edited by George T. Kurian, Miles Orwell, Johnnella E. Butler, and Jay Mechling, 4:310–16. New York: Grolier, 2001.

Scurati, Antonio. "Dire addio alle armi: Forma giuridica e retorica della Guerra in Schmitt e Hemingway." In *Le parole e le armi*, edited by Giorgio Mariani, 291–326. Milan: Marcos y Marcos, 1999.

Seelye, John. "Flashing Eyes and Floating Hair: The Visionary Mode in Early American Poetry." *Virginia Quarterly Review* 65.2 (1989): 189–214.

Shalev, Eran. *Rome Reborn on Western Shores: Historical Imagination and the Creation of the American Republic*. Jeffersonian America. Charlottesville: University of Virginia Press, 2009.

Shan, Te-Hsing. "Life, Writing, and Peace: Reading Maxine Hong Kingston's *The Fifth Book of Peace*," *Journal of Transnational American Studies* 1.1 (2009): article 14.

Shaw, Mary N. "Apprehending the Mystery in Stephen Crane's 'The Mystery of Heroism.'" *CLA Journal* 39.1 (1995): 94–103.

Shay, Jonathan. *Achilles in Vietnam: Combat Trauma and the Undoing of Character*. New York: Scribner, 1993.

———. *Odysseus in Vietnam: Combat Trauma and the Trials of Homecoming*. New York: Scribner, 2002.

Sheardy, Robert, Jr. "The White Woman and the Native Male Body in Vanderlyn's *Death of Jane McCrea*." *Journal of American Culture* 22.1 (1999): 93–100.

Sherman, A. J. "Schools for Scandal." *New England Review* 26.3 (2005).

Sherry, Vincent. *The Great War and the Language of Modernism*. New York: Oxford University Press, 2003.

Shounan, Hsu. "Writing, Event, and Peace: The Art of Peace in Maxine Hong Kingston's *The Fifth Book of Peace*," *College Literature* 37.2 (2010): 103–24.

Siebers, Tobin. *The Ethics of Criticism*. Ithaca, N.Y.: Cornell University Press, 1988.

——. Review of *Writing after War: American War Fiction from Realism to Postmodernism*, by John Limon. *Criticism* 37.3 (1997): 505–8.

Slotkin, Richard. *The Fatal Environment: The Myth of the Frontier in the Age of Industrialization, 1800–1890*. New York: Atheneum, 1985.

——. *Gunfighter Nation: The Myth of the Frontier in Twentieth-Century America*. New York: Atheneum, 1992.

——. *Regeneration through Violence: The Mythology of the American Frontier, 1600–1860*. Middletown, Conn.: Wesleyan University Press, 1973.

Smith, Helen Zenna. *Not So Quiet . . . Stepdaughters of War*. New York: Feminist, 1989.

Smith, Julian. "A Source for Faulkner's *A Fable*." *American Literature* 40 (1968): 394–97.

Solecki, Ralph. *Shanidar: The First Flower People*. New York: Knopf, 1971.

Sollors, Werner. "'Eager to Acquire Disks'? American Studies in War and Peace." *American Studies and Peace: Proceedings of the 25th Austrian Association of American Studies Conference*, edited by Dorothea Steiner and Thomas Hartl, 23–40. Frankfurt: Lang, 2001.

Solomon, Eric. "From Christ in Flanders to *Catch 22*: An Approach to War Fiction." *Texas Studies in Language and Literature* 11 (1969): 851–66.

Spanier, Sandra Whipple. "Hemingway's Unknown Soldier: Catherine Barkley, the Critics, and the Great War." In *New Essays on* A Farewell to Arms, edited by Scott Donaldson, 75–108. American Novel Series. Cambridge: Cambridge University Press, 1990.

Spanos, William. *The Errant Art of Moby-Dick: The Canon, the Cold War, and the Struggle for American Studies*. New Americanists. Durham, N.C.: Duke University Press, 1995.

Spielberg, Stephen. "Battlegrounds." In "A Century on Screen Supplement," *Newsweek* 131 (Summer 1998): 66–68.

Spivak, Gayatry Chakravorty. *Death of a Discipline*. Wellek Library Lectures. New York: Columbia University Press, 2003.

Springfield Republican. Unsigned review of *The Backwash of War*, by Ellen N. La Motte. October 2, 1916: 6.

Stack, George J. *Nietzsche and Emerson: An Elective Affinity*. Athens: Ohio University Press, 1992.

Stallman, R. W. *Stephen Crane: An Omnibus*. New York: Knopf, 1952.

Stallybrass, Peter, and Allon White. *The Poetics and Politics of Transgression*. Ithaca, N.Y.: Cornell University Press, 1985.

Sten, Christopher. *Sounding the Whale: "Moby-Dick" as Epic Novel*. Kent, Ohio: Kent State University Press, 1996.

Stein, Gertrude. *Autobiography of Alice B. Toklas*. New York: Vintage, 1970.

Stessel, Edward. "The Soldier and the Scholar: Emerson's Warring Heroes." *Journal of American Studies* 19.2 (1985): 165–97.

Stewart, Garrett. "Digital Fatigue: Imaging War in Recent American Film." *Film Quarterly* 62.4 (2009): 45–55.

Stone, Robert. "Me and the Universe." *Triquarterly* 65 (1986): 229–34.

Tate, Trudi. "The First World War: British Writing." *The Cambridge Companion to War Writing*, edited by Kate McLoughlin, 160–74. Cambridge Companions to Literature. Cambridge: Cambridge University Press, 2009.

Thompson, Lawrance. *Melville's Quarrel with God*. Princeton, N.J.: Princeton University Press, 1952.

Thoreau, Henry David. *Resistance to Civil Government*, 1849.

Tichi, Cecelia. *New World, New Earth: Environmental Reform in American Literature from the Puritans through Whitman*. New Haven, Conn.: Yale University Press, 1979.

Tompkins, Jane. *West of Everything: The Inner Life of Westerns*. New York: Oxford University Press, 1992.

Tosel, André. *Kant rivoluzionario*. Rome: Manifestolibri, 1999.

Trafton, John. "The 'Anti-War Film' and the 'Anti-War-Film': A Reading of Brian De Palma's *Redacted* (2007) and *Casualties of War* (1998)." *Journal of War and Cultural Studies* 4.1 (1989): 113–26.

Traverso, Enzo. "Le armi nonviolente." *Il Manifesto*, September 25, 2010: 11.

Tritle, Lawrence A. *From Melos to My Lai: A Study in Violence, Culture and Social Survival*. London: Routledge, 2002.

Trumbo, Dalton. *Johnny Got His Gun*. New York: Citadel, 1994.

Turner, Brian. "The Bomb within Us." *New York Times*, March 4, 2010. Available at http://opinionator.blogs.nytimes.com/2010/03/04/home-fires-the-bomb-within-us (accessed March 10, 2015).

———. *Here, Bullet*. Highgreen: Bloodaxe, 2007.

———. *Phantom Noise*. Highgreen: Bloodaxe, 2010.

———. "Verses in Wartime (Part 2: From the Home Front)." *New York Times*, October 24, 2007. Available at http://opinionator.blogs.nytimes.com/2007/10/24/verses-in-wartime -part-2-from-the-home-front (accessed March 10, 2015).

Twain, Mark. *Mark Twain's Notebook: The Complete Works of Mark Twain*. Vol. 22. New York: Harper, 1935.

———. "The War Prayer." In *The Norton Anthology of American Literature*, 2nd ed., edited by N. Baym, R. Gottesman, et al., 260–63. New York: Norton, 1985.

Tylee, Claire M. *The Great War and Women's Consciousness: Images of Militarism and Womanhood in Women's Writings, 1914–64*. Iowa City: University of Iowa Press, 1990.

Urgo, Joseph. *Faulkner's Apocrypha: A Fable, Snopes, and the Spirit of Human Rebellion*. Jackson: University Press of Mississippi, 1989.

Valladão, Alfredo. *The Twenty-First Century Will Be American*. London: Verso, 1996.

vanden Heuvel, Katrina. "Obama's 'Kill List' Is Unchecked Presidential Power." *Washington Post*, June 11, 2012.

Vernon, Alex. *Soldiers Once and Still*. Iowa City: University of Iowa Press, 2004.

Vincent, Jonathan. "'Tendrils of Association': World War I Narrative and the U.S. Political Imaginary." *American Literature* 82.3 (2010): 553–81.

Voelz, Johannes. *Transcendental Resistance: The New Americanists and Emerson's Challenge*. Hanover, N.H.: Dartmouth College Press, 2010.

Vonnegut, Kurt. *Slaughterhouse-Five; or, The Children's Crusade: A Duty-Dance with Death*. London: Vintage, 1991.

Wachtell, Cynthia. *War No More: The Antiwar Impulse in American Literature, 1861–1914*. Baton Rouge: Louisiana State University Press, 2010.

Wald, Priscilla. "Hearing Narrative Voices in Melville's *Pierre*." *Boundary 2* 17 (1990): 100–132.

Weil, Simone. *The Iliad; or, The Poem of Force*. Translated by Mary McCarthy. Wallingford, Pa.: Pendle Hill, 1956.

Weiser, Elizabeth M. "Burke and War: Rhetoricizing the Theory of Dramatism." *Rhetoric Review* 26.3 (2007): 286–302.

White, R. S. *Pacifism and English Literature: Minstrels of Peace*. Basingstoke: Palgrave, 2008.

Whitman, Walt. *Specimen Days: Complete Poetry and Collected Prose*, edited by Justin Kaplan. New York: Library of America, 1982.

Whittier, Gayle. "Childbirth, War and Creativity in *A Farewell to Arms*." *LIT* 3 (1992): 253–70.

Wiener, Jon. *Historians in Trouble: Plagiarism, Fraud, and Politics in the Ivory Tower*. New York: New Press, 2005.

Williams, William Carlos. *In the American Grain*. New York: New Directions, 1956.

Williamson, Joel. *William Faulkner and Southern History*. New York: Oxford University Press, 1993.

Wills, Garry. "Spiking the Gun Myth." *New York Times*, September 10, 2000.

Wilson, James. *Vietnam in Prose and Film*. Jefferson, N.C.: McFarland, 1982.

Wink, Walter. *Engaging the Powers: Discernment and Resistance in a World of Domination*. Minneapolis: Fortress, 1992.

Winter, Aaron McLean. "The Laughing Dove: Satire in 19th-Century Anti-War Rhetoric." PhD dissertation. University of California at Irvine, 2008.

——. "The Laughing Doves of 1812 and the Satiric Endowment of Antiwar Rhetoric in the United States." *PMLA* 124.5 (2009): 1562–81.

Wolfe, Alan. "Anti-American Studies." *New Republic*, February 10, 2003: 25.

Wright, Nathalia. *Melville's Use of the Bible*. Durham, N.C.: Duke University Press, 1949.

Wright, Robert A. "'History's Heavy Attrition': Literature, Historical Consciousness and the Impact of Vietnam." *Canadian Review of American Studies* 17.3 (1986): 301–16.

Zatti, Sergio. *Il modo epico*. Bari: Laterza, 2000

Ziegler, Valerie H. *The Advocates of Peace in Antebellum America*. Macon, Ga.: Mercer University Press, 1992.

Zinn, Howard, ed. *The Power of Nonviolence: Writings by Advocates of Peace*. Boston: Beacon, 2002.

Zins, Daniel L. "Imagining the Real: The Fiction of Tim O'Brien." *Hollins Critic* 23 (1986): 1–12.

Zizola, Giancarlo. "La Bomba e il Vangelo." In *Culture della pace e della guerra*, edited by Andrew Arato et al., 126–53. Milan: Angeli, 1984.

Zolo, Danilo. "Prefazione: La profezia della guerra globale." In *Il concetto discriminatorio di guerra*, by Carl Schmitt, edited by Stefano Pietropaoli, v–xxxii. Bari: Laterza, 2008.

Index

GIORGIO MARIANI is a professor of American literature at the Sapienza University of Rome. He is the author of *Spectacular Narratives: Representations of Class and War in Stephen Crane and the American 1890s.*

The University of Illinois Press
is a founding member of the
Association of American University Presses.

———————————————————————

Composed in 10.5/13 Marat Pro
by Lisa Connery
at the University of Illinois Press
Manufactured by Sheridan Books, Inc.

University of Illinois Press
1325 South Oak Street
Champaign, IL 61820-6903
www.press.uillinois.edu